Transactions of the Royal Historical Society

FIFTH SERIES

38

LONDON 1988

British Library Cataloguing in Publication Data

Transactions of the Royal Historical Society.
   —5th series, vol. 37 (1987)
   1. History—Periodicals
   I. Royal Historical Society
   905   D1

ISBN 0-86193-109-2

Made and printed in Great Britain by Butler & Tanner Ltd, Frome and London

CONTENTS

TRANSACTIONS OF THE

ROYAL HISTORICAL SOCIETY

PRESIDENTIAL ADDRESS

By G. E. Aylmer

COLLECTIVE MENTALITIES IN MID SEVENTEENTH-CENTURY ENGLAND: III. VARIETIES OF RADICALISM

READ 20 NOVEMBER 1987

SINCE the terms radical and radicalism were not in use before the nineteenth century, it may fairly be asked what they signify when applied to the mid-seventeenth century. The simplest answer is a pragmatic one: by radical I mean anyone advocating changes in state, church or society which would have gone beyond the official programme of the mainstream puritan-parliamentarians in the Long Parliament and the Westminster Assembly of Divines. In the Parliament I therefore exclude here the 'political Independents', alias the War Party, other than the handful of pre-1647–8 republicans. In the Assembly I exclude the 'Five Dissenting Brethren', who were the spokesmen of moderate Congregationalism, but outside it I include some religious Independents whose radicalism will be presently defined. To borrow another nineteenth-century figure of speech, if we look to the Left of the mainstream Puritans and Parliamentarians, what a bewildering profusion of groups and individuals appears. It is scarcely necessary to have studied the period at all to be familiar with the names of many such sects or movements, if not perhaps of all: Anabaptists, Antinomians, Behmenists, Brownists, Comenians, Diggers, Familists, Fifth-Monarchy Men, Grindletonians, Levellers, Mortalists, Muggletonians, Quakers, Ranters, Seekers, and Socinians. Yet simply to reel off such a list is to omit many interesting and remarkable groups and individuals: would-be reformers of the professions and of law, medicine and education, free-traders, agricultural improvers, philo-semites and proto-feminists, to mention only some of the most obvious. Any reader of Thomas Edwards' *Gangraena*[1] and

---

[1] Conveniently reprinted by The Rota (Exeter, 1977).

other contemporary comminations[2] or of Christopher Hill's *The World Turned Upside Down* and his other writings[3] will be familiar with most of them and no doubt with others too. The question for the historian is whether any pattern can be discerned, any general explanation offered of where these people and their ideas came from and what they signified.

Given the discipline of our subject, we should look first to the chronological dimension. Did their open emergence on the public scene from 1641 on merely represent the re-appearance under more favourable conditions of ideas long latent among sections of the population, now freed from censorship and other constraints, indeed positively encouraged to seek articulate expression? Or were they to a greater extent the short-term product of a conflict within the traditional ruling class, which split apart the upper and middle levels of society, thereby stimulating those below them in the social hierarchy to put forward their own contributions to solving the country's problems? Clearly the answer is a bit of both, but more of one than of the other in different instances. The tradition of Protestant religious separatism has been traced back to the earliest days of the English Reformation, if not to Lollardy and other medieval heresies long before that.[4] The idea of religious toleration had emerged in the sixteenth century and, although repressed or held within strictly defined boundaries, had not disappeared even in the generation before 1640.[5] On the other hand the sects of the Interregnum bear only a limited resemblance to the Separatists of Tudor times; likewise the range of arguments for and

---

[2] The 'anti' literature is voluminous. Besides Edwards, I have consulted the following: Robert Baillie, alias Baylie, *A Dissuasive from the Errours of the Time* ... (1645); Daniel Featley, *The Dippers Dipt* ... (1645); Ephraim Pagitt, *Heresiography* ... (five editions 1645–54); William Prynne, *Twelve Considerable Serious Questions touching Church Government* ... (1644); *Independency Examined, Unmasked, Refuted* ... (1644); *A Fresh Discovery of new-blazing Firebrands* ... (1645); Samuel Rutherford, *A Survey of the Spirituall Antichrist* ... (1648); *A Free Disputation. Against pretended Liberty of Conscience* ... (1649). And this is to omit works by Benjamin Bourne, Thomas Gataker, Obadiah Howe, John Tickell and others.

[3] Christopher Hill, *The World Turned Upside Down Radical Ideas during the English Revolution* (1972); see also *Puritanism and Revolution* (1958); *Change and Continuity in 17th-century England* (1974); *Milton and the English Revolution* (1978); *The Experience of Defeat* (1982); *Collected Essays* (3 vols., Brighton, 1985–7).

[4] In order of appearance: A. G. Dickens, *Lollards and Protestants in the diocese of York 1509–1558* (Oxford, 1959); *The English Reformation* (1964), ch. 2; Margaret Aston, *Lollards and Reformers: Images and Literacy in Late Medieval Religion* (1984), 'Lollardy and the Reformation' (first published 1964); B. R. White, *The English Separatist Tradition* (Oxford, 1971); C. Hill, 'From Lollards to Levellers', in M. Cornforth (ed.), *Rebels and their Causes* (1978), repr. in Hill, *Collected Essays*, vol. 2, ch. 7.

[5] J. Lecler, *Toleration and the Reformation* (2 vols. Engl. translation 1960); W. K. Jordan, *The Development of Religious Toleration in England* (4 vols., Cambridge, Mass., and London, 1932–40; repr. Gloucester, Mass., 1965); H. Kamen, *Rise of Toleration* (1967).

against toleration goes well beyond those of the sixteenth-century forerunners. Turning if you will from the world of Grace to that of Nature, there had been peasant uprisings in England extending at least from 1381 to 1607, but these had been aimed chiefly at the maintenance or restoration of traditional customary rights, and can hardly be said to have encompassed the demands of the Diggers and other Utopians, nor *pari passu* those of all the would-be 'Improvers'. There had been criticisms of abuses and failings in the law and in the system of office-holding, and even periodic attempts at limited reforms from mid-Tudor times to the Personal Rule of Charles I, but these again were hardly an anticipation of the variety and scope of the legal and administrative reforms demanded during the 1640s and 1650s. There had been campaigns for free trade (namely the liberation of the outports from the privileged domination of the great London companies)[6] and against monopolies during the reign of James I, but the concept of a monopoly developed by Lilburne in 1645[7] and the kind of free trade envisaged by Robinson and others[8] went so much further as to be in effect qualitatively different. So too with some of the post- or neo-Baconian schemes discussed by Charles Webster[9]: some followed logically enough from the 'Great Instauration', indeed perhaps arose directly from the publication of Bacon's works in 1640 and after, but others went well beyond anything to be found in his writings. At the most general level perhaps we can only say that some manifestations of Interregnum radicalism do seem to follow naturally from earlier traditions of criticism and dissent; others may appear to borrow ideas from the ancient world or from contemporary Europe but are substantially novel on the English scene. A few seem to have no precedent anywhere at all. So if the chronology of these ideas turns out to be more like a spectrum than a single line of measurement, can we find any other, more satisfactory framework of explanation?

Insofar as the radical ideas of the 1640s and 1650s can be located

[6] T. K. Rabb, 'Sir Edwyn Sandys and the Parliament of 1604', *Am. Hist. Rev.* lxix (1963); R. Ashton, 'The Parliamentry Agitation for Free Trade in the opening years of the reign of James I', *Past and Present*, xxxviii (1967); debate between Rabb and Ashton, *ibid.*, xl (1968), xliii (1969).

[7] John Lilburne, *Englands Birth Right Justified Against all Arbitrary Usurpation whether Regall or Parliamentary, Or under what Vizor soever* (October 1645), pp. 8–11, reprinted in W. Haller (ed.), *Tracts on Liberty in the Puritan Revolution 1638–1647* (3 vols., N.Y., 1934, repr. 1965), iii, 257–307, esp. pp. 266–9.

[8] J. P. Cooper, 'Social and Economic Policies under the Commonwealth', in G. E. Aylmer (ed.), *The Interregnum The Quest for Settlement 1646–1660* (1972; repr. 1974), 121–42, 211–12, 226–8; Joan Thirsk and J. P. Cooper (eds.), *Seventeenth-Century Economic Documents* (Oxford, 1972) nos. V, 37, 39, VII, 10; Joyce O. Appleby, *Economic Thought and Ideology in Seventeenth-Century England* (Princeton, 1978).

[9] Charles Webster, *The Great Instauration. Science, Medicine and Reform 1626–1660* (1975).

in specific sectors of the social and cultural milieu of pre-Civil War England, where might we expect to find them? Obviously in greater London, the one truly urban society in the whole country; only less obviously in the forest, moorland and fenland areas, where rural industry was often located and where the social control exercised through the structure of the parish and the manor was often weak or even non-existent.[10] It may be an over-crude form of economic or rather geographical determinism to expect a direct congruence between the presence of radical popular ideas and settlements in woodland, wealden and other non-fielden districts. However, unless some such correspondence can be found, it seems legitimate to question the whole hypothesis. Hill himself cites the Grindletonians as a sect, in fact the only sect named after a place not a person or a concept.[11] He also suggests links between Elizabethan Familists and later separatist congregations lurking in out of the way woodlands, and reminds us of Lollards having survived in the Chilterns and elsewhere. But these parts of England were not exactly like the Himalayas or the Amazonian jungle: the truth is that there were no remote hide-aways then, any more than there are now, outside 'safe houses' in the larger towns and cities or, as Charles II had good cause to know in 1651, scattered across the countryside. Any notion that what went on in the Forest of Dean, let alone in the Weald of Kent and Sussex was somehow concealed from the authorities is frankly implausible. True, George Fox enjoyed his earliest sensational successes as a revivalist in Cumbria; but, short of digging in above the snow line, such hills as we have in England (and in most of Wales) are simply too small and too bare to have provided 'cover', even in times before the helicopter gunship. Inaccessible tracts of mountains, forest or marsh cannot be invoked to explain anything when they did not exist.[12] This is not to deny that some places were less accessible than others. General George Monck's brilliant counter-insurgency campaign of 1654 in the Highlands of Scotland was only won because he was unencumbered by a

---

[10] See Joan Thirsk, 'Industry in the Countryside', in F. J. Fisher (ed.), *Essays in the Economic and Social History of Tudor and Stuart England* (Cambridge, 1961); 'Seventeenth-Century Agriculture and Social Change' in *Land, Church and People: Agricultural History Review*, Supplement, xviii (1972); Alan Everitt, *Change in the Provinces in the Seventeenth Century* (Leicester, 1969); Everitt, 'Nonconformity in country parishes', in *Agricultural Hist. Rev.* xviii, Supplmt. (1972). A comprehensive range of references down to *c.* 1970 can be found in Hill, *World Turned Upside Down*, ch. 3, 'Masterless Men', esp. pp. 35–45. See also B. Sharp, *In Contempt of All Authority Rural Artisans and Riot in the West of England, 1586–1660* (Berkeley, Call., 1980), and, most recently, for a rather different topographical approach, David Underdown, *Revel, Riot and Rebellion: Popular Politics and Culture in England 1603–1660* (Oxford, 1985).

[11] C. Hill, *World Turned Upside Down*, ch. 5. s. 2, pp. 65–8.

[12] H. C. Darby (ed.), *A new historical geography of England* (Cambridge, 1973).

heavy siege train. And returning for a moment to Fox, he did of course have a 'safe house', if not at the very beginning from an early date, with Thomas and Margaret Fell. Differences in topography and thus in historic settlement patterns, sometimes going back for thousands of years[13] may indeed have helped to produce distinctive social, political and religious characteristics, in some cases favouring the nurture of non-conformity in its various manifestations. The reverse might also be true: masterless-men, marginal people, those on the run, dissidents might be attracted to such settlements. As the whole debate about Tudor vagrancy demonstrates, the evidence is uncertain to say the least.[14]

If a geographical interpretation is of only limited use, may a sociological explanation prove more helpful? We know a lot about the family background, upbringing and pre-Civil War careers of some well-known figures: e.g. John Goodwin, Samuel Hartlib, Hugh Peter, Henry Robinson, but very little in the case of others: e.g. Richard Overton, John Wildman, and many of the early Quakers. It may certainly be helpful to distinguish those who had been to a university, and a notch down below that those with grammar-school or equivalent education, from the completely self-taught. It seems fair to distinguish those with direct access to the learned languages (Latin, Greek, occasionally Hebrew) from those limited in their reading to available English translations. There were a few, most often of mercantile background, or refugees from the Continent, who had one or more modern European languages but knew no Latin. Unfortunately this does little to explain why particular individuals came up with the ideas they did, though it may determine preconditions. William Walwyn tells us that he knew no foreign languages and was therefore dependent entirely on works in English;[15] but by the 1640s this included a very wide range of classical and modern authors. Nor did all grandsons of bishops who had gone into trade in London evolve in the same intellectual directions as Walwyn.

It is tempting to look for modern parallels. There is something in the 'dissidence of dissent' and the tendency of sects to divide and multiply. Beyond that, and maybe rather too easily, there is the

---

[13] See most recently Christopher Taylor, *Village and Farmstead. A History of Rural Settlement in England* (1983; paperback 1984), and the great pioneering work of W. G. Hoskins, *The Making of the English Landscape* (1955; paperback Harmondsworth, 1970).

[14] A. L. Beier, *Masterless Men The Vagrancy Problem in England 1560–1640* (1985), pp. 33–9; P. A. Slack, 'Vagrants and Vagrancy in England, 1498–1664', *Econ. Hist. Rev.*, 2nd ser. xxvii (1974), 360–79.

[15] W. Walwyn, *Walwyns Just Defence against the Aspersions cast upon him ...* (1649), reprinted in W. Haller and G. Davies (eds.), *Leveller Tracts 1647–1653* (N.Y., 1944); see pp. 362–4.

parallel drawn by 'Mercurius Oxoniensis' in the *Spectator* between the most radical of the sects, such as the Ranters and Fifth-Monarchists, and the student revolutionaries of the 1960s and early 1970s; in some ways a more fitting comparison might be with the Chinese 'Red Guards' in the so-called Cultural Revolution. It is probably a mistake for a historian to pursue such lines of thought very far. A more general observation may safely be ventured: there are bodies of ideas and ways of thinking by which large numbers of people are influenced which can only exercise any real force in a specific historical context. Selective conscription for the Vietnam War did not cause student militancy, but without it that movement would have taken a very different course, at least in the United States. Proposed conscription for service in Ireland did not cause the politicisation of the New Model Army in 1647 but surely acted as a catalyst for its inception.[16] To carry such an analysis a little further, it may seem to some egregiously anachronistic to intepret Millenarianism as an example of what Marx meant by false consciousness, or to see Thomas Venner, the Fifth-Monarchist wine cooper, as the prototype of the twentieth-century ideological terrorist. I happen to find these helpful historical metaphors; others may not.

Anyone who experienced a brief mood of mental intoxication for a day or two last month, wondering whether Marx had been right after all and half believing that this really was the final crisis of capitalism, should have some sense of the eschatological or millenarian temper. The conviction that the last days were in truth at hand struck different individuals at different times during the 1640s and 1650s; for George Fox this feeling seems to have been at its strongest when he wrote *The Lamb's Officer* in 1659.

The main elements in a functional intellectual analysis are familiar enough. They have been so well described by other historians that I can lay claim to no originality at all:[17]

1. the tradition of the post-reformation sects, with whatever admixture of older Christian heresies;
2. the indigenous tradition of popular protest, even occasional

---

[16] See M. Kishlansky, *The Rise of the New Model Army* (Cambridge, 1979), esp. chs. 7–8; and now Austin Woolrych, *Soldiers and Statesmen The General Council of the Army and its Debates 1647–1648* (Oxford, 1987), mainly chs. i-iv.

[17] Besides the works already cited by Hill and others, see J. Frank, *The Levellers: A History of The Writings of Three Seventeenth-Century Social Democrats: John Lilburne, Richard Overton, William Walwyn* (Cambridge, Mass., 1955; repr. N.Y., 1969); W. Haller, *Liberty and Reformation in the Puritan Revolution* (N.Y., 1955); D. M. Wolfe, *Milton in the Puritan Revolution* (N.Y., 1941); K. Thomas, 'The Levellers and the Franchise', in Aylmer (ed.), *The Interregnum*, 57–78, 207–8, 219–22.

revolt, but also of normal participation in local affairs, at the level of township, manor or parish;

3. some awareness of recent and contemporary European happenings, whether or not correctly understood: the Spanish *comuneros*, the German peasants and Anabaptists, the Dutch Revolt, the French Wars of Religion.

Setting these influences in the context of 1641–42, may we not simply say that when the masters and mistresses fall out, the lads will play? If aristocrats and others from the propertied and educated élite could not only criticise the King and his ministers or the bishops, but put forward comprehensive and far-reaching schemes for reformation in church and state, why should not ordinary people have a go too? In the broadest sense this is self-evident. Once more it is so wide an explanation as not to take us very much further. It fails to account adequately for the speed with which certain ideas appeared, in some cases actually anticipating the outbreak of civil war. Indeed the reverse has been cogently argued: that the threat which this potential popular upsurge was felt to pose contributed directly to the outbreak of war by its polarising effects within the ruling class.[18] Perhaps we should think of the two processes—popular response to upper-class divisions and élite polarisation precipitated by popular upsurge—as having been concurrent or anyway overlapping. In the case of the sects it was the content of their forms of worship, the implications of their calls for liberty of conscience, and the kinds of people that they were, such as women and other lay preachers, which combined to make them so alarming. But less dramatically some of the arguments for free trade and for educational reform soon outstripped anything that the Long Parliament was ready to contemplate.[19]

By 1643 or 1644 a new element is discernible: what may fairly be called the ideology of disillusionment or disappointment. This influence continued to operate with varying force until 1649, if not 1653, and again briefly in 1659–60. It is expressed most clearly in the pamphlets of those who would later be called Levellers towards the parliamentarian leadership in 1645–6, and then with bitter virulence

---

[18] B. S. Manning, 'The Nobles, the People and the Constitution', *Past & Present*, ix (1956); (ed.), *Politics, Religion and the English Civil War* (1973), chs. 2–3; *The English People and the English Revolution* (1976), chs. 1–3, 8. C. Hill, *The Century of Revolution. A History of England 1603–1714* (Edinburgh, 1961; rev. edn. London, 1980), ch. 8; and R. Ashton, *The City and the Court, 1603–1642* (Cambridge, 1979), ch. 7.

[19] G. H. Turnbull, *Hartlib, Dury and Comenius. Gleanings from Hartlib's Papers* (Liverpool and London, 1947); H. R. Trevor-Roper, 'Three Foreigners, the Philosophers of the English Revolution', repr. in *Religion, the Reformation and Social Change* (1967), ch. 5; C. Webster, *The Great Instauration*; 'The Authorship and significance of '*Macaria*', *Past & Present*, lvi (1972); (ed.) *Samuel Hartlib and the Advancement of Learning* (Cambridge, 1970).

towards both the parliament and the high command of the Army in 1647–9. But this feeling, I would suggest, ran much wider than that. Many ordinary people must have felt that they had ventured all and had sacrificed much in the Parliament's cause, and that very little if anything had been delivered in return. By 1649–50 most Crown and church lands had been sold, but most people were no better off. Indeed the level of taxation, especially of the monthly assessment and the even more unpopular excise, remained at unprecedented levels. *Cui bono?* With some this produced a pro-royalist reaction, first visible among the Clubmen of the south-west during 1644–5 but far more widespread and militant in 1646–8, over much of the country.[20] But we must not forget that such disillusionment took a radical direction also, reaching its greatest intensity perhaps in 1649–50 but evident most of the time from 1645 to 1660. If we ask what specific promises the Long Parliament had made and broken, the circumvention of the Self-Denying Ordinance with all its implications of private pockets being well lined at the public expense is much the clearest case. Otherwise it was perhaps more the general tenor of parliamentarian propaganda against episcopacy and royal government that was increasingly felt to be in conflict with the realities of life under puritan-parliamentary rule, and subsequently within the fetters of what Lilburne was so eloquently to call 'England's New Chains',[21] forged by the self-styled 'Commonwealth' of 1649. None the less the mere fact of disillusionment or disappointment, emotionally powerful and embittering as it was, does not account for the radical ideas which were advanced.

A familiar and no doubt superficial distinction may be drawn between those who were more concerned with religious truth, theology and the life to come, and those more taken up with life in the temporal world on earth. Again, at the extremes this is easy enough to apply: Saltmarsh, Biddle, Reeve and Muggleton, perhaps Bunyan towards one end of the scale, Hartlib, Culpepper, Wildman towards the other. But it is quite inadequate and unsatisfactory when applied to many others, to most of the Levellers, moderates like Parker and Robinson,[22] Winstanley and Fox, to mention only some of the most obvious. Another contrast might be discerned between those who looked back to some kind of golden age in the past and those who anticipated a

[20] J. S. Morrill, *The Revolt of the Provinces 1630–1650* (1976); (ed.), *Reactions to the English Civil War* (1982); R. Ashton in *ibid*, ch. 8 and in C. Jones, M. Newitt and S. Roberts (eds.), *Politics and People in Revolutionary England* (Oxford, 1986), ch. 7.

[21] J. Lilburne, *Englands New Chains Discovered ... Parts One* and *Two* (Feb. and Mar. 1649), repr. in Haller & Davies, *Leveller Tracts*, pp. 156–70, 171–89.

[22] For whom see W. K. Jordan, *Men of Substance A Study of the Thought of Two English Revolutionaries* (Chicago, 1942).

better world in the future, but one located in this life not the next. If anything, this is still less satisfactory. Just occasionally, as in the moving, now much quoted letter by Milton's friend, Moses Wall,[23] or in some of Overton's writings, there is a clear anticipation of future developments and a positive rejection of the past. But in far more cases a harking back, whether well or ill-founded in historical reality is another question, is inextricably bound up with a vision of the future, sometimes with specific policies for its attainment.

There are other themes around which we might attempt to categorise the elements in this otherwise bewildering kaleidoscope, not as a rigid classification but as a way of grouping together those less unlike each other. The very decision to use the words radical and radicalism suggests one of these, the extent of class feeling and social resentment. Almost anything that one can say here will arouse strong disagreement: to address this topic is the historiographical equivalent of the proverbial bull in a china shop, or perhaps of starting to dance on a ballroom floor of thin-shelled eggs. I shall be both middle-of-the-road and controversial, it being one of the stranger heresies to which our own age is heir that these two things are incompatible! Considering the extent of social inequality, the extremes of wealth and poverty, the steep gradations of status and the economic difficulties of the previous century or so, early Stuart England was a remarkably well integrated society, with surprisingly little violence, disorder or evident class hatred. Reading one interesting recent symposium[24] induced a feeling that historians might do well to discard the phrase social control altogether. Only a philosophic anarchist can believe in a society without restraint, and that perhaps only at the price of excessive self-control. We need to imagine ourselves back in a country with about one ninth of today's population, admittedly with only one large urban community but with no standing army, no professional police force and virtually no full-time bureaucracy at the local level. Given such conditions, how tranquil life was for most people in England and Wales for most of the time between 1558 and 1642! This is not to

---

[23] For the full text see D. Masson, *The Life of John Milton* ... (7 vols., Cambridge and London, 1859–94), v, 602–3, quoted by Hill, *World Turned Upside Down*, p. 291; and *Some Intellectual Consequences of the English Revolution* (1980), p. 86. For Wall, see also D. M. Wolfe (ed.), *Leveller Manifestoes of the Puritan Revolution* (N.Y., 1944), no. 16, p. 344, as an assessor to appoint electoral commissioners, January 1648/9; W. R. Parker, *Milton. A Biography* (2 vols. Oxford, 1968), p. 1069, n. 89; D. S. Katz, *Philosemitism and the re-admission of the Jews to England 1603–1655* (Oxford, 1982), pp. 31, 144, 186–7, 188–9; J. Thirsk (ed.), *The Agrarian History of England and Wales,* V, ii (Cambridge, 1985), 555–7.

[24] A. J. Fletcher and J. Stevenson (eds.), *Order and Disorder in Early Modern England* (Cambridge, 1985); contrast this with J. Brewer and J. Styles (eds.), *An Ungovernable People* (1980).

imply that there were no social tensions, no feelings of class fear and resentment. For the preoccupations of the upper classes, the privileged minority, one need only turn to the dramatists; or for an individual witness from the civil war years to the diary of Sir John Oglander.[25] Yet recent studies of disturbances in the fenlands of eastern England have shown how difficult it is to equate these with straightforward class divisions, indeed what little headway radical ideologists made even when the circumstances might seem to have been propitious for them.[26] This is not to imply that the common people were somehow natural Anglicans and royalists, although they may as a whole have been conservative with a small c. The reaction of the later 1640s, the hostility shown towards soldiers, committee-men, excise officials and sequestrators was not any more representative of popular radicalism than the Clubmen had been earlier, who had really had no programme beyond getting the rival armies off their backs.[27]

I have said enough last year about the difficulties in identifying popular royalism, which is not to deny the genuineness of Charles II's welcome home in 1660. What the sources tell us about crowds and mass demonstrations has to be weighed against other evidence, about popular reading habits,[28] and the repeated alarm shown by the authorities and the propertied classes as a whole. Of course I accept that popular and radical were not identical, in the seventeenth century any more than they are so today; but they are not antithetical or mutually exclusive either.

Let us turn back to the content of what was being expressed. For some conservative contemporaries, as for at least one present-day scholar, everything else arose from the demand for religious toleration.[29] However, as is well known, that itself could mean very

[25] F. Bamford (ed.), *A Royalist's Notebook: The Commonplace Book of Sir John Oglander of Nunwell* (1936), pp. 104, 105–6, 109. For references to pillaging in Essex in 1642, see W. Hunt, *The Puritan Moment* (Cambridge, Mass., 1983), ch. 11.

[26] K. Lindley, *Fenland Riots and the English Revolution* (1982); C. Holmes, *Seventeenth-Century Lincolnshire* (Lincoln, 1980), and 'Drainers and Fenmen', ch. 6 in Fletcher and Stevenson, *Order and Disorder*.

[27] See note 20 above; also D. Underdown, 'The Chalk and the Cheese. . . .', *Past & Present*, lxxxv (1979); R. Hutton, 'The Worcestershire Clubmen in the English Civil War', *Midland History*, v (1979–80); P. Gladwish, 'The Herefordshire Clubmen: a re-assessment', *Midland History*, x (1985).

[28] Margaret Spufford, *Small Books and Pleasant Histories* (1981); D. Cressy, *Literacy and the Social Order, Reading and Writing in Tudor and Stuart England* (Cambridge, 1980); K. Thomas, 'The Meaning of Literacy in Early Modern England', in G. Baumann (ed.), *The Written Word: Literacy in Transition* (Wolfson College Lectures, 1985. Oxford, 1986), ch. 4, pp. 97–131.

[29] Edwards, *Gangraena* and other works cited in n. 2 above; J. C. Davis, ch. 6, in Manning (ed.), *Religion, Politics and the English Civil War;* and 'The Levellers and Democracy', *Past and Present*, xl (1968).

different things to different people and to the same people in different contexts. For the orthodox Puritan it meant no more than the right to replace prelacy with presbytery, or with some modified erastian presbyterian-congregationalist compromise as it was to turn out. For all Particular (or Calvinist) and for some General (or Arminian) Baptists, it comprised the right of their own gathered churches to worship as they wished and to practise adult sprinkling or immersion. What the attitude of Baptists would have been towards Presbyterians and Independents in the unlikely event of their having themselves gained majority support, or having seized control of the machinery of state, is an entirely hypothetical question; we can only say for certain that they would not have had a single agreed answer. In practice the leading questions of the time were whether toleration should extend to Anglicans, alias Prelatists, and to Papists. At a more theoretical level the issue of toleration involved the very nature of a true church or a godly community. If by definition this could only be a select, voluntary body which individuals opted to join, then any notion of a state church, with compulsory financial maintenance, let alone attendance at its worship, must fall. Some sects, like the Fifth-Monarchists, claimed a monopoly of revealed truth; others, such as the Seekers, were sincere pluralists. A few individuals but scarcely any organised groups took the principle to its logical conclusion, arguing against any coercion or discrimination on religious grounds, extending this even to Papists, non-Christians and unbelievers.

In this respect the attitude of the early Quakers is obscure. Clearly they wanted a let-up on persecution, an amnesty in effect. But in what sense Fox and Naylor and their associates would have tolerated 'professors' and others worshipping in 'steeplehouses', if they themselves had really gained the upper hand, again is open to debate. Even the Levellers and Winstanley were not prepared to tolerate the advocacy of counter-revolution. For the former, attempts to overthrow the Agreement of the People once it had been accepted, for the latter the re-introduction of buying and selling and the private ownership of land were to be offences beyond the pale. It would be all too easy to sneer at them for inconsistency, but I suspect that for most of us too toleration is a value, not the value; and that, if we are honest with ourselves, we set limits to it which are defined by our other values. Perhaps for Milton in the *Areopagitica*, as for the modern liberal, any opinion however eccentric or outrageous could be advocated, any form of worship practised, so long as it did not have any practical implications. And the question then arises, who is to decide about this, and to weigh conflicting values in the balance. Even the Levellers, thoughtful as they were about these issues, did not specify who was to adjudicate in dubious cases as to whether or not the Agreement was being infringed. The removal of civil disabilities on those who do not belong or conform to the majority faith or to the established church is of course a much more limited objective, where some of the Interregnum radicals certainly were in advance of their time; but this principle too, however admirable and unexceptionable it may be, raises its own difficulties: should those whose own views would entail the suppression of the freedoms of others be allowed to propagate these and in particular to do so with the advantages of holding places of trust in a free society? Some mid-seventeenth-century tolerationists faced these issues; others either did not see them or shied away. I am not sure that we have got much further.

Linked to the issue of toleration in this world is that of salvation in the next. It is tempting to see a dichotomy in the whole radical Protestant tradition between élitist intolerant predestinarians and populist, tolerant antinomians, Arminians and 'universalists'[30] as their enemies sometimes called them. But this is probably too neat and tidy a view of the past. Not all predestinarians were intolerant; some were more radical on social and other secular matters than some anti-predestinarians. The doctrine of election, even more that of double predestination—to eternal reprobation as well as salvation—had its own upside-down turning implications, within families, communities, even whole realms.

It is difficult to see how some of what was being demanded in the 1640s could be said to have arisen from the campaign for religious toleration. The claims which were made to enjoy the rights of free-born Englishmen, above all for equality before the law, were only related coincidentally to the ecclesiastical issues of the time. Whether or not such demands would have arisen without the religious divisions and conflicts, we simply cannot tell. Lilburne's attack on monopolies, which he held to include privileged control over access to the Bible, may suggest a link between the two.[31] On the other hand reform of the legal system, to establish an equal rule of law at least for all free males, which in turn led on to demands for parliamentary and constitutional change, seems at most only tangentially related to the struggles of churches and sects over theology, liturgy and ecclesiology. Free trade and legal equality, like religious toleration, could no doubt mean different things to different people; but as objectives they owed much more to the debate over 'fundamental laws' conducted by King and Parliament back in 1641–2 than they did to the future of bishops or the prayer book.

Perhaps, as with those of other persuasions, it is possible to make a

---

[30] Obadiah Howe, *The Universalist Examined and Convicted* ... (1648).
[31] See note 7 above.

distinction between authors who seem mainly to be responding to
outside pressures and events, including the influence of other people's
writings, and those who express their own ideas more or less independently of any external influences. A moment's reflection tells us
that 'no man is an island', and that the notion of a 'Robinson Crusoe'
type of thinker is quite unreal. None the less some writers are more
acted upon, some are more of an influence upon others. Then there
is the further distinction between those who express their views on a
variety of topics and those who stick to one. John Cook, Solicitor at
the King's Trial and executed as a regicide in 1660, wrote successively
on the law and legal profession, the Independent or congregational
churches, how to achieve peace between the conflicting parties and
justice for all in the context of 1647, provision for the poor, justification
of regicide and the abolition of monarchy, excessive legal costs and
other faults in the law.[32] Can any common theme be discerned in
these works, spanning the years 1646 to 1655? Cook writes on legal
reform as a practising lawyer, later as a judge, and as a practical,
moderate reformer. In wanting justice to be available to all on fair
terms, yet within the framework of the common law and the existing
structure of courts, he never waivers. Likewise, his concern for the
poor, not to abolish gradations of wealth and status, let alone to
tamper with private property, but to alleviate the lot of those worst off
by reducing the extremes of wealth and poverty, is another consistent
theme. By contrast, his concern for religious toleration, which is to be
enforced by the civil magistrate, seems to have arisen from alarm at
presbyterian pretensions and the threat, as he perceived it, of a new
ecclesiastical tyranny. His conversion to republicanism too would
seem to have followed from his utter disillusionment with Charles I
during the course of 1647-8. This is not to doubt the sincerity of
Cook's commitment to religious freedom or to republican ideals, only
to suggest a contrast between the beliefs which he seems to have held
in his own right and those which he apparently developed in response
to current circumstances. Even so, Cook might not have written, or
at least published at all on any of these topics without the general
stimulus of

these (commonly called) unhappy times .... and I confess in
many respects so they are, though for my own particular, I looke

[32] *The Vindication of the Professors and Profession of the Law* ... (1646); *What the Independents
would have* ... (1647); *Redintegratuio Amoris, or, A Union of Hearts* ... (1647); *Unum
Necessarium: Or, The Poor Man's Case* ... (1648); *Monarchy No Creature of God's Making*
... (1652); Bodleian, Rawlinson MS. A 189, fols. 383–406; E. MacLysaght, *Irish Life
in the Seventeenth Century* (2nd edn. Cork, 1950), Appendix, pp. 417–46; G. E. Aylmer,
The State's Servants ... 1649–1660 (1973), pp. 76, 368. This long, very revealing letter
written to Fleetwood in August 1655, was not cited in the *D.N.B.* article on Cook.

upon them as the most glorious times that ever were since the Apostles. . . .[33]

His defence of his own profession and discussion of the qualities needed in judges are tempered by his realism about human nature: 'what if the best lawyers be not the best men?' As for reform of criminal procedure and the law of debt; 'me thinkes these necessitous times should be as a golden key to open the doore of hope for poor prisoners'. On political theory he praises William Ball's *Sphere of Government*, except for its dangerous opinion that there might be circumstances when the counties of England would be justified in resisting an act of parliament (which had received the assent of both Houses and the Crown), by armed force. He argues that Ball

> mistakes the nature of democracy, where the power resides in the people (as all lawfull power originally is) they may nominate what Governours they please, and may prescribe in what form they will be governed, but when they have settled a forme and elected Governours, they may not displace and change that Government.[34]

Cook's congregationalism was not merely Erastian but theologically low-key and almost non-sectarian:

> He desires no Toleration for any Errours against Religion or State-Policie, but of some Errours in Religion which do not raze the foundation, conceiving liberty to be the best means to cure all such differences . . .

In the context of 1647 he is predictably critical of the Commons majority for their hostility towards the Army. He denies that he would extend toleration to Roman Catholics unless they would take an oath of political loyalty and were incapable of doing any harm. In his opposition to presbyterian orthodoxy, he introduces a medical metaphor: 'is it not better to be healed by an Emperick, than to be poysoned by a Physitian?' He favours the reconquest of Ireland and the punishment of known rebels there, but laments the genocidal undertones

---

[33] *Vindication*, p. 1.

[34] *Ibid.*, pp. 53, 77, 87–9. William Ball the pamphleteer was not the recruiter M.P. for Abingdon of that name, who died in the spring of 1648, but is described as Esquire of Barkham in 1646 and was still alive in the 1650s (*Catalogue of the Pamphlets . . . collected by George Thomason, 1640–1661* (2 vols., 1908), Index, II, 468; D. Wing, *Short-Title Catalogue . . . 1641–1700*, vol. I (2nd edn. N.Y., 1972), B586–598; *Victoria County History of Berkshire*, iii, 201, 238, 361; D. Brunton and D. H. Pennington, *Members of the Long Parliament* (1954), 33, 207, 226; *Cal. S.P. Dom., 1651*, p. 503, *1656–7*, p. 580).

of some preaching on this subject.[35] So far he has no doubts about a settlement including the King, even if imposed in part by the Army. Indeed it might be said that the only unrealistic, in the sense of unrealisable policy advocated by Cook anywhere in his writings was precisely this: a settlement which Charles I would accept and by which he would then honestly abide. It is Cook's proposal that the poor should receive free medical treatment which has led Charles Webster to include him under the heading, 'The Prolongation of Life'.[36] Ironically Cook's schemes for social welfare required an ethic of paternalism arguably nearer to that of the pre-Civil War monarchy than was to be attained under the Republic or indeed after the Restoration. We must of course beware of making him look more modern than he was: although 'I believe there are more godly women than men in the world', his argument against hereditary monarchy saw it as 'against the Law of God and nature to make Millions of men subject to the commands of a woman'.[37] His reforms perhaps came nearest to achievement in Ireland under Ireton and later Henry Cromwell, and in England during the early months of the Protectorate. His failing was to believe that men would in general act against their own material interests through intellectual and moral persuasion alone.

Whatever we make of Hugh Peter—his personality, his part in the King's trial and execution, his conduct at his own trial and execution—a similar range of concerns is to be found in his writings. Peter put forward proposals encompassing educational changes which were to be related to the advancement of true religion, measures related to social welfare together with economic improvements, and various legal reforms, some quasi-Mosaic, others limited and pragmatic.[38] Only with regard to the law and in advocating the indirect election of M.P.s did he diverge from other moderate reformers. And for the former deviation he was gently reproved by Cook, who in other respects accorded Peter greater originality than he claimed for himself. To call Peter a Utopian, as does his best modern biographer,[39] surely implies that even relatively limited reforms were unattainable. In disagreeing with this, I do not totally exclude the contrary implication: that in certain historical situations moderate reformism may

---

[35] *What the Independents would have....*, p. 9; *Redintegratio Amoris*, pp. 36–7, 46, 54, 78–9.

[36] *Great Instauration*, ch. IV.

[37] *Monarchy No Creature*, p. 35.

[38] His works are conveniently summarised in R. P. Stearns, *The Strenuous Puritan Hugh Peter 1598–1660* (Urbana, Ill., 1954). There are also numerous references to him, as to Cook, in Webster's *Great Instauration*.

[39] Stearns, pp. 264, 381.

be just as unrealisable as more sweeping and drastic schemes, which might more accurately be designated Utopian, or revolutionary.

The Army officers who ventured into print to express their continuing discontents after Putney and Ware, are by no means a homogeneous group, beyond having that much in common. Nicholas Cowling, like Ireton a Commissary-General, is usually described as an Antinomian.[40] Yet by the summer of 1650 he was calling for a range of practical reforms comparable to Cook's, with the addition of abolishing tithe payments in kind besides other changes in the law and in poor relief.[41] Colonel John Jubbes moved furthest in a Leveller direction, producing his own version of an 'Agreement of the People'.[42] Major Francis White helped in the suppression of the pro-Leveller mutinies in 1649, having been pardoned for saying earlier that all power was now in the sword; but he continued to defend military intervention as a political means to achieve reforms. To this end, and to prepare for the eventual Fall of the Beast and Rule of the Spirit,

a forme is necessary both in divine and civill things; for God is the God of order, and rules the world by order, for if every man's spirit should be his rule, few would be ruled.[43]

Captain John Vernon reacted to the Whitehall Debates of December 1648 by reiterating his support for the Agreement and opposing the magistrate having any restrictive, let alone compulsive power in matters of religion.[44]

Disagreement about the use of juries illustrates some of the differences between conservative and radical reformers. Henry Robinson's arguments for more trials to be conducted by judges or professional assessors have a modern ring to them. Jurors are ignorant, apathetic,

[40] E.g. Gertrude Huehns, *Antinomianism in English History with special reference to the period 1640–1660* (1951), index entries, all relating to his first work, *The Saints Perfect in this Life, Or Never* (dated by Thomason 7th Nov. 1647).

[41] *A Survey of Tyrannie: Or, The Anatomizing of Tyrants* ... (1650. Dated by Thomason 9th August).

[42] For a convenient reprint, see John Jubbes, 'Several Proposals for Peace and Freedom By an Agreement of the People' (22 Dec. 1648), Doc. 14 in D. M. Wolfe (ed.), *Leveller Manifestoes of the Puritan Revolution* (New York, 1944; repr. 1967), pp. 311–21).

[43] *The Copies of Severall Letters Contrary to the Opinion of the present powers, presented to the Lord General Fairfax and the Lieutenant General Cromwell* (London, 1648. Dated by Thomason 20th March 1648/9), p. 17, supporting the Agreement; *A True Relation of the Proceedings in the Business of Burford With other Discourse of Publike Concernment* (his text is dated London, 17th September 1649) p. 16. *For the Sacred Laws of the Land* (Thomason, 28th November 1652), by Francis Whyte (sic), is much more conservative and seems likely to be by another author.

[44] *The Sword's Abuse Asserted: Or, A Word to the Army* (Thomason, 19th December 1648). He is discussed in Jordan, *Religious Toleration*, iv, 332–5.

corruptible and over-suggestible.[45] William Walwyn's reply is equally predictable: men of honesty and sufficiency are amply available for jury service, and juries provide bastions of English liberty.[46] A blunter, more forthright defence of the system is given in the Levelleresque work by 'Divers affectionate Persons to Parliament, Army and Commonwealth, inhabiting the cities of London, Westminster, Borough of Southwark and places adjacent, Presenters in the behalf of themselves and others', to Cromwell and the officers of the Army on 28th January 1653 as *The Onely Right Rule for regulating the Lawes and Liberties of the People of England*, where in this respect as in others they maintain

> there is not perfection to be expected in any Government in this world, it being impossible for the wisest men that ever were to compose such Constitutions, as should in every case warrant a just event [that is, guarantee the right verdict or decision].[47]

Yet on annual parliaments and annual rotation in office, as on trial by jury, they allow no doubts. Interestingly Robinson's next work, which contains his most comprehensive range of proposals both for law reform and economic development, omits any mention of juries.[48]

The writings of the 'improvers', most of all in relation to agriculture and the countryside, demonstrate how rights and freedoms could lead to conflict as easily as to consensus. The right to enclose land, to improve wastes, commons and fens, to disafforest, to drain, to engross in severalty, might all represent freedom for some individuals to make the best use of their own property, and no doubt in the long run bring benefit to the majority through the consequent increase in total wealth and productivity. But this could often only be at the cost of the customary rights of others, who might equally well have supported the parliamentary cause in the naive belief that their interests would thereby be protected, maybe even advanced.[49]

One final thought here: in view of the emphasis on new manu-

---

[45] *Certain Considerations In order to a more speedy, cheap, and equall distribution of Justice throughout the Nation* (London, dated 14th November 1651), pp. 2–3.

[46] *Juries Justified* ... (London, dated 2nd December 1651). In style and force of argument this is far below the level of Walwyn's best tracts of the 1640s.

[47] The authors name themselves as George Baldwin, Simon Turner, Philip Travers, William Tennant, Isaac Gray, and Robert Everard. The quotation is from p. 5.

[48] *Certain Proposals In order to a new Modelling of the Lawes, and Law-Proceedings ... As Also: Certain Considerations for the Advancement of Trade and Navigation* (submitted to Parliament, London, 1652–3). The two pieces are separately paginated.

[49] Webster, *Great Instauration*, especially ch. V; Thirsk, 'Plough and Pen: Agricultural Writers in the Seventeenth Century', in T. H. Aston *et al.* (eds.), *Social Relations and Ideas* (Cambridge, 1983), and ch. 16, 'Agricultural Policy: Public Debate and Legislation', section B, in Thirsk (ed.), *Agrarian History*, v, ii and the older work by G. Fussell, *The Old English Farming Books from Fitzherbert to Tull, 1523 to 1730* (1947).

factures by Robinson, Wall and others, might the later, most damaging split between finance and industry, by which English society was to be bedevilled, have been somewhat lessened if progress had continued along the lines marked out by these reformers, whatever their differing degrees of radicalism?

Apart from William Clarke's inimitable record of the Army debates, our evidence comes overwhelmingly from contemporary pamphlets and newsbooks. And this is a reminder of the key role played, especially in enabling the expression of extreme, minority views, by the radical publishers. Chief among these were William Larner and Giles Calvert.[50] Indeed a cynic might be tempted to argue that these two between them invented the popular movement in the English Revolution! Whether they, or others unknown, were responsible for the anonymous printing and publishing of similar works, we can only surmise. There might be different motives for anonymity, but evading the attention of government is surely the most likely. The probably spurious Rotterdam imprint of *Tyraniprocrit*[51] was contemporaneous with the activities of John Crouch, who used pornography to maintain a clandestine royalist readership.[52]

This leads on to the question which it would be cowardly not to ask, but hopelessly rash to try to answer: who read the pamphlets and newsbooks of the Interregnum? Unless we are to suppose that the publishers and booksellers (I assume them, rather than the printers) were left-wing philanthropists, like Victor Gollancz subsidising the Left Book Club out of non-political best sellers in the 1930s,[53] prepared to back whatever sectarian or good cause it might be, entirely regardless of sales, then we must assume a market to have existed. It makes much better sense of the available evidence, and is generally less implausible on common-sense grounds, to suggest that some publishers, perhaps even printers too, were committed in differing degrees to various sects or movements; but that few, if any, could or

[50] P. G. Morrison, *Index of Publishers, Printers and Booksellers in Wing's STC ... 1641–1700* (Charlottesville, Va., 1955); anon, 'George Calvert's publishing career', *Journal of the Friends of Historical Society*, XXXV (1938), 45–9; H. R. Plomer, *Dictionary of Printers and Booksellers ... from 1641 to 1667* (1907), pp. 42–3, 113.

[51] August 1649. Only two copies are recorded as having survived; parts are reprinted in G. Orwell and R. Reynolds (eds.), *British Pamphleteers* (1948) I, 81–112; Walwyn's authorship is canvassed in H. N. Brailsford, *The Levellers and the English Revolution*, ed. C. Hill (1961), p. 71 n. and in O. Lutaud, *Cromwell, Les Niveleurs et la République* (2nd edn. Paris, 1978), pp. 79–88.

[52] M. Gimelfarb-Brack, *Liberté, Egalité, Fraternité, Justice. La vie et l'oeuvre de Richard Overton* (Berne, 1979), Annex 4. See microfilms of the Thomason Tracts for '*The Man in the Moon*', *Mercurius Democritus, Fumigosus*, etc.

[53] The evidence is just short of conclusive, but seems overwhelmingly probable (see Ruth Dudley Edwards, *Victor Gollancz. A Biography* (1987), esp. p. 257).

would have gone on producing works for which there was no demand at all. An alternative hypothesis is that well-to-do patrons, individual or corporate, met part of the costs. Insofar as this is applicable at all, it would surely be least so the more radical the works in question. It would be fascinating to find the Fell family transmitting funds from Cumberland to London, so that Giles Calvert and others would continue to produce what we know as the early Quaker writings. I can see no reason why this should not have happened, but am unaware of any evidence that it did. As to authors having subsidised their own works, this might apply to the more affluent on what I have by implication labelled the 'Moderate Left', but hardly among the more radical, with the possible exception of William Walwyn, though again there is no evidence that he did do so. It is hard to think of anyone else on the more extreme Left of whom this might have been true. During the period (probably for some months in 1648) when the Levellers may have raised small individual subscriptions from their supporters,[54] some of this money may well have been used to help produce Petitions, Agreements or other tracts. Were the economics of *The Moderate*, during its Leveller phase, any different from those of any other newsbook?[55] Once more, we simply do not know. In the huge corpus of modern scholarly writings on John Milton, I am unaware of any sustained consideration of how his prose works were financed, other than the semi-official or commissioned anti-monarchical pamphlets of 1649–54.[56] Did the divorce pamphlets pay for themselves, or did they receive a subvention from the Milton family funds; hardly from the Powells of Forest Hill and the unpaid marriage portion! And what of his republican tracts of 1659–60? Insofar as there is more material still to be worked on, relating to the history of the book trade,[57] more evidence may come to light. Lacking it, we

---

[54] 'A Declaration of Some Proceedings of Lt. Col. Lilburne and his Associates' in W. Haller and G. Davies (eds.), *The Leveller Tracts 1647–1653* (N.Y., 1944), pp. 100–1.

[55] See D. E. Brewster and J. Howell, 'Reconsidering the Levellers: The evidence of *The Moderate*', *Past and Present*, xlvi (1970); J. Frank, *The Beginnings of the English Newspaper 1620–1660* (Cambridge, Mass., 1961), pp. 154–82 passim; A. N. B. Cotton, 'London Newsbooks in the Civil War: their political attitudes and sources of information', Oxford. D.Phil. thesis, 1971, which corrects Frank, e.g. on the editorship of *The Moderate*.

[56] W. R. Parker, *Milton*; J. M. French, *the Life Records of John Milton* (5 vols. New Brunswick, N.J., 1949–58); John Milton, *Complete Prose Works* (8 vols. New Haven, 1953–80), see especially vols. II, *1643–1648*, ed. E. Sirluck, and VII, *1659–1660*, ed. A. Woolrych. Needless to say, there are many works on Milton which I have not consulted.

[57] In an important paper, delivered in Oxford in May 1987, but unfortunately not published, Ms Sheila Lambert has suggested that this is so, and has offered some instances where drastic revision of previous views may be necessary, though I cannot claim her support for anything that is said here.

can only suppose that publishers and booksellers, like printers, were businessmen, although some were better at it than others. The Levellers in particular may have exaggerated the size of their imprints for propaganda purposes. But when Henry Parker attacked Lilburne in 1649, he said that the Leveller leader had a following of between 10,000 and 20,000 people;[58] this might easily imply a potential readership plus oral audience of listeners two to three times that, or say 50,000 in all give or take: equivalent in today's population to 450,000. We should have to move forward in time to John Wilkes and Tom Paine, to find radical authors of comparable popularity. And just to repeat myself, since every historian should always be vigilant against her or his personal bias: the evidence of ballads and chapbooks is ample reminder, if any were needed, of what I have already said: radical does not equal popular or *vice versa*.

It is worth remembering how extraordinarily wide a range of reforms were under discussion, and how relatively modest a place the franchise had among them. To illustrate this, works by those not of the first rank may be the more revealing. Let us consider briefly the thirty one proposals made by the Quaker, Edward Billing in his *Mite of Affection*, which appeared in 1659.[59] Besides religious freedom for all Christians (who remain undefined), his points include the consideration of all servile tenures and of copyhold and their reduction to consistency with a free Commonwealth provided that everyone's existing property is respected; forced labour instead of the death penalty for theft; indirect election of M.P.s *via* parishes and hundreds; taxation to be reformed in proportion to people's wealth; persecutors and delinquents only to be banned from voting and from holding office; annual rotation plus annual parliaments; the whole of the British Isles to constitute a single 'free trade' area. This is only a selection.

Almost equally remarkable are the two sets of propositions, one presented to the Barebones by Samuel Hering in 1653 and the other by the even more obscure William Hickman to Cromwell as Lord General in 1651. Hering, who purports to have been in a mystical trance when the message came to him, wanted—as Hill and others have pointed out—two colleges in each university devoted exclusively to studying the writings of Jacob Boehme and similar authors. His call for discrimination against wine-drinkers, for old people's homes

---

[58] Henry Parker, *A Letter of due censure and redargution to Lieut. Coll: John Lilburne* ... (1650), p. 39.

[59] Reprinted in H. Barbour and A. O. Roberts (eds.), *Early Quaker Writings 1650–1700* (Grand Rapids, Michigan, 1973), Part D. no. 9, pp. 407–21. Most of the work for this paper had been done before I read B. Reay, *The Quakers and the English Revolution* (1985), in which this and other pamphlets cited here are discussed.

and workhouses to contain the idle young, for salaried officials, all to be chosen by the 'Godly Party', for strict sumptuary laws, the abolition of hereditary titles of honour, and the drastic decentralisation of the structure of law and government may appear little more than a mish-mash of extreme sectarian Puritanism and functional, far from 'fanatical' or Utopian remedies for contemporary disorders.[60] Hickman covers a narrower range, and displays an even more intense religious fervour, especially in his bloodthirsty attitude towards the Irish and in his sense of Antichrist being at work all around in the world, even (surprisingly) in the Congregational churches. Yet when he turns to the things of this life, and in particular what he perceives as Cromwell's mission to settle the government of the country, his analysis is clear and cogent; he sees that a republic requires a greater measure of equality and independence among its people than is necessary or indeed appropriate for a monarchy. He argues that fundamental changes is the legal and social systems are essential if the country is not to return to kingship. Other specific reforms which are needed will follow from these more general requirements.[61]

It will be obvious that there is more than one possible definition of radical. For Christopher Hill it describes

> those who rejected any state church: both separatist sectaries, who opposed a national church on religious principle, and others ... whose opposition was part of a more general political, social and economic programme.

Elsewhere he writes:

> In the radicals' mode of thought two strands are twisted. One is belief in the evolution of truth, continuous revelation; ...

while the second principle is

> reliance on the holy spirit within one, on one's own experienced truths as against traditional truths handed down by others.

This should be related to another well-known passage in the same work:

> There was, however, another revolution which never happened, though from time to time it threatened. This might have established communal property, a far wider democracy in political and legal

---

[60] J. Nickolls, Junior (ed.), *Original Letters and Papers of State Addressed to Oliver Cromwell ... Found Among the Political Collections of John Milton* (small folio. 1743), 99–102.

[61] *Ibid.*, 29–33. Unlike Hering, apparently a lay London Baptist, Hickman is not in R. L. Greaves and R. Zaller (eds.), *A Dictionary of English Seventeenth-Century Radicals* (3 vols. Brighton, 1982–4), and is untraceable in other standard works of reference.

institutions, might have disestablished the church and rejected the protestant ethic.[62]

Clearly a number of those with whom I have been concerned this afternoon do not survive as radicals at all by these somewhat stringent, exacting standards. I have been encouraged, should I say emboldened, by a recent article of William Lamont,[63] to take this a little further. Can we discern a potential programme of moderate reform, short of Hill's abortive popular revolution, but more substantial than what was achieved by successive regimes from 1640 to 1660? On the question of a state church, the levying of compulsory tithes might seem to have been the decisive obstacle. It would certainly be a mistake to underrate their contentiousness.[64] On the other hand it is worth reminding ourselves that the Levellers and even Winstanley envisaged salaried school-teachers, who were also to be religious and ethical instructors.[65] Might some compromise not have been possible for the commutation or amortisation of tithes, such as was progressively achieved during the nineteenth and twentieth centuries? If the Maintenance Trustees of the 1650s had had at their disposal all the assets realised by the sales of capitular lands and perhaps the fruits of some additional redistributive measures, then an alternative to tithes other than complete voluntaryism could have been attained. Moreover a modified episcopacy, along the lines advocated in 1641,[66] would have been a practical possibility if Charles I had accepted the Heads of the Proposals and had made an honest attempt to help implement them. As to the law, there were surely changes to be effected in the legal system and the profession going well beyond the limited achievements of 1650–53 (proceedings in English, documents in normal handwriting, civil marriage and parish registers, limited protection for poor debtors) and the partial reconstruction of Chancery (effective 1655–8), yet stopping far short of what would have satisfied either the Diggers or

---

[62] Hill, 'The Radical Critics of Oxford and Cambridge in the 1650s', in *Change and Continuity in 17th-century England* (1974), p. 132; Hill, *World Turned Upside Down*, pp. 296–8, 12.

[63] W. M. Lamont, 'The Left and its Past: re-visiting the 1650s', in *History Workshop Journal*, xxiii (1987), pp. 142, 151.

[64] Margaret James, 'The Political Importance of the Tithes Controversy in the English Revolution', *History*, xxvi (1941), 1–18; C. Hill, *Economic Problems of the Church From Archbishop Whitgift to the Long Parliament* (Oxford, 1956), esp. chs. V, VI, XI, XII; Eric J. Evans, *The Contentious Tithe* (1976): J. F. McGregor and B. Reay (eds.), *Radical Religion in the English Revolution* (Oxford, 1984), references from the Index.

[65] D. M. Wolfe (ed.), *Leveller Manifestoes* (N.Y., 1944); G. H. Sabine (ed.) *The Works of Gerrard Winstanley* (Ithaca, N.Y., 1941).

[66] By the committees associated with Archbishops Ussher and Williams: see W. A. Shaw, *A History of The English Church during the Civil Wars and under the Commonwealth* (2 vols., 1900), i, 65–73, ii, 287–94.

the Fifth-Monarchy Men. In addition to the Heads, I would suggest that the elements of such a programme can be extracted from the Officers' Agreement of January 1649, the Army Petition of August 1652, the draft bills prepared by the Hale Commission in 1652–3, and other schemes submitted to the Rump, the Barebones and the Protector.[67] Many such items are to be found in the pamphlets of John Cook and Hugh Peter and John Hall, as well as in those of Henry Robinson, in the fragmentary remains of Henry Marten,[68] the published and unpublished writings of Samuel Hartlib, the works of the 'improvers' especially Blith and Yarranton. For example, land tenure could have been rationalised without sacrificing the rights of commoners or proletarianising cottagers. Restrictive practices in trade and industry could have been swept away, but safeguards created against oligopoly and exploitation. This would have constituted an economic policy, not revolutionary, by some criteria not even radical, but much more comprehensive and far-reaching than the meagre harvest of 1649–51: namely the London Poor Relief Act, the Navigation Act and that for lowering the rate of interest. Not merely do measures such as these seem pragmatic rather than Utopian, but I would argue that they were potentially realisable, either if Henry Ireton had survived to succeed Cromwell, or if the Protector had taken the plunge and nominated Lambert as his successor before the fiasco of the Militia Bill and the Humble Petition. Mention of political leaders is a reminder that I have said little here about constitutional reform, at either national or local level. Clearly the Instrument of Government was an unsatisfactory compromise. The franchise should have been standardised in the boroughs as well as in the counties. Whether any nearer approach towards universal suffrage was possible, let alone necessary or desirable, without its causing more alarm and opposition than it was worth, seems highly doubtful. But then it was only briefly and perhaps fortuitously the central issue in 1647.[69] The Officers' Agreement was probably more sweeping than the Rump's lost draft Bill, certainly than the Instrument; none the less well this side of Utopia. As to local government, if England's American colonies could begin to move towards elected magistrates and other officeholders during the later seventeenth and eighteenth centuries, would this have been logically impossible in Old England too? It was by no

---

[67] D. Veall, *the Popular Movement for Law Reform 1640–1660* (Oxford, 1970); N. L. Matthews, *William Sheppard: Cromwell's Law Reformer* (Cambridge, 1984).

[68] C. M. Williams, 'Henry Marten: the anatomy of a radical gentleman' in D. H. Pennington and K. V. Thomas (eds.), *Puritans and Revolutionaries: Essays presented to Christopher Hill* (Oxford, 1978), 118–38.

[69] On which see now Austin Woolrych, *Soldiers and Statesmen The General Council of the Army and its Debates 1647–1648* (Oxford, 1987), which supersedes all previous accounts.

means unthinkable for some contemporaries. The ballot, that is secret voting as opposed to choice by lot for office as advocated by Harrington and others, is the great lacuna in almost all these schmes. Yet, if the Council of State could be elected by secret ballot of M.P.s from 1651 to 1653, the principle was surely extendable.[70] It conflicted of course with that favourite image, should one say myth, of Lilburne and others, the free-born Englishman, afraid of no one as he gave his voice at the hustings. And we have seen the sovereignty of general meetings with open voting re-asserted in our own time. But in the context of the seventeenth century it needed only a very small transference of thought, a tiny leap of the political imagination, to see the ballot as protective of those very rights that Lilburne cherished; always assuming of course that voters were intended to have a choice, rather than accept aristocratic selection, as we have recently been reminded.[71] The ballot and the attack on corrupt electoral practices really need not have waited for Gladstonian reforms in the 1870s and 1880s.

So much for speculation. The realities, as we know, were far otherwise. Here the evidence from 1659, even the early months of 1660, is instructive. The radical, indeed the revolutionary ideas are still there, but they lack any basis in political reality. Only a millenarian or a military dictatorship, of Vane and/or Lambert, offered any alternative to the restored and partially repentant but now fatally discredited Rump of the Long Parliament. And it was not one with which the rank and file of the Army, or many of the common people of England were prepared to 'live and die', to adapt Cromwell's words about his own relations with the Army.

In conclusion, how close did the world come to being 'turned upside down'? The most plausible answer is, not so nearly as some alarmed contemporaries feared. Whether to go further than this, and to eschew use of the phrase 'popular movement' altogether is another matter. We should not be surprised by the haltings and uncertainties, the limitations and inconsistencies evident in seventeenth-century radical

---

[70] W. L. (William Leach of the Middle Temple, Gent.), *A New Parliament, or Representative* ...... (1651), Wing L775A, pp. 4–6, contains an ingenious scheme for handing in paper slips with only the names of the voters' preferred candidates showing; Edmund Leach of New England, Merchant, *A short Supply or Amendment To the Propositions for the New Representative* (dated by Thomason 2 Nov. 1651. E. 644/9), pp. 5–7, glosses this (a) to guarantee the sitting Members of the Rump, (b) always to have a carry-over of $\frac{1}{2}$ or 1/5 of MPs from one parliament to the next, and (c) only to allow the voters to ballot for two out of four nominees for each constituency. For the references to the two Leachs I am grateful to Professor Austin Woolrych's *Commonwealth to Protectorate* (Oxford, 1982), pp. 21–2, although my emphasis is slightly different from his.

[71] Mark A. Kishlansky, *Parliamentary Selection Social and Political Choice in Early Modern England* (Cambridge, 1986), for 1640–60 see particularly ch. 5.

thought and propaganda. Whether our own reactions are sympathetic or the reverse, we can as historians only be impressed by its amazing range, vitality and eloquence, which were not to be equalled, still less surpassed for many a long year. As his son-in-law and friend, Dr Brooke wrote of Walwyn:

> He hath studied the Peoples Freedoms so radically, and hath brought to light Principles so supportive thereof, and so essential therunto, that no other Designe but their good, can with any pretence be fixt upon him; ...[72]

Could anyone wish for a better epitaph?

[72] Dr Humphrey Brooke, 'The Charity of Church-Men ....' (1649), in Haller and Davies (ed.), *Leveller Tracts*, p. 345.

CONSPICUOUS CONSUMPTION AND WORKING-CLASS CULTURE IN LATE-VICTORIAN AND EDWARDIAN BRITAIN

By Paul Johnson

READ 30 JANUARY 1987

IN the last decade, as economic orthodoxy has shifted from a Keynesian-influenced study of demand towards the monetarist concern for the supply side in the economy, so history seems to have moved in the opposite direction. After many years studying the role of production and supply in the economic development of Britain, historians have belatedly turned their attention to demand, and have been discovering, or rediscovering, the history of consumption. The advent of consumerism in Britain has been positively identified by Joan Thirsk in the seventeenth century, and by Neil McKendrick in the eighteenth.[1] Putting a date to the consumer revolution has become a highly competitive business; W. Hamish Fraser, and before him Peter Mathias, have identified just such a transformation in the second half of the nineteenth century, while Derek Aldcroft prefers to locate this change in the inter-war years.[2]

Consumerism is clearly a flexible concept, flexible enough to describe changes across four centuries of British history in the scale and nature of demand for manufactured goods, purchased for cash in the market economy. Despite the different time periods looked at by these historians, their intentions and interests have been similar—a desire to explain significant changes in the level of manufactured output in the British economy by reference to changes in tastes and increases in real incomes for at least a section of the population. The focus of this paper is rather different; it will look at consumption not in order to develop explanations of macro-economic growth, nor to identify abrupt changes in the social order, but instead to examine the dynamic nature of social relationships among a particular group

---

[1] Joan Thirsk, *Economic Policy and Projects: The Development of a Consumer Society in Early Modern England* (Oxford, 1978); Neil McKendrick, 'The Consumer Revolution in Eighteenth-Century England' in Neil McKendrick, John Brewer and J. H. Plumb, *The Birth of a Consumer Society: The Commercialization of Eighteenth-Century England* (1982).

[2] W. Hamish Fraser, *The Coming of the Mass Market, 1850–1914* (1981); Peter Mathias, *Retailing Revolution* (1967); Derek Aldcroft, *The Inter-War Economy, 1919–1939* (1970), 367–69.

of consumers—in this case urban working-class families in Britain between 1870 and the First World War.

Much historical investigation of the working-class population in this late-Victorian and Edwardian period has been concerned with the closely linked worlds of work and politics, and has focused on the rise of the Labour Party, the role of trade unions, and, more recently, on investigation of the labour process.[3] The academic predominance of this research has tended to divert historical attention away from the equally important worlds of domestic and community life. By directing relatively less attention to experience beyond the workplace, historians have appeared to belittle the worlds of married women, of children and the elderly, and of workers during their leisure hours. For some years social historians have been trying to redress this imbalance by reconstructing the history of people's non-working lives, though in many cases their efforts have told us more about the ideas of middle class administrators than they have about the actions of working-class subjects.[4] One problem that British social historians have faced has been, ironically, the wealth of readily available historical evidence. The almost obsessive propensity of Victorian administrators to conduct enquiries and collect statistics on a whole range of social issues from sanitation to sexual disease has provided a legacy of historical evidence which is easily accessible to researchers but frequently remote from the everyday experience of working-class people. And, conversely, the evidence of everyday life left by late-Victorian and Edwardian households is relatively sparse, hence the heavy reliance by historians on illuminating but exceptional sources such as Robert Roberts's *The Classic Slum*.

Yet there is a vast amount of historical information about the everyday lives of the British population that can be gleaned from the records of how people spent their money; that is, by looking at their consumption patterns. The (relatively few) historical studies of working-class consumption in Britain that exist tend to focus rather narrowly on the poverty of the manual workforce, and on the gradual improvements in living standards that came about at least from the middle of the nineteenth century.[5] This is not surprising, since much of the data on working-class expenditure has been drawn from social

---

[3] For a brief review of this literature, see the editor's introduction in Jay Winter (ed.), *The Working Class in Modern British History* (Cambridge, 1983), vii–xii.

[4] Editors' Introduction in Pat Thane and Anthony Sutcliffe (eds.), *Essays in Social History: Volume 2* (Oxford, 1985). vii–xxxiv; David Thomson, 'Welfare and the Historian', in Lloyd Bonfield, Keith Wrightson and Richard Wall, *The World We Have Gained* (Cambridge, 1985), 355–78.

[5] John Burnett, *Plenty and Want* (1966), chapter 8; T. C. Barker, J. C. McKenzie and J. Yudkin (eds.), *Our Changing Fare* (1966), chapter 2.

surveys that were designed to investigate the nature and extent of working-class poverty. The emphasis, then, has been on the proportion of this population living on a subsistence or below-subsistence income, and how they spent their money to make ends meet. But this is a very narrow and economistic way of looking at expenditure, since virtually all people, even the very poor, use their power to consume not just to meet their basic needs for food, clothing and shelter, but also to define their social position. The clothes we wear, the food we eat, the type of house we live in and the way we decorate it, the clubs and associations we join, are all aspects of our pattern of consumption which help to establish our social reputation. Beyond the workplace, individuals define themselves primarily by the way they spend their money.

This idea of consumption as a vital aspect of social existence, a primary way in which an individual interacts with a broader social environment, is not new to social science. It has long been a commonplace to social anthropologists and sociologists,[6] though most economists tend to view consumption in a narrow financial light, which is not surprising given the highly individualistic assumptions that underpin most economic analysis.[7] Some historians have made important progress in their attempts to place working-class consumption patterns in a social context by recognising that consumption expenditure is not simply the means to individual sustenance and gratification, but is also part of a social dynamic.[8] Yet in the main historians have followed economists in viewing consumption primarily in a quantitative and individualistic way, rather than as a means of studying social interaction.

It is, perhaps, surprising that historians of the late-nineteenth and early-twentieth centuries have taken so long to recognise this social element of consumption expenditure—surprising because one of the earliest, and certainly one of the most striking, analyses of the social role of consumption was written in this period. In 1899, the maverick American economist Thorstein Veblen published *The Theory of the Leisure Class* in which he developed the idea of conspicuous consumption, or consumption of goods and services done primarily for the

[6] Erving Goffman, *The Presentation of Self in Everyday Life* (1969); Mary Douglas and Baron Isherwood, *The World of Goods: Towards an Anthropology of Consumption* (1979).

[7] Notable exceptions to this are the relative income hypothesis of James Duesenberry, and the development of psychological economic analysis by George Katona. See James S. Duesenberry, *Income, Saving and the Theory of Consumer Behaviour* (Cambridge, Mass., 1949); George Katona, *Psychological Economics* (New York, 1975).

[8] See, for instance, Eric Hobsbawm, 'The Making of the Working Class 1870–1914' in his *Worlds of Labour* (1984), 194–213; Gareth Stedman Jones, 'Working-class culture and working-class politics in London 1870–1900: Notes on the remaking of a working class', *Journal of Social History*, vii, Summer 1974, 460–508; Harold Perkin, *The Origins of Modern English Society* (1969).

notice and approbation of other members of the community.[9] Veblen's book is a critique of consumerism in late-nineteenth century America, though it is written as a general analytical account that has relevance to all developed or developing consumer societies. At its heart is Veblen's belief that consumption is a social activity, and that 'The motive that lies at the root of ownership is emulation'[10]. He points out that this is initially true only for the richer members of society, but that in industrial societies even the 'impecunious classes' will spend substantially on non-essential items. The reason why even the relatively poor direct resources away from fulfilling basic subsistence needs is that 'the members of each [social] stratum accept as their ideal of decency the scheme of life in vogue in the next higher stratum, and bend their energies to live up to that ideal'[11]. People attempt to live up to these ideals through the conspicuous consumption of goods and services. Veblen stresses that:

> No class of society, not even the most abjectly poor, forgoes all customary conspicuous consumption.The last items of this category are not given up except under stress of the direst necessity. Very much squalor and discomfort will be endured before the last trinket or the last pretense of pecuniary decency is put away.[12]

The world Veblen paints is a world of competition and struggle, but the struggle is not between monolithic classes in the capitalist system, but between adjacent strata that are distinguished only by minor gradations of possession and consumption. It is a hierarchical world, where movement up or down the hierarchy is dependent on pecuniary strength, and the ability to display that strength in some tangible way. Veblen's critique of consumerism appealed to many of his American contemporaries, and influenced the work of a number of subsequent historians in their investigations of living standards and consumption patterns in modern America.[13] Here, however, his work received short shrift; *The Theory of the Leisure Class* was not published in Britain until 1925, and was never accorded the honour of a review in the *Economic Journal*. Yet Veblen's idea of conspicuous consumption as a motivating force at all levels of the economic hierarchy is a potentially powerful

[9] Thorstein Veblen, *The Theory of the Leisure Class* (New York, 1899). All page references are given to the 1970 English edition. On Veblen's social and economic philosophy, see John P. Diggins, *The Bard of Savagery: Thorstein Veblen and Modern Social Theory* (Hassocks, 1978).

[10] Veblen, 35.

[11] Ibid, 70.

[12] Ibid, 70.

[13] Richard Wightman Fox and T. J. Jackson Lears (eds.) *The Culture of Consumption* (New York, 1983); Daniel Horowitz, *The Morality of Spending* (Baltimore, 1985).

analytical device which can be used to throw light on consumption patterns of workers in late-Victorian Britain. The next three sections of this paper will examine the expenditure of this working-class population on 'necessities', luxury goods and luxury services, in an attempt to gain some insights into the importance of hierarchy and competition within working-class culture.

Necessities

it may seem odd to suggest that conspicuous consumption could affect the purchase of necessities, given what we know of expenditure patterns from family budgets collected around the turn of the century. The investigations of Charles Booth in London, Seebohm Rowntree in York, Maud Pember Reeves in Lambeth and the Liverpool Economic and Statistical Society on Merseyside all showed that, on average, over half the total expenditure of poor urban workers in these areas went on food, while rent took twenty to thirty per cent, fuel and light accounted for nine per cent of expenditure, and clothing between three and seven per cent; very little indeed seemed to be left for any other sort of consumption, conspicuous or otherwise.[14]

The idea of conspicuous consumption of foodstuffs seems even more far-fetched when set against the evidence about the poverty of many working-class households in this period. The social investigations of Booth and Rowntree, which found almost one third of families living in poverty and having insufficient income to maintain physical efficiency, have been taken to imply that income could be used to purchase only the most basic foodstuffs. Rowntree, in fact, believed that he had scientifically proven this to be the case, by using the most advanced nutritional evidence from the United States to calculate a minimum nutritionally adequate diet, and then working out the cost of this. His well-known conclusion was that a family of five in York in 1899 needed at least 21s. 8d. to live on, of which 12s. 9d. was required for food.[15] But a re-estimation of Rowntree's calculations shows that they were nowhere near as scientific as has commonly been assumed. His poverty measure 'was essentially impressionistic and based on *a priori* moral explanations', and his minimum expenditure was not a bare subsistence standard, since minimum dietary needs could have been achieved with about half the expenditure on food that Rowntree

---

[14] Details taken from Charles Booth, *Life and Labour of the People in London* (17 vols., 1902), vol. 1, 131–40; B. S. Rowntree, *Poverty. A Study of Town Life* (4th ed. 1902), chapter 8; Maud Pember Reeves, *Round About a Pound a Week* (1913) *passim*; Liverpool Joint Research Committee, *How the Casual Labourer Lives* (Liverpool, 1909), summary table.

[15] Rowntree, 110.

actually allowed.[16] Built into Rowntree's minimum budget, therefore, was a large discretionary element for palatability and variation in individual taste.

This discretionary element could be and often was used for various types of non-necessary expenditure. From an analysis of 1024 urban working-class household budgets collected in Britain around 1890 by the U.S. Commissioner of Labor, it is possible to calculate the extent to which families exercised discretion over their food expenditure.[17] Taking the common economic criterion that an expenditure category with an elasticity greater than one is a luxury[18], and a necessity if it has an elasticity under one, then food, rent, fuel and light were all necessities for urban workers in Britain in the 1890s, while clothing and furniture were luxuries.[19] But within the food category, there was considerable variation, with tea, sugar, milk, bread, potatoes and meat all counting as necessities (with lard appearing as an inferior food), and eggs, vegetables, fruit and fish coming into the luxury category.[20] The existence of some luxury foodstuffs within working-class budgets shows that there was scope (albeit often rather limited) to use diet as one element of conspicuous consumption within working-class communities. As Margaret Loane, a district nurse and writer on London's poor, observed in 1908, 'Schoolchildren are constantly forbidden to tell one another what they have had to eat—unless occasionally, when there may be something to boast of'[21]. Details about money matters and expenditure on food were generally kept secret, she noted, so that families could maintain their self-respect and independence during periods of financial pressure.

In a world where the financial security of almost all households was precarious, where sickness, strike or a downturn in the trade cycle could lead to rapid impoverishment, and where average savings could

[16] Ian Gazeley, 'The Standard of Living of the Working Classes, 1881–1912: The cost of living and the analysis of family budgets', Oxford University D.Phil. thesis, 1984, 371; J. H. Veit-Wilson, 'Paradigms of Poverty: A Rehabilitation of B. S. Rowntree', *Journal of Social Policy* 15 (1986), 69–99.

[17] Sixth and Seventh Annual Reports of the U.S. Commissioner of Labor, for 1890 and 1891 (Washington, Government Printing Office, 1891 and 1892).

[18] A good has an expenditure elasticity greater than one when the proportion of income spent on that good rises more rapidly than total income, and an elasticity less than one when the proportion spent on the good rises less rapidly than income. An inferior good is one on which the proportion of income spent falls when income rises.

[19] A. Fishlow, 'Comparative Consumption Patterns, the Extent of the Market, and Alternative Development Strategies' in E. Ayet (ed.), *Micro-Economic Aspects of Development* (New York, 1971); Mark Thomas, 'The Liberal Social Reforms and the Distribution of Income, 1906–10', Paper presented to the S.S.R.C. Quantitative Economic History Study Group, Essex University, September 1981.

[20] Gazeley, 318.

[21] Margaret Loane, *From their point of view* (1908), 75.

seldom sustain a family through more than a month or two of unemployment,[22] self-respect and community status could best be maintained by concealing evidence of financial hardship (such as a restricted diet), and by taking every opportunity to demonstrate economic good fortune. As Veblen wrote, 'The basis on which good repute in any highly organized industrial community ultimately rests is pecuniary strength'[23], but this pecuniary strength had to be displayed in the most effective way possible to maximise social advantage. When possible, food and diet were used to display pecuniary strength; more frequently, though, this was done through the other major necessary item of expenditure for all families—housing.

In his work on Victorian Kent, Michael Winstanley has written that

> People were slotted into the appropriate rung on the social ladder by a variety of factors: their jobs, income, cleanliness, material welfare, whether they had lace curtains up, whether they had a table cloth or a newspaper on their dining table, whether they frequented the pub or not, and most important of all, where they lived.[24]

Where someone lived was perhaps the most obvious and visible sign of their pecuniary strength. The Victorian age was a time of residential segregation, of the sorting out of towns and cities into distinct residential areas where different sorts of accommodation were provided at different rents for different income groups and classes.[25] But this was not, as has sometimes been suggested, simply a segregation between working class and middle class; it was as much a segregation between finely divided strata within the same broad class group. In Edwardian Wapping, according to one resident:

> If you crossed the Dock Bridge, or lived beyond it, you were said to be 'on the other side'. Neither the grown ups nor the children 'on the other side' had anything to do with us. They were a community on their own and so were we, although we were all in one parish.[26]

South of the Thames the same was true: one woman who grew up in New Cross recalled:

---

[22] Paul Johnson, *Saving and Spending; the working-class economy in Britain 1870–1939* (Oxford, 1985), 205.

[23] Veblen, 70.

[24] Michael Winstanley, *Life in Kent at the turn of the century* (Folkestone, 1978), 165.

[25] Donald J. Olsen, *The Growth of Victorian London* (Harmondsworth, 1979), chapter 1.

[26] Grace Foakes, *Between High Walls* (1972), 22.

We all had our districts, and the very fact that you lived at New Cross meant you were someone better than the people who lived in Deptford. I mean, the Deptford people would in their way think themselves someone who was better than those that came from the other side of the river. Anyone the other side of the river were rough people. You imagined so.... You were made to know your districts in London, but the districts kept themselves socially apart.[27]

Within the same districts, residential segregation and the social divisions this implied could be just as sharp. In one street just off the Commercial Road in the East End:

There was snobbery even among the working classes, and the boys from Morrison Buildings who were a little better off than we were and a little better dressed, used to sneer at our rags.[28]

Even single streets were divided by their inhabitants into 'rough' and 'respectable' ends, distinguished both by physical features such as bay windows, and by presumed differences in social behaviour[29], and residents would frequently demonstrate improvements in their economic status by moving to slightly better accommodation in the same or an adjacent street.[30] Some sorts of accommodation were open demonstrations of financial sufficiency—tenement blocks run by philanthropic housing trusts, for instance, required rent to be paid in advance, and tenants in arrears were immediately evicted, so these sorts of buildings tended to be occupied by workers with slightly higher, or more importantly, more secure incomes than the average.[31] But elsewhere, in mean streets of small and apparently identical houses, subtle but pointed distinctions were drawn by the inhabitants by their labours in colouring their doorsteps and windowsills with hearthstone, planting windowboxes and putting up curtains. Why did they do this? One former resident of a street of poor terraced houses in the centre of Bolton explained that 'It was as though there was a competition as to who could produce the best result, even though there wasn't any prize on offer'[32]. But Mrs Pember Reeves, in her description of living conditions in Lambeth, gave a clear hint about the nature of the social rewards or costs from this apparently benign competition when she wrote:

[27] Winstanley, 163.

[28] Jim Wolveridge, 'Ain't it Grand' (Stepney, 1976), 19.

[29] Ron Barnes, Coronation Cups and Jam Jars (1976), 31–43; Patrick McGeown, Heat the furnace seven times more (1967), 19.

[30] Lady Bell, At the Works (1907), 68; David Green, 'A Pauper Community in Victorian London', KCL Geography Department Occasional Paper 26, June 1986.

[31] Gareth Stedman Jones, Outcast London (Harmondsworth, 1976), 184–7.

[32] Bill Horrocks, Reminiscences of Bolton (Swinton, 1984), 6.

The inhabitants keep themselves to themselves, and watch the doings of the other people from behind window curtains, knowing perfectly that every incoming and outgoing of their own is also jealously recorded by critical eyes up and down the street.[33]

Luxury Goods

Since some elements of competitive and conspicuous expenditure are identifiable even within the closely constrained fields of food and housing, it would not be surprising to find that expenditure on other goods was even more obviously directed towards the twin goals of social approbation and social emulation. One of the most notable examples of this was the typical late-Victorian habit of wearing special clothes on a Sunday. A broad range of authors testify to the social importance of being properly dressed on the Sabbath. For the children of an Irish Catholic family in Liverpool, wearing the right clothes for attendance in God's house was what mattered:'What a sense of shame' recalled one such person, 'for a boy or girl to appear at mass on Sunday morning in the same old weekday rags'.[34] For a labourer in Edwardian Poplar, the motivation was somewhat different: 'He had to keep up appearances when he visited the pub for the weekend session with his mates'[35]. Alexander Paterson, writing of South Londoners in 1911, thought that:

On Sundays they are enslaved by a similar tradition. It is a day for better clothes, for starched collars and bright boots, whether they be black or yellow. The mother, with a sense of bitter pride, will not allow her family to stray into the main streets should a week of depression have ended in the pawning of their Sunday clothes.[36]

Dressing up on Sunday was a near-universal habit, but it was not the only opportunity to use clothing in a consciously public way. The social conventions varied from place to place, but the purpose was the same. In Lancashire, girls were put in new white dresses so they could walk with pride in the Whit Parade; in Craigneuk, near Glasgow, babies were carried wrapped in shawls, the colour and quality of which were a public indication of their family's worth.[37] But just as some clothes were a sign of financial sufficiency, other clothes, equally standardised in their cut and colour, could signal distress and poverty. In many workhouses, for instance, everyone 'was dressed in a uniform, the men in thick navy suits and the women in

[33] Pember Reeves, 5.
[34] Pat O'Mara, *Autobiography of a Liverpool Irish Slummy* (1934), 63–4.
[35] John Blake, *Memories of Old Poplar*, (1977), 11.
[36] Alexander Paterson, *Across the Bridges* (1911) 37.
[37] McGeown, 18.

thick navy dresses; you always knew where they lived the moment you saw them—their clothes gave them away.'[38] Was the social importance attached to clothing in this period surprising? Not to Veblen, who thought that

> at no other point is the sense of shabbiness so keenly felt as it is if we fall short of the standard set by social usage in this matter of dress. It is true of dress in even a higher degree than of most other items of consumption, that people will undergo a very considerable degree of privation in the comforts or the necessaries of life in order to afford what is considered a decent amount of wasteful consumption.[39]

To standard forms of dress for Sunday wear were added adornments such as the skilled worker's fob watch, and other more sombre trappings necessary for a decent funeral. The enormous economic edifice of industrial life assurance that was built on the penny-a-week contributions of working men and women was designed to provide the wherewithal for a decent funeral, and a decent funeral meant good refreshments and black clothes.[40] Putting on appropriate mourning dress was vital because funerals were, in the words of Lady Bell, 'one of the principal social opportunities' of the working class, one of the few formal chances they had to show off to friends and neighbours.[41]

Clothes were a very effective form of social display—of competition and emulation rolled into one—and they were effective because of their very portability. This was important in a society where the degree of geographical mobility was high, because clothes could serve as the sort of visible character reference that could not otherwise be obtained. Also important, though often less obvious and visible, was the type of decoration and furnishing provided in the family home. As a survey of casual workers in Liverpool found in 1909.

> The instinct of housepride seems almost never wanting ... Some attempt at ornament is always made, and coloured prints, photographs, and dust-collecting knickknacks often abound in houses from which the more pawnable articles of useful furniture have been stripped.[42]

Note here the telling middle class mixture of approval for the sentiments of housepride, but disapproval for the unnecessary and waste-

---

[38] Foakes, 21; Alice Linton, *Not Expecting Miracles* (1982), 49.

[39] Veblen, 119.

[40] Johnson, 14. By 1910 working class subscribers were paying almost £19m. a year for burial insurance.

[41] Bell, 77.

[42] Liverpool Joint Research Committee, xxiii.

ful accumulation of dust-collecting ornaments. This was even more clearly expressed by Mrs Samuel Barnett, who complained of working-class households that

> In most rooms there is too much furniture and there are too many ornaments ... I have counted as many as seventeen ornaments on one mantelpiece—three, or perhaps five are ample. She who aims to be thrifty will fight against yielding to the artificially developed instinct to possess.[43]

But it is far from clear that the instinct was artificially developed. Advertising directed at the working-class readers of the *News of the World* at the turn of the century focused on selling branded tea, cocoa and soap, not on selling patterned plates or china ornaments. Yet the idea of domestic decoration was common to all working-class households, though the exact form varied with both income and regional location. For prosperous workers who could afford it, the front room or parlour was the ultimate symbol of respectability, displayed to all who walked past the front window, and used only on Sundays. In this room were located all the possessions that were most expensive and flamboyant—gaudily covered chairs, patterned lino, large, extravagantly framed paintings, and a huge mirror extending from the mantelpiece to the ceiling. The whole purpose of the room was to be filled with possessions, and the bigger, brighter, brasher and more noticeable they were the better.[44] In poorer households—two-room tenements, for example—where there was neither the space nor the money for the luxury of the front room, there was still some attempt at decoration and display, all designed to demonstrate pecuniary strength. According to Walter Besant's account of such households in East London at the turn of the century, there would be a table, chairs, a chest of drawers, and

> On this chest stands a structure of artificial flowers under a glass shade. This is a sacred symbol of respectability ... So long as we have our glass shade with its flowers we are in steady work and beyond the reach of want. On each side of the glass shade are arranged the cups and saucers, plates and drinking glasses, belonging to the family. There are also exhibited with pride all the bottles of medicine recently taken by the various members.[45]

---

[43] *Thrift Manual* (1906), 20.

[44] Daisy Noakes, *The Town Beehive* (Brighton, 1978), 23–4; Raphael Samuel, *East End Underworld: Chapters in the Life of Arthur Harding* (1981), 97–8; Jerry White, *Rothschild Buildings* (1980), chapter 2.

[45] Walter Besant, *East London* (1901), 120.

The medicine, it should be noted, was important not just because it was an expensive good in its own right but also because it often signified the recent receipt of even more prestigious services from a doctor.[46]

Luxury Services

Medical attention was just one of the many luxury services with an expenditure elasticity greater than one that appear in working-class budgets in this period, but the two main categories were expenditure on amusements of all sorts, including holidays and outings, sports and hobbies, and expenditure on club and society membership.

Working-class holidays, trips to the seaside, charabanc outings from the local pub, all had one thing in common—they were done in a group, *en masse*. This was partly for reasons of economics—mass consumption is cheaper than individual consumption—but partly for reasons of display and emulation. There was little point in taking a holiday or a day-trip alone, as no-one was there to witness it, and no point in taking it with strangers, as they could not know who you were. So holidays became community events: by 1900 most Lancashire cotton towns went *en masse* to the seaside for the annual holiday outing.[47] The collective holiday was the culmination of collective saving, as the money to pay for the outing was accumulated throughout the year in the mill- or pub-based 'going off' clubs which proliferated from the 1880s.

Other collaborative activities that had an underlying economic rationale of cost-sharing were also heavily weighed down with an ethos of collective display. Of chief importance here were the major working-class institutions of the nineteenth century, the friendly societies and trade unions, though, as Stephen Yeo has pointed out in his detailed study of Reading, the same impetus to visible participation was present across a much wider range of clubs and associations.[48] In the nineteenth century, it should be remembered, both friendly societies and trade unions devoted most of their effort and money to providing life assurance and sickness benefit, rather than organising trade disputes. This insurance system was of vital importance to manual workers with a precarious income, and membership was taken out by all who could afford the regular contributions (and, judging from the high lapsing rates, many who could not).[49] But in the

---

[46] Johnson, 74.

[47] John K. Walton and Robert Poole, 'The Lancashire Wakes in the Nineteenth Century' in Robert D. Storch (ed.), *Popular Culture and Custom in Nineteenth Century England* (1982), 100–124.

[48] Stephen Yeo, *Religion and Voluntary Organisations in Crisis* (1976), 167.

[49] Johnson, chapters 2 and 3.

competitive world of any working-class community, the economic security that came from friendly society or trade union membership had to be publicly and conspicuously displayed for it to bring the maximum degree of social prestige and advantage. So, some sort of show—typically a public parade—was organised at least once a year, and from the 1860s these parades became increasingly elaborate as members adorned themselves with sashes, ribbons and medallions, and carried banners before them as they processed around the town. The large friendly societies excelled at this sort of pomp and ceremony, by the 1890s organising parades of over 1000 members and half a dozen brass bands at their annual congresses.[50]

Members also had personal emblems to display in their homes, alongside the other decorations in the front parlour. From the 1870s, friendly societies and trade unions developed an array of large, ornate and often very beautiful membership certificates, which were designed to be framed and hung in a prominent place at home, so that visitors or passers-by could see evidence of membership and, by implication, evidence of financial security.[51] Even the insurance books issued by penny-a-week life insurance companies would be hung up in the home, to let visitors see that the household was well insured and therefore respectable.[52] Because resources were so scarce in virtually all working-class households, every item of expenditure—for food, rent, clothing, holidays or even for insurance—had to be turned into something visible and tangible[53], so that its utility could be maximised.

To whom was all this effort at social display and conspicuous consumption directed? Was it for the itinerant middle-class social observer, priest or charity worker, who would jot down his or her observations with greater or lesser moral censure? Although the writing of Mayhew, Dickens and Gissing made slumming an exciting experience for a few of the West End wealthy in London, it seems most unlikely that working-class housewives would scrub the front doorstep or working men put on their 'Sunday Best' just to amuse passing tourists. The purpose of this social display was to impress the local community, the peer group. In an environment where so many people owned virtually nothing, almost any possession and the display

[50] The parades held at the major friendly society conferences are reported in the *Quarterly Reports* of the Ancient Order of Foresters and the Independent Order of Oddfellows.

[51] Eric Hobsbawm, 'The Transformation of Labour Rituals' in his *Worlds of Labour*, 66–82.

[52] Johnson, 46.

[53] Paterson, 47–8.

of this possession, was a way of broadcasting and establishing one's social worth. As one worker, describing life at the end of the First World War, explained, 'if you were keeping up with the Joneses, you had a piano and had your front door open so that people could hear'[54].

This is why households would put up with hardship, even to the extent of damaging their health, in order to keep up appearances. Rowntree found that some of the poorest families in York in 1899 were starving, and hastening their own death, in order to maintain the insurance payments that would let them have a really good funeral.[55] And every Monday morning throughout Britain, thousands of bundles of Sunday clothes would be deposited with the pawnbroker, and then redeemed the following Saturday at enormous long-term cost, just to maintain appearances on the Sabbath. Writing of working-class families in Middlesbrough, Lady Bell noted that most people were 'living under conditions in which the slightest lapse from thrift and forethought is necessarily conspicuous'[56], so it was not surprising that strenuous and costly efforts were made to hide such lapses, and every opportunity taken to indulge in the conspicuous display of financial sufficiency. It was for this reason that thrift institutions like friendly societies developed colourful public rituals which were functionally unrelated to their role as insurance clubs.

This (necessarily brief) analysis of working-class expenditure patterns has shown that even among poor working-class households before the First World War, income was sufficient to allow some discretion in expenditure, and this discretion could be exercised quite consciously to promote a family's social as well as physical wellbeing. Social wellbeing was related to the position of any family on the local pecking order of social status, and status was very largely determined by the ability to possess goods and utilise services. The financial insecurity of practically all manual workers in this period meant that status was linked less to qualitative judgements about taste and style (as is typical among secure middle-class households) than to quantitative judgements about ability to consume. By displaying pecuniary strength through conspicuous expenditure, the good repute of a family was enhanced. But the display was to a very local community, the increase in status apparent often only to neighbours close in economic and cultural terms, as well as close geographically.

This, perhaps, is why many middle-class observers in the late-nineteenth and early-twentieth centuries came to condemn so forcefully working-class profligacy. They saw the extravagant funerals, the

---

[54] John Langley, *Always a Layman* (Brighton, 1976), 11.
[55] Rowntree, 213.
[56] Bell, 52.

charabanc outings, the ornaments, in strictly economic terms, because they were not part of the working-class cultural world that placed high social value on these forms of conspicuous consumption. It is also, perhaps, one reason why political organisation within working-class communities was, in the eyes of many leaders of the labour movement, so backward and so difficult to stimulate. Although working-class life beyond the workplace was a harsh one of competition and struggle, the competitive horizons were very limited. Competition was with social neighbours, the struggle was to gain a slight improvement or prevent a slight reduction in financial security and social status. When friendly society members put on their Sunday best, adorned themselves with sashes and medallions, and paraded round the town, they did it to show their workmates that they were that little bit better off, that little bit more financially secure. When Durham miners organised their annual gala, they were saying as much or more to their fellow workers about their own social and economic prestige, as they were to mine owners about the symbolic conquest of the working class.[57]

The cultural distinctiveness of working-class life which was so much a function of the financial insecurity of manual workers has been taken by a number of historians as a proof of distinctive class consciousness. To quote Eric Hobsbawm:

> Where, in all this world of cramped, enduring, stoic and undemanding men and women, do we find class consciousness? Everywhere. The lives of British workers were so impregnated with it that almost every one of their actions testified to their sense of difference and conflict between 'them' and 'us'.[58]

But this study of the actions of workers and their families in spending and consuming highlights not the solidarity of workers but the degree of competition within their ranks. It suggests a working class decomposed into many strata with slightly different value systems, aspirations, interests and incomes. It suggests a world of competition and struggle centred around the everyday act of spending, but of competition and struggle *within* the working class, rather than *between* workers and owners of capital or managers. Workers and their dependants in late-nineteenth century Britain, just like those written about by Veblen in late-nineteenth century America, defined their social position by the way they spent their money. Shifting the historical focus away from the worlds of work and politics, and away from

---

[57] Hobsbawm, 'Transformation of Labour Rituals', 76.
[58] Eric Hobsbawm, 'The Formation of British Working Class Culture' in his *Worlds of Labour*, 190.

concern about production and income, towards the worlds of domestic and community life, of consumption and expenditure, presents an altogether more fragmented image of the British working class than is commonly seen in writing on this period.

But does this fragmentary pattern of social stratification matter, except for those historians who busy themselves studying the minutiae of working class social interaction? It is always possible to identify complex status hierarchies in any society, but it is not always the case that these run counter to more fundamental class divisions.[59] In late-Victorian and Edwardian Britain, however, the immediacy of the status divisions at all levels of working-class society, and the precarious nature of most families' income and social respectability, acted as a barrier to the development of a more cohesive working-class outlook. This was not false consciousness, it was real life.

[59] For a critique of this neo-Weberian view of social stratifiation, see Frank Parkin, *Class Inequality and Political Order* (1972), chapter 1. For a discussion of neo-Weberian analyses of nineteenth-century Britain see chapter 5 of Robert Gray, *The Aristocracy of Labour in Nineteenth-century Britain c. 1850–1914* (1981).

POWER, STATUS AND PRECEDENCE:
RIVALRIES AMONG THE PROVINCIAL ELITES
OF LOUIS XIV'S FRANCE

By Roger Mettam

READ 6 MARCH 1987*

DURING the past thirty years most historians have acknowledged that it is anachronistic to describe Louis XIV as an absolute monarch. Many of them have turned their attention towards the various élite groups whose power and privileges coexisted with those of the crown in the very different, and sometimes fiercely separatist, provinces which formed the kingdom of France. A few have attributed such great influence to local nobles and institutions that the royal government seems to have been reduced to impotence. This impression, clearly too extreme, has been created first by a preoccupation with those issues and periods where the crown was in conflict with many, or in the case of the Frondes with almost all, of its leading subjects, and a disregard for the more numerous occasions when the king and at least some élite groups had identical or compatible purposes. Secondly, it has arisen from a neglect of the informal channels of communication which were often more important than the formal administrative structure for linking the court and the provinces, and for conducting the everyday routine of government. The most important of these was the network of 'brokers', often influential governors and bishops, by which provincial requests for highly prized royal patronage—whether titles, orders, offices, privileges or pensions—

---

* This paper, as read to the Society, has been abbreviated here because of constraints on space in *Transactions*. In order to preserve most of the text, it has been necessary to include only a minimum of footnotes. Most of the argument is based on buildings and paintings, whose location is clearly stated, and it is not dependent on interpretations advanced by other scholars. Nevertheless general acknowledgement must be made of information about architects and painters, the dates of their works and the men who commissioned or subsequently owned them, and matters related to their construction or production. Most of these factual details have been drawn from documentation compiled by the Caisse nationale des monuments historiques et des sites in Paris, but debts must also be recorded to the Musée des Grands Augustins in Toulouse, the Musée des beaux arts in Lyon, the Musée d'art et d'histoire in Narbonne, and the Bibliothèque historique de la ville de Paris. The remarks about French society and social priorities at the beginning of this paper have been expanded, with full references to archival sources and to the work of other historians, in Roger Mettam, *Power and faction in Louis XIV's France* (Oxford, 1988).

were conveyed to the ministers and to the king himself. The possibility of personal advancement was a vital consideration for members of the upper social échelons as they calculated their responses to ministerial instructions and enquiries.

There are three ways of categorising élites in the seventeenth century, none of them mutually exclusive. There are social strata—nobility, clergy and bourgeois; professional and institutional affiliations, such as army officers, royal officials and municipal councillors; and, perhaps the most significant, family and clientage networks. An individual had to balance the need to defend the status of his social group against his best interests as a member of an institution or profession, and at the same time to consider how to advance his family and retain the support of his patrons and clients—a set of often conflicting priorities. The social categories of nobles, clergy and Third Estate were terms in common use, because the *Etats-généraux* and the provincial estates in the *pays d'états* were constituted according to this tripartite division. Yet each estate included men of widely differing resources and status, only the most senior of them being represented at these assemblies.

At the summit of the nobility were the *princes du sang*, closely followed by the *princes étrangers* who came from sovereign houses which had either been absorbed into the French kingdom or were still ruling in other parts of Europe. In order to preserve their superiority, they regularly married into other sovereign houses, thereby being the only nobles in France whose family prestige and quest for greater power depended on international links. Thus they were alone in seeking to influence that most kingly of functions, the making of foreign policy, and were duly regarded by French kings as potentially the most dangerous of subjects. Fortunately for Louis XIV, when he assumed personal control of the government in 1661, most Frenchmen no longer supported the ambitions of these grandees. The princely Fronde had exposed the selfishness of their motives. They had agreed to oppose Mazarin, but they could not decide which of their number should dominate the government in his place, and they had certainly shown no concern for the best interests of the wider population. Not for many years would princes be able to persuade large areas of provincial France to take up arms against the central government. Many Frenchmen had strongly resisted the attempts of Mazarin to use arbitrary powers, and would similarly challenge ministers in the future, but they did not think that a government of self-seeking and factious princes would be an improvement.

The rest, the greater part, of the estate of the nobility had ambitions which lay entirely within the kingdom. Most nobles did not want to participate in the policy-making councils at the centre, although they were quick to sense and to resist any attempts by ministers to undermine their extensive legal and fiscal privileges and their jurisdictional rights. They were not a homogeneous group, as their ranks included all nobles from great dukes to humble provincial *seigneurs*, men of widely differing resources, wealth, prestige and influence. Yet all of them claimed to belong to a social order whose origins lay in the distant past—1400 was the date which conferred true respectability on a noble genealogy—and to one which had been instituted to honour military valour. If that initial bravery had been supplemented by further chivalrous deeds in subsequent centuries, the family would have built up a cumulative repository of virtue, and of noble sentiment, which it could bequeath to later generations in the same manner as it passed on its hereditary titles and estates. The nobility was not only forbidden by law, but it also disdained, to be involved in the base bourgeois world of commerce and industry. The aristocratic landlord was largely master of his own property, having his own seigneurial court on whose judicial functions the crown had no desire to encroach. Only in the imposition of taxes did the king interfere in the economic relationship between the peasant and his lord, and in time of expensive wars these levies became the principal cause of animosity, uniting the noble and his tenants against the royal government.

The order of clergy was equally varied, ranging from cardinals and bishops to humble parish priests, and including privileged groups like the orders of monks and friars, as well as the troublesome theological faculty of the Sorbonne. The Third Estate, as it was represented in the provincial estates and on local hierarchies, was also diverse, including the corporations of merchants and craftsmen, professional men such as bureaucrats and lawyers, and that highly self-conscious élite, the elected councillors of the towns with their extensive control over urban affairs.

The one social stratum which was difficult to classify was the senior bureaucracy, composed of men who, like all royal officials, had not only purchased their offices and could pass them on to their heirs as if they were any other piece of property but who had the right to sell their posts to another man without reference to the king, even though the purchaser would then become a royal official in his own right. These senior *officiers*, through a combination of the length of service given by their family in the bureaucracy and the prestige of the offices that its members held, were also members of the nobility, the *noblesse de robe*. Or were they? The officials themselves, the king who had authorised the conferment of this status, and the leading bourgeois who aspired to enter these uppermost ranks of the bureaucracy would have insisted that this *noblesse* was undeniable. The old military families would have none of it. The bureaucrats could not produce genealogies of sufficient antiquity and they were totally lacking in inherited military valour. Moreover they worked for their living— they had even worked in order to acquire their so-called nobility— and such a way of life was intolerable to any true aristocrat. No one denied that a great official, like a *président* of the *parlement* of Paris, was a man of immense social status who could be invited to associate with ducal families in the most illustrious aristocratic *hôtels*. Indeed, in a society where the high entertained the lower, but the more humble were never so presumptuous as to invite their superiors, a great noble might even visit the house of the *premier président* of the *parlement* of Paris. But was it solely the prestige of the office which made such meetings socially acceptable? The aristocratic visitor would undoubtedly have said so, but the host would have insisted that it was a combination of his official prestige and his noble rank. Certainly a family like the Lamoignon, at the summit of the Parisian judicial hierarchy, felt that they could live in the aristocratic *quartier* of the Marais, and not among their fellow *parlementaires* on the Ile Saint-Louis.

If we return to my three ways of categorising élites, it will soon be evident that there were many sources of tension and rivalry. Within a purely social classification of first, second and third estates, there were many points to be disputed by the members of these strata. For example the Longueville family was demanding to be ranked among the *princes du sang;* the La Rochefoucauld to be recognised as *princes étrangers;* the nobilities of sword and *robe* closely observed and often challenged each other's pretensions; the lower clergy was aggrieved about the excessive wealth and powers of the bishops; the various levels of bourgeois were watchful lest some of their number sought to claim excessive social prestige—the list was almost endless. The three estates also regarded each other with suspicion. One of many grievances which could be cited was the resentment of great nobles that cardinals took precedence over them. They therefore became doubly aggrieved when a royal minister received the red hat, and could exercise social superiority over them as well as using the authority associated with his ministerial post. For that very reason it was vital for ministers like Richelieu, Mazarin, Dubois and Fleury to be cardinals. So too it was essential for Retz to gain entry to the Sacred College as he launched his unsuccessful bid to replace Mazarin as *premier ministre*.

When élites are classified by their institutional function the causes of rivalry are equally easy to discern. The hierarchy of institutions and jurisdictions in France had grown up haphazardly. On many occasions the crown, impoverished in time of war, had perceived a short-term advantage in creating and selling new offices, rights and privileges. Such posts and liberties were often ill-defined, provoking much dispute, either immediately or when unforeseen issues arose at a later date, about which person or institution had the right to exercise which functions. If the confrontation became serious, as it often did, the parties would seek a legal resolution of their differences, a process made all the more complicated because the jurisdictions of the courts themselves were ill-defined, and a case between two litigants might give more than one court an opportunity to challenge the competence of its rivals to hear it. A plaintiff who flattered one group of judges by insisting that they alone had the appropriate jurisdictional authority might receive a sympathetic hearing from them, while his opponent might be faring equally well in the rival court where he had started proceedings. Then the *parlement* might intervene and evoke the entire case to its own chamber, to the fury of both the lesser tribunals. Daily life in Paris and the provinces was therefore enlivened by numerous jurisdictional disputes—between secular and ecclesiastical courts, between bishops and the Sorbonne, between the Sorbonne and the Paris *parlement*, between different *parlements*, between *parlements* and the royal council, between the municipal authorities and the local royal courts, between the town councils and the gilds, the permutations were endless but the process was always very expensive.

My third classification of élites, in terms of family and clientage groups, had rivalry as its driving force. Patrons sought to demonstrate their influence through the favours they could obtain, and families tried to outdo each other in their social status, the number and quality of their offices, the extent of their property and wealth, and the prestige of their marriage alliances. The kinship group worked as a unit, guided by a family council, and its success was judged by the whole range of prizes it had obtained for its members and for its clientèle, and not by the achievements of one illustrious individual within it. Many of these ambitious rivals were seeking to advance themselves only in their own restricted geographical area; some had a desire to move on, to Paris or to the royal court; a few high-ranking nobles, like Saint-Simon, centred their lives almost entirely on the court; but most great aristocrats kept one foot firmly in the entourage of the king and the other in a province where they had considerable property and influence. It was these great nobles, some of them also being bishops, who formed the crucial links between court and province, helping both the king to govern his realm and the local élites to obtain royal patronage. Even when a family had ambitions to establish its position more firmly but only in its own immediate area, there were still many desirable positions of influence or of profit which were in the royal gift. They ranged from great prizes like governorships and bishoprics, to lesser ones like the position of prioress in a rich religious house, or the office of colonel in the army, or, on a purely monetary level, the award of a contract to a tax-farmer. In appointing, say, a bishop, the king knew that he would have to choose a member of one of the leading families in the diocese, because it was essential that the man of his choice should already be influential in local society. Despite this limitation, there was usually more than one suitable candidate, and not all were from the same aristocratic house, so that the man who was appointed would feel some gratitude to his sovereign for honouring his family in preference to others. Yet this feeling of obligation would fade unless it was revived by further grants of favour in the not too distant future.

Louis XIV was in all these matters a conservative. He deplored rapid social mobility—it destabilised society, made men too ambitious, and offended against his love of hierarchy and order. During his personal rule, there were very few instances of *robe* nobles being appointed to positions which were traditionally the preserve of the sword; aristocratic titles were not bestowed on men who were socially unworthy; ministers did not become cardinals or dukes; intermarriage between *robe* and sword was firmly discouraged, with the king willing to give financial aid to any old noble house which had fallen on such hard times that a marriage into the wealthy and socially ambitious *robe* had seemed to be the only remedy. Above all Louis XIV had considerable success in following the policy which, as he stated in his memoirs for 1661, was his first priority on taking charge of the government. He determined to distribute his patronage evenhand-edly, favouring no single family or clientèle to an excessive degree, and giving everyone reason to hope that all who were worthy of royal favour would be justly rewarded.[1]

Marriages across social divides, *mésalliances*, were generally disliked by the élites of French society, with the exception of those individuals who were currently arranging just such a socially or financially advan-tageous match. Similarly they disapproved of rapid mobility, especially when they saw others overtaking them, although they were prepared to seize such opportunities for themselves. On balance, the evidence from commentators at the time suggests that most people preferred a more static society, in which their own ambitions would be curtailed along with those of their fellows, to a turbulently mobile world where greater prizes were obtainable but might go to rivals who would thus become dangerously powerful. Increasingly, therefore, in the seventeenth century, society became more rigidly stratified, and

[1] Louis XIV: *Mémoires for the instruction of the dauphin*, intro., trans. and notes by Paul Sonnino (New York, 1970) 24, 31–7.

fewer people married outside their immediate social group. That does not mean merely that sword married sword, and *robe* married *robe;* suitable partners were selected from even narrower categories. Thus sons of dukes usually chose daughters of dukes; *parlementaire* houses intermarried but rarely selected spouses from other areas of the upper office-holding *noblesse de robe;* town councillors of merchant stock married within their own group of families, but did not forge alliances with their fellow councillors whose careers had been in the legal profession. Nor did many men change their professional rank; for example in the *parlements,* the barristers and *avocats* seldom became judges.

All of these tendencies towards a static society led to these social sub-strata living very self-contained lives, and this was reflected in the geographical pattern of their dwellings. Most *quartiers* of towns were peopled by men of similar background or profession. During the reign of Louis XIV the high aristocrats were busily building and rebuilding in the Marais, the *parlementaires* were similarly engaged on the Ile Saint-Louis, and the ministerial families were congregating around the Louvre. In Toulouse, when during the seventeenth century the great *parlementaire* families established themselves in a newly built *quartier* of splendid mansions along the rue de la Dalbade, the lesser members of the legal profession moved into the houses which the judges had recently vacated, and the great merchants acquired the properties of the barristers and *avocats*. The social integrity of these *quartiers* remained, but the various élites had all moved westwards.

It will already have been remarked that the assertion of social prestige could be expensive, whether it took the form of lengthy law suits or of lavish new houses, and these two forms of expenditure greatly worried the king. The royal government was perfectly willing to allow the local institutions and élites to carry out their traditional functions in running the daily administration and life of their area. The crown could therefore confine itself to kingly matters such as war, peace, diplomacy, the defence of the realm, and indeed any matter which had an international dimension, which included colonial expansion and issues like the power of the Holy See. Only in Paris, the court's own locality, did the royal government show an interest in the minute details of everyday living, the policing of the streets, the confinement of the potentially seditious poor, and similar problems. The one aspect of government which caused the king to pay close attention to the behaviour of the provincial élites was the collection of royal taxation. Not only was he concerned to improve the quality and the safety of roads, so that taxpayers, tax-collectors and the revenues themselves might travel unmolested, but he deplored both fiscal corruption and any lavish expenditure which consumed funds that he would have preferred to see in his treasury. The nobles were exempt from direct taxation as were some, but not all, of the other élite groups in society, and the crown dared not undermine these long-standing and cherished exemptions. Yet such men might be prepared to advance money to the king, in the form of government bonds, loans or sums which would anticipate the regular revenues. To the annoyance of the finance ministers, these wealthy subjects were in no position to do so because they were expending enormous amounts, first on litigation as they defended their own rights and resisted the encroachments of rivals, and secondly on the trappings of life as they sought to glorify their family, institution or social group. Louis XIV had little success in restraining these excesses, except at court, and even there he did not prescribe regulations which would offend his courtiers because he was always careful to avoid tactless and needless provocation.

In the wider kingdom he made a sustained attempt to rationalise jurisdictions, so that at least law cases would be concerned with the grievances of the litigants and not also with the rivalries of different courts, but most of his initiatives came to nothing. Too many vested interests were involved. He ameliorated the situation slightly by appointing suitable candidates to high office and by spreading his favours among different clientèles, causing families to seek his patronage rather than, as had often happened under Richelieu, combining their efforts to thwart a royal nominee whom they regarded as both alien and unsuitable. Louis asked his bishops and governors to try to resolve some of these local disputes, offering further royal favours to those who would accept such mediation, and he even expressed his own willingness to play the role of supreme arbitrator. Some groups accepted one of these invitations, but many preferred not to do so lest the decision go against them. They thought it better to pursue their campaign in the confused world of the local courts where it was difficult to win a case but almost impossible to lose one. The main purpose of these confrontations was that a family or institution was actively defending its own rights and challenging the pretensions of its rivals, even if a conclusive outcome was unlikely. So the overlapping jurisdictions and the conflicting privileges remained, and the expensive legal squabbles continued.

Those resources which were not spent on litigation were devoted to ostentatious display, and to such an extent that town councils, nobles and élite groups frequently had to borrow heavily to sustain this expenditure. As a result, they could not honour their fiscal obligations, and certainly not lend money, to the crown, and the municipalities were unable to repair many roads and bridges or to maintain security. Colbert laboured to reduce municipal debts during his twenty-two years as finance minister, but had to admit that little success had crowned his efforts. In the peaceful 1660s he had waived the fiscal obligations of the towns for a year or two, on the understanding that the council would use the sums instead for the repayment of outstanding loans. The councillors gratefully accepted this royal concession, but all too often Colbert subsequently learned, from the *intendant*, the bishop or the governor, that they had not repaid part of their debt. They had preferred to extend or refurbish the town hall, give a lavish banquet or hold a spectacular procession and entertainment—further expenditure on display.

There is no doubt that outward splendour was an essential element of the prestige and ambition of all the élites in seventeenth-century France. Yet it was also subject to hierarchical strictures. If social mobility was destabilising, so too excessive ostentation in disregard of social origins was deeply offensive. The king had to live more luxuriously and bestow greater generosity than anyone else, and his prudent housekeeper, Colbert, who complained so bitterly about the extravagance of war, never begrudged the money spent on royal display and patronage, no matter how hard it was for him to balance the budget. This expenditure was vital to the reputation and influence of the king in his kingdom. Below the monarch, there was a hierarchy of ostentation. Great nobles lived more splendidly than lesser ones, and all were quick to petition the king if one of their number broke these social rules. Thus Louis XIV, after receiving representations on the matter from other nobles, rebuked both the duc de Rohan and the duchesse de Bouillon for the excessive gilding on their carriages. The king also decreed that at court some restraint would be shown in dress, not so much for economy as to enable him to honour great courtiers by permitting them to wear what was forbidden to others. The prince de Condé was singled out from a general prohibition on the extravagant wearing of fabrics made with gold and silver, and Louis himself prescribed the exact details of the elaborate apparel that Condé was to be permitted to wear. Yet, as in most aspects of royal rule in France, it was possible to enforce at court what could never be imposed in the wider realm.

In Paris, in the *quartier* of the Marais, the great aristocrats were seeking to outdo each other in their building and rebuilding plans. Latest fashions in architecture had to be accommodated, and an elaboration of court etiquette necessitated a similar, if more modest, change of behaviour in the noble household. Little gatehouses were built or refurbished to house Swiss guards, just like those who served the king. Some grandees did hire native Swiss, others engaged a variety of motley foreigners, and a few had to content themselves with Frenchmen from distant provinces who masqueraded as exotic imports. The more elaborate the etiquette, at court and in the *hôtels particuliers* of the capital, the more there were opportunities for the monarch or the noble to give small tokens of his favour to those who attended upon him. The invitation to hold the master's shirt at the morning *levée*, for example, was one such sign, and would be duly noted by all those present because their competitive instincts were never put to rest for a moment. Sometimes, of course, a noble family could not sustain its ostentation because its creditors had finally refused further aid, and in that case there was no alternative but to return to its country estates. In high society there was nothing wrong with living beyond one's means, if one could do it, but it was impossible to be seen to live in a style below one's rank.

The nobles of the *robe* similarly built and rebuilt palatial town houses, hoping that these dwellings would enhance their aura of nobility, at least in the eyes of their equals and inferiors, for they would never convince the aristocracy of the sword. Occasionally a wealthy parvenu would intrude, geographically, into the highest social échelons by building an *hôtel particulier* in a *quartier* peopled by the great *noblesse*. This audacity would not lead to his acceptance into aristocratic circles, but it would impress those of his own social group who were invited to his elaborate *soirées*. Such a house is the hôtel Aubert de Fontenay, recently opened as the Musée Picasso, and familiarily known now, as in the 1650s when it was built, as the hôtel Salé because it was constructed by a farmer of the salt tax. Indeed the outcry against the finance minister, Nicolas Foucquet, was prompted not only by accusations of ministerial mismanagement but by the offensive ostentation of his life style at Vaux-le-Vicomte, and his impertinence at inviting the king himself to the extravagant *fête* which finally assured his downfall.

In the case of the *robe* and the municipal élites, their lavishness was channelled in two directions, towards the private house and the place of work, the sword nobles of course having only the former. Thus not only personal property but also palaces of justice, town halls, gild halls, commercial exchanges, customs houses and many other buildings were sumptuously ornamented as tributes both to the power of the institution and to the prestige of those who worked within it. The same was true for the higher clergy, where the bishop enjoyed a personal life style of great pomp in his extensive palace, next door to the ecclesiastical buildings which were also being adorned ever more elaborately as a symbol of the institutional power of the church. Even more money was spent on *fêtes* and banquets so that one élite group could impress its rivals and inferiors, and every ceremonial procession was a manifestation of these hierarchical concerns. Indeed one historian has defined the word 'élite' in this period by saying that élites are those who participate in these ceremonies, non-élites are those who watch.[2] Sometimes these events raised such major problems of precedence that plans had to be abandoned, compromises reached or remedies devised. For example doorways had to be widened so that rival notables did not have to give way. On one occasion the prince de Condé feigned an attack of gout and went to open the estates of Burgundy by carriage, because an apparently irresoluble dispute about the precedence in the procession which would escort him, if he walked to the ceremony, threatened to prevent the opening of the assembly.

The provinces were just as preoccupied as the court and the capital with these questions of hierarchy, except that they had an additional concern—to defend their provincial liberties against anything which savoured of royal or Parisian interference, whether it be the levying of new taxes or the imposition of artistic or architectural norms. They knew that the Parisian salons sneered at the rusticity of life away from the capital, and yet some of these distant towns had a fine scholarly, literary and artistic tradition of which they were fiercely proud.

In the serious business of municipal self-assertion, a local rival might at times be an asset. A town which had a bishop, or better still an archbishop, had much greater status than one which had neither, although the councillors and the prelate might often be at odds about their respective rights and jurisdictions. Both sides would play on this ambiguous relationship as it suited their immediate purposes. For example in the case of Narbonne, there was no doubt that the cathedral and the presence of an archbishop gave the town primacy in its immediate region. Also he was one of the two alternate presidents of the estates of Languedoc, and could promote the interests of the municipality at the assembly, unless he and the councillors were currently locked in dispute. Yet for four hundred years the Narbonnais had been contenting themselves with half a cathedral, running from the sanctuary to the crossing, because the building of the nave would have breached the walls of the town and encroached on municipal territory. The need for adequate urban defences was cited as the reason in 1272, but that could not seriously be sustained under Louis XIV because the fortifications of the archiepiscopal palace more than adequately protected the town on this side. The archbishop continued his battle unsuccessfully throughout the eighteenth century, even building the structure for the first bay of the nave, but that was as far as he could go. In the nineteenth century the town took its revenge and made the walls of the palace into the towers of its new town hall.

[2] Jean-Marie Apostolidès *Le roi machine: spectacle et politique au temps de Louis XIV* (Paris, 1981)

If many fortifications were becoming less necessary, they still had a symbolic significance. All the principal southern bishops lived in fortresses more appropriate to medieval prince-bishops, inside whose walls they now built ever more gracious palaces and formal gardens. Cities too did not extend their walls but adorned them with impressive ceremonial gateways. Not to be left out, the king did the same. A good example is the fortress of Salses in Roussillon, a province only recently acquired by France. As the great engineer Vauban reveals in his correspondence, this stronghold was vital to the Spanish when they ruled this area on the French side of the Pyrenees, but was of no practical use to Louis XIV now that his territory went as far as those mountains, where other fortifications took the strain. Nevertheless the Roussillonais had to be reminded of the power of their new sovereign, and Salses was made to look much more impressive by what were purely theatrical, rather than militarily effective, additions, for that is how Vauban himself describes them.[3]

The crown was determined to assert its influence over the provinces in the visual, as in other fields, and the learned academies in the capital sent out the latest strict rules for good architectural and artistic practice. The glee with which the provinces ignored, overtly disobeyed or modified these prescriptions knew no bounds. Towns deliberately engaged architects from countries with which they had close economic contacts, in order to demonstrate that their links with these other lands were stronger than those with Paris and the court. Some Provençal municipalities found their architects in Tuscany, disobeying the royal policy that all Italian influences should be gallicised in Paris or at the French School in Rome. There might be even stronger political overtones to such artistic actions. Collioure, the Roussillonais town recently transferred to France, hastily built a massive new church on the waterfront, facing the royal castle, and enlisted the services of a Barcelona architect who provided it with a riotously elaborate, Catalan baroque interior. The examples are legion, and the rest of this paper looks in detail at a few of these visual battles which were part of wider social, administrative and judicial rivalries.

In 1984, the Caisse nationale des monuments historiques mounted an exhibition in Paris entitled 'La place royale'. It described the planning of a number of grand squares, in Paris, and the provinces during the seventeenth and eighteenth centuries, whose purpose—or so we were assured by the absolutist art historians who mounted the display[4]—was to glorify the king by creating an enormous space whose

---

[3] Facsimiles of letters by the maréchal de Vauban relating to the fortresses of Roussillon, in the collection of the fortress at Collioure.

[4] M.-F. Poullet, avec contribution de C. Cosneau et B. Sournia, *La place royale* (Paris, 1984).

centre-piece was a statue of his royal person. That may have been true for the Parisian examples, but it was certainly not the motive in all the provincial instances. There the prime intention was, in this period when stately urban promenades were being created for the pleasure of citizens, to demonstrate the sophistication of the town and the grandeur of its schemes for improving the environment. Statues of the king did make an appearance, but they were not always welcomed, and certainly not originally envisaged, by the planners of these great visual enterprises. Indeed their purpose in Lyon was to build the largest square in the kingdom, bigger than anything in the capital, and this they did achieve.

The planning of these public works and their execution is almost always a chapter in the history of rivalries among local élites, often including interventions by the crown. One of the most complex stories is that of the Place royale in Dijon, where the city and the crown were in favour of its construction but other powerful local interests were not. Dijon was the principal city of Burgundy, the seat of the royal governor and the meeting-place of the provincial estates. Being a *pays d'états*, the province was largely administered by the elected estates, and by the officials they appointed and supervised. The crown, through its governor, negotiated with the estates which, often having forced him into a hard bargain, especially on levels of taxation, then implemented the agreement through their own officials—and frequently with neither enthusiasm nor urgency. They seldom defied the king, but they were expert at failing to carry out policies and decisions that they disliked. In Dijon therefore, there resided the royal governor, the prestigious estates when in session and their permanent officials who were there all the time, the proud city council, the *parlement* and various other élite groups.

In 1674 the estates decided that their permanent officials needed a more splendid building, both to impress the populace and to permit the orderly conservation of all the archival materials relating to their administration of the province and to its liberties and privileges.[5] They voted the sum of 20,000 *livres* for this purpose, to which would be added the return from the sale of the building that the officials currently occupied. At their next meeting the estates, fearing that these combined amounts would not be sufficient for the erection of a suitably grand edifice, added a further 10,000 *livres*. The governor, the prince de Condé, was unhappy about this decision on two counts.

[5] I am indebted for some of the factual detail on the construction of the Dijon palais des états and the place royale, although not for the interpretation of its significance, to Yves Beauvalot, *La construction du palais des états de Bourgogne et de la place royale à Dijon—de Daniel Gittard à Robert de Cotte: l'oeuvre de Jules Hardouin-Mansart* (Dijon, 1981).

First France was at war, and these funds would undoubtedly be diverted from the possible tax yield of the province. Secondly they were being spent on the glorification of the already difficult estates. In 1679 the assembly added another 14,000 *livres* because they had now decided to include in the new building a chamber for their own plenary sessions. With 6,000 from the sale of the existing *bureau*, the total had risen to 50,000 *livres*, equal to about one-tenth of the sum which was paid each year by the whole province in direct taxation. Moreover the estates resolved that they would authorise additional expenditure as necessary.

At this point the governor stepped in and offered them the site for their building, within the land occupied by the royal palace which was virtually empty save for the officials of the mint. This gift meant that the entire sum could be spent on the process of construction, and the estates were well aware that to have purchased a site in the town would have cost them much money. Their one reservation was that, as the land was royal, it was under the administrative control of the *trésoriers de France*. These fiscal officials had wide powers in *pays d'élections* but played no part in the collection of taxes in the *pays d'états*. The estates were therefore reluctant to have any dealings with them, as it would mean acknowledging the authority of a group which had no place in the normal administration of Burgundy. The governor calmed their fears by agreeing to locate the officials of the mint at one end of the site, in a new building of their own, and giving an assurance that the *trésoriers* would be concerned solely with them and would have no interest in the palace of the estates. Accordingly the assembly went ahead with the plans for its splendid meeting place, but it also decided to purchase a little more land in order to build a special chamber, beyond the assembly hall, in which its officials could hold their regular meetings. Condé tried to dissuade them on the grounds of expense, but the estates enlisted the aid of some wealthy benefactors who agreed to advance them the money on long loan, so that no further expenditure would be needed at the moment. The governor knew exactly what the estates were plotting, because this extra piece of adjacent land was outside the boundaries of the royal palace and beyond the reach of its officials. Decisions made in the new chamber would therefore be taken within the jurisdiction of the estates alone, even if access to the room was across royal land.

Until this moment the architectural designs had been prepared by an assistant of the great architect of the king, Jules Hardouin-Mansart, who had also worked for the governor, Condé, at Chantilly. Towns and provinces were not averse to employing such a man. Far from appearing to be subservient to the crown, they felt that their prestige was reinforced by employing the greatest practitioner of this art in the entire realm. Hardouin-Mansart had nevertheless decided that this project should be delegated to one of his assistants, but now the king and Condé, determined to curb the pretensions of the estates, insisted that he take personal charge because no one was a better royal propagandist than he.[6]

Mansart rapidly evolved three plans of action, all of which soon irritated the estates. The impressive exterior, too impressive, was almost completed in 1685. He accordingly designed an enormous *place royale* in front of the new palace, but not to add to its splendour. The square was not to be centred on its imposing façade, and the sight lines led the eye away from it towards the statue of the king which would dominate the new space. The city council was delighted to co-operate because this project would enhance their town, and the councillors had long been annoyed by the arrogance of the estates. Mansart quickly produced a design for the equestrian statue of Louis XIV and for an elaborate plinth, which included the message that the estates of Burgundy had ordered the erection of this monument in 1685, when they had made no such decision. Secondly, speaking as a structural engineer, he said that the minting presses were so heavy that they would have to be in ground-floor rooms, and therefore that the mint would have to occupy the whole of the ground level of the entire palace, and not the planned special building at one end of the site. Thirdly he began with great haste to decorate the interior and exterior. The estates had asked for an austere chamber, suitable for their dignified and lofty purposes, and they were horrified by what they saw. Over the entrance to their assembly hall were the arms of the royal orders of Saint-Michel and the Saint-Esprit, and facing it was the shield of the prince de Condé. Inside, over the door of the vestibule, Mansart had created an elaborate design with the royal arms at its centre. In the hall, between the windows, there were garlands of flowers incorporating, at the centre of each one, a beaming sun emblem. The great gateway from the outside into the whole palace complex was seen to be adorned with the royal arms, a globe bearing the fleur-de-lys and surmounted by a huge sun, and on one side the figure of military glory, on the other that of History recording the deeds of Louis le Grand. It was a veritable *arc de triomphe* listing all the victories of the king. Nowhere in any of the decorative scheme was there a mention of the province or of the estates.

The members of the assembly were furious, but they could hardly take down references to their own sovereign. Mansart had achieved a successful *fait accompli*, but the estates were not prepared to give way

---

[6] All the designs of Hardouin-Mansart for the Dijon palais and place royale are collected as Ms 1501, Bibliothèque de la Sorbonne.

so easily. They purchased a bust of Louis XIV by Coysevox, and told the governor that they wished to make it into the principal feature of their assembly hall, whose furnishings had not yet been finally resolved. They expressed the hope that, in return for this display of loyalty, the governor might persuade the king to relocate the officials of the mint, so that the estates might have occupation of the entire building. Condé was amenable to this request, and it was only when Mansart turned his attention to the furnishings of the hall that he discovered their plot. There was only one suitable site for the Coysevox bust, and that was the centre of the far wall, but when the thrones of the governor, the bishops and the great nobles were in position on the dais, the sculpture would be completely hidden from view. After lengthy discussions, Mansart had to assert that the bust could not be in the hall, to the delight of the estates. There were many more confrontations of this kind, until the 1730s when the estates rebuilt the staircase and the approach to their meeting place on the grounds that their style was no longer architecturally fashionable.

Meanwhile Mansart and the city council had pressed on with the *place royale*, and by 1690 it was completed. The great equestrian statue of Louis XIV was finished, and awaiting its 300-kilometre journey from Paris to Dijon. The officials of the estates now announced that, as a token of their loyalty and their enthusiasm for the scheme, they would arrange and pay for its transport. They did not hurry to fulfil their commitment, but in 1692 the statue had arrived in the province and was at Auxerre. After a further year's delay it set off once more, but after only a few miles the carts became bogged down at the village of La Brosse. The officials declared that any advance would be impossible until the roads could be improved, adding that as France was involved in a major war they wished to give any spare funds to the king for the war effort. They duly rented a barn from Monsieur Chacheré, villager of La Brosse, and there the equestrian Louis resided until 1720. Only then was the statue finally brought to Dijon, at which point the estates said that the original plinth, with its fulsome tribute to the valour and achievements of the king, was clearly out of fashion, and so a simple one was designed which merely said that, at the behest of the governor, the three estates of Burgundy had commissioned this statue of Louis le Grand as a monument for posterity—hardly an elaborate panegyric. By this time the estates had negotiated the removal of the mint into a house in the town, and had the palace to themselves. Indeed their own officials were still hard at work, trying to purchase more property in order that they and the assembly could carry out their duties in even greater style.

Further south, the city of Lyon was busy adorning itself and asserting its civic pride. It had just built the largest square in the kingdom,

the place Bellecour, 310 metres long and 200 metres wide. The municipal council, with great reluctance, had been persuaded by the
governor, the respected and popular duc de Villeroy, that it should
place a statue of the king in the centre of this new space. Their
enthusiasm can be gauged by the fact that, when a similar project
was being discussed in Montpellier, the royal architect wrote to the
Montpelliérain councillors, warning them to avoid following the
example of Lyon. There, he complained, the statue had been placed
on such a low plinth and was so well screened that it was impossible
to see it from most parts of the square.

Of more interest here is the reason why the governor had insisted
on the Bellecour statue, and that was prompted by the rebuilding of
the town hall, further up the peninsula. Old Lyon had grown up in
the narrow strip between the hill of Fourvière and the right bank of
the Sâone. As an expanding commercial community it had been
forced to colonise the land between that river and the Rhône, whose
status as the new city centre had been recognised by the construction
there of a new hôtel de ville in 1653. After a severe fire in 1674, that
building was now being redecorated and considerably extended. Lyon
was a proud metropolis. Many Frenchmen would have acknowledged
it to be the second city in the kingdom, but the Lyonnais were
disinclined to be so modest. The Roman settlement, with its great
amphitheatres on the hill, testified to the antiquity of the town, as did
the title of primat des Gaules, which was still borne by the archbishop
because the cathedral had been founded in A.D. 117. Only Lyon and
Paris boasted a mayor with the title of *prévôt des marchands*, so that in
every way Lyon was equal, or superior, to the capital. As there were
neither estates nor a *parlement* there, the city council was the supreme
élite body, and needed to display itself in a manner fitting for that
position. The predominant themes of its new ostentation were to be
Roman, and not just because of Lyon's ancient past. The crown, too,
was fond of classical imagery, not least because such references were
more comprehensible to foreigners, who might be less well versed in
the lives of St Louis and other French heroes.

On the exterior of the restored hôtel de ville, the dominant motif
was that of the fasces of the Roman lictors, symbolising the power as
magistrates of the councillors who held court within. Royal imagery
was totally absent. Inside the city displayed its pride in a variety of
ways. The director of the decorative scheme and the executor of much
of it was Thomas Blanchet, the official painter of Lyon, for most great
cities had their civic artist to record their doings. Blanchet was one of
a number of painters who, though Parisian by birth, chose to develop
their career in a provincial centre. Most of these men had studied in
Italy, but had found themselves inhibited by the gallicised version of

Italian art which was favoured in the Parisian academies and at the French School in Rome. In Lyon Blanchet could paint as he wished and, a year after becoming civic artist, he began to plan an academy of painting there, knowing that its Italianate style of art, like his own works, would irritate the Paris academies. His decorative scheme for the town hall was the antithesis of that devised by Hardouin-Mansart for the Dijon palace. Aided by a team of French-born artists who had studied in Italy, Blanchet designed a ceiling for the grand salon according to the formula used by Annibale Carracci in the Palazzo Farnese. One enormous panel of it was entitled 'the city of Lyon, surrounded by allegorical personages, offering her hand to the god Mercury', a reminder that, whereas in most cities the council was composed of men from the professions, the Lyonnais élite was largely drawn from the merchants, of whom Mercury was the god. On the ceremonial staircase he painted a tribute to the Rhône and the Sâone, the lifelines of this commercial centre; another of the great fire which destroyed the town under Nero; a further picture which portrayed 'love begging the ancient gods to put out the fire'; and finally the assembly of the gods, clustered round a map of seventeenth-century Lyon, planning the rebuilding of the city. Another ceiling displayed 'the consular grandeur of Lyon', showing the modern councillors amid various Roman images and with Mercury presiding once again. Yet royal imagery inside the town hall was not totally lacking but it appeared in an impertinent form. There was an enormous ceiling depicting 'monarchy sustained by the affection of Lyon' and, as the focal point of the salle consulaire, an impressive fireplace, which was dominated by a large coat of arms bearing three small fleur de lys at the top and a large lion underneath, the whole design supported by a large lion's head. It was after seeing this series of self-congratulatory tableaux that the governor began to insist that the councillors should install a statue of the king in the place Bellecour.

If the Lyonnais councillors made these less than flattering references to the crown, the arrogant city council of Toulouse mentioned neither the king nor France in the latest decorative scheme for their town hall. The Toulousains were not only eager to assert the maximum degree of independence from Paris and the central government but also wished to challenge some bitter rivals in the province of Langue-doc. Chief among these was Montpellier, the other principal admin-istrative city in the region. Toulouse was the seat of the *parlement*, while Montpellier was the residence of the officials of the provincial estates and often, though not always, the meeting place of that assembly. Narbonne was also a rival, because the archbishops of Toulouse and Narbonne took turns to preside over the estates, an apparent equality which had to be challenged. There were also conflicts about rights and jurisdictions between Toulouse and some nearby towns, especially Castres and Montauban, the *parlement* frequently interfering in their affairs and the Castrais and Montalbanais vigorously protesting to the estates, to the governor, to the *intendant*, even to the king—to anyone in fact who would listen.

The artistic activity of the Toulousain councillors took account of many of these challenges. The Roman past of the city was always in their minds because, uniquely among French civic élites, they were not *échevins* or *consuls* but *capitouls*, and they had not an *hôtel de ville* but a Capitole. This building, and the palais de justice of the *parlement*, were the twin foci of their artistic enterprises. They were not themselves rivals because, unlike in some *parlementaire* centres, the *capitouls* were almost always drawn from the families of the *parlement*. Just inside the Narbonne gate, the palais de justice was always being extended and adorned, and the judges had also taken over the former palace of the inquisition, making it into their own prison which therefore symbolised their victory over ecclesiastical jurisdiction. The secular courts never ceased to challenge those of the church. In self-defence, the crown had recently erected a large building of its own on the opposite side of the square, so that it was the first major edifice which would greet the visitor entering the city. It was to house the royal financial officials, but they needed only a fraction of the space in what was primarily a display of royal prestige. The capitole, like the palais de justice, was also subject to regular alteration and refurbishment. Having been made more impressive under Henri IV, further improvements were made during the reign of Louis XIV. Although that building was completely rebuilt under Louis XV, inside and outside, acquiring the appearance it has today, the *capitouls* preserved all the paintings they had commissioned in the seventeenth century, and most may now be seen in the magnificently restored Musée des Grands Augustins.

Their subject matter is fascinating. With a few exceptions, they concern either the Roman past of the city or the great deeds of the medieval *comtes* of Toulouse, before the area was incorporated into the kingdom of France. The Toulousains were not pleased that the title of comte de Toulouse, born by the brave in the middle ages, had been conferred by Louis XIV on one of his illegitimate sons. They prided themselves on the fact that the arms of the medieval counts had been adopted as those of the province of Languedoc, stressing the role of their city as unofficial capital of the province. The French regarded Toulouse as having been the third city of Roman Gaul, after Paris and Lyon, but the Toulousains accepted no such classification. The Roman themes in the paintings of the capitole all concern the Tectosages, the brave and warlike native inhabitants of Narbonnian

Gaul, Gallia Narbonensis, of which Toulouse always insisted that it, and not Narbonne, had been the chief city. The Tectosages were great travellers. The end wall of the great gallery shows the 'fondation d'Ancyre' in Asia Minor by the tribe; others portrayed it on the march, at the foundation of a town in 'Germanie', taking prisoner Sosthène, king of Macedonia, and many other events. The Sosthenes picture is not without irony because he was a general, not a king, was not taken prisoner, but was killed in a battle at which his army, despite his own death, routed the Tectosages. The medieval topics include Raymond, comte de Toulouse, taking the crusading vow, and the defeat of Henry II of England before the walls of Toulouse, among many other subjects. Further glories of the city's past were represented by a portrait of Pope Urban II coming personally to consecrate the church of Saint-Sernin in 1097, a building which still claims to be the largest Romanesque basilica in Europe, and another of the town's own Saint Louis—Saint Louis, évêque de Toulouse. In these medieval subjects there was a strong religious theme, and that is to be found in the only painting to refer to relatively recent times. It concerned 'the expulsion of the Huguenots by the citizens of Toulouse on 17 May 1562'. Whatever the past record of Toulouse for involvement with heterodoxy, the *parlement* was fiercely anti-Huguenot during the personal rule of Louis XIV, and this attitude greatly affected its bitter relations with Castres and Montauban. This picture was clearly partly conceived with those towns in mind. Yet in all the paintings in this series, there was not a mention of king or kingdom.

There are, of course, thousands of examples of the assertion, in art and architecture, of social prestige in seventeenth-century France, and extensive records of elaborate festivals and processions. Enormous sums were spent on them, and every élite group watched closely to see what its rivals were doing. Every quarrel between families, social groups or institutions would have its visual aspect, and town centres were dominated by the evidence of their spending on architectural display. Yet, if such ostentation was a permanent preoccupation of competitive élites, imagine the effect of the collective result on the humble townsman and on the country peasant coming to market!

THE 'MOTHER GIN' CONTROVERSY IN THE
EARLY EIGHTEENTH CENTURY

By Peter Clark

READ 24 APRIL 1987

DURING the second quarter of the eighteenth century there were successive waves of public agitation over the spirits trade—in 1726, 1728–9, 1735–8 and again in 1748–51. Opponents of 'Mother Gin' and her supporters waged a multi-media propaganda war, through tracts and sermons, broadsides, ballads, satirical verse, petitions, posters and prints (though Hogarth's *Gin Lane* and *Beer Street* came only as a final, splendid coda to the attack on gin, in 1751).[1] Parliament in this period enacted a series of measures to deal with the problem. The most dramatic and draconian of these was the 1736 Gin Act, which was hurried through Parliament in a few weeks and threatened to close down the spirits trade overnight. The Act, with secondary legislation in 1737 and 1738, caused such a landslide of protest and opposition in the capital that it had to be abandoned and later repealed. In this paper I want to concentrate on the 1736 Act, looking at its background and aftermath. As we shall see, the controversy raises important questions not only about the organisation of the drink trade and consumption patterns in the early eighteenth century, but also about the social and political processes of legislation—the activity of interest groups, the attitude of government, and the problems of enforcement.

The subject has surprisingly received only patchy treatment from historians. The standard account remains that of Dorothy George in her *London Life in the Eighteenth Century* (1925). This broadly accepts the assertions of critics of 'Mother Gin' in the 1730s, emphasising the scale of the trade and the social and order problems it created, and concludes that it would be 'hardly possible to exaggerate the cumulatively disastrous effects of the orgy of spirit-drinking between 1720 and 1751'.[2] Equally pessimistic, T. S. Ashton claimed in 1955 that the growth of spirits at this time caused 'a steep rise in the number of deaths and a demoralisation, of rich and poor alike, so great as to lead to fears ... for the future of civilised life in Britain'. More recently,

---

[1] I am grateful to Professor A. Newman, Professor J. Plumb, Professor W. Speck, Dr J. Innes, Dr D. Hayton, Mr A. Hanham, and Dr J. Landers for their advice and communications. For Hogarth see R. Paulson, *Hogarth's Graphic Works* (2 vols., New Haven, 1965), i.206–11.

[2] M. D. George, *London Life in the Eighteenth Century* (1925), 41–55, quotation at p. 51.

Hans Medick has talked of the destruction of traditional plebeian sociability and solidarity through the new consumer economy of Gin Lane, but he only recycles the evidence presented by Dr George.[3]

To begin, we need to put the controversy into perspective by examining the rise of gin consumption and retailing. In the sixteenth century spirits—mostly rough aqua vitae—was very much a minority drink in England: most distilling was undertaken for medicinal purposes. During the next century, however, spirit drinking became increasingly common, as in other European countries, for reasons discussed elsewhere.[4] In the 1680s the exciseman, Charles Davenant, noted that consumption was widespread across southern England. But most supplies at this time came from abroad and French brandy dominated the market after the Restoration.[5] The Revolution of 1688 and the outbreak of war with Louis XIV led to punitive duties on imported brandy but the gap in the market was increasingly filled by colonial rum and the growing output of home distilleries. After 1689 the London Company of Distillers effectively lost its control over the industry and anyone could set up as a distiller provided he paid the excise duties.[6] Though wholesale distilling of raw spirits remained in the hands of major producers, compound distilling (rectifying gin and brandy) was highly profitable and attracted large numbers of small men. In the 1730s London was said to have 1500 distillers, of whom a hundred had equipment worth more than £1000 and 1200 had stills and the like worth under £100. In contrast, the brewing industry was much less open, increasingly dominated in London by large-scale, capitalist producers.[7]

Expanding output of spirits was matched by rising demand. In 1688, duty was levied on half a million gallons of British spirits; by 1720 the amount was about 2.5 million gallons and growing.[8] An

---

[3] T. S. Ashton, *An Economic History of England: the 18th century* (1955), 6; H. Medick, 'Plebeian culture in the transition to capitalism', in *Culture, Ideology and Politics*, ed. R. Samuel and G. S. Jones (1982), 96–108. G. Rudé, ' "Mother Gin" and the London riots of 1736' in *idem, Paris and London in the 18th century* (1970), 201–21 has little new to say on the gin controversy; the account in P. Clark, *The English Alehouse: a Social History 1200–1830* (1983), 239–42 also relies heavily on George.

[4] C. A. Wilson, 'Burnt wine and cordial waters', *Folk Life*, xiii (1975), 59–63; Clark, *Alehouse*, 95–6, 211–12.

[5] British Library, Harleian MSS. 5120, fos. 36, 43; 5121, fos. 6v, 41v, 48; *A Brief Case of the Distillers and of the Distilling Trade* (1726), 22.

[6] Cambridge University Library, Cholmondeley (Houghton) MS.P28/8; E. B. Schumpeter, *English Overseas Trade Statistics 1697–1808* (Oxford, 1960), 48–53; *An Impartial Enquiry into the Present State of the British Distillery* (1736), 5–6.

[7] *Impartial Enquiry*, 7–8; P. Mathias, *The Brewing Industry in England 1700–1830* (Cambridge, 1959), ch.1.

[8] *Parliamentary Papers*, 1870, xx, Report of the Commissioners of Inland Revenue, 382.

important factor in the popularity of spirits was their cheapness. As one observer remarked in 1737, 'dram-drinking has been a practise among the poorer sort because they could be made merry with distilled spirits cheaper than they could with any other liquor'. This price advantage was due in large measure to the high increases in excise duties on ale and beer which doubled between 1688 and 1710; as a result, the price of a quart of beer rose from 2d in the 1680s to 3d or more by the 1720s. In contrast, British spirits paid only a few pennies a gallon in tax.[9] But one should not overstate the significance of the price differential. Though there is continuing uncertainty about wage rate movements in the eighteenth century, it is difficult to avoid the impression that lower class incomes were advancing in the decades after 1700, albeit with short-term fluctuations. Many ordinary people had more money to spend on consumer items and were, as Joan Thirsk and others have shown, increasingly sophisticated in their tastes and demands.[10] Elias Bockett made the important point that in drinking 'the little vulgar imitate the manners of the vulgar great'. Not only was spirits a fashionable drink (with the upper class imbibing punch and expensive citron waters and cherry and raspberry brandies) but the consumer could choose from a great variety of liquors with gin sweetened and softened by juices, spices and juniper berries.[11] Finally, there may have been a growing preference for more fiery 'shorts' over blander, longer drinks, the former popularised by seamen drinking spirits on long voyages.

With demand so buoyant, spirit retailing was clearly a profitable trade. It was also a more open trade than its established rival— alehousekeeping. By the early Hanoverian period, the alehouse business was increasingly regulated and difficult to enter. Under the 1552 Act and later laws, alehousekeepers had to obtain annual licences from local justices, who by the early eighteenth century had intro- duced stern measures against illicit victuallers. Magistrates also acted to curb the number of premises, to prevent poorer folk setting up in the trade, and to limit the economic and social activities taking place there. As we know, alehouses had become larger and more elaborate by this time, partly because of official controls and partly because of other factors (including the rising affluence of customers). They

---

[9] *Gentleman's Magazine*, vii (1737), 214; Mathias, 369; *Parl. Papers*, 382.

[10] Cf. L. D. Schwarz, 'The standard of living in the long run: London, 1700– 1860', *Economic History Review*, new series, xxxviii (1985), 25 et. seq.; P. Mathias, *The Transformation of England* (1979), ch. 8; J. Thirsk, *Economic Policy and Projects* (Oxford, 1978), ch. 5 et seq.; N. McKendrick et al., *The Birth of a Consumer Society* (1983), esp. ch. 1.

[11] [E. Bockett], *Blunt to Walpole* (1730), 30; *Brief Case*, 46–7; *A Supplement to the Impartial Enquiry* (1736), 22.

offered not only a greater range of drinks but food and accommodation as well. They were better equipped and furnished with specialist rooms such as games and club rooms. By George II's reign, the landlord was often quite a respectable figure with some capital behind him and family connections in the trade.[12] By comparison, anyone setting up as a gin-seller faced few obstacles. Spirit-sellers were exempt from the usual licensing laws and other controls imposed on victuallers. In addition, since most gin sellers did not offer food and accommodation, they needed less elaborate premises and less capital than established victuallers. Distillers may also have been willing to help newcomers with stock. No wonder so many people moved into the trade.[13]

By the early 1720s the Middlesex justices were already expressing concern at the spread of dram-selling in the capital. In 1721 Middlesex sessions heard that brandy shops caused 'more mischiefs and inconveniences to this town than all other public-houses joined together'. In January 1726 a special committee of justices from that county collated returns by parish constables and claimed there were over 6,000 retailers within the Bills of Mortality (apart from the city and Southwark), though half of these were licensed victuallers. In 'some parishes, it was asserted, every tenth house, in others every seventh, and in one of the largest every fifth house' was a gin-shop; others sold from wheelbarrows and street stalls.[14] The committee's report may have presaged a move to lobby Parliament to control the trade, but nothing seems to have happened at this time, probably due to opposition from the distillers. Two years later, however, the Middlesex justices were involved, with the government, in a new campaign against disorderly alehouses, lodging houses and the 'extravagant multitude' of gin shops. In 1729 Parliament passed legislation imposing controls on the gin trade. Under the law retailers had to pay £20 for an annual licence, while a new duty of 5s. a gallon was levied on spirits.[15]

The 1729 Act was not successful. Only a few hundred people took out the new licences. The Distillers' Company campaigned vociferously against the law, appointing in 1731 a parliamentary committee to lobby for repeal and distributing pamphlets against the measure among M.P.s. Critics complained that the Act had depressed the legal trade in spirits while allowing the proliferation of illicit retailers. There

---

[12] Cambridge Univ. Lib., Cholmondeley MS. P51/109; Clark, *Alehouse*, ch. 9.
[13] George, 42–3.
[14] Greater London Record Office, MJ/OC 1, fos. 130v–2; MJ/OC 3, fos. 41–3.
[15] GLRO, MJ/OC 3, fos. 152–4v, 160–4; *Commons Journals*, xxi. 262 *et passim*; *Statutes at Large* (24 vols., Cambridge, 1765), xvi. 27; see also M.J. Jubb, 'Fiscal Policy in England in the 1720s and 1730s' (unpublished Ph.D. thesis, Cambridge Univ., 1978), 275.

is also evidence to indicate that part of home demand was also being met now by imported or smuggled spirits.[16] Repeal in 1733 encouraged a major revival of home production and consumption: in 1730 duty was levied on 3.8 million gallons of British spirits; in 1733 the figure was 4.8 million and two years later 6.4 million.[17] By the summer of 1735 there were renewed cries of upper-class concern. In May the court of aldermen in the City of London ordered beadles to return names of unlicensed retailers, and in June the bishops of Bristol and Gloucester, Sir Joseph Jekyll and others, made representations to Queen Caroline about the pernicious consequences of the trade. At Michaelmas the grand juries at the various metropolitan sessions called for action against the problem.[18] Within a short time the campaign against Mother Gin had taken off. In January 1736, as ten years before, the Middlesex justices at Hicks Hall drew up a detailed indictment of the trade, using returns by parish constables. They claimed that there was a growing epidemic of gin-selling, affecting many lesser trades, and this was one of the chief causes of the 'vast increase of thieves and pilferers' and of beggars and parish poor in the capital. They ordered copies of the report to be printed in the *Daily Advertiser* and *London Evening News* and presented Parliament with a petition for legislation.[19] The Middlesex report was also reprinted in Thomas Wilson's crusading *Distilled Spirituous Liquors the Bane of the Nation*, which passed through two editions in the spring of 1736, and played an influential part in orchestrating support for action in Parliament.[20]

However, before we consider the sources of support for legislation, we need to focus on the spirits trade itself, to see how far the allegations against the structure and impact of the trade were justified. The evidence is rather scrappy and more dependent than one would like on official returns, but certain points can be made. In the first place, numbers of gin shops. How far was it the case, as critics like Wilson and others alleged, that society was being swamped with gin shops by the 1730s?[21] In the provinces one can find clusters of specialist gin

---

[16] Public Record Office, CUST 48/13, p. 99; Guildhall Library, Distillers' Company Papers, MS. 6207/1A (unfol.); *The Case of the Distillers Company...* (?1735), 2; *The Distillers' Petition to his Majesty* (?1733); PRO, CUST 48/12, p. 443.

[17] *Statutes at Large*, xvi. 383–7; *Parl. Papers*, 382, 384.

[18] City of London Record Office, Repertories, cxxxix, pp. 185, 213; *Grub Street Journal*, 26 June 1735; T. Wilson, *Distilled Spirituous Liquors The Bane of the Nation* (1st ed., 1736), appendix, 3–14.

[19] GLRO, MJ/OC 4, fos. 54–7v.

[20] Wilson, *Liquors* (1st ed.), app., 14–24; *The Diaries of Thomas Wilson, DD.*, ed. C. L. S. Linnell (1964), 148, 152.

[21] Wilson, *Liquors* (1st ed.), 9, 14, 58; app., 11; *The Trial of the Spirits* (1736), 23–4.

sellers in the larger towns and ports.[22] But the impression so far is that most retailing outside the capital was done by established victuallers. In a mock debate in the *Craftsman* in August 1736, Mr. Hearty admitted that gin drinking 'has got too much footing amongst us in the country', but he adds, 'not to such a degree as some people seem to imagine'.[23] In 1736 no provincial centre joined in the parliamentary clamour against Mother Gin. For London the evidence is more detailed. According to the Middlesex justices in 1736, there were 7044 premises vending spirits in the county, but of these nearly half were established victuallers: only 3835 sold gin and brandy alone. This is broadly supported by William Maitland's figures for drinking houses within the Bills of Mortality (including the City and metropolitan Essex and Surrey as well as Middlesex). Maitland's source is not clear, but he may have used excise records, at least for the licensed victuallers. He calculated that there were 8659 brandy-shops in the capital (compared with 5975 alehouses), but with marked local variations in their incidence. The density was particularly high in Southwark and the East End, especially around Whitechapel where there were twice as many gin-sellers as alehousekeepers; in Southwark brandy-shops numbered 2105 (or 1:7.5 houses) as against 932 alehouses: But elsewhere in the capital the situation was less acute. In the City the number of brandy-shops was half that of alehouses with only one to every 38.4 houses. In the respectable western suburbs established victuallers were on a numerical par with the dram-shops.[24]

What about the social background of the retailers? What are we to make of charges that they came from inferior and impoverished trades? Here we have as evidence lists of the occupations of gin-sellers and victuallers drawn up by the constables in 1735–6 at the behest of the Middlesex justices; most of the detailed returns are for the East End.[25] The data are tabulated in the Appendix. Comparing the occupational background of gin-sellers and victuallers, there are few signs of any great influx of labouring poor into the spirits trade any more than into established victualling. Nor, despite official complaints, was there a large contingent of textile workers among the dram-sellers—the proportion was higher in victualling; this reflected the continuing importance of the cloth trade in the East End. Not surprisingly, with the vital contribution of the port to London's economy, shipping and

---

[22] *Read's Weekly Journal*, 2 Sept. 1738; London School of Economics, Archives Dept., Webb Collection, v, 350; R. East, *Extracts from the Records . . . of Portsmouth* (Portsmouth, 1891), 730–4.

[23] *Craftsman*, 14 Aug. 1736.

[24] GLRO, MJ/OC 4, fos. 54–7v; W. Maitland, *The History and Survey of London* (2 vols., 1756), ii. 719, 735.

[25] Wilson, *Liquors* (1st ed.), app. 17, 21; GLRO, MR/LV 6/43–63.

allied workers were well represented in the lists of gin-sellers, but again the victuallers had a higher share. On the other hand, two trades were clearly more important among the spirit-sellers: distillers and chandlers. Chandlers also figure prominently among gin-sellers in the City in 1751.[26] One newspaper correspondent wrote in 1737 that chandlers' shops required 'neither much money nor experience to set up, [and] afford an easy means of relief to indigent people who, being reduced either by infirmities or else bred to no trade, are unable to get their livelihood any other way'. Campbell in the *London Tradesman* declared: the 'chandler's shop deals in all things necessary for the kitchen in small quantities; he is partly cheesemonger, oil-man, grocer, distiller etc.' These small general stores multiplied in town and countryside during the eighteenth century responding to rising demand and reflecting the growing sophistication of inland trade.[27] Some, no doubt, as commentators said, were little establishments kept by poor folk, but surviving inventories for East London chandlers from the later seventeenth century indicate that there could also be more substantial traders. Thomas Fluck, for instance, of St James, Clerkenwell, had a well-stocked shop selling brandy and other spirits, Cheshire and Warwickshire cheeses, butter, bacon, mops, soap, candles and thread, and had an estate worth nearly £44 at his death— partly in outstanding debts. Writers commented how orderly many of these shops were kept.[28]

Where the poor and destitute may have been more active was in street-trading. There are many complaints of poor women, immigrants and others, selling from barrows, stalls and bulks in the street or from small boats plying the Thames.[29] We have less detail about these people, though street-traders of all kinds were increasingly numerous in eighteenth-century towns. But apart from such people, there is not much evidence to substantiate claims that specialist gin retailing was dominated by the impoverished and disorderly. Occupational backgrounds were often not very different from those of established victuallers. Moreover, there were significant numbers of respectable traders engaged in the business, including apothecaries and grocers.

The relative respectability of many dram-shop keepers in the 1730s is confirmed when we correlate them with lists of ratepayers and the

[26] CLRO, MS. 82.17.

[27] *Grub Street Journal*, 27 Jan. 1736/7; R. Campbell, *The London Tradesman* (1747) (Newton Abbot, 1969), 280; I. Mitchell, 'The development of urban retailing 1700–1815', in *The Transformation of English Provincial Towns*, ed. P. Clark (1984), 270–5.

[28] Guildhall Lib., Probate Inventories, MS. 9898/3; also MS. 9174/5,14; *Grub Street Journal*, 27 Jan. 1736/7.

[29] *Daily Post*, 13 Nov., 19 Nov. 1736; *Read's Weekly Journal*, 23 Oct. 1736, 12 March 1736/7; GLRO, MR/LV 6/49.

poor. Thus, in Bethnal Green, an apparently major centre of the trade, comparison of retailers in 1735 with a scavenger's rate a few years before indicates that they paid at a median rate significantly higher than for the area as a whole. Admittedly, poor people may have been exempt from the rate, but only two or three of the gin-sellers in 1735 had previously received a parish pension.[30]

The lists of London gin-sellers do however highlight one contrast with victuallers: the larger proportion of women involved in spirit retailing. In 1725–6 24 per cent of a sample of Middlesex spirit sellers were female (compared with 10 per cent of victuallers); in 1735–6 women comprised 23 per cent of spirit-sellers (and 15 per cent of victuallers). Among unlicensed spirit-sellers in the City in 1751, the female proportion was nearly one third.[31] This last might suggest that poorer traders were more likely to be women, a point which is supported by evidence of committals to the Westminster House of Correction to Tothill Fields under the 1736 Act. Of those gin-sellers imprisoned by J.P.s in 1738–9 because of their inability to pay the £10 fine, three quarters were women.[32] These figures doubtless help to explain the 'Mother Gin' image of the trade. One factor behind heavy female participation may have been their progressive exclusion from the licensed victualling trade over the previous two centuries. But another reason was the growing migration of women into towns in the late seventeenth and early eighteenth centuries, creating a significant surplus over men; many women moved into newer, less regulated craft and service trades.[33]

What about official complaints that gin shops were often located in squalid premises—in cellars and sheds—compared to the spacious, well-equipped alehouses? Here there is an absence of direct evidence but in the few cases where we have the rental value of dram-shops, they were not especially low, and no doubt the grocers and apothecaries engaged in the trade had substantial premises. The Bethnal Green evidence already cited points to considerable numbers of respectable establishments.[34] As we know, however, where the spirits trade was different from orthodox victualling was in the number of street vendors: the Gin Act and later measures were particularly concerned with the problem of hawkers.

[30] GLRO, MR/LV 6/55; Tower Hamlets Library, London, Bethnal Green MSS.257, 306. A list of recipients of parish relief in 1737 also includes only one or two retailers (B.G.MS. 307).
[31] GLRO, MR/LV 6/43–63; CLRO, MS. 82.17.
[32] GLRO, Westminster Sessions Papers, WJ/CC/R 7–12.
[33] Clark, *Alehouse*, 79, 203; D. Souden, 'Migrants and the population structure of later seventeenth-century provincial cities and market towns', in *Transformation*, ed. Clark, 152 et seq.
[34] Eg., Kent Archives Office, U 655, E3; Tower Hamlets Lib., B.G. MS. 257.

As for the consumers, we have already indicated the likely significance of rising living standards and consumer consciousness in stimulating the appetite for gin. It seems likely that many of the customers were not the indigent, as opponents of the trade claimed, but skilled workers like those described by Tom Brown in his account of a dram-shop in the 1720s.[35] More convincing is the critics' stress on women drinking at the dram-shop—'servant maids and labouring men's wives'. In the eighteenth century women tended to visit alehouses on their own only on special occasions. If women did visit gin-shops more often it may have reflected greater female involvement in the trade and the identification of spirits from an early time as a 'female' drink.[36]

In general then, the spirits trade was more limited in its scale and conventional in its organisation than alarmist propagandists asserted. They also misrepresented its effects. Gin became the progenitrix of most of the social and economic problems afflicting the country, particularly in the 1730s. Three charges were frequently reiterated: that the trade had caused an upsurge of crime and disorder; that the national population had declined; and that agriculture had suffered.

On the first count, the grand jury at the City sessions alleged that 'most of the murders and robberies lately committed have been laid and concerted at gin-shops', while there were reports by Wilson and others of men and women dead-drunk littering the streets.[37] It is true there were some notorious headline cases at this time—including one incident where an Irish gin-seller started a fire in an alley off St Martin's Lane which destroyed much of the neighbourhood. But recent research on metropolitan crime has not indicated any particular increase of criminal prosecutions in this decade.[38] On drunkenness the Bills of Mortality, cited in the newspapers, recorded an increase of deaths ascribed to excessive drinking from 17 in 1725 to 69 in 1735, but this rise may have reflected greater official consciousness about the problem; after 1736 recorded numbers fell back despite mounting levels of consumption. The famous story of a dram-shop with the sign 'Drunk for a penny, dead drunk for two pence' was discredited as apocryphal soon after it appeared.[39]

[35] T. Brown, *The Works* (5 vols., 1720), ii. 227–8.

[36] *Calendar of Treasury Books, 1735–8,* 47; also T. Wilson, *Distilled Spirituous Liquors The Bane of the Nation* (2nd ed. 1736), vii; Brown 177, 182.

[37] *Read's Weekly Journal,* 30 Sept. 1735; Wilson, *Liquors* (2nd ed.), vi, app., ix; R. Drew, *A Sermon Preached to the Societies for Reformation of Manners* (1735), 16.

[38] *Read's Weekly Journal,* 14 June 1735; J. M. Beattie, *Crime and the Courts in England 1660–1800* (Oxford, 1986), 108, 214–17, 514.

[39] *A Collection of the Yearly Bills of Mortality from 1657 to 1758,* ed. T. Birch (1759); *Supplement,* 13.

At first sight the claim that Mother Gin had inaugurated a demo-graphic recession through higher morbidity and mortality and reduced fertility seems better substantiated.[40] The Bills of Mortality for the early decades of the eighteenth century suggest a marked rise in mortality levels within the metropolis and a more sluggish movement in baptisms. As several supporters of the spirits trade pointed out, the advance in mortality was not constant—the number of burials dipped in the early 1730s. But London's demographic deficits were almost certainly expanding from the start of the eight-eenth century. This is confirmed by parish register evidence for St James, Clerkenwell, an important gin-selling area, where the demo-graphic deficit doubled in the years 1710–40. It is problematical, however, whether gin-drinking was a significant factor in this deteri-oration. The high levels of infant mortality at this time were mainly associated with endemic levels of smallpox and typhus; adult mortality rates remained relatively stable. Nationally, the 1730s were a time of accelerating population growth.[41]

In the case of agriculture, increased distilling possibly contributed to a fall in beer production in the early 1730s, notably in London, and this in turn may have depressed corn and malt prices. Distilling used less malt than brewing, and distillers increasingly substituted grain for malt. However, there can be little doubt that the prime factor in falling corn prices in the 1730s was rising agricultural pro-ductivity and a succession of good harvests in 1730–4.[42]

Thus the mounting campaign during the mid-1730s against the spirits trade was exaggerated and often sensationalist: the social reality was much more modest. Public scepticism about the attack was articu-lated in newspapers and tracts, though predictably the strongest counter-blast came from the distillers.[43] Nonetheless, the reformist movement made rapid headway. On 20 February 1736 the petition

---

[40] S. Hales, *A Friendly Admonition to the Drinkers of Brandy* (2nd ed., 1734), 4 et seq.; Wilson, *Liquors* (1st ed.), 10, 28 et seq.

[41] J. Marshall, *Mortality of the Metropolis* (1832), 62, 72–3, 75–7; *Daily Post*, 9 April 1736; *Supplement*, 42, 61; J. M. Landers, 'Some Problems on the Historical Demography of London 1675–1825' (unpubl. Ph.D. thesis, Cambridge Univ., 1985), 32–72; R. Hovenden, *A True Register of all the Christeninges, Mariages and Burialles in the Parishe of St James Clerkenwell* (Harleian Soc., 9, 10, 19, 20, 1884–5, 1893–4); E. A. Wrigley and R. S. Schofield, *The Population History of England 1547–1871* (1981), 495.

[42] Mathias, 544; in contrast beer production was stable in the Birmingham area: PRO, CUST 48/13,p. 209; *Agrarian History of England and Wales: V(2)*, ed. J. Thirsk (Cambridge, 1984), 830–1; W. G. Hoskins, 'Harvest fluctuations and English economic history 1620–1759', *Agricultural History Review*, xvi (1968), 31.

[43] Cf. *Daily Post*, 27 March, 30 March, 1 April, 3 April, 9 April 1736; *Daily Journal*, 1 March, 5 March, 27 March 1736. *Impartial Enquiry; A Proper Reply to the Trial of the Spirits* (1736).

of the Middlesex justices against the gin trade was referred by the
House of Commons to a Committee of the Whole House which
approved the main points of statutory action. On 29 March, Sir
Joseph Jekyll introduced the bill and it completed all its stages in the
Commons three weeks later. Opposition in the House was small-scale,
though the distillers and powerful West India interests (concerned at
the likely cut-back in rum and molasses imports) lobbied and petitioned against the Bill. Passage through the Lords was even swifter:
the Bill received its third reading there on 4 May. The Gin Act, with
its introduction of heavy duties on spirits, a £50 licence fee for retailers,
and fines for street-traders, would come into effect on 29 September.[44]

How does one explain the remarkable success of the anti-spirits
campaign? It must be said at once that there was not any widespread
grass-roots agitation in support of parliamentary action. Vestry and
town meeting minutes—even in districts like St James, Clerkenwell,
Stepney and Mile End Road, where gin-selling was apparently rife—
have virtually no references to the problem, no calls for legislation.
The exception was St James, Piccadilly, whose vestry issued an order
against geneva shops in June 1735, but here the rector was the Bishop
of Bristol, a prominent opponent of the trade.[45] At the magisterial
level, the associated Westminster justices supported the Middlesex
bench in their onslaught on gin, but other metropolitan magistrates
were less vocal in their criticism.[46] Outside the capital there was
general magisterial silence.

The role of the Middlesex bench was obviously central. Doubtless
they were influenced in part by a growing concern for improvement
in the metropolis, particularly in the suburbs, exemplified by the
building of Westminster bridge after 1737, the flurry of nightly watch
acts for West End parishes in 1735–6, the introduction of street lighting
to drive away crime, and the growing concern with dirt and squalor.[47]
But other factors encouraged the Middlesex and Westminster magistrates to act. Sir John Gonson, the chairman of the Westminster
bench, had taken an active part in attacking the gin trade in 1728–9

[44] *Commons Journals*, xxii. 582 et passim; see below, p. 78; *Lords Journals*, xxiv. 653,
654, 658, 659; *Statutes at Large*, xvii. 22–31.
[45] Finsbury Library, London, Archives Dept., St James Clerkenwell Vestry Minutes
1725–75; Tower Hamlets Lib., Stepney MSS. 201, 816; Victoria Public Library,
Westminster, D1759, pp. 420, 421, 426. In 1735 many Middlesex parishes were locked
in conflict with quarter sessions over vagrancy rates.
[46] *Read's Weekly Journal*, 11 Oct. 1735; CLRO, Repertories: cxxxix, pp. 314–15; cxl,
p. 51; I am grateful to Mrs E. Stazicker for checking the Surrey sessions records for me.
[47] George, 107, 109; *Statutes at Large*, xvi. 510; xvii. 6–8, 10–11, 13–20; *Daily Post*, 7
Jan. 1736/7.

and he repeated this performance in 1735–6. In his charge to the Westminster grand jurors at Michaelmas sessions 1735, he encouraged them to condemn the spirits trade. Gonson may have had a connection with the Societies for the Reformation of Manners.[48] Early in 1735 Robert Drew, in a sermon to the London societies, had castigated the drunkenness and crime associated with gin-drinking. But by this time the societies were in terminal decline and played no significant part in the campaign against spirits.[49] More crucial probably was Gonson's connection with the Society for Promoting Christian Knowledge.

Gonson was a regular attender at S.P.C.K. meetings in the early 1730s. In 1735 he introduced another Middlesex justice, Benjamin Burrowes, as a member and he may also have had a hand in the admission of the lawyer Thomas Lane of the Inner Temple the same year.[50] Like Burrowes, Lane was a prominent dissenter; he was also subsequently chairman of Middlesex sessions and was closely involved in the public attack on the spirits trade at Michaelmas 1735. This attack seems to have been coordinated by another leading member of the S.P.C.K., Thomas Wilson, the son of the Bishop of Sodor and Man.[51] Overall, members of the Society took a leading role in the propaganda war against gin-selling. One of the first fusillades against the trade in the 1730s came from Dr Stephen Hales, the scientist and medical writer, whose *Friendly Admonition to the Drinkers of Brandy* (1734) had passed through five editions by 1751; copies were widely distributed by the society.[52] Thomas Wilson borrowed from Hales' work and consulted other members like Lane and James Vernon, an excise commissioner, when drafting his own influential tract *Distilled Spirituous Liquors* which appeared early in 1736; the costs of the second edition were paid for, in part, by Sir John Phillips, a leading member, and by donations apparently obtained through Hales. Though the Bishop of Durham warned against 'our society's meddling with things foreign to their proper business', it is evident that a leading group was deeply implicated in the campaign.[53]

Several members of the S.P.C.K. active over the gin question had long-standing connections. Hales, Vernon and James Oglethorpe had

[48] J. Gonson, *Five Charges to Several Grand Juries* (1730), 59, 78, 94–7, 103; *Read's Weekly Journal*, 11 Oct. 1735.

[49] Drew, 16–17.

[50] Society for Promoting Christian Knowledge, London, Minutes, xvi, pp. 72, 146.

[51] Guildhall Lib., MS 3083/1, p. 49 *et passim*; Wilson, *Liquors* (1st ed.), app., 24; *Wilson Diaries*, 132 et seq. Wilson had early links with the Wesleys Keble College, Oxford, Keble Correspondence: 197, Wilson Diary I (letters: Nov. 1731).

[52] D. G. C. Allan and R. E. Schofield, *Stephen Hales: Scientist and Philanthropist* (1980), 23–4, 80–1.

[53] *Wilson Diaries*, 133, 143, 146–8, 152.

been associated with Dr Thomas Bray and his campaign for prison reform in the late 1720s (Oglethorpe was chairman of the Commons' Gaol Committee in 1729). They were also prominent in the subsequent project for the settlement of Georgia. For instance, Vernon acted as liaison between the S.P.C.K. and the Georgia trustees.[54] Others supporting the plantation included Gonson and Wilson.[55] No less interesting, prominent supporters of the Georgia project who were not apparently involved in the S.P.C.K. took part in the campaign against 'Mother Gin'. Thus in the autumn of 1735, Oglethorpe went with Wilson to consult Sir Joseph Jekyll, the Master of the Rolls, over tactics. In May 1735 Jekyll had supported the Georgia society's petition to Parliament and remained a warm advocate of settlement.[56] The Georgia project brought together upper-class people who were interested in moral and religious reform; like the Gaol Committee before it, it served as an important political focus for independent Whigs.[57] As such, it was a major conduit of support for the campaign against Mother Gin.

Jekyll, an old-fashioned Whig, was to play a key role in the successful passage of the Gin Act. Having won his legal reputation in the prosecution of Sacheverell in 1710 and the Jacobite rebels in 1716–17, Jekyll had become Master of the Rolls in 1717. By the 1730s he was in his eighties and pursued his own independent political course, quite often upsetting Walpole. Lord Hervey sneered that he had 'no great natural perspicuity of understanding and had, instead of enlightening that natural cloud, only gilded it with knowledge, reading and learning, and made it more shining but not less thick'. Yet, as Hervey admitted, Jekyll enjoyed a considerable reputation in Parliament 'from his age and the constant profession of having the public good at heart'.[58] As well as supporting the Georgia plantation, he had a recognised interest in the welfare of the lower classes, advocating poor law reform, serving as governor of several city hospitals, and becoming president of the Westminster Infirmary (where he issued orders against the admission of gin drinkers). He was also strong on

---

[54] H. P. Thompson, *Thomas Bray* (1954), 97 et seq.; Allan and Schofield, 67–8, 70–5; *Commons Journals*, xxi. 237–8; S.P.C.K. Minutes, xvi, pp. 88, 139; *Gentleman's Magazine*, ii (1732), 1032.

[55] *Gentleman's Magazine*, ibid; S.P.C.K. Minutes, xvi, p. 175; *Wilson Diaries*, 211–12.

[56] *Wilson Diaries*, 132–3; *HMC*, Egmont Diary, i. 373, 374; *Grub Street Journal*, 11 July 1734; BL, Additional MS. 35, 586, fo. 37.

[57] For the political importance of the Gaol Committee see L. Namier, *England in the Age of the American Revolution* (2nd ed., 1961), 188.

[58] R. Sedgwick, *The House of Commons 1715–54* (2 vols., 1970), ii. 174–5; *DNB*, Jekyll, Sir Joseph; *Some Materials towards Memoirs of the Reign of King George II by John, Lord Hervey*, ed. R. Sedgwick (3 vols., 1931), ii. 419–20; see also Sir Thomas Robinson on Jekyll: *HMC*, Carlisle MSS., 147.

moral issues, opposing state lotteries and urging the passage of the Licensing Act (enforcing stage censorship) in 1737.[59]

But Jekyll's signal success was undoubtedly the Gin Act; Edward Harley reported in his diary that he was the 'chief promoter'. In June 1735 he had joined the delegation to the Queen and in the early autumn he was talking with Wilson about bringing in a Bill. He encouraged the Middlesex justices to act, sending Wilson to speak to them and consulting with Lane. In December he again went to see the Queen and got her support. Soon after he was advising Wilson on his tract and he paid for the first edition. In February 1736 he arranged for the presentation of the Middlesex petition and may already have drafted a Bill. In the Commons Committee he proposed the most stringent penalties and introduced the eventual legislation. Little wonder that when the Act became law, large numbers of troops were stationed near the Rolls Chapel.[60]

One should not underestimate Jekyll's political skill. As well as working closely with the Middlesex justices and members of the S.P.C.K., he probably mobilised other sources of support. He had important nonconformist connections.[61] His marriage ties with Lord Hardwicke, Chief Justice of King's Bench and later Lord Chancellor, gave him access to the ministry. Despite his political unreliability, his support for Walpole during the excise crisis of 1733 may also have helped.[62]

Walpole took part in the debate on the gin question in the Committee of the Whole House and was one of the drafting committee for the Gin Bill. His position was circumspect, concerned at the loss of government revenue if spirit consumption fell and sceptical of the view that the growth of distilling had damaged the brewing industry or landed interest. But his support when it came was crucial. By his insistence that the Civil List had to be compensated for any possible loss of revenue following legislation, the measure became a money bill. In consequence, petitions against the Bill by the West India merchants and others were given short shrift and thus opposition

---

[59] *Wilson Diaries*, 148; *Daily Post*, 6 April 1737; *Grub Street Journal*, 29 May 1735; *DNB*, Jekyll, Sir Joseph; BL, Add. MS. 35, 586, fo. 19. For the background to the Licensing Act see J. Hopes, 'The Debate on the English Stage 1690–1740' (unpublished Ph.D. thesis, Newcastle Univ., 1980).

[60] Cambridge Univ. Lib., Additional MS. 6851, fo. 39; *Grub Street Journal*, 26 June 1735; *Wilson Diaries*, 132–4, 143, 146–7, 149, 150; *HMC*, Egmont Diary, ii. 257; PRO, SP43/22, fo. 135; *Hervey Memoirs*, ii. 569–70.

[61] Leicestershire Record Office, Barker Papers, DE730/2, fos. 70, 85-v; J. E. Force, *William Whiston: Honest Newtonian* (Cambridge, 1985), 20, 27.

[62] N. C. Hunt, *Two Early Political Associations* (Oxford, 1961), 119 claims that Jekyll was a dissenter, but does not give any evidence.

was effectively thwarted.[63] A variety of factors may have influenced Walpole. One (stressed by opponents) was an apparent concern to use the measure to improve the income of the Civil List (compensation under the Act was over-generous). Another factor was the strong tide of reformist opinion in the House. At the same time, the bill allowed Walpole to conciliate the Dissenters, traditional advocates of moral reform, who were upset by his refusal to support their latest attempts to repeal the Test and Corporation Acts and by the failure of the Tithe Bill. Interestingly, Lane, the Middlesex justice and a leading opponent of the spirits trade, was a prominent member of the Committee of Dissenting Deputies.[64] Curbing the spirits trade might also help reduce the smuggling problem which preoccupied the Treasury and Excise Board at this time—important legislation against smuggling was also passed in 1736.[65] One of the surprises, however, is that neither the Treasury nor, for that matter, Parliament, consulted the Excise Board about the problems of enforcing the gin legislation (in 1729 excise officials had been called in to advise the Commons). Admittedly, Vernon, one of the commissioners, was involved in the circle of reformers at the S.P.C.K. but the measure was to suffer sorely from this lack of administrative consultation and advice.[66]

To ensure the success of the Gin Bill in Parliament, the lobbying of the moral reformers and the Middlesex justices and the support of Walpole were not enough. It needed the backing of substantial numbers of rank and file M.P.s, Whigs and Tories, and this is what it received. As one newspaper claimed, the Act 'was lately made by all parties in the House as something to preserve the health of the people'.[67] Landowners spending several months a year in the capital attending Parliament and the Court were clearly sympathetic to alarmist propaganda about an increasingly disorderly metropolis. Substantial numbers moreover had estates in the arable regions where falling corn prices from the 1720s had depressed rents and incomes; they were thus responsive to the claim that distilling was the prime cause. There was also a growing consciousness among the ruling classes about moral and religious issues, a consciousness which was soon to lead to the emergence of Methodism. Speaker Onslow, always influential with backbenchers, had discussed the gin question with Thomas Wilson and Hales before the session began and had given his backing for reform.[68]

[63] HMC, Egmont Diary, ii. 257; Wilson Diaries, 150; Commons Debates, ix. 159; London Magazine (1736), 539 et seq., 596–7.
[64] Jubb, 436–40; Hunt, ch. 7, p. 149-n.
[65] PRO, CUST 48/13, pp. 40–4, 60, 70–2; also Read's Weekly Journal, 19 June 1736.
[66] Commons Journals, xxi, 358, 360; Wilson Diaries, 146–7.
[67] Daily Gazetteer, 9 Oct. 1736.
[68] Wilson Diaries, 139–40.

Not that the opponents of Mother Gin had the political field to themselves. Unlike the brewers who stayed out of the public debate, though they were in touch with the moral reformers and may have paid for some of their propaganda,[69] the distillers threw themselves into the fray. In July 1735 the Distillers Company appointed a committee to lobby the Treasury, the City authorities and Parliament with a proposal to curb excesses in the trade by enlarging the company's powers. The company also disbursed large sums on pamphlets, broadsheets and petitions against the new law, while its agents swarmed about the Palace of Westminster, button-holing M.P.s. There was a report that the distillers had paid £5000 to an opposition M.P. to attack any Bill.[70] The West India merchants petitioned against the measure's impact on colonial imports. In the Commons itself the harshest criticism came from William Pulteney who, though accepting the need for controls, questioned the likely efficacy of the new law and urged instead the revival of the 1729 Act. Other protests emanated from Tories and independent Whigs who resented the way that Walpole was manipulating the Bill to increase the Civil List. As one writer commented, this increase 'put a stop to the unanimity which had long reigned upon this subject'. One detects a growing feeling in Parliament and outside that the law was being rushed through with undue haste.[71] But critics were mollified by talk that the measure could be amended or repealed the following session.[72]

During the summer of 1736 agitation against the new Act increased. On 17 July, Jacobite conspirators set off an explosive device in Westminster Hall while the courts were in session, scattering libels against the Gin Act and other recent laws as 'destructive of the product, trade and manufactures of this kingdom' and tending to 'the utter subversion of the liberties and properties of the kingdom'. Though the issue figured only sporadically in the anti-Irish riots later that month, the Tory *Craftsman* published several hostile articles during the summer, on 11 September asserting the act would ruin 'infinite numbers of people'.[73] *The Fall of Bob: Or, The Oracle of Gin* by 'Timothy Scrubb' published about this time had a scene in which ordinary people were urged to take to the streets in protest; later in the month Jacobite letters tried to whip up similar action. Worried at

[69] *Wilson Diaries*, 143; Guildhall Lib., MS. 5445/27.

[70] Guildhall Lib., MS. 6207/1A (unfol.); *Read's Weekly Journal*, 10 April 1736.

[71] *Commons Journals*, xxii. 674–5, 679; *Commons Debates*, ix. 153–7; *London Magazine* (1736), 316, 320, 347–53; also Jubb, 436–40.

[72] *London Magazine* (1736), 349–50, 596–7.

[73] *Memoirs of the Life and Administration of Sir Robert Walpole*, ed. W. Coxe (3 vols., 1798), iii. 346–7, 350; PRO, SP 43/20, fos. 48–9v; Rudé, 204 et seq.; *Craftsman*, 5 June, 26 June, 14 Aug., 11 Sept. 1736.

the prospect of widespread disorder in the metropolis, the government mobilised large numbers of troops at Michaelmas when the Act came into effect.[74] In London, some retailers made 'a parade of mock ceremonial for Mother Gin's lying in state' and there were also processions at Bristol and Norwich, while ballads and prints lamented the life and death of Madam Geneva. In the capital there were cries of 'No Gin, No King', but in general there was little serious trouble.[75]

The next few months, however, quickly exposed the deficiencies of the Act. Although the Excise Board was not consulted, prime responsibility for enforcing the law in the metropolis was in their hands. Within the Bills of Mortality the Board had the power to try and fine (up to £100) all unlicensed traders. Magistrates had summary jurisdiction over street traders who could be fined £10 or committed to Bridewell. Outside London, enforcement was the work of local justices. Opposition to the Act from the spirits trade was near universal: only two or three people took out licences in the capital and nobody elsewhere. Spirit traders clearly judged that it would be impossible to sell profitably on a licensed basis. Some attempted to move into wine or beer, but the majority simply tried to evade the Act.[76] The Excise Board took a firm line, convicting 416 unlicensed retailers from Michaelmas 1736 to June 1737. In November 1736 one of the commissiones boasted 'we have acted with so much impartiality, vigour and resolution against all sorts of offenders that I believe before Christmas we shall entirely break the drinking of it'. But most of those prosecuted before the board seem to have been well established and respectable traders, distillers, apothecaries, grocers and so on, easily detected by the authorities. Petty dramshops and street vendors continued to do a flourishing business with little or no restraint. One writer later asserted that the Act had transferred the trade from 'those who have legal settlements, pay all taxes, do all offices, to those who have no settlement at all, but are many of them on the poor's book'.[77]

By August 1737, 587 persons had been convicted before the Excise Board but only 127 had been committed to Bridewell by the London

[74] T. Scrubb, *The Fall of Bob: Or, the Oracle of Gin* (1736), 24–5; Rudé, 213–15; *Walpole Memoirs*, iii. 359; PRO, SP 43/22, fo. 135-v.

[75] *Gentleman's Magazine*, vi (1736), 550; *London Magazine* (1736), 579; *Daily Gazetteer*, 5 Oct. 1736; *Read's Weekly Journal*, 2 Oct. 1736; *An Elegy on the Much Lamented Death of ... Madam Gineva* (1736).

[76] *Statutes at Large*, xvii. 23 et seq.; PRO, CUST 48/13, p. 215; *Calendar of Treasury Books, 1735–8*, 193; *Daily Gazetteer*, 13 Oct. 1736.

[77] PRO, CUST: 48/13, p. 395; 47/166, p. 116 et seq.; *HMC*, Carlisle MSS., 175; *Read's Weekly Journal*, 23 Oct., 30 Oct. 1736; *Daily Gazetteer*, 1 Dec. 1736; *A Short History of the Gin Act* (1738), 6.

justices. In the provinces, prosecutions were infrequent. While the Excise Board concerned itself with better-off traders in the capital, magistrates and constables showed a general reluctance to act against small people fearful perhaps of triggering disorder. In London, magisterial action seems to have been confined to a few determined government supporters like Colonel Thomas de Veil at Bow Street.[78] However, by now the government appears to have felt committed to making the law work, blaming opposition to Jacobite and Tory intrigues; hopes of distillers and others that the legislation would be repealed proved groundless. The Sweets Act passed in the 1737 session empowered the Excise Board to offer rewards to informers.[79]

This new measure unleashed a tidal wave of informing in the capital. By November 1737 it was said 350 persons were in the Bridewell for retailing spirits. In the summer of 1738 there was a report that 7,000 had been convicted by the justices within the Bills since 1736, with another 5,000 penalised by the Excise Board, but these figures were wild exaggerations; under 1,300 retailers were fined by the Excise in the whole period 1736 to 1740. Nonetheless the number tried by the justices rose sharply. In April 1738 the number committed to Westminster House of Correction stood at 25 (20 per cent of all committals); by June the figure was 57 (35 per cent) and in October, 66 (35 per cent).[80] Informing became a highly organised and professional operation. Edward Parker reportedly had 30 informers working for him who made allegations against 1,500 persons. Excisemen hired poor people to bring charges against innocent traders. Informers invented a variety of dirty tricks to entrap retailers. Gangs travelled into the provinces to catch out local people. The memoirs of the most energetic of the Middlesex justices, de Veil, complained later that the law had set 'loose a crew of desperate and wicked people who turned informers merely for bread'.[81]

Attacks on informers became increasingly widespread. In January 1737 a chairman's effigy was carried around St George's, Hanover Square, and burnt before a vast crowd, but with the passage of the new Act several informers a month suffered brutal physical assaults.

[78] Read's Weekly Journal, 20 Aug. 1737; PRO, SP 36/39, fo. 152-v; R. Paley, 'The Middlesex Justices Act of 1792: its origins and effects' (unpublished Ph.D. thesis, Reading Univ., 1983), 150.

[79] Daily Gazetteer, 3 Aug., 15 Dec. 1737; Statutes at Large, xvii. 104 et seq.; Read's Weekly Journal, 11 June 1737.

[80] Craftsman, 12 Nov. 1737; Gentleman's Magazine, viii (1738), 379; Read's Weekly Journal, 29 July 1738; PRO, CUST 48/13, p. 395; GLRO, WJ/CC/R 7-9.

[81] Read's Weekly Journal, 14 Oct., 4 Nov. 1738, 6 Jan. 1738/9; Daily Post, 30 Dec. 1737; Short History, 48; R. Sabourn, A Perfect View of the Gin Act with its Unhappy Consequences (1738), 17-19; T. Deveil, Memoirs of the Life and Times of Sir Thomas Deveil, Knight (1748), 39.

The attacks frequently had a ritual character with the victims being dragged through the mire in the street and then repeatedly ducked under pumps or in ponds. One mob hauled a man 'through all the channels along Aldersgate Street, beat him with sticks, kicked him about in a terrible manner, dragged him to a dung-hill in Bishop's Court, St Martin's, and there buried him for some time with ashes and cinders'. At Bristol, an informer was tarred and feathered. Women as well as men suffered; several reportedly died from their injuries. Crowds sometimes widened their attack to include excisemen and magistrates, but the main target were informers.[82]

Informers clearly incensed ordinary people. In the seventeenth century there had been hostility to individuals prosecuting economic offenders for their own profit. At the turn of the century the efforts of the Societies for the Reformation of Manners had foundered on popular resentment at individual informing against sexual miscreants and others to the authorities. In 1730 Francis Hare, preaching to the societies, admitted that the 'low condition and the mean circumstances of these people have greatly helped to make the name of informer odious', even among well-meaning persons. Public opinion was reinforced by judicial hostility to informing.[83] To employ informers in such a controversial matter as the Gin Act was to court disaster.

At the same time, informing was not the sole cause of widespread public hostility to the Gin Act. There was, from the start, a strong sense that the law was a class measure. One writer declared that 'getting drunk will for the future be a great sign of a man's riches'; 'the generality of the people will think themselves oppressed'. There was a long-standing hatred of the arbitrary activities of the excise, loudly and widely ventilated during the excise crisis in 1733. There was a belief that the London justices were exceeding their powers, trying not only hawkers but 'housekeepers and people of credit': not just the poor but respectable citizens were being ruined. In 1737 an attorney declared to a mob outside de Veil's house that it was 'a great hardship upon the subject that people should be convicted for such offences'. The Act was mentioned in the same breadth as the notorious Black Act of 1723, a draconian measure rushed into law with scant regard for public liberties.[84]

[82] *Daily Post*, 18 Jan. 1736/7; *Read's Weekly Journal*, 13 Aug., 20 Aug. 1737; *Craftsman*, 29 Oct. 1737; *Read's Weekly Journal*, 15 Oct. 1737, 7 Jan. 1737/8; *Daily Post*, 5 Nov. 1737.

[83] M. W. Beresford, 'The common informer, the penal statutes and economic regulation', *Ec. H.R.*, new series, x (1957–8), 221–37; T. C. Curtis and W. A. Speck, 'The societies for the reformation of manners', *Literature and History*, no. iii (1976), 45–64; F. Hare, *A Sermon Preached to the Societies for Reformation of Manners* (1731), 15–17; *ex inform.* Joanna Innes.

[84] *London Magazine* (1737), 23, 26; see also Pulteney's criticism of the class bias of the

The government blamed the Jacobites and distillers for stirring up popular agitation and there may have been some truth in this. But it is also evident that by 1738 opposition to the measure embraced not only the poor but many respectable householders as well. Neighbourhoods acted to rescue or help offenders. A Southwark retailer 'well beloved in her neighbourhood' had her fine paid to save her from jail. When a Covent Garden landlady was sent to Bridewell 'a hundred of her neighbours went, some in coaches and others on foot, and redeemed her and brought her home in triumph'. Some of the middling people giving succour to victims of the Act may have been among those London supporters of the patriotic opposition to the ministry in the 1730s described by Dr Rogers.[85] In the summer of 1738 several vestries repaid to convicted offenders part of the fines which had come to the parish. In May 1738 Roger Allen, who had led a large mob in attacking de Veil's house, was accquitted by a jury in King's Bench.[86]

In the spring of 1738 a royal proclamation called for the strict enforcement of the law. The Middlesex and other metropolitan justices agreed to meet several times or more a week to try cases, to limit the opprobrium to individual magistrates. Further legislation was passed to overawe popular resistance: constables could be fined for inaction and rioters transported.[87] But the official position was increasingly desperate. Consumption of British spirits which had dipped in 1737 was rising sharply again by 1738. Even in previously favourable newspapers, reporting of prosecutions became openly critical, particularly where informers were involved. By April 1739 committals to Westminster House of Correction had fallen to 20 (12 per cent of all committals); by July the number was down to two (3 per cent). The number of cases before the Excise Board also fell.[88] With the outbreak of war with Spain, growing ministerial instability, and the calamitous harvest failure of 1739 creating the risk of major public disorder, the Gin Act was put on one side.

---

legislation in 1736: *Commons Debates*, ix. 156–7. P. Langford, *The Excise Crisis* (Oxford, 1975), ch. 10; Sabourn, 22–6; *Read's Weekly Journal*, 15 Oct. 1737; *Craftsman*, 11 Sept. 1736. Cf. E. P. Thompson, *Whigs and Hunters: the Origin of the Black Act* (1975), esp. 21 et seq.

[85] *Read's Weekly Journal*, 4 March 1737/8, 8 April, 22 July 1738; *Daily Post*, 17 June, 24 Sept. 1737; N. Rogers, 'Resistance to oligarchy', in *London in the Age of Reform*, ed. J. Stevenson (Oxford, 1977), 5–9.

[86] *Read's Weekly Journal*, 13 May, 5 Aug. 1738; Deveil, 41–2.

[87] *London Magazine* (1738), 203; *Read's Weekly Journal*, 1 April, 8 April 1738; *Statutes at Large*, xvii. 200 et seq.

[88] *Parl. Papers*, 384; *Read's Weekly Journal*, 3 Feb. 1738/9; GLRO, WJ/CC/R 11, 12; PRO, CUST 48/13, p. 395.

Despite vociferous lobbying and a coalition of support within Parliament, the legislation of 1736 failed to attain that consensus of acceptance in the country as a whole which was essential if it was to be enforceable. Rather, attempts to reinforce its effectiveness only managed further to undermine its public acceptability. Parliament soon recognised reality and in 1743 repealed the measure, replacing it with more liberal controls. Spirit sellers could now obtain a licence for £1. Unlike in 1736 the Excise Board was consulted and the new Act brought some order to the trade. It was not the end of the story, however. The number of licensed retailers rose quickly from under 23,000 in 1744 to nearly 29,000 in 1750, with a significant spread of retailing in the provinces.[89] By 1750–1 there was a renewed outcry against spirits. As before, the Middlesex justices were involved, but the lead now was taken by the City corporation, with Westminster and a number of London parishes in support. There was also important petitioning by major provincial centres such as Norwich, Bristol and Manchester.[90] The 1751 Act increased spirit licences to £2 per annum, restricted retailing to respectable occupiers, and raised the duty on spirits. This time the measure worked. Consumption fell sharply, the number of retailers stagnated and there was no popular opposition. Part of the explanation may be the fact that with the spread of large-scale gin retailing into the provinces, there was greater national recognition of the seriousness of the problem, creating a stronger public consensus. The new measure was carefully drafted, following lengthy committee meetings and consultation with interested parties, and as a result was politically astute. The licence fees and duties though higher were not excessive; the principal thrust was directed at the distillers not the retailers; the Excise Board was not given any special powers of enforcement.[91] No less important, by the mid-eighteenth century the brewing industry was mounting a powerful commercial reply to spirits. In London and southern towns brewers were extending their control over the drink trade through the start of tied house networks. Meantime, the great brewers in the capital were marketing a new high-quality beer—porter. Through mass production and important technical innovations, the real price of porter fell steadily in this period, helping to to dominate the market. To compound the distillers' problems, bad harvests and grain shortages in the 1750s and afterwards prompted the government to ban distilling

[89] *Statutes at Large*, xviii. 78–84; PRO, CUST 48/13, pp. 398, 414; *Parl. Papers*, 436.
[90] GLRO, MJ/OC 5, fos. 225-v; CLRO, MS.82.17; *Commons Journals*, xxvi. 55 *et passim*; *A Dissertation on Mr Hogarth's Six Prints* (1751); *Wilson Diaries*, 257; *General Evening Post*, 23–29 Jan., 16–19 Feb., 23–6 Feb. 1750/1.
[91] *Statutes at Large*, xx. 234–51; *Parl. Papers*, 384, 436; *Commons Journals*, xxvi. 112 *et passim*.

periodically, thus disrupting the trade.[92] Changing fashions in drinking taste and market forces finally brought 'Mother Gin' to her knees where all the might of Parliament in the 1730s had failed.

APPENDIX

Table: Occupations of Retailers of Spirits in London 1735–6

	gin-sellers %	victuallers %
chandlers	40.9	1.5
clothing trades	4.0	2.9
distillers	9.1	0.0
misc. distributive	2.3	0.0
food and drink	4.7	19.5
gardeners	1.1	4.8
labourers	4.9	4.4
misc. service	3.2	2.9
shipping and port trades	5.7	9.7
textiles	15.4	30.5
misc. wood trades	2.4	8.3
misc.	6.3	15.5
sample	530	205

(entries collated from GLRO, MR/LV 6/43–60a)

[92] Mathias, 12 *et seq.*; Clark, *Alehouse*, 183–4; George, 51.

THE FIRST ARMY PLOT OF 1641

By Conrad Russell

READ 29 MAY 1987

ON 11 May 1641, Maurice Wynn reported that 'some plott or other' had been discovered to the Commons.[1] The vagueness of his reaction seems to have been characteristic of much assessment of the army plot ever since. There is a general sense that there is enough smoke to make it probable that there is some fire, but we are not extremely clear who plotted with whom to do what. This is, in part, because of a very justifiable caution. It is felt that Charles I's plots, like his grandmother's lovers, are capable of growing in the telling, especially when the tellers are people to whom belief in popish conspiracy comes with eagerness distressing to a modern ear. Pym and Hampden's later readiness to exploit such mare's nests as the Beale plot at crucial moments in the debate on the Grand Remonstrance adds further to the wariness with which plot stories from the Long Parliament are treated.[2] Wariness is an entirely justified reaction with any Long Parliament plot, but wariness may stop short of incredulity. Above all, a belief that plots should not be taken on trust is no substitute for an examination of the sources.

The key source consists of the body of depositions presented to the Commons in Nathaniel Fiennes' report from the Close Committee on 14 June 1641. These depositions were subsequently published as part of the propaganda war of 1642,[3] and have normally been used in their printed version. The provenance of this printed version, as part of the paper war of 1642, has not added to its credibility. However, it is not necessary to rely on the printed versions. The original MSS, signed by the deponents on each sheet, survive, and are divided between the Braye MSS and the Nalson MSS, now in the Bodleian. There are a very few discrepancies between the printed and manuscript versions. The last page of Goring's deposition does not now survive, but the fact that the surviving MS differs from the printed version only in the sort of trivial errors which normally arise in transcription suggests that this is an accident of survival rather than any nefarious interference with the sources. There is only one interesting piece of information in

---

[1] National Library of Wales, Wynn of Gwydir MSS, no. 1685.
[2] *Journal of Sir Symonds D'Ewes*, ed. W. H. Coates (New Haven 1942) (hereafter '*D' Ewes* (C)), pp. 148, 149, 151, 167.
[3] *C.J.* ii 573. All subsequent references are to vol. ii.

the manuscript depositions which has been suppressed in the printed version. This information, which is crossed out in the MS itself, is that Henry Jermyn had been seen visiting his laundress at three in the morning. It was not only Jermyn's reputation as a dandy which might have made the Parliament doubt whether his motives on this occasion were primarily political.[4] We are perhaps dealing here with a reminder that this was still a struggle between gentlemen.

These depositions, though they are known through the report which presented them to the Commons, were in fact taken, as the signatures on them prove, by the Lords' committee for examinations, which enjoyed the advantage over the Commons of being able to administer an oath. It consisted of Bath, Essex, Warwick, March, Saye, Wharton, Paget, Kimbolton, Howard of Charlton and Howard of Escrick with Attorney General Herbert and Serjeant Glanvill to take the examinations.[5] The majority of these, with some significant exceptions, such as the deposition of Sir William Balfour, Lieutenant of the Tower, are confessions of the minor conspirators. We have another confession by the Earl of Northumberland's brother Henry Percy, which was not taken by the committee, but was extracted from Percy by his brother in return for a blind eye to his escape. This confession exists in two versions, one in Northumberland's papers, and the other printed in London in the summer of 1641.[6] The difference between the two versions is disappointingly small, and consists mainly in the greater clarity of the second.

Confessions as evidence have their limitations, and it is fortunately possible to check them against some other sources. The best of these is a series of letters, now in State Papers, addressed to Northumberland and Conway by Sir John Conyers, Lieutenant General of the Horse, who had a ringside view of the plot developing, and did not like what he saw. This can be supplemented by a limited amount of record evidence in the State Papers, the Signet Office docket book, and the Queen's accounts in the National Library of Wales. There is a very

---

[4] Bodleian Library MS dep. C. 165 (Nalson MS 13) item 9 *C.S.P.D. 1633–4*, vol. ccxxxviii, no. 35 examination of Eleanor Villiers: 'he never promised her marriage, for she loved him so much that she never asked him'.

[5] *L.J.* iv 235 (subsequent references are to vol. iv unless otherwise stated). The peculiarity of this committee is that it contained no bishops. This need not be a statement of political hostility, since the committee's work could be regarded as coming close to the giving of judgements of blood.

[6] Alnwick Castle MSS vol. 15 (British Library Microfilm 286) f. 223a–b. I am grateful to His Grace the Duke of Northumberland for permission to examine these MSS. The MS is not in Henry Percy's hand, but in that of someone who was in England on 11 May (see below n. 85). There is no name on it, but the description of the occasion when 'Goring and I' went to see the King makes the identity clear. Percy's public confession is in SP 16/481/41.

limited amount of correspondence between the conspirators in the papers of William Legge, Lieutenant General of the Artillery, now in Stafford Record Office. In addition, the Scottish Commissioners in London and Newcastle and the French ambassador had enough interest, and a close enough view, to count as first hand sources on a number of points.[7] Fortunately, it seems to be possible to cross-check enough points to decide how far the confessions should be believed.

During the early months of 1641, the King's main English objectives were to preserve some form of episcopacy, and to save the life of the Earl of Strafford. During the weeks before the army plot began, the King had learnt painfully that he was unlikely to achieve these objectives by merely political means. In the third week of February 1641, prospects had looked brighter for a settlement than they did in any other week of the Parliament. The passage of the Triennial Act and the first subsidy bill, on 15 February, were rapidly followed by the appointment of seven new Privy Councillors on the 19th. Most of these new Councillors immediately made token gestures in favour of Strafford, and Charles, by his own subsequent confession, believed that preferment would lead them to drop their opposition to episcopacy also.[8] What Charles hoped, the Scots feared, and for a few days, it seemed as if the Parliamentary-Scottish alliance which had brought Charles to his knees was about to break.[9]

This optimism was shattered by the publication of the Scottish paper of 24 February, demanding the death of Strafford and the abolition of episcopacy in England, and by the refusal of the Parliamentary leaders to condemn this paper in the hard-fought debate of 27 February. The King's disappointment can be measured by the depth of his anger: in Johnston of Wariston's words, 'the king hes run stark mad at it'.[10] What Charles learnt in the two weeks after 24 February was that he could not settle with his critics on any terms he would find acceptable. Instead, he began plans to fight back. On 3 March 1641, in conversation with Walter Stewart, he committed himself to the intrigue with Montrose, designed to end Covenanter control of Scotland, which was to culminate in the Incident.[11] In

[7] The French ambassador's main informant was the Earl of Holland, who became Lord General in the middle of April, but he also enjoyed numerous sources in the queen's household, including Father Philip, the queen's confessor.

[8] *His Majesties Declaration* (12 Aug. 1642) BL, E. 241(1) p. 517. On the behaviour of the new Privy Councillors, see Staffs. R.O. D 1778/1/i/14, O'Neill to Legge, 23 Feb. 1641. I am grateful to the Earl of Dartmouth for permission to use his family papers.

[9] Robert Baillie, *Letters and Journals*, ed. D. Laing (Bannatyne Club, Edinburgh, 1841–2), i. 305–6 (hereafter cited as '*Baillie*').

[10] David Stevenson, *The Scottish Revolution* (Newton Abbot, 1973), 219. I hope to discuss this matter at length elsewhere.

[11] National Library of Scotland, Wodrow MS Fol. 65, f. 72a–b.

England, the issue of episcopacy was one on which he could afford to wait while Hyde, Digby, Culpepper, Strangeways, Bristol and Williams harnessed a growing anti-Scottish reaction to his service. On the issue of Strafford, he could not afford to wait, and it was precisely at the moment when this realisation was becoming urgent that growing discontent in the English army in the north presented Charles with a golden opportunity to exploit.

The English army felt that its honour had been wounded by the defeat at Newburn, and it had already suffered a hiatus in its pay caused by the City's reluctance to lend money until it had procured the execution of Goodman the priest. It was also suffering severe disciplinary problems because of absence of martial law, and the soldiers' deep sense of the hostility of civilian justice to the military. Conyers warned Conway on this subject on 13 February, adding that 'I would I had stayed at Bredae'.[12] On top of this already simmering discontent, the City now decided to withhold loans of money for *both* armies until they had justice on the Earl of Strafford.[13] This move caused severe problems in both armies, and made the competition between them for what money was available even more acute than it was before. This competition became urgent in the Parliamentary debate of 6 March. The House was about to send a sum of money to the English army when it received a demand for money from the Scots, backed by a threat to advance further if they did not get it. On the motion of William Purefoy and Secretary Vane, the House diverted £10,000 from the English to the Scottish army. This vote appears to have produced an explosion of anger among the English army officers in the House. Strode found Willmott and Ashburnham 'much discontented' in Westminster Hall: from such conversations the House took alarm at what it had done. They were too late: Henry Percy, another army officer highly discontented, had been sent to see the King as a one-man deputation on the Algiers pirates, and he enjoyed the opportunity to share his discontent with the King.[14] The real lesson of the day was that the Commons were vulnerable to military pressure.

On 20 March the English army officers submitted a memorial of

---

[12] Public Record Office, State Papers (hereafter SP) 16/477/26 (also 12 and 54). I am grateful to Dr Ronan Bennett for a helpful discussion of the attitudes of civilian courts to soldiers.

[13] SP 16/477/46: Valerie Pearl, *London and the Outbreak of the Puritan Revolution* (Oxford 1961), 198–207. I have not added significantly to Professor Pearl's account of this episode.

[14] *Journal of Sir Symonds D'Ewes*, ed. Wallace Notestein (New Haven, 1923), 448–52 (hereafter *D'Ewes(N)*). BL Harleian MS 163, f. 837a (Strode speaking on 13 Aug. 1641).

their discontents to the Lord General. 'First', they said, 'wee com-
playne as gentlemen that by the long neglect of sending our paie wee
have bene enforced contrary to our disposicions, and the qualities of
our former lives, to oppresse a poor countre, and live upon the curtesie
and at the discretion of strangers, which both they and wee are weary
of'. They complained that their former address by way of petition
had found no credit and brought no remedy, touched in passing on
the 'perverse endeavours' of those who crossed their proceedings,
expressed a desire to recover their military honour, and complained
of judges 'unexperienced and not practiced in our way and profession'
beseeching the Parliament to preserve them from those that would
impose such innovations on them.[15] This letter was brought to London
by a junior officer called Captain James Chudleigh, and from his
arrival in London, on 21 March, the army plot took off. Chudleigh
first met William Davenant the poet, who told him it was 'a matter
of greater consequence that he imagined', adding that 'the Parliament
was so well affected to ye Scotts, as yt there was no lyklihood the army
should have satisfaction so soone as they expected it'. Davenant then
put him in contact with Henry Jermyn and Sir John Suckling. Jermyn
asked to show a copy of the army letter to the Queen, and asked if he
might bring Chudleigh to see her. Chudleigh very properly refused
the second request, saying it was the task of Lord General Northumberland, to whom the letter was addressed, but he does not tell
us his response to the first. Suckling told him the King would be
well pleased if the army would receive Goring as their Lieutenant
General.[16]

Meanwhile, it seems, Henry Percy had begun a second conspiracy,
involving himself, Commissary Willmott, Captain Pollard, John Ashburnham, Sir John Berkeley and Daniel O'Neill. This group, according
to Pollard, began meeting 'about the beginning of Lent', which was
on 10 March. This is a group of minor courtiers and junior army
officers (Henry Percy was Master of the Horse to the Prince, and
Daniel O'Neill a Gentleman of the Privy Chamber extraordinary).[17]
The key common factor of this group seems to be that four of the six
were among the limited group of army officers who were also members
of Parliament, and at least three of those four were present and
indignant at the debate of 6 March. The key to the thinking of this
group was the desire to imitate the Scots: they had seen the Scots able
to bend the Parliament by petitions with the sword behind them, and

---

[15] House of Lords Main Papers, 20 March 1641.
[16] House of Lords Record Office, Braye MSS 2 147v. A clumsy passage in this
testimony is the result of a correction to eliminate hearsay.
[17] SP 16/480/14: PRO LC5./134, p. 300.

intended to see whether what the Scots could do, they could do better.[18] Henry Percy arrived at their first meeting with the heads of a petition already drawn. It asked to preserve the bishops' functions and votes, that the Irish army should not be disbanded until the Scots were too, and that the King's revenue should be improved 'to that proportion was formerly'. Pollard confessed that 'what was meant by the king's revenues, I understand not, unless how to improve it'. Even without Pollard's testimony, it would be possible to doubt whether these articles originated spontaneously with those who were offering them. These articles so much measure royal preoccupations that it seems highly likely that the articles Henry Percy brought to the first meeting came from the king. There is only one of the king's major preoccupations missing, and this may be because the conspirators had cold feet about it and rejected it. Willmott and Ashburnham both insisted that they had not agreed that anything should be done towards the saving of Strafford; or, Willmott added, to the prejudice of the Parliament. Had they felt otherwise, it is likely that we would have known Percy's petition with four heads and not with three. This sounds a law-abiding picture, and it is one Charles later admitted to in relation to the second army plot, saying that 'the commanders and officers of the army had a mind to petition our Parliament, as others of our people had done'.[19]

While Henry Percy was organising his petition, Jermyn, Suckling, Davenant and probably Goring were organising a more far-reaching plan to take control of the Tower and bring the English army southwards. These two were always described by the conspirators as a single plot. The king, probably on 29 March, organised a meeting which was meant to bring these two conspiracies together. This meeting brought together Percy, Willmott, Pollard, Ashburnham, O'Neill and Berkeley from one conspiracy with Jermyn and Goring from the other. Percy's company appear to have refused a request to admit Suckling. It is perhaps in their accounts of this meeting that the conspirators' accounts need to be read with most caution, since they were all concerned to establish that the more shocking propositions came from somebody else, preferably somebody safely abroad. In particular, Percy and Goring, who turned state's evidence, may have been more deeply implicated than their own confessions suggest. On the other hand, the fact that when the plot became public, at the beginning of May, Jermyn, Suckling, Davenant and Percy fled before anyone had accused them is itself evidence for thinking that they were more deeply implicated than those who stayed behind.

[18] Bodleian MS dep. C. 165, ff. 30–41: SP 16/481/41.
[19] L.J. 667.

According to Goring, he was recruited for this meeting through a preliminary approach from Jermyn and Suckling. They took him to see the Queen, who in turn took him to see the king. 'His Majesty asked him, if he was engaged in any cabale concerning the army: to which he answered, that he was not: whereupon his Majesty replied, I command you then to joyne your self with Percy and some others, whom you will find with him'.[20] The King did not attend the subsequent meeting in Percy's chamber, which seems to have been a difficult one. Without necessarily accepting that Willmott, Ashburnham and Percy were quite as holier than thou as their subsequent accounts suggest, we may believe that what they heard gave them cold feet. Pollard said that 'we were afraid to know their proposicions', and that Willmott and Ashburnham had argued that the bringing up of the army to London would lead to 'inconveniences' to king and subject. Ashburnham, by contrast, said that at this meeting he never heard of bringing the army to London, but admitted there were 'some extravagant discourses' so wild they were dissented from. He supplied no particulars of what these discourses were.[21] Percy, in his confession from abroad, said Jermyn and Goring were considering 'a way more sharpe and high, not having limits either of honour or law'. Percy's original manuscript confession, now in Northumberland's papers, is a little franker on this point, though hard to use because the burning of the edge of the paper has destroyed some key words. He said 'there was an intention to ——[1 word] the army and to putt it in a posture of being able ——[2 words] of beeing willing to interpose in the proceedings ——[2 words]'. He concludes 'this I thought unlawfull' to interpose in the proceedings of the House.[22] Goring denied responsibility for the propositions of bringing the army south and taking the Tower, but admitted they were put forward by Jermyn.

It is at least agreed that there was considerable dissension at this meeting, and Percy tells us that he and Jermyn, as representatives of the two rival designs, went to see the King, who told Jermyn and his fellows that 'these ways were vain and foolish, and (he) would think of them no more'.[23] It seems probable that the King said this, and that it was what he wished Percy and his fellows to believe, but it is not what happened. A full understanding would involve an ability to explain why there were two plots. It is possible that this is simply an example of the difficulties conspiracy suffers through secrecy. It is also

[20] Braye MSS 2, f. 158 ff.

[21] Bodl. MS dep. C. 165, ff. 14–41. Ashburnham appears to contradict himself.

[22] SP 16/481/41: Alnwick MSS vol. 15, f. 223b. There is an intriguing suggestion in the last line of the Alnwick confession that Percy may have told Northumberland about the plot before his flight.

[23] SP 16/481/41.

possible, however, to see them as having been initially the king's plot and the queen's plot. Percy's plan for army petitions represented something the king was prepared on a later occasion to admit to having done, whereas by contrast he always vehemently and totally denied any involvement in any plan to bring up the army. This interpretation would turn the king's command to Goring to join himself with Percy into an attempt to merge the queen's wilder plot into his own more responsible plot. It would involve believing that the king spoke truth when he told Goring and Percy that 'these wayes were vain and foolish, and (he) would think of them no more.'

This interpretation solves some difficulties, only to create others. It explains the two plots, and the king's conduct, but it does not explain why the more serious plot managed by Jermyn and Suckling was not brought to a halt by the king's ostensible veto. The plan to bring the army south continued at least for another week, and when Chudleigh came back from the army on 4 April, Suckling took him to report to the king. It would be possible to explain this by saying that Chudleigh had already left for the army before Goring and Percy spoke to the king, and that orders countermanding the plot waited for his return from the north. According to Chudleigh's testimony, he stayed in London eight or nine days from his arrival on 21 March. This would mean he left on the 29th or 30th. Since we do not know how long after the meeting of 29 March Goring and Percy reported to the King, it is impossible to tell which event happened first. It is then possible to explain the failure to stop the plan to bring the army south without disbelieving the king. It is a more serious difficulty that the king's disavowal, as reported by Percy, applied equally to the plan to bring the army south and to the plan to take the Tower. The plan to take the Tower we know he continued, operating through Suckling. On this point, his disavowal must be taken as for public consumption only. Since we must disbelieve half the disavowal, I am inclined to disbelieve the other half, and regard the king as a full participant in the plan to bring the army south.

At this point, Goring chose to impart 'the mayn of the business', though not the particulars, since he had taken an oath of secrecy, to his brother-in-law Lord Dungarvan, then to the Earl of Newport Master of the Ordnance, and finally to Bedford, Saye and Mandeville.[24] From the first week of April onwards, the army plot was conducted in full view of the House of Commons. On 6 April the Commons voted, in the first use of a form of words which was to have a long, if not honourable, history during 1642, that no one was to move the king's army or the Yorkshire trained bands 'without special

---

[24] Goring's deposition, as above.

order of his Majesty, with the advice and consent of both Houses of Parliament'.[25] The fact that this very public notice did not bring the Army Plot to a halt is one of the most intriguing facts about it.

On the same day, Conyers gave warning of a meeting of officers at Boroughbridge, which had taken place on 3 April, though he said he could not find out what had happened at it. He also gave warning of a plan to make Goring Lieutenant General, and gave warning that neither he nor Astley would serve under him. He asked, if Goring should come to the army, for leave to come to London to tell his story.[26] Fortunately, we have other descriptions of the Boroughbridge meeting. Colonel Vavassor said Chudleigh said that the Parliament had taken great offence at the letter of 20 March, that those who had written it would be questioned for it, and that there was small hope of money for the present. He also brought them a letter ready drafted, addressed to Goring, saying that if the king should appoint him Lieutenant General, they would be willing to receive him. Chudleigh confirms the story of the letter asking for Goring to be Lieutenant General, and says he brought it back to London on 4 April, with the signatures of Colonels Vavassor and Fielding and a few others, and that Suckling brought him to kiss the King and Queen's hands. He also spread a report that the Earl of Newcastle was to be their general, and that the King would pawn his jewels to get them pay. His handling of the meeting was not inconsistent with the advice Suckling had given him, that the army 'did undiscreetly to show their teeth, except they could bite'.[27] Shortly afterwards, another officers' meeting was organized at York, at which they were offered a ready drawn declaration 'of their readinesse to serve his Majesty', 'but not findinge any great cause for it, it was after torne'.[28] It is, perhaps, not fanciful to hear a lack of enthusiastic support behind these words. It looks as if the failure of the York and Boroughbridge meetings dampened the plans to bring the army to London.

When Chudleigh returned from Boroughbridge, on 4 April, he brought a letter to Goring from some of the officers, offering to serve under him as Lieutenant General. Not finding Goring in London, Chudleigh took this letter to Suckling, who in turn took it to the king,

---

[25] *C.J.* 116 and other refs. For the origins of this resolution, see B.L. Harl. MS 164, f. 951b. Stapleton and Holles who moved it, regarded it in part for the protection of the Scots. See also SP 16/479/27.

[26] SP 16/479/13, 13.1, 19, 88. No. 88, which is an extract taken from a letter by Conyers not now in State Papers, says that Percy, as well as Holland and Goring was expected at the army. This probably means that Chudleigh or his colleague Sergeant Major Willis told the officers so, but it need not follow that we should believe them.

[27] Braye MSS 2, ff. 147–9. Depositions of Chudleigh and Col. Vavassor.

[28] *ib.* f. 151, deposition of William Legge.

'and afterwards brought him to kiss ye kg. and queenes hands'. 'Within a day or two', the letter was returned to Chudleigh, who took it on to Goring at Portsmouth. On 4 April the plan to bring the army southwards was still alive. By 9 April, when a new Lord General was appointed, it was dead.[29] This timing is compatible with two explanations for calling off the plan to bring the army south. It could represent the king's first chance to bring Chudleigh (and his wife) into line. It could simply represent a recognition, which the evidence would warrant, that the Boroughbridge meeting had not shown enough support to make the design a practical possibility. What seems clear is that the plan to bring the army south did not advance further after 4 April. When a new general was appointed to replace Northumberland, who had malaria, it was not the hard-liner Newcastle, but the much more flexible Earl of Holland, whose appointment had been proposed on 29 March by Percy. Nothing more was heard of some of the rumours spread by Chudleigh and others, of the Prince's going to the army, of French support from Frenchmen around London, or of 1,000 horse financed by the clergy.[30] A rumour continued to circulate through April that the King had sent money to the army, and might go to the army in person, but there is no secure provenance for this rumour.[31] There is only one more suggestion of bringing the army south, in an ambiguous letter from Sir John Berkeley to Legge, written on 1 May.[32] The plan to bring up the army was a genuine plan, but one which failed. Since the Boroughbridge meeting, at which the plan was definitely still in progress, came after Charles's assurance to Henry Percy that he would think of the plan no more, it seems overwhelmingly probable that it was lack of support in the army, rather than Charles's own moral scuples, which brought

[29] SP 16/480/9.
[30] Chudleigh's deposition, ff. 147–8. The plan to make Newcastle general was discussed at the London meeting, but Willmott, Ashburnham and Pollard denied that these other propositions had been discussed there. Chudleigh's suggestion that Newcastle would feast the troops in Nottinghamshire, where his estates were, raises the possibility that the army might have been moved far enough south to cause alarm, but not far enough to burn its boats.
[31] *Calendar of State Papers, Venetian 1640–42*, pp. 142, 145; *H.M. Twelfth Report (2)*, 280.
[32] Staffs. R.O. D 1778/1/i/18, Berkeley to Legge, York, 1 May 1641. This letter deserves quotation in full: 'Deare Will, I have ordered my officers to meete me at Doncaster, and therefore cannot stay. I have performed what was agreed on last night, you know there hath been many occasions of our delay but none from me although I of all men were most excusable if I had, being told by Capt. Palmes that I was mistaken if I thought the rest did not discent as much as he: then which in my judgement nothing could be more. However as I have not been backward heretofore so I will not be for the future in any honourable resolution that shall be approved on by such persons so itt be undertaken roundly and heartily and so you may assure all or any of them from thy Jo. Berkeley'.

the plan to a halt. It is the scuples of the army, unpaid and angry as they were, which are truly impressive evidence of the instinctive constitutionalism of the English.

What undoubtedly continued after the first week of April was the plan to secure Strafford's escape and gain control of the Tower. Sir William Balfour Lieutenant of the Tower, 'our good kind countrieman', as Baillie called him,[33] was unwilling to agree to any such suggestion. He remained unwilling even when Strafford, three or four days before his death, offered him £20,000 and a good marriage for his son to agree to it.[34] If Strafford could be got out of the Tower, his brother Sir George had a ship waiting down river ready to get him away. On one occasion, Strafford and Sir George Wentworth were overheard making plans for an escape. Elizabeth Nutt, wife of a merchant of Tower Street, confessed in an examination on 4 May[35] that she and two other women had gone into the Tower to peep through the keyhole in the hope of seeing Strafford, 'and they then peeping through the keyhole and other places of the dore to see the said Earle did heare him and the other partye conferring about an escape as they conceived, and saying it must be done when all was still and asked the said partie where his brothers shippe was—and doubted not to escape if something which was saied concerninge the Lieutenant of the Tower were done, but what was, as also where they might bee in twelve hours, they could not know by reason that when they talked further off they could not perfectly heare'. Like Sir William Balfour, I find this testimony convincing: the refusal, in spite of palpable frustration, to make up what they could not hear carries conviction. Mrs Nutt also, more questionably, heard the Earl say 'that if this fort could bee safely guarded or overwritten for three or four months there would come aid enough'.

The problem, then, was to gain physical control of the Tower without alerting everyone by going through the ritual of dismissing Balfour. This task was undertaken by Sir John Suckling, in collaboration with an officer from Strafford's Irish army called Captain Billingsley.[36] On Easter Eve 24 April, Billingsley, in the name of Sir John Suckling, approached a certain John Lanyon to recruit him for mercenary service for the King of Portugal, telling him that the king's leave for him to quit royal service could be procured, and he should bring as many cannoneers as he could. Unfortunately for Suckling

---

[33] *Baillie* i. 282, Balfour's deposition, Braye MS 2, f. 156 r–v.

[34] BL Harl. MS 163, f. 500a; *L.J.* 229–30.

[35] Braye MS 2, f. 144 r–v. This was not taken by the Lords' committee for examinations, but by Balfour and Newport as Lieutenant and Constable of the Tower. In acting as Constable, Newport was twenty-four hours premature.

[36] Bodleian Library MS Carte 1, f. 182v.

and Billingsley, Lanyon went to check the story with the Portuguese ambassador, who said that they were very willing to have men, but that he knew nothing of Suckling or Billingsley, and had given them no commission to raise men. After this, Lanyon seems to have avoided turning up at meetings with Billingsley, and received nothing more from him than an offer to buy arms.[37] Others seem to have been less cautious than Lanyon, and by the end of April, Billingsley had a hundred men in his service. These were more than enough to over-power the forty Yeoman Warders of the Tower, and Balfour viewed them with an alarm which can only have been increased when Strafford told him it might be dangerous to refuse to let them in. On 3 May Balfour's resistance was supported by a petition to the House of Lords, from the citizens, who kept a very close watch on what happened at the Tower. The Lords immediately sent Essex, Hamilton and Holland to the king to ask him to withdraw Billingsley's men. There can be no better evidence of the intensity of Charles's deter-mination to save Strafford than the fact that, even at this late date, with the plot in effect discovered, and the weight of the Lords against him, he still demurred. It was reported that 'upon discourse between him and the Lieutenant of the Tower concerning the great concourse of people that resorted about the Tower, his Majestye did think fitt for the better preserving the munition in the Tower, to putt 100 men under the commande of Captain Billingsley into the Tower to garde the munition, but if any jelousie should arise by puttinge those 100 men, his majestie is willing to heare whate advice their lordships will give him in it'. This reply provoked the Lords to send an immediate further deputation, consisting of Pembroke, Bath, Essex, Hamilton, Warwick, Bristol and Saye, 'humblie to desire his majestie' that Billingsley's men should be immediately discharged. Before the depu-tation returned, the Lords ordered Newport to go and take command of the Tower.[38] The next day, Newport reported smugly from the Tower that 'Suckling and his desines are discovered, and I am assured he will pay for it if he stay by it.' He added, with even greater smugness, that the Lords had sent him to take command of the Tower, the King was making him Constable, and 'I have behaved myself so well, I am trusted by both'.[39] For all his smugness, Newport's condemnation of Suckling should be taken seriously.

Even this defeat did not bring the king and queen to a halt, and

---

[37] Braye MS 2, f. 146 v–r (*sic*) (Lanyon's deposition).
[38] Paul Christianson, 'The "Obliterated" Portions of the Lords' Journals', *E.H.R.* xcv (1980), 346–8. I have taken the liberty of changing Professor Christianson's reading of 'Lord Chancellor' on p. 347, since there was no such officer at the time. 'Lord Chamberlain' appears a more probable reading. Original Journals, vol. 16, p. 222.
[39] Staffs. R.O. D 1778/1/i/21.

the plan to send the queen away to Portsmouth, which Goring had fortified with her money, persisted for several days longer. This plan had been some time in gestation. Henry Browne, the queen's servant, testified on 6 May that he had packed up all the queen's plate the week before Easter (18–25 April),[40] and his testimony may have had something to do with the Lords' decision, on the same day, to send Bristol and Holland to the king to stay the queen's journey.[41] It was the day *after* this appeal, Saturday 7 May, that the French ambassador found the queen's carriages waiting at the door, and her most precious things all packed up. He implored the Bishop of Angoulême to stop her, saying flight would only hasten the dangers she feared, to which Angoulême replied undiplomatically that he agreed, but the queen would not listen.[42] He sent the ambassador to see Father Philip, whose letter of the previous day appealing for French help had been intercepted, and is now in State Papers.[43] He decided, after a long conversation, that Father Philip had a hand in the queen's decision. It was only two hours later that he learnt that the queen had changed her mind. What the queen's objectives were is not clear. It may be that the king simply wanted her out of the way, in the hope that he might then be able to refuse to sign the attainder bill without fear for her safety, but the fact that she was withdrawing to a place newly fortified and in the direction of France was bound to make people fear the worst.

The Parliamentary committee which investigated the plot claimed that the plot also included a plan to obtain French help. This was not true, but the king and queen had only themselves to blame for the spreading of the story, since they and their allies had industriously circulated it. The queen had in fact wented to obtain help from France, and had been spreading the rumour that she would go to France, presumably to get help, ever since February. Richelieu, in March, had told the queen bluntly that such a visit would be *'mal à propos'*, and warned her that *'en telles occasions qui quitte la partie le perd'*. He advised the queen *'de se donner un peu de patience, jusques a' ce que le mal qui la presse soit sur son retour'*.[44] This advice annoyed the queen so

---

[40] Bodleian MS dep. C 165, no. 9.

[41] *L.J.* 236.

[42] PRO 31/3/72, f. 552 r–v.

[43] SP 16/480/18.

[44] PRO 31/3/72, p. 458, but see *ib.* pp. 460–2 for the emasculated official form which this advice was transmitted to the Queen. For the deliberate circulation of the rumour, see *ib.* p. 416 (Jan. 28/Feb. 7), when the French ambassador reported that it was thought she hoped to inspire some jealousy in the Parliament. See also *Baillie* i. 295, PRO 31/3/72, pp. 423–4, 435, 436, *H.M.C. De L'Isle and Dudley* vi. 386 and Kent Archive Office U 1475/C 114/7. I am grateful to Viscount De L'Isle and Dudley, V.C., K.G., for permission to quote from his family papers. For the Queen's anger at Richelieu's response, see PRO 31/3/72, pp. 465, 482.

much that she started the rumour that she was going to go to Ireland instead.[45] The French ambassador, on 7 May, industriously circulated a denial of French intervention through Holland,[46] but Jermyn, Suckling and others had circulated it enough to make it hard to kill. It is also doubtful, in spite of the French ambassador's optimism, whether the Parliamentary leaders really wanted to kill it. There is an endorsement on Father Philip's intercepted letter of 6 March, which suggests that on this one issue, they were behaving in the way royalist propaganda has always attributed to them. There are two notes on the dorse of this letter. One says '*pca 25 Junii*', presumably meaning that it was read in the Commons on 25 June, when the impeachment of Father Philip was discussed. The other reads 'fit to be read. To incense the French'.[47] This can only mean a desire to increase French irritation with Charles and Henrietta Maria for claiming French help when they knew it was not available. If members knew that this letter would incense the French, they knew that the charge it was sustaining was not true, and were spreading a false accusation in the hope that mud would stick. They were clearly quite capable of behaving in this way: it is only the fact that the King happened to be guilty on the other charges which meant they did not need to. Another item which gave rise to misplaced alarm was the delivery of new guns at the Tower in the first week of May: the order had been placed in the aftermath of Newburn.[48]

There is further evidence of the King's complicity. During the weeks when the army plot was in gestation, he granted annuities to Percy, Willmott and O'Neill. The week of Henry Percy's flight, facing a potential treason charge, he altered Percy's grant from a grant to him direct into a grant to feoffees to his use, thereby ensuring that a conviction for treason would not make Percy lose it.[49] In June, reports were circulating that the king wished to bring back Jermyn and Percy, and in the autumn Jermyn, jointly in survivorship with his father, was granted the Keepership of Hampton Court Park. It is a small

---

[45] *C.S.P. Ven. 1640–2*, p. 127.

[46] PRO 31/3/72, p. 554.

[47] SP 16/480/18. It is not clear why a House of Commons document is now in State Papers.

[48] PRO (Kew) WO 55/455 (26 Sept. 1640). This order carries a note that Browne's men were to be paid extra wages because of the need for haste. Payment is noted on 20 April 1641. For the order of 10 Dec. for new gun platforms for these guns, PRO WO 49/72, 10 Dec. 1640 (payment 8 May 1641). For the original desire to fortify the Tower after Newburn see SP 16/464/45 and 466/2 and 11, and Bodleian MSS Clarendon 1418 and 1423.

[49] PRO SO 3/12, ff. 142 v, 144 v: SP 16/480/48 and 15.

grant, but one not normally made to exiled traitors.[50] During the Civil War itself, many of the plotters, notably Jermyn, Willmott, Ashburnham, Berkeley, Goring and O'Neill showed every sign of remaining in favour. In August 1641 the King intervened to secure the payment of O'Neill's pension out of the Irish hanaper.[51] Lunsford, who had been involved on the fringes of the meeting at Boroughbridge, was clearly still in the King's favour in December. A final and unexpected witness in favour of the genuineness of the plot is Edward Nicholas, in his history of the Long Parliament, where he says that Jermyn and Goring, and interestingly, also Percy and Willmott 'advised—how the English army might be assured to the King, and if it pleased him, to be persuaded to march southward'.[52] He is a man who is not likely to have repeated the charge lightly.

Another question worth thought is where the money came from. Some of it was raised by a method of delightful simplicity. There was a regular procedure for officers whose pay was in arrears to jump the queue by getting a warrant to receive their back pay directly from Uvedale in London, instead of waiting in the queue to receive it at York. Many innocent people used this procedure, but those taking advantage of it also included Goring, Ashburnham and Chudleigh, who again used the cover story of mercenary service for the King of Portugal. This money, though, is unlikely to have gone far.[53] The report, circulated by the Venetian ambassador, that the king sent money down to the army at York, cannot be confirmed,[54] but since the Treasurer of the Chamber's accounts and the Privy Purse accounts do not survive, the lack of evidence is not conclusive. What is rather more suggestive is the note by Sir Richard Wynn the Queen's Receiver that on 24 March 1641, £1,300 was issued into the queen's own hands. Once it was in her own hands, it no longer needed to be accounted for, and could be spent without creating any further record. It should be said that this is not the only sum issued into the queen's own hands: there is a regular issue at the end of the year for New Year's Gifts, and an unusual one in 1642 to do with the repayment of the loan the queen had made for the Bishops' Wars. However, the entry about the loan is noted in Wynn's warrant book for what it is. There is no such note for the payment of 24 March, but instead a most unbureaucratic note that the receipt was 'written with the

---

[50] Bedfordshire Record Office St John MSS J 1382. PRO C. 233/5, f. 87v.

[51] PRO SO 3/12, f. 169v. See PRO Wards 9/431, f. 387v for the payment of Willmott's pension.

[52] BL Add. MS 31954, fo. 184a.

[53] SP 16/480/11 (Chidley) and 41 (Goring and Ashburnham).

[54] *C.S.P. Ven. 1641–2*, p. 142.

Queen's own hand'.[55] Combined with Chudleigh's testimony that the queen had sent Goring money for fortifying Portsmouth, this is very nearly conclusive.

It is also necessary to ask the question Professor Hibbard has often asked me: how are we to interpret plotting conducted as much in public as Louis XIV's dressing? From 6 April onwards, if not earlier, the plotters should have known that the House of Commons was alert to their activities. Billingsley's activities around the Tower were plain for all the citizens to see. There is no sign that Goring, for all his public leaking, ever suffered any significant royal disfavour, nor that Willmott ever lost the king's confidence for the indiscreet remark, on 19 April, on the floor of the Commons, that all the army officers were sent for to the army very suddenly.[56] This question should be considered alongside the question why Goring chose to leak the plot almost as soon as he was embarked on it. The chronology does not seem to make it easy to explain Goring's leaking in the terms suggested in his deposition, of pique at not being made Lieutenant General, since his appointment as Lieutenant General was still on the cards at Boroughbridge, several days after he had leaked the plot. It is possible that Goring, like Willmott and Ashburnham, gave evidence out of genuine shock at what he had been asked to do. It is true that it is dangerous to underestimate the constitutionalism of any Englishman in 1641, not excluding the army plotters, but it is not easy to regard this as the sole explanation of Goring's conduct. It would square a good many circles if we were to consider the hypothesis that Goring leaked the army plot because the king asked him to. The whole pattern of the politics of 1640–42, for Pym as much as for Charles, is the pattern of the use of threat to force compliance. In almost every example of this process, the initial object of the exercise was not to carry out the threat: it was to achieve the compliance. The lengthy prehistory of the Grand Remonstrance is a classic example of this process. So is the lengthy prehistory of the militia ordinance, first threatened by Pym on 23 June 1641.[57] So is the lengthy prehistory of the attempt on the Five Members.[58] It is only when the deployment

---

[55] National Library of Wales, Wynnstay MSS vol. 165 p. 10 (Wynn's book of pound-age); vol. 173 pp. 12–13 (Wynn's warrant book). The warrant book records £1,400 not £1,300 as delivered into the Queen's hands. I am grateful to Professor Caroline Hibbard for drawing my attention to these MSS. The brief of Wynn's annual account, SP 16/484/48, shows £9,500 as delivered into the Queen's own hands. Of this, £4,200 is not accounted for in the poundage book or the warrant book. In December 1641, when Balfour was offered £3,000 to leave his place at the Tower, the money was channelled through Sir Richard Wynn. D'Ewes(C) p. 330.

[56] C.J. 123.

[57] Bodl. MS Rawlinson D 1099, f. 86a.

[58] See my The Fall of the British Monarchies 1637–1642 (forthcoming).

of these threats failed to induce any compliance that it became necessary to carry them out. The Civil War itself is the ultimate example of
this history of the called bluff. This, perhaps, is the pattern into which
the army plot should be fitted. It was Charles's primary objective
to save Strafford who had trusted in him, and bishops, who had
been entrusted to him. It is likely that Charles believed, as he may
have believed as late as the summer of 1642, that the mere threat
of force, as soon as he could get it to be believed, would be enough
to bring the recalcitrant into line. In the reign of Henry VIII, this
assumption would almost certainly have been correct. It is the real
peculiarity of the reign of Charles I that throughout it, the threat
of force increased, instead of diminishing, the recalcitrance of his
opponents.

This is something many of the plotters seem to have appreciated
better than their leader. Suckling, in his anonymous memorandum of
February or March 1641, told the King there was no other way to
preserve his ministers but by being first right with his people. He
advised Charles that 'it will not be enough for ye kinge to doe what
they desire, but he must doe something more, for yt will showe ye
heartiness, I meane by doeinge more, the doeinge something of his
owne, as throwing away things they call not for'. He added pointedly
that 'to make itt appeare perfect & lasting to ye kingdome, it is
necessary ye Queene really joine'.[59] Henry Jermyn, too, had been
deep in the settlement negotiations of February 1641, even to the
extent of trying to make money out of Leicester's desire for office, by
selling himself, literally, as the man who got him the job.[60] There is
only one among the whole list of plotters of whose thinking this desire
to secure compliance by the threat of force is characteristic, and that
is Charles I himself. Even if the direct evidence did not lead to a belief
in Charles's own involvement, the design so much bears his hallmark
that the burden of proof must rest on those who would suggest that
he was not responsible.[61]

This suspicion can only be strengthened by the suggestion that the
army plot may have had a Scottish dimension, since the king was
alone among the conspirators in having the *locus standi* to have a
Scottish policy. Such a dimension clearly existed in the second army
plot of July 1641, which was in many respects a pale carbon copy of

[59] SP 16/478/82. Gardiner, who is usually accurate on the Army Plot, is at his most
Gladstonian in commenting on this memorandum; *History of England*, ix. 311–2 (1893).
[60] *H.M.C. De L'Isle and Dudley*, VI 367, 382.
[61] Scottish Record Office, Hamilton MSS G.D. 406/1, 1437 and other refs.

the first. When Daniel O'Neill, from the king, lobbied Sir Jacob Astley with plans to move the army southwards, Astley made the obvious objection that 'they must fight with the Scotts first and leave them before they could move southward', to which O'Neill replied 'what if the Scotts could be made neutrall'?[62] If Charles had such a design in the spring of 1641, he at least had material to work with. The City's withholding of money until the death of Strafford had the ironic effect of disabling the Scots as a fighting force, and had contributed substantially to their retreat from the paper of 24 February.[63] Their impatience to finish their business and go home was growing more intense, and was being expressed with an increasing eloquence.[64] They were, moreover, vulnerable to royal attempts to intrigue behind their backs in Scotland. They had been well aware from the beginning that the Covenanters were very far from representing a united Scottish nation, and that the anti-Covenanter cause needed only leadership to make itself effective. They were aware that Montrose, who was one of the leading commissioners with the army at Newcastle, had had a supposedly secret correspondence with Charles since 1639.[65] The beginning of negotiations, on 3 March, with Montrose's allies on a plan which appeared to lead to Montrose's supporters getting the leading Scottish offices may well have been meant as a threat to the Covenanters in the same way as the army plot was meant as a threat to the English, to induce them to adopt a more compliant negotiating posture. The Covenanters were well aware of the strength of what Baillie called 'our unfriends' about Charles.[66] When Charles, on 21 April, told the Scottish Commissioners he meant to come to Edinburgh to complete the treaty, he was raising both hopes and fears: he appealed to the hope that his presence at Edinburgh might signal a greater willingness to make concessions, but also to the fear that it might give him a greater opportunity to pursue the policies he ultimately adopted in the Incident, of spiking the Covenanters' guns by doing a successful deal with their Scottish opponents.[67] The carrot and stick character of Charles's policy is highlighted by the fact that, shortly after starting his intrigue with Montrose, he tempted the Covenanters with the one concession which would have made Montrose's strategy impossible: an agreement that the Scottish great officers and Council should be appointed from a list of nominees made

[62] Astley's deposition 29 Oct. 1641, Braye MS 2, ff. 203–4.
[63] National Library of Scotland, Adv. MS 33.4.6, ff. 132v, 134r.
[64] L.J. 231, BL Harl. MS 457, f. 72r and Stowe MS 187 f. 63r.
[65] Scottish Record Office, Hamilton MSS G.D. 406/1/878 and 1096.
[66] Baillie i. 350; Edinburgh University Library MS D.c.4.16., f. 89v.
[67] National Library of Scotland, Adv. MS 33.1.1 vol. XIII no. 80: David Stevenson, op. cit., 223.

by the Scottish Parliament.[68] He was, in effect, offering the Scots control of their own affairs in return for the end of their meddling in English affairs: the same offer he made to Loudoun and Argyll in the autumn. The withdrawal of the Scottish army from England was an essential condition of any such offer.[69] At the same time, he was threatening, through rumours spread by the Earl of Holland, to use the Irish army against the Scottish if the Scots should fight to secure the death of Strafford.[70] If Charles hoped in April, as he did in July, that the Scots could be made neutral, his hope was not unrealistic: he had put a lot of intelligent effort into securing it. This aspect of the plot was less reported than the others, since the English Parliament lacked the authority to investigate it, but all the clues suggest that it was probably as genuine as the rest.

In the event, the army plot did nothing but defeat all those objectives for which it had been undertaken. It contributed significantly to the death of Strafford, and Strafford's own final letter, 'I beseech your Majesty, for prevention of evils which may happen by your refusal to pass this bill',[71] is plain advice to the king to give up the plot. If Gardiner's date of 4 May is correct, this letter was written the day after Billingsley had failed to gain admission to the Tower, and probably immediately after Elizabeth Nutt had revealed his plans to escape. If so, Strafford probably had little choice in the matter. The circulation of stories about the Irish army during April must have contributed to the Lords' willingness to convict Strafford on that charge, and Strafford can hardly have benefited from the fact that the story of Billingsley's designs on the Tower broke, by Charles's timing and not by Pym's, on the day before the third reading of the Attainder Bill.

Among Charles's potential moderate supporters, the army plot caused a deep dismay. On 3 May Sir John Culpepper, probably the King's most distinguished supporter in the Commons, moved 'for the remonstrance, and peticion of rights to be forthwith read, and then to goe to the Lords and by that we may try the affeccion of the kinge, and that if we should be dissolved, that we might be found doeinge the service we were hither sent for'.[72] Sir Thomas Roe, the Stuarts' Greek chorus, was even more eloquent: 'the tydes returne with every

---

[68] Harl. MS 457, ff. 77r, 80r: National Library of Scotland, Wodrow MS Quarto 25, f. 160v. It is worth noting that this offer was not made at a formal meeting of the negotiators, but at a private meeting between Charles and the Scottish Commissioners.

[69] Hamilton MSS, GD 406/1/1585 and 6.

[70] PRO 31/3/72, fo. 513 (8/18 April). This rumour is unlikely to have helped towards Strafford's acquittal on the Irish army charge.

[71] S. R. Gardiner, op. cit. ix 362 and n.

[72] BL Harl. MS 477, f. 28r.

season, but obedience will be long lame, if ye Parlament every way restore it not'. He hoped for things to improve, but added 'if not I shall envy those that perish with honour than they yt outlive the honour and peace of their countrye'. Roe spoke with feeling, since he had been turned out of the great cabin in his ship by the fleeing plotters, who 'soldier-like, mean to live upon their quarter'.[73] Since Roe, on diplomatic service, possessed the only exemption to the order stopping the ports, it was an obvious move for the fleeing plotters to batten on him. It is, of course, possible that Roe also spoke with fuller information than is available to the rest of us.

The bill against the dissolution of the Long Parliament, without which the Civil War would have been nearly impossible, was another consequence of the army plot. Sir John Culpepper was not alone in fearing that the plot involved a plan to dissolve the Parliament, and when Black Rod came to the Commons to summon them to hear the King's speech, on 1 May, he soothed fears by saying 'fear not, I warrant yow'.[74] The need for security for payment of the armies was an important motive for the Act against Dissolution, but it can hardly be a coincidence that it was passed at the height of a major dissolution scare. Moreover, the need for security for the armies is unlikely to explain the Commons' success in totally rejecting a Lords' amendment to restrict the life of the bill to two years.[75] The disbandment of the Irish army, announced on 7 May, looks like another reaction to the army plot, but curiously, it is not: it is simply a belated acceptance that there was no longer the money to keep it together.[76]

The Protestation, on the other hand, patently is a reaction to the army plot. The proposal for an oath of association was moved by Marten, Wray, Harley and Perd, in the middle of the debate on the plot, and the preamble of the Protestation itself sets out what it is: a declaration of readiness to resist a royal *coup d'état*.[77] At the same time, it was something the Scottish party had failed to obtain in more settled times: it was, as Baillie put it, 'I hope in substance our Scottish Covenant'.[78] The Protestation achieved this synthesis by weaving the army plot together with the 'designs of the priests and Jesuits and other adherents of the see of Rome', and reiterating the case Pym

---

[73] SP 16/480/26.

[74] BL Harl. MS 163, f. 512a.

[75] *C.J.* 138–40, BL Harl. MS 477, ff. 43r, 45v, 47r. It is intriguing to imagine the course of the Civil War if this amendment had been carried.

[76] SP 63/274/21 and 2.

[77] S. R. Gardiner, *Constitutional Documents of the Puritan Revolution* (Oxford repr. 1979), 155–6.

[78] *Baillie* i. 351.

and Rous had been repeating since 1628, that the subversion of the fundamental laws was being attempted because the fundamental laws were an obstacle to the introduction of popery.[79] This was in part an attempt to assimilate the unacceptable to a familiar context, symbolised by Tomkins' motion on 10 May to search the cellars.[80] It is in part also a result of the necessary conventions of seventeenth century political speech. Leading members knew perfectly well, in the first week of May 1641, that what they were facing was a royal plot. Idiom did not permit them to say so, so they had to find a code method of describing it. It cannot have done Charles any good that the code word for 'royal plot' became 'popish plot'. This sort of displacement aggression may also help to explain why, in the weeks after the plot, there was a sudden turning on the bishops from people not all of whom would have been expected to be their natural enemies. Perhaps the most intriguing example of this process is that crusty old anti-Puritan Sir John Conyers. On 28 May, he wrote to Conway that 'I feare so longe as the bishops have any power the church of Ingland will hange toward that of Roome, and will never be aright settled to the true service of God'.[81] On June 14 Baynham Throckmorton, a future royalist, was saying he hoped to hear of the 'the turninge out ye bishops altogether since now there is no other remedy for cure of the disease'.[82] In this way, the army plot presented the godly with numerous unexpected allies.

Perhaps the biggest contribution the army plot made to the coming of civil war was in the contribution it made to convincing respectable members of the House of Lords that true loyalty might take the form of taking authority, and especially military authority, out of the king's hands. The decision, on 3 May, to send Newport to take command of the Tower before he had the King's consent was the first such decision, and it led to others. Also on 3 May, the Houses sent Mandeville to secure Portsmouth and Earle to secure the trained bands of Dorset. The resemblance to the Houses' actions over Hull a year later is very close. The two Houses asked Charles to change the Lords Lieutenant in Yorkshire, Dorset and Hampshire, appointing Essex instead of Strafford in Yorkshire, and Salisbury and Southampton in addition to Cottington and Richmond in Dorset and Hampshire. On 7 May the Lords called in the trained bands of Wiltshire and Berkshire to secure Portsmouth, while instructing those of Sussex and Dorset to

[79] Caroline Hibbard, *Charles I and the Popish Plot* (Chapel Hill, 1983), 194–6.
[80] BL Harl. MS 163, fo. 544a.
[81] SP 16/480/73.
[82] Bristol Record Office, Smyth of Long Ashton MSS, no. 136(e). 'Cure of' is an interpolation in the MS.

remain in readiness.[83] On 7 May there was also an almost unique example of a proclamation issued on the 'advice' of the House of Lords.[84] On 8 May the committee for the defence of the kingdom directed the Lord Admiral to give command of ships to 'men of trust.' The Lords seem to have believed in the first two weeks of May 1641 that the kingdom was on the edge of an immediate civil war, as they told Charles not too obliquely on 11 May. In reply to the king's final request for a reprieve to Strafford, the Lords told him that his wish could not be 'without danger to himself'.[85] This story does not only illustrate the danger of civil war at the beginning of May 1641. It also illustrates two very deep seventeenth century political assumptions. One is the Lords' view of themselves as a government-in-waiting, ready to take over authority whenever the king could not cope. In this line, their measures of May 1641 foreshadow much of what they did during 1642. The other assumption it illustrates is that whenever the body politic was divided to the point of danger, the king was thought to have a special responsibility for making the concessions necessary to restore unity. It was not only the king who had used the threat of armed force to get his way in English politics: his opponents, in alliance with the Scots, had done so quite as much as he had. Yet, because more was expected of kings than of ordinary mortals, the king suffered for it in a way his opponents never did. Above all, the army plot left many responsible politicians with a feeling that politics were too important to be left to kings. Since this was an assumption Charles could not share, it ultimately became one against which he had to fight.

[83] *L.J.* 238, 241 and 235–246 *passim*; *C.J.* 135. The Lords Lieutenant asked for were duly appointed: PROC 231/5, ff. 447, 450, 451.

[84] *Stuart Royal Proclamations*, ed. James F. Larkin (Oxford, 1983), ii. 742–3.

[85] Alnwick MSS vol. 15 (BL Microfilm 286), f. 221; *L.J.* 245, Original Journal, vol. 16, p. 24.

THE EMPRESS MATILDA AND CHURCH REFORM

By Marjorie Chibnall

READ 1 JULY 1987

Magna ortu, majorque viro, sed maxima partu
Hic jacet Henrici Filia, Sponsa, Parens[1].

MATILDA'S epitaph, proclaiming her the daughter, wife and parent of a Henry, great by birth, greater in marriage, and greatest of all in her offspring, epitomises her standing among her contemporaries. It also explains some of the difficulty any historian must experience in attempting to penetrate her character and motives. Her role was seen essentially as an auxiliary one. The relatively few years when she played a leading part in English politics as 'domina Anglorum', with one very brief and ill-advised attempt to act as 'regina Anglie', years to which modern historians have devoted most of the pages they have allowed her, counted for virtually nothing in the summing up of her influence made in 1167. As a woman involved in politics she was assigned a woman's place: important and influential, but limited, variable, and always secondary.

This corresponds partly to reality, partly to the conventions of chroniclers. Her property rights, even as a king's daughter, emperor's wife and count's widow, were restricted to dower, marriage portion and assigned revenues. An element of uncertainty may have hung over the grants she made out of the English royal demesne in the years of opposition to Stephen, sometimes in her own name, sometimes jointly with her son. Twenty years later that had been smoothed over; whether or not she had ever had the right to wear the crown as her father Henry's heir, she had unquestionably transmitted it to her son Henry. Her career could be neatly fitted into a pattern acceptable to custom, as the contemporary sources for her reign also reveal. The comments of chroniclers, so varied that they scarcely seem to describe the same person, depend on the particular conventional woman's role in which each writer pictured her. To German chroniclers, who saw her as a potential intercessor with her husband the emperor and a patron of religious houses, she was pious, beneficent and even (for

---

[1] *Matthaei Parisiensis monachi sancti Albani Chronica majora*, ed. H. R. Luard (Rolls ser. lvii, 1872–83), ii, 324.

good measure) beautiful. The historians of Normandy, where she passed the last twenty years of her life, took the same line. Contemporary English chroniclers, on the other hand, saw her as an aspirant to the throne; and perhaps because, as Karl Schnith has suggested, they were opposed to rule by a woman, they found her haughty, choleric, and a bad influence on her son.[2] In Castille-León Queen Urraca had an equally bad press in some quarters. But unlike Urraca and some Merovingian queens, Matilda was never denounced as Jezebel.[3] The reason may be that, unlike the queens Brunhild and Bathild, she never incurred the hatred of any very powerful prelate. And that in itself may be an important clue to her actual treatment of the church. Her own voice is rarely heard, but her influence and the opinions that directed it can be seen fairly clearly in the way in which she exercised such patronage as she was able to command. Both her benefactions to religious houses and her attitude to episcopal elections (an important source of patronage to any twelfth-century ruler) are relevant to this enquiry. Both bear on the question of church reform.

Patronage of monasteries was the less politically-charged aspect of reform. Lay benefactions were divided between the older Benedictine monasteries and the new orders of monks and canons, but whichever order might be favoured there were always two sides to lay patronage: a genuine desire for spiritual benefits and a wish for some practical, worldly advantage from the surrender of property. It would have been difficult for anyone as politically alert as Matilda to have been in Germany between 1114 and 1125 without being aware of the

[2] Karl Schnith, 'Regni et pacis inquietatrix', Journal of Medieval History, ii (1976), 136–7, comments on the contrasting views. The most violent criticism is in the Gesta Stephani, ed. K. R. Potter, intro. R. H. C. Davis (Oxford Medieval Texts, 1976), 121–3. Henry of Huntingdon (Henrici archidiaconi Huntendunensis Historia Anglorum, ed. T. Arnold (Rolls ser. lxxiv, 1879), 58, wrote, 'Erecta est autem in superbiam intolerabilem'; and there is malicious later gossip in Walter Map, De Nugis Curialium, ed. M. R. James, revised C. N. L. Brooke and R. A. B. Mynors (Oxford Medieval Texts, 1983), 478–81, 484–5. William of Malmesbury, Historia Novella, ed. K. R. Potter (Nelson's Medieval Texts, 1955), 58, is more restrained. Norman chroniclers were laudatory; see Robert of Torigny's interpolations in the Gesta Normannorum ducum of William of Jumièges, ed. J. Marx (Soc. de l'Hist. de Normandie, Rouen, 1914), 280–1, 299–300; Le Dragon Normand et autres poèmes d'Étienne de Rouen, ed. H. Omont (Soc. de l'Hist. de Normandie, Rouen 1884), 120–2. For favourable German comment see F. J. Schmale et I. Schmale-Ott Anonymi Chronica Imperatorum Henrico V dedicata (Ausgewählte Quellen zur Deutschen Geschichte des Mittelalters, xv, Darmstadt, 1972), 262.

[3] Urraca was denounced as Jezebel by the author of the Historia Compostelana (E. Florez, España Sagrada (Madrid, 1747–1879), xx), 204, 324, 333. For the Merovingian queens see J. L. Nelson, 'Queens as Jezebels: the careers of Brunhild and Bathild in Merovingian history', Medieval Women, ed. Derek Baker (Studies in Church History, Subsidia I, 1978), 31–78.

way in which her husband's kinsfolk, the Dukes of Zähringen, were consolidating their power in the Black Forest by the foundation of reformed monasteries.[4] In any case the use of monastic patronage to initiate or consolidate political control in disputed territory was a long-established practice all over western Europe. The vassals of Matilda's grandfather, William the Conquerer, had founded and endowed religious houses in the Vexin and Le Perche as they struggled to extend the frontiers of Normandy.[5] New orders, in particular the Cistercians, who deliberately sought a geographical no less than a spiritual wilderness, become specially favoured for very mixed motives, practical no less than pious. The monastic foundations of Stephen's reign, though certainly important in the history of religion, are also one side of the struggle for power in a country more regionally divided than it had been for several generations.[6]

As patron of monasteries and other churches Matilda had a dual role. Some gifts were personal, made out of her own private resources; others were made in virtue of her office as regent at different times in England or Normandy, or as 'lady of the English'. Towards the end of her life her benefactions were mostly private, and her own personal religious preferences naturally appear most strongly in her last years, when piety and *timor mortis* prevailed over secular considerations, and in any case her power had passed to her son and her influence over him had diminished. But during her struggle with Stephen it was important for her to assert her right to control the royal demesne, and to deny the validity of any gifts made by Stephen out of the inheritance she claimed. Consequently her more official benefactions were determined by the regions where she could exercise real authority, and they were often prompted by the wish of the recipients to legitimise their holdings by securing confirmations from all possible authorities. The English religious houses that sought charters from her lay in the regions where she and her supporters had control at some period in the early 1140s: the upper Thames valley, Gloucestershire, Worcestershire, Somerset, parts of Wiltshire and Shropshire, with a few brief outliers in London and Exeter.[7]

---

[4] The story was told in detail by Theodore Mayer in his inaugural lecture to the University of Freiburg (translated by Geoffrey Barraclough, *Medieval Germany 911–1250* (2 vols., Oxford, 1938), ii. 182–9.

[5] David Bates, *Normandy before 1066* (1982), 177; M. Chibnall, *The World of Orderic Vitalis* (Oxford, 1984), 51–2.

[6] See for example E. King, 'The Anarchy of King Stephen's reign', *T.R.H.S.*, 5th ser. xxxiv (1984), 133–54. There is some discussion of the problem in Bennett D. Hill, *English Cistercian Monasteries and their patrons in the twelfth century* (Urbana, 1968), 36–41; though unfortunately he confuses the Empress Matilda with Stephen's queen Matilda (p. 182).

[7] Some charters were a response to special circumstances; Matilda's writ to the barons

Bordesley Abbey is the most striking example of her use of monastic patronage to strengthen political control in a region of wavering allegiance.[8] Count Waleran of Meulan, one of the first to support Stephen, was rewarded by Stephen with extensive gifts out of the royal demesne in Worcestershire and, in 1138, with the earldom of Worcester. Before the end of that year he used part of his booty to found a new Cistercian abbey at Bordesley, and his endowment was confirmed by Stephen. After the victory at Lincoln, Matilda was able to grant the shrievalty of Worcester to William de Beauchamp, in return for his liege homage 'against all mortal men, and specifically against Waleran count of Meulan'[9]. Bordesley presented her with a problem; she could not suppress a thriving new Cistercian house even had she wished to do so without alienating the church, but she could not recognise the foundation as it stood without conceding the legitimacy of Waleran's title to royal demesne received from Stephen. She therefore took over the abbey and, in effect, refounded it herself. Count Waleran, who at that moment had come over to her side, had to witness her new charter of foundation. She did not attempt to remove the abbot, who was and remained a friend of Waleran's, but from that time Bordesley was an abbey of the royal foundation, and the king exercised the rights of a patron in further elections.

There was a postscript to the Bordesley story a little later in Normandy, when Matilda appropriated a Cistercian abbey that Waleran had attempted to found on a site disputed by the abbey of Mortemer. Aided by Archbishop Hugh of Rouen, Matilda forced Waleran to withdraw. The story has been very well told by David Crouch, though he is inclined to be indulgent towards Waleran's motives and over-critical of Matilda's.[10] Her alleged vow to found a Cistercian abbey may well have been genuine; there can have been few prominent persons who, in the scramble to escape from the rout at Winchester, did not vow to found a monastery of some kind, the Cistercians were

---

and sheriff of London confirming a pension of 50 marks in silver from the ferm of London to the nuns of Fontevrault (*Regesta Regum Anglo-Normannorum*, ii. ed. Charles Johnson and H. A. Cronne, iii. ed. H. A. Cronne and R. H. C. Davis (Oxford, 1956, 1968), iii, no. 328) may, as the editors suggest, have been 'a desperate command to a rebellious city'. But Matilda may have been given some rights over city ferms when her father was grooming her for succession; his original charter to Fontevrault (*Regesta*, ii. no. 1581; *Calendar of Documents preserved in France*, ed. J. A. Round (1899), no. 1052) was separately confirmed by Matilda, and a grant to Cluny out of the ferms of London and Lincoln (*Regesta*, ii. no. 1691; *CDF* no. 1387) received her separate subscription; such special notice by her was unusual in Henry I's charters.

[8] For the foundation of Bordesley Abbey see *V.C.H. Worcs.* ii. 154; David Crouch, *The Beaumont Twins* (Cambridge, 1986), 39–40, 51; *Regesta*, iii. nos. 114, 115, 116.

[9] *Regesta*, iii. no. 68.

[10] Crouch, *Beaumont Twins*, 69–71.

widely favoured, and Matilda's personal gifts show a devotion to the Cistercian order that seems stronger than mere pious fashion. She had every reason to suspect Waleran, who had strong interests in the kingdom of France. Since he had once been pardoned by her father for rebellion and treason he had a special obligation of loyalty to him; yet he had supported Stephen against her and had wavered more than once in his allegiance to any side. In her view, a new Cistercian abbey in Normandy ought to be a royal foundation. Waleran had to surrender; it is to his credit that he did so with a good grace.

The case of Bordesley is particularly striking because it involved taking over the patronage of a new foundation. But that was a typical act of assertion of right at a time of political instability, and was common practice. In Wales whenever the Welsh princes conquered territory formerly held by Normans they took over the patronage of the Norman abbeys.[11] Many of Matilda's charters to English houses, whether established or newly-founded, had the same purpose of neutralising Stephen's gifts out of royal demesnes and revenues.[12] On more than one occasion she and her son Henry took over a tentative new foundation favoured by Stephen and refounded it on a new site. Anchorites settled at Radmore were made the nucleus of a Cistercian abbey moved to Stoneleigh.[13] Arrouasian canons at Donnington Wood were transfered to Lilleshall.[14] Occasionally, as young Henry became more active in government, he and his mother went a stage further and used royal demesnes for new foundations on the frontiers of the regions they controlled. At Wallingford they made an abortive attempt to establish a house of Augustinian canons.[15] A Cistercian abbey (later to be transferred to Stanley) was founded by the Empress at Loxwell in Wiltshire.[16]

Besides the strongly political element due to the civil war in Matilda's benefactions, there was also an element of normal aristocratic and royal patronage in her almsgiving in both England and Normandy.

---

[11] See F. G. Cowley, *The Monastic Order in South Wales 1066–1349* (Cardiff, 1977), 25, 38; D. Crouch, 'The slow death of kingship in Glamorgan, 1067–1158', *Morgannwg*, xxxix (1985), 35.

[12] *Regesta*, iii. *passim*. There is a fairly wide dating limit for some of the charters, which makes it difficult to determine whether Stephen's or Matilda's came first. In Shropshire, where Matilda slowly regained some influence after Stephen's initial victory at Shrewsbury in 1138, the later dating of two Shrewsbury charters (*The Cartulary of Shrewsbury Abbey*, ed. Una Rees (Aberystwyth, 1975), nos. 40, 50) is to be preferred to the dating in *Regesta*, iii. nos. 820, 821.

[13] *Regesta*, iii. nos. 838, 839, 840.

[14] *Regesta*, iii. nos. 460, 461, 462; *V.C.H. Shropshire*, ii. 70–1.

[15] *Regesta*, iii. no. 88, correcting date in P. Walne, 'A "Double Charter" of the Empress Matilda and Henry, duke of Normandy c. 1152', *E.H.R.*, lxxvi (1961), 649–53.

[16] *Regesta*, iii. nos. 836, 837; *V.C.H. Wilts.* iii. 269.

Family foundations were maintained or enlarged. Sometimes, owing to the influence of new religious movements, older foundations were changed to conform to newer rules. William I's secular canons at Notre-Dame-du-Voeu near Cherbourg were replaced by Augustinian canons.[17] Such benefactions by Matilda were normal and frequently little more than conventional. For any indication of her own personal wishes we must look at the endowments made out of her own private resources.

These, apart from one or two early gifts to abbeys in the Empire during her first husband's lifetime, were almost all in Normandy. Her resources were in cash rather than land; sometimes she purchased lands to give away.[18] The jewels, regalia and relics that she brought back from Germany went to various monasteries, notably to Bec.[19] The special place of the abbey of Bec in her affection is a subject too large to be more than briefly touched here.[20] Though independent in origin, it was under ducal protection; and the subject priory of Notre-Dame-du-Pré outside Rouen was a royal foundation. Adjacent to the park of Quevilly, where Henry I built and Henry II enlarged a royal residence, it provided Matilda for long periods in her father's reign and for the years from 1148 to 1167 of her retirement in Normandy with the only really settled home she ever knew. As early as 1134, when she lay ill at Rouen and her life was in danger after the birth of her second son, the monks of Bec were around her. She bequeathed her finest jewels and regalia to the abbey, and insisted, against her father's wishes, that when she died she should be buried there.[21] The gift of the churches and manors at Ogbourne in Wiltshire by her closest adherents, Matilda of Wallingford and Brian fitz Count, was soon followed by the establishment of a small priory,[22] and no doubt helped to keep open her regular contacts with monks of Bec when she was in England during the 1140s.

Apart from Bec the main recipients of her private bounty were the newer orders of regular canons (favoured by both her parents)[23] and

---

[17] *Regesta*, iii. 168; *Gallia Christiana*, xi. Instr. 229; *CDF* nos. 933–8.

[18] *CDF* no. 934; *Regesta*, iii. no. 607.

[19] A. A. Porée, *Histoire de l'Abbaye du Bec* (2 vols., Évreux, 1901), i. 650–1, prints the list of treasures given to Bec.

[20] It is dealt with in my paper, 'The Empress Matilda and Bec-Hellouin', forthcoming in *Anglo-Norman Studies*, x (1988).

[21] Torigny, Interpolations, ed. Marx, 304–5.

[22] M. Morgan, *The English Lands of the Abbey of Bec* (Oxford, 1946), 31 and *passim*.

[23] Her mother, Queen Matilda, had actively furthered the foundation of Merton (J. C. Dickinson, *The Origin of the Austin Canons and their Introduction into England* (1950), 117; and her chaplain Ernisius, was one of the first religious at Llanthony (Cowley, *Monastic Order*, 30) Nostell was founded with the help of Adelulf, chaplain of Henry I, who became the first bishop of Carlisle, King Henry's new bishopric established with

the Cistercians. She held some of the revenues once forfeited by Robert of Bellême, which included dues from Argentan and the forest of Gouffern, and used them to provide for a new foundation of Premonstratensian canons at Silly-en-Gouffern. Her interest in the Premonstratensians went back to her early days in Germany, when the founder of Prémontré, St Norbert, sometimes attended her husband's court. There Drogo, one of her Norman knights, became Norbert's friend. After his return with Matilda to Normandy he entered the cloister as a Premonstratensian canon, helped to instigate the foundation of Silly, and became its first abbot. Matilda had the normal interest of any great magnate in assisting a member of her household who had taken monastic vows; besides this she may have remembered Norbert himself with respect and admiration. She bought lands and a house to add to the revenues from Argentan and Gouffern that she gave to the new abbey.[24] But it was the Cistercians who were, after the monks of Bec, most favoured by her. If there was a political element in her interest in Bordesley, Radmore, Loxwell, and even in Le Valasse there was no secular motive in her final foundation of La Noë. In the last year of her life she bought lands from the vassals of Robert count of Meulan and Richer of L'Aigle to provide a site for the new monastery.[25] Although she might have considered any vow taken in the stress of war to have been fulfilled when she put her resources into the house that Waleran of Meulan had attempted to found at Le Valasse, she may still have felt an obligation to establish a house with less tainted motives. In any case, with health declining and the end of her life so near, she showed a clear wish for the prayers of Cistercian monks. This preference for a reformed order is entirely in line with the views on moral reform in the church that she expressed about the same time to Nicholas of Mont-St-Jacques (to which I shall return). Traditional though she was, and tenacious of regalian rights, she could appreciate new movements of reform in both the monastic and the secular church.

The other side of her church policy appears in her treatment of episcopal elections. She was in Germany and the Empire during some of the bitterest years of the investiture contest. When a compromise was reached at Worms in 1122 it still left many rough edges and

---

a chapter of Augustinian canons. See M. Brett, *The English Church under Henry I* (Oxford, 1975), 25–6); and for the patronage of Augustinian houses by Matilda's uncle, King David of Scotland, G. W. S. Barrow, *The Kingdom of the Scots* (1973), 178–84.

[24] There is a full account in Thomas Stapleton, *Magni Rotuli Scaccarii Normanniae sub regibus Angliae* (2 vols., 1840), i. pp. lxix–lxx. For charters see *Regesta*, iii. nos. 824–6.

[25] *Regesta*, iii. 607; *GC* xi. App. 133, where it is wrongly dated 1144.

unresolved questions.[26] There was even some doubt as to how far the concessions were binding after the death of the participants. Since Henry V's renunciation of investiture with ring and crozier, and his promise to allow canonical election and free consecration were made to the Roman church, not to any individual pope, they were in principle binding on his successors, but his successors did not always see it that way. There was more doubt about the concessions made to Henry personally by Calixtus, that elections should take place at the imperial court and that he might grant the regalia with the sceptre before consecration. But even if these concessions lapsed, the force of the pre-existing custom which they recognised would remain. The emperor retained considerable control in elections whenever he was strong enough to exercise it; but at any time political realism might restrain him from attempting to make use of his theoretical rights. And, like the kings of England after the earlier compromise at Bec in 1107, the German emperors showed some reluctance to relinquish the regalian customs ceremonially implied in investiture. Henry I of England was said to have felt resentment towards Anselm for depriving him of his investitures; and it was only in 1133 that the Emperor Lothar finally gave up his attempt to have the right of investiture restored to him.[27] Matilda cannot have been blind either to the regret with which the symbols were renounced in both regions, or to the fact that the real issue was now the right to grant licence to elect, exercise any customary rights of regale pertaining to the temporalities, and receive the fealty of the new prelate.[28] As with the compromise at Bec, the battle was not ended by the truce at Worms, but the battle-lines had shifted.

Only for a few weeks in 1141, after the capture of Stephen at the battle of Lincoln and Matilda's acceptance as 'lady of the English', was she in a position to influence episcopal elections directly, and to invest bishops with the temporalities. Her direct influence is recorded for London and Durham.[29] The London election was the more straightforward. The see had been vacant since 1134, and after the attempted election of Anselm, abbot of Bury St Edmunds, had failed

---

[26] The two main documents issued at Worms in 1122 are printed *MGH Const.* I, nos. 107–8, pp. 159–61. For some assessments of the Concordat see Adolf Hofmeister, 'Das Wormser Konkordat: Zum Streit und seine Bedeutung', *Forschungen und Versuche zur Geschichte des Mittelalters und der Neuzeit: Festschrift Dietrich Schäfer* (Jena, 1915), 64–148; R. L. Benson, *The Bishop-Elect* (Princeton, 1968), 228–37; Karl Leyser, 'England and the Empire in the early twelfth century', *TRHS*, 5th ser. x (1966), 61–83.

[27] Benson, *Bishop-Elect*, 251–6; Lothar Speer, *Kaiser Lothar III und Erzbischof Adalbert I von Mainz* (Cologne, Vienna, 1983), 59–66.

[28] See M. E. Howell, *Regalian Right in Medieval England* (1962), 24–9.

[29] A. Saltman, *Theobald, Archbishop of Canterbury* (1956), 95–7; *Placita Anglo-Normannica*, ed. M. M. Bigelow (London, 1879), 147; Migne, *PL*, clxxx. 1248–9.

in 1138, partly on the grounds that the dean had not given his consent, no attempt had been made to fill the vacancy. Henry of Winchester administered the see with papal agreement as dean of the province. Matilda's candidate was Robert de Sigillo, her father's keeper of the seal, who had become a monk at Reading. His election made no stir. The Worcester chronicler recorded that when Matilda reached Westminster in June 1141 she immediately took steps, as was proper, to provide for the needs of the church in consultation with worthy persons, and gave the church of London to a certain monk at Reading, a venerable man called Robert, with the approval of his abbot Edward who was present.[30] There is no record of who was consulted, but though the nomination was clearly Matilda's the election was apparently regular in form and the candidate a man of good character, who was praised by St Bernard and Pope Eugenius III nò less than by the English chroniclers.[31] We do not know with what symbol Matilda restored the temporalities, or whether he did homage to her; it is likely, in view of his later refusal of fealty to Stephen, that he had at least sworn fealty. Archbishop Theobald made no bones about consecrating him, and he made the customary profession of obedience to the church of Canterbury.[32] Not surprisingly, Stephen made difficulties. St Bernard had to write to Pope Innocent on behalf of Robert in 1142, when he was obstructed by officials holding the temporalities.[33] Although shortly afterwards he was transacting business in his see, Stephen pressed for a form of fealty that he felt unable to give after consecration, and excluded him from his diocese. In 1147 Eugenius III wrote commanding Stephen to be satisfied with a simple promise of loyalty.[34] It is noteworthy that all through Robert's troubles both Bernard and Eugenius spoke of him as a bishop lawfully occupying a see which, in Bernard's words, had fallen to his lot by the will of God. Stephen's action damaged his own standing with the pope; whereas whatever the part of Matilda in the election, she certainly did nothing to offend even the strictest reformers in the church.

The Durham election should be seen against this background. It was different, because there was a disputed election and Matilda was

---

[30] *Florentii Wigorniensis monachi Chronicon ex Chronicis*, ed. B. Thorpe (2 vols. 1849), ii. 131 (continuation of John of Worcester).

[31] *S. Bernardi Opera* ed. J. Leclercq, C. H. Talbot, H. M. Rochais (8 vols. in 9, Rome, 1957–77), viii. 70 (ep. 211), 'antiquus amicus, fidelis servus, devotus filius'; Eugenius III (Migne *PL*, clxxx, 1248–9), ep. 199, 'vir sapiens et honestus et religionis amator'; *Henrici Hunt.* 316, 'vir animo magnus'; John of Hexham, who wrongly calls him Henry I's chancellor, 'vir bonus' (*Symeonis monachi opera omnia*, ed. T. Arnold (Rolls ser. 1882–5), ii. 309.

[32] *Canterbury Professions*, ed. M. Richter (Cant. and York Soc. 1973), 42 (no. 84).

[33] Bernard, *Opera*, viii. 70 (ep. 211).

[34] Eugenius III, ep. 199, 200 (Migne, *PL*, clxxx, 1248–9); Jaffé, 9088–9).

in part responsible for trying to intrude an unwanted if not unsuitable candidate. Her uncle, King David of Scotland, attempted to force the election of William Cumin, a clerk of the former archbishop Geoffrey who had become his own chancellor. The cathedral clergy, who preferred another candidate, refused to accept such an irregular procedure without the consent of the papal legate, Henry of Winchester. Both parties dispatched envoys to find the legate and the Empress, who at that moment were acting in collusion. When the envoys reached Westminster Matilda was prepared to approve the election; the legate was not there. He arrived shortly afterwards and refused to invest Cumin on the reasonable grounds that the election had been irregular. Matilda refused to give way. Caught between her two kinsmen at a time of mounting crisis, she was unwise enough to lean towards David of Scotland, who was exerting secular pressure on the Durham chapter. What exactly was said or planned we do not know; there is nothing to judge by except a hearsay report of intention. According to the Durham chronicler, a hostile critic writing far away in Durham, Matilda was preparing to invest Cumin with ring and staff when the Londoners rose against her and she was forced to retreat from Westminster taking Cumin with her.[35] If this is a true record she was indeed reactionary as well as foolish, but we do not know whether she would have gone to the length of investing Cumin or what symbol she would have used. She may have uttered threats; but if in a fit of anger she spoke rashly, perhaps telling her cousin the legate that if he wouldn't invest Cumin she would do so herself, this is not a reliable guide to her views on reform. It would be no more a proof that she clung obstinately to lay investiture with ring and staff than Boniface VIII's alleged remark that he 'would rather be a dog than a Frenchman' proved his disbelief in the immortality of the human soul. Experienced in giving advice, Matilda was relatively inexperienced in exercising power, and acted hastily at a moment of mounting passions and political crisis. She was undoubtedly guilty with her uncle David of trying to intrude Cumin into the bishopric. Yet it is on this one episode, and in part on the word of a hostile chronicler, that her reputation as an old-fashioned opponent of church reform largely rests.

The balance of evidence for the two sees of London and Durham does not prove that Matilda attempted or wished to reintroduce the

---

[35] *Sym. mon.* i. 143–8 (*Continuatio prima*). There is a later, shorter account (ibid., 161–7), written probably thirty or forty years later. As Benson observed (*Bishop-Elect*, 256 n. 20), 'Most of the evidence for investiture with ring and staff after 1133 is questionable'. He merely refers to R. H. C. Davis, *King Stephen* (1967), 61, for Matilda's threatened investiture with ring and staff of Cumin; and in fact the evidence for this is as questionable as the rest.

practice of lay investiture. For further evidence, it is worth looking at elections to other prelacies in which, though she did not have the power of granting the temporalities, she may have been able to exert indirect influence. The two regions of special interest are the parts of England where her forces had the upper hand in the period between King Stephen's release and her own departure for Normandy, and the duchy of Normandy after her husband Count Geoffrey won effective control in 1141.

In the province of Canterbury two elections are particularly relevant.[36] Salisbury had been a bone of contention between Stephen and his brother Henry since the death of Bishop Robert in 1139. Stephen had rejected Henry's candidate, and Henry in his turn had prevented the consecration of Stephen's man, his chancellor Philip of Harcourt.[37] When Philip was given the bishopric of Bayeux in 1142 the way was clear for a new election, and Jocelin de Bohun was chosen.[38] An archdeacon of Winchester and protégé of Henry of Blois, but also a kinsman of Robert earl of Gloucester, he was politically a good compromise candidate for a see whose territory was a battle-ground between opposing factions. Fighting very near Salisbury coincided with some divisions in the cathedral chapter;[39] nevertheless the election appears to have passed off regularly enough for archbishop Theobald to consecrate the bishop elect, and King Stephen to receive his homage.[40] Whether or not the Empress attempted to influence the election, she accepted the outcome and for the most part worked smoothly with the new bishop, even after Devizes, the great castle that Stephen had forcibly taken from Bishop Roger, fell to her forces. Between 1141 and 1148 her occupation of the bishop's lands at Canning (where Devizes was situated) and Potterne was balanced by her enlargement of the prebends of Heytesbury. In 1148 she attempted, on instructions from the pope, to secure the restoration of all the lands claimed by the bishop.[41]

Hereford came nearer than any other to being an Angevin see after 1141. Bishop Roger of Bethune died abroad during the Council of Rheims in 1148, and Pope Eugenius III nominated Gilbert Foliot,

---

[36] Although Stephen's capture led to complications over the installation of the bishop of St Asaph's, Matilda had no influence in north Wales (Saltman, *Theobald*, 94–5).

[37] *The Ecclesiastical History of Orderic Vitalis*, ed. M. Chibnall (Oxford Medieval Texts, 1969–80), vi. 536; S. E. Gleason, *An Ecclesiastical Barony of the Middle Ages* (Cambridge, Mass., 1936)', 27–31.

[38] Saltman, *Theobald*, 97–8; Orderic, vi. 536 n.4; A. Morey and C. N. L. Brooke, *Gilbert Foliot and his Letters* (Cambridge, 1965), 55–6.

[39] *The Letters and Charters of Gilbert Foliot*, ed. A. Morey and C. N. L. Brooke (Cambridge, 1967), no. 31.

[40] Richter, *Canterbury Professions*, 43, no. 85.

[41] *Regesta*, iii. nos. 791–4, *VCH Wilts.*, x. 237–8.

abbot of Gloucester, as his successor. Gilbert had worked amicably though independently with the Angevin party which controlled Gloucester, and was personally acceptable to Matilda's son. Young Henry, then in Normandy, agreed to confirm the election and restore the regalia on condition that the new bishop would do fealty to him within a month of consecration and not do fealty to King Stephen. Gilbert was duly consecrated at St Omer by the archbishop assisted by a number of French bishops; but on his return he was persuaded by Theobald to disregard the undertaking to Henry and do fealty to Stephen. In the words of John of Salisbury, the archbishop 'appeased the duke and persuaded him that a bishop had no right to cause schism within the church by refusing fealty to the prince approved by the Roman church'.[42] At this date although young Henry, on the brink of his investment as duke of Normandy, was beginning to take more initiative, he was still strongly under the influence of his mother. The fact that he was persuaded, however unwillingly, to accept a papal directive is an indication of her growing appreciation of the areas in which papal authority was effective, and of her need for papal and ecclesiastical support as the only means of securing the English crown for her son in preference to Stephen's son.[43]

Though Normandy was the region with which Matilda became most familiar and where ultimately she made her home, she was never in a position to exercise ducal power directly; she could only transmit it, or act as regent for an absent father or son. By 1135 when Henry I died the overlordship of the king of France was an acknowledged fact. Henry's son William had done homage to Louis VI, though after his death Henry himself never repeated the ceremony.[44] But it is not likely that the king of France would have accepted homage for Normandy from a woman; and in any case Stephen had forestalled her by persuading Louis VII to receive the homage of his son Eustace.[45] After 1141, however, Stephen's authority was merely nominal. Once Normandy was conquered Geoffrey Plantagenet, Matilda's husband, assumed the ducal title as a first step to recognition by King Louis.[46]

He was remarkably successful in upholding the ducal prerogatives

---

[42] The *Historia Pontificalis* of John of Salisbury, ed. M. Chibnall (Oxford Medieval Texts, 1986), 47–51; Saltman, *Theobald*, 107–10.

[43] Cf. R. Foreville, *L'Église et la Royauté en Angleterre sous Henri II Plantagenet* (Paris, 1943), 11.

[44] On the position of Henry I in Normandy see C. Warren Hollister, 'Normandy, France and the Anglo-Norman Regnum', *Speculum*, li (1976), 202–42.

[45] *Henrici Hunt.*, 260; Robert of Torigny, *Chronicles of the Reigns of Stephen, Henry II and Richard I*, ed. R. Howlett (Rolls ser. 4 vols. 1884–9), iv. 132.

[46] C. H. Haskins, *Norman Institutions* (Harvard Historical Series, xxiv, 1925), 127–35.

without pressing any claims against the church to an intolerable point. The first episcopal vacancy occurred in 1141, just when the tide was turning in Geoffrey's favour though his position was still precarious. John, bishop of Lisieux, one of Henry I's most loyal and long-serving officers, died on 21 May 1141, only a few weeks after making peace with Geoffrey. Orderic Vitalis, writing the last pages of his *Ecclesiastical History*, commented sadly that he did not know when or by what kind of a bishop the see might be filled.[47] It was filled before the end of the year by Arnulf, archdeacon of Sées and brother of John, bishop of Sées.[48] The election was probably canonical, but Arnulf and his family were strong supporters of Stephen against the Angevins. Only two years previously Arnulf had argued Stephen's case before Innocent II at the Lateran Council, and had even challenged Matilda's legitimacy by alleging that her mother was a nun. Whether or not Stephen had been in a position to press his candidature, Geoffrey was sufficiently in control to appeal to the pope and refuse Arnulf entry to the temporalities for over two years because he had been consecrated without his consent. He did not give way until Arnulf recognised him as duke of Normandy, and then he took a fine of more than 900 livres. Once reconciled, the two men saw that their interests lay in working together; and Matilda, who had been trained in too hard a school to indulge in the luxury of vindictiveness, also made her peace with Arnulf. In 1149 he was sent by Abbot Suger to negotiate with King Louis on behalf of the Angevins. His shuttle diplomacy between the Empress and her son in Normandy, Geoffrey in Anjou and King Louis in Paris successfully brought about a reconciliation.[49] He also used his influence with friends in England; in the summer of 1149 he wrote to Robert Chesney, the newly elected bishop of Lincoln, urging him to favour the cause of the new young duke of Normandy, 'who ought to succeed to the kingdom of England by hereditary right'.[50] The change of sides was not surprising, for it furthered his own interests and, like his secular lord and lady, he combined a hard-headed pragmatism with a genuine interest in some aspects of church reform. These included encouragement of the new orders, respect for the observance at least of the letter of canon law, and a firm belief in the dignity of

[47] Orderic, vi. 550-3.
[48] For the Lisieux election see *The Letters of Arnulf of Lisieux*, ed. F. Barlow (Camden 3rd ser. lxi, 1939), pp. xix–xx, 209; *Recueil des historiens des Gaules et de la France*, new edn, ed. L. Delisle (Paris, 1869–1904), xv. 582-5, 603-4. By 1143 Arnulf dated his charters from Geoffrey's reign, not Stephen's.
[49] Abbot Suger was also involved in the negotiations (*Recueil des historiens*, xv. 520–2).
[50] *Letters of Arnulf*, 7 (no. 4).

the episcopal office.[51] They were entirely compatible with the view that Caesar also had his rights.

Geoffrey's other involvement was with the election of a new bishop of Sées in 1144. There were irregularities in this election which led to an appeal to Rome. Geoffrey, whose licence had not been sought, sent his officers to intervene, and the violence of their attack on the unfortunate intruder, Gerard, shocked even the party hostile to him. Again, Geoffrey took the course of prudence; he disowned the actions of his servants and agreed that they should be judged in an ecclesiastical court.[52] At Easter, 1147, he met Pope Eugenius in Paris; Archbishop Theobald was there at the same time, and their meeting may have helped to promote understanding between them.[53] Geoffrey succeeded in asserting his interest without alienating powerful parties in the papal curia. The process of canonical election was allowed to run its course, even when it produced a candidate not of his own choice; but he insisted on his right to give the licence to elect and to invest the new bishop with the temporalities.[54]

In all this Matilda remains in the background; but Geoffrey's actions and the whole of his administration of Normandy show, as Haskins pointed out, that he regarded himself as a regent holding the duchy in trust for his eldest son, to whom he surrendered it formally early in 1150.[55] She is likely to have been consulted on critical issues and, with her knowledge of her father's rule in Normandy, she certainly exercised a powerful influence on her son in the early years of his independent government. And one common factor that emerges in many of these elections during the 1140s bears the stamp of Matilda's experience and perception. She recognised the increasingly effective power of the papacy and realised that, though the popes would tolerate much in the interests of peace, to press any dispute beyond the point that they would tolerate was sheer folly.

From the first weeks of Stephen's reign the pope was involved in the succession question. Between 1139, when Matilda took her case to the Lateran Council, and 1153, when her son's succession was finally assured, relations with the papacy were one of her constant preoccupations. She might in any case, owing to the uncertainties surrounding female succession, have been ready to look to Rome for ratification, as did Queen Urraca of Castille-León.[56] Since Stephen

[51] *Letters of Arnulf,* p. xxxii and *passim.*

[52] *Letters of Arnulf,* 4–5 (no. 3), 21–2 (no. 16).

[53] H. Gleber, *Papst Eugen III* (Jena, 1936), 71.

[54] See H. Böhmer, *Kirche und Staat in England und in der Normandie im XI und XII Jahrhundert* (Leipzig, 1899), 310–25.

[55] Haskins, *Norman Institutions,* 135.

[56] Bernard F. Reilly, *The Kingdom of León-Castilla under Queen Urraca 1109–1126* (Princeton, 1982), 364.

moved quickly, her hand was forced by his immediate appeal for support from Innocent II. This was desirable for him in a case where oaths were involved, and he acted hastily to make good a dubious right. Although the evidence is not clear, Matilda probably sent envoys to protest to Innocent in 1136; her formal appeal was made three years later in 1139, when she was about to invade England and lay claim to the throne.[57] The outcome is well known. Her attempt failed; Stephen's envoys won the first round, and Innocent refused to change his mind. What is a little less frequently remembered is the manoeuvring of Matilda's party at the papal curia during the following years.

Some of the Roman clergy had become known to her through their activities as legates in Germany.[58] Whatever views she may have held about the theoretical position of the reforming papacy, she had experienced at first hand the political power a strong pope might enjoy throughout a great part of the western church and the dangers of incurring excommunication. John of Salisbury's *Historia Pontificalis* gives an interesting hint that her agents were active in Rome. Some of the cardinals were not convinced by the arguments of Stephen's envoys in 1139; one of these was Guy, cardinal priest of St Mark, who four years later was elected pope as Celestine II. His promotion was made, John wrote, 'favore imperatricis'.[59] This may imply more influence than the Empress actually exercised, since Guy was elected unanimously immediately after Innocent II's death; but John's statement shows that she was in close touch with the papal curia, and was keeping alive her cause in that influential quarter. Although Celestine's pontificate lasted only five months he wrote, according to John, to Archbishop Theobald forbidding him to make any change in the matter of the English crown, since the transfer had been justly denounced and the case was still pending. His successors, Popes Lucius and Eugenius, repeated the prohibition. These letters have not survived, but John was in a position to know something both of papal business and of the business handled by Archbishop Theobald, and

---

[57] The dates of proceedings in the papal court have been the subject of much debate; see the recent assessment by Giles Constable, *The Letters of Peter the Venerable* (2 vols. Cambridge, Mass., 1967), ii. 252–6. The events at the Lateran Council are described by Gilbert Foliot in a letter to Brian fitz Count (*Letters of Gilbert*, 65–6), and by John of Salisbury, *Historia Pontificalis*, 83–5, discussed by M. Chibnall, 'John of Salisbury as historian', *The World of John of Salisbury*, ed. M. Wilks (Studies in Church History, Subsidia 3, 1984), 172–4.

[58] Both Lambert, cardinal-bishop of Ostia (later Pope Honorius II), and Gregory, cardinal-deacon of S. Angelo (later Pope Innocent II), had been legates in Germany in 1122 (G. Meyer von Knonau, *Jahrbücher des Deutschen Reiches unter Heinrich IV und Heinrich V* (7 vols., Leipzig, 1890–1909), vii. 199–206).

[59] *Historia Pontificalis*, 85–6.

his story would explain the reluctance of successive popes to commit themselves to Stephen's cause.

The election of Eugenius III in 1145 brought to the papal throne a Cistercian pope, a friend of St Bernard, with whom Stephen rapidly became embroiled.[60] At this stage in the struggle in England, with the country divided into regions of differing allegiance, the control of church elections became more important than ever. Stephen, needing a stronghold in the north against the danger of a renewed Scottish invasion, wished to put his own man into the archbishopric of York. He also needed a complaisant archbishop, and Theobald of Canterbury had made it clear from the outset that he would not give way to political pressure from either side. Standing firmly for the unity of the church, he held the bishops of the province of Canterbury together in a way that was to Stephen's advantage, but he insisted on obeying papal precepts even against the king's will. So the York election was doubly important to Stephen.[61] The opponent of his candidate was the Cistercian, Henry Murdac, protégé of St Bernard; and Stephen's resistance brought down upon his head and that of his brother Henry of Winchester the wrath of that formidable opponent.

Although at the height of the Lisieux dispute, when Bernard wrote to Innocent II on behalf of Arnulf, he described Count Geoffrey of Anjou as *malleus bonorum, oppressor pacis et libertatis ecclesie*,[62] this was related specifically to his refusal to admit Arnulf to the temporalities; and Bernard's language was mild in comparison with his corruscating attack on the opponents of Henry Murdac, when he described Bishop Henry of Winchester as (amongst other epithets) 'that old whore of Winchester'.[63] Matilda herself avoided alienating Pope Eugenius, and there were good relations between her family and St Bernard. Her half-brother, Robert earl of Gloucester, founded the Cistercian abbey of Margam in south Wales. At a solemn ceremony in 1147 Robert symbolically handed over lands for the purpose of founding the abbey to St Bernard's brother Nivard.[64] It must have been during Nivard's journey through England that he enlisted Matilda's support for the monks of Cerne, who were involved in a long and complicated case

[60] Gleber, *Papst Eugen III*, 71, 96–7.

[61] For the York election see David Knowles, *The Historian and Character* (Cambridge, 1963), 76–97; Gleber, *Papst Eugen III*, 163–4. St Bernard's attitude is discussed by Christopher Holdsworth, 'St Bernard and England', *Anglo-Norman Studies*, viii (1986 for 1985), ed. R. Allen Brown, 149–52.

[62] St Bernard, *Opera*, viii. 291–3 (ep. 348).

[63] St. Bernard, *Opera*, viii. 480–1 (ep. 520); Holdsworth, 'St Bernard and England', 149.

[64] R. B. Pattison, *Earldom of Gloucester Charters* (Oxford, 1973), no. 119.

against their abbot, which had finally gone to Rome. Matilda, politically in control of much of the diocese of Salisbury, wrote on behalf of the monks to her friend Gilbert Foliot, then abbot of Gloucester, whose former prior was the abbot elect of Cerne. Gilbert replied in deferential but firm terms.[65] He was certain that if Nivard had known all the facts he would never have taken up the case of the rebellious monks, who were acting in defiance of the pope. Gilbert had been instructed by the pope himself to have them removed to another monastery. He pointed out respectfully that he was ready to obey the Empress in every way that was right and possible, but she must hold him excused from defying the authority of the pope. No more is heard of Matilda's involvement in the affair. The episode reveals friendly contacts between her and a brother of St Bernard, as well as showing that a plea to respect the normal processes of appeal to the papal court had some influence on her actions. A year later she and her son accepted a similar argument from Gilbert Foliot, when he did fealty to Stephen as bishop of Hereford in spite of his earlier undertaking to young Henry. It was a wise course; at the very moment when Stephen was fatally weakening his position at Rome by his unsuccessful attempt to prevent Archbishop Theobald attending the Council of Rheims, Matilda discreetly lay low. Stephen subsequently failed to secure papal consent to the coronation of his son, even after he had made his peace with Henry Murdac. The popes continued to uphold Celestine II's decision to suspend judgement, waiting on events; and meanwhile Matilda's party steadily strengthened their position. Although the attempt of Geoffrey of Anjou in 1148 to challenge Stephen's usurpation failed, Stephen never secured the coronation of Eustace;[66] when the young man died in 1153 no attempt was made to have his younger brother William crowned. Patience and prudence had won the day. Military and feudal considerations, important as they were, are not the subject of this paper; but on the ecclesiastical side the way had been well prepared for the truce of Wallingford and Stephen's acquiescence in young Henry's claim to succeed him on the English throne.[67]

How far was this due to Matilda's influence? Her later actions suggest a view of church reform and the rights and limits of papal power entirely in keeping with the course pursued during those difficult years. She had a clear appreciation of the place of the pope in

---

[65] *Letters of Gilbert Foliot*, 98 (no. 63), App. III, 507–9. The editors suggest that the monks of Cerne probably enlisted the help of Nivard, who was abbot of Clairvaux, on their way back from the papal curia; but since he visited England at the time of the dispute it is more likely that the meeting took place on his way to or from Margam.

[66] *Historia Pontificalis*, 83; Gleber, *Papst Eugen III*, 163–5.

[67] *Regesta*, iii. 97–9, no. 272.

the complex pattern of European political relationships. When in April 1165 Henry II received ambassadors of the schismatical emperor Frederick Barbarossa at Rouen, the Empress refused to give them an audience, even though one of the objects of their visit was to negotiate a marriage between her granddaughter Matilda and Henry duke of Saxony.[68] She was less prepared than her son to have personal dealings with the enemies of Alexander III. Of her refusal Archbishop Rotrou of Rouen wrote to Cardinal Henry of Pisa, 'Do not imagine for a moment that she will vacillate in any way.'[69]

A strict reformer might perhaps have charged her with inconsistency in her attitude to schismatics, for she used the title of empress in spite of the fact that her only imperial coronation had been at the hands of an anti-pope. Like her Norman forebears, she was essentially pragmatic; she would have endorsed the assertion of the first Earl of Stockton in his maiden speech in the House of Lords: 'Pragmatic politics are the only good ones.' When her actions happened to be in line with those of reformers in the church, it was frequently because practical prudence pointed in the same direction. This appears in her attitude to royal title and coronation.

The place of the church in the supreme moment of kingmaking was a central theme in the writings of church reformers. The Norman kings, punctilious in their attempts to legitimize an authority that might seem to rest on military conquest, had made it an essential first step in succession to the throne.[70] Stephen's trump card was his coronation by the archbishop of Canterbury. This act brought the English church to his side; he could not have been deposed without papal sanction, and even that might have been challenged in some quarters. Matilda's attitude was at times inconsistent, partly because she was learning from experience as the years passed, but she was ready to learn.

She had been crowned and anointed queen in a ceremony of unquestionable validity once or at most twice in her life. When in 1110 as an eight-year-old bride she came to Germany she was solemnly betrothed to King Henry V and crowned queen by the archbishops Frederick of Cologne and Bruno of Trier. Archbishop Bruno lifted her up in his arms to be anointed.[71] After her marriage in 1114 she was again crowned queen at Mainz.[72] She had not been in Rome with

---

[68] R. W. Eyton, *Court, Household and Itinerary of King Henry II* (1878), 78; *Materials for the History of Thomas Becket*, ed. J. C. Robertson *et al.* (7 vols. Rolls ser. 1875–85), vi. 80.

[69] *Materials*, v. 194–5.

[70] Karl Schnith, *Journal of Medieval History*, ii (1976), 135–58.

[71] Torigny, Interpolations, ed. Marx, 280–1.

[72] *Anonymi Chronica Imperatorum* ed. Schmale, 262; Florentii Wigorn., ii. 67.

her betrothed husband when, in 1111, he received the imperial crown from the unwilling hands of Pope Paschal II; she had remained in Germany to learn the language and customs of her new country. When in 1117 she accompanied Henry to Rome relations between Pope and Emperor had become so hostile that only the most sanguine could have hoped for any signs of papal favour. Henry was determined to be seen as emperor, with an empress at his side. But before the imperial armies reached Rome, Pope Paschal withdrew. Only one prelate, the Archbishop of Braga, later anti-pope, remained to conduct the ceremony in St Peter's and place crowns on the heads of Henry and Matilda.[73] Even this may have been more a ceremonial crown-wearing than a coronation; on two occasions, at Easter and Pentecost, they showed themselves crowned in Rome. Matilda did not then adopt the imperial title; in her charters and on her seals she was 'regina Romanorum'. But this may not mean that she regarded herself as less than Empress, however, dubious the validity of the ceremonies in Rome. Her husband sometimes used the title 'rex Romanorum' after his earlier valid coronation, and evidently regarded it as having imperial overtones.[74] She used the title 'imperatrix' from soon after her return from Germany in 1125 up to the end of her life, and was constantly called empress in sources as varied as the letters of prelates and the Pipe Rolls, and even by some German chroniclers. It may have been something of a courtesy title, but it was never challenged. There was some misunderstanding in the West about what happened in Rome in 1117; Robert of Torigny said that the imperial crown had been placed on her head by the pope and she had twice gone crowned through the streets of Rome.[75] He is the writer who has left the fullest details of her various coronations and anointings, and there can be little doubt that he had the information, directly or indirectly, true or false, from Matilda herself. Whatever significance she attached to

---

[73] Meyer von Knonau, *Jahrbücher*, vii. 30–3; C. J. Hefele, *Histoire des Conciles*, ed. H. Leclercq (Paris, 1907 ff.), v (i), 553–62.

[74] Schnith, *Journ. Med. Hist.*, 148: idem. '*Domina Anglorum*, Zur Bedeutungstreite eines hochmittelalterlichen Herrscherinentitels', *Festschrift für Peter Acht* (Münchener Historische Studien, Abt. Geschicht. Hilfswissenschaften 15, 1972), 101–11. R. L. Benson, 'Political *Renovatio*: Two models from Roman Antiquity', *Renaissance and Renewal in the twelfth century*, ed. R. L. Benson and Giles Constable (Cambridge, Mass., 1982), 373. I shall discuss Matilda's title more fully in my forthcoming book on the Empress Matilda.

[75] Torigny, Interpolations, ed. Marx, 304–5; the Worcester chronicler wrote that she was crowned empress in 1114 ('et in imperatricem est coronatus', Florentii Wigorn, ii. 67). In Germany the *Annales Patherbrunnenses*, ed. P. Scheffer-Boichorst (Innsbruck, 1870), 334, gave her the title of empress, 'Godeboldus Traectensis episcopus gratiam imperatoris per interventum imperatricis . . . obtinet'.

the actual ceremony of crowning and anointing, she certainly believed it important to be seen wearing the crown.

When she first came to England in 1139 her son Henry was still a young child, and she made what was probably a mistake of claiming the throne for herself. Reilly, writing the history of Queen Urraca of Castille-León, emphasised Urraca's wisdom in associating her equally young son with her government almost from the beginning.[76] It is possible that in one or two early charters Matilda described herself as 'Anglorum regina'.[77] This would have been a break with tradition. Although Karl Schnith was not quite right when he claimed that no Norman king had used the title *rex* before his coronation, the only exception—very briefly—was Stephen. In his first so-called 'charter of liberties' issued at London when he had arrived with his count of Mortain's household, he described himself as 'rex Anglorum'.[78] The document was hastily drawn up and witnessed only by his steward; plainly he had not yet learnt the ropes, and his coronation followed so quickly that he had no time to make the same mistake again. If either of the charters in which the title 'regina' occurs was authentic, Matilda must have been told by her advisers that it was a mistake; in any case she rapidly settled for 'domina Anglorum'. She still hoped for a proper regal title, and took steps to secure it. We cannot be sure what kind of ceremony was planned to take place at Westminster in June 1141, before the defection of the legate and the Londoners. Stubbs, followed by Karl Schnith, suggested that it might have been more a solemn crown-wearing than coronation and unction.[79] This would have put it roughly on a par with the ceremonies in Rome in 1117, and it might have satisfied her. But whatever her intention, or the interpretation of the chroniclers who called it a coronation, it never took place. After Stephen's release it became clear that the English church would never tolerate the deposition of an anointed king who, in spite of his quarrels with later popes and even a threat of excommunication, was never in serious danger of deposition by the pope. Her only hope was to prevent the coronation of Eustace, and to work for the recognition by the church of her son Henry's hereditary

---

[76] Reilly, *Urraca*, 334.

[77] Schnith, *Journ. Med. Hist.*, 149; *Regesta*, iii. no. 343, a charter for Glastonbury, c. 3 March 1141 (a cartulary copy, so even here the title may not be authentic). The title *regina* is also used in no. 699, but the authenticity of the charter is doubtful. According to Ashmole the legend on the seal (now lost) of her first charter to Geoffrey de Mandeville was 'REGINA ANGLIÆ' (*Regesta*, iii. no. 274).

[78] Schnith, *Journ. Med. Hist.*, 148; *Regesta*, iii. no. 270.

[79] W. Stubbs, *The Constitutional History of England* (3rd edn, 3 vols., 1880–4), i. 339–40.

right. These were practical ends based on a realistic assessment of papal power rather than on any theory.

Towards the end of her life reformers sometimes saw her as a useful ally for practical reasons. The fullest statement of her views is preserved in the letters relating to the Becket dispute. She was said by some of the bishops to have opposed the election of Becket as archbishop of Canterbury, though on what grounds is not known.[80] They may have been pragmatic. Young as she was when the Emperor Henry V's formerly devoted servant and chancellor Adalbert was rewarded with the archbisopric of Mainz and immediately took up the cause of reform against his master, she had seen something of the consequences of his rebellion and the way that a man might change on appointment to an office with both new spiritual responsibilities and new temporal interests.[81] She may have feared that Becket would become a threat to Henry. On the other hand she may have thought him unworthy of high office because of his notorious pluralism and the ostentation of his former way of life.[82] The fact that her objections, whatever they were, went unheeded, is a sign that her influence over her son was waning. Nevertheless many of Becket's friends believed that she was worth cultivating and that she might be able to provide effective mediation. Becket himself applied to her, and Pope Alexander III also asked her to attempt to make peace between her son and the archbishop.[83] She was thought to be fair-minded and able to see both sides, and with some reason. She warned Becket that he was suspected of attempting to raise rebellion against her son in England, and that only a humble and submissive approach would restore him to favour.[84] On the other hand she gave cautious support to a few of his exiled friends;[85] and when her son brutally intercepted, tortured and imprisoned one of Becket's messengers charged with a secret mission she insisted on the release of the unfortunate man.[86] When in 1164 Nicholas of Mont-Saint-Jacques at Rouen crossed the river Seine to seek her out in her retirement at Le Pré, hoping to secure her support against the Constitutions of Clarendon, she gave her views fully and

---

[80] *Materials*, v. 410. Thomas replied (ibid., v. 516–17) that if the Empress had raised any objections they had never been made public.

[81] F. Hausmann, *Reichskanzlei und Hofkapelle unter Heinrich V und Konrad III* (Schriften der *Monumenta Germaniae Historica*, Stuttgart, 1956), 25–35.

[82] F. Barlow, *Thomas Becket* (1986), 44–5.

[83] *Materials*, v. 201; *The Letters of John of Salisbury*, ii, ed. W. J. Miller and C. N. L. Brooke (Oxford Medieval Texts, 1979), pp. xxvii, xxx, nos. 144, 157, 179.

[84] *Materials*, vi. 128–9.

[85] Barlow, *Becket*, 127.

[86] Barlow, *Becket*, 161.

frankly. The account of the interview which Nicholas sent to Becket is worth examining in detail.[87]

He began by giving her a verbal report of the contents of the Constitutions, explaining that his copy of them had been mislaid. He assured her that some were contrary to the faith of Jesus Christ and almost all to the liberty of the church, so that both she and her son were in danger of eternal damnation as well as facing worldly difficulties. This résumé was not good enough for the practical Empress: she demanded to see a copy of the Constitutions. Nicholas conveniently succeeded in finding his copy that evening, and took it to her next day. She ordered him to read the clauses to her in Latin and explain them in French. 'She is a woman of the race of tyrants', Nicholas wrote, 'and she approved some clauses, particularly the prohibition of excommunicating justices and other ministers of the king without his permission.' He added that he had had to remonstrate with her, quoting scripture, at this point. Then his tone softened. She had condemned many of the clauses, and above all she was displeased that they had been written down and the bishops compelled to promise to observe them: such a thing had never been done before. In the end she had agreed with him that the best way to restore peace would be for the king to consult with reasonable persons and find a moderate compromise, whereby the written record and the promise might be withdrawn and the ancient customs of the kingdom observed; with the proviso that secular justice would not take away the liberty of the church and the bishops would not abuse that liberty.

The Empress, Nicholas wrote, had cunningly defended her son, excusing his conduct by adducing his zeal for justice and the malice of the bishops, but she had shown herself reasonable and discreet in uncovering the roots of disturbance in the church. She said some things that Nicholas heartily endorsed. Bishops were reckless in ordaining clerks without title to any benefice, and the great multitude of impoverished clergy brought disgrace on the church. They could commit crimes with impunity, having no benefice to lose; they did not fear the bishop's prison, since the bishop did not want the trouble and expense of guarding them. Yet there were pluralists who had four or more churches or prebends, in defiance of the canons that forbade anyone to hold even two. The bishops kept silent on the abuse because they gave benefices to their kinsfolk as laymen did to their servants. They took fines to which they were not entitled by the canons. Nicholas concluded by admonishing Becket, 'If you love the freedom of God's church, show by your words and deeds that you disapprove of such things.' This reads like the language of the Empress; Becket's new way

[87] *Materials*, v. 148–50.

of life was not widely known, and Matilda's criticism of the bishops seems to have had him in mind.

Her proposals impressed Nicholas as reasonable; they were shrewd and traditional. The reforms were the moral reforms of the first stages of church regeneration—the attack on simony, nepotism and pluralism. Respect for custom had been the way of her grandfather William the Conqueror; his canons of Lillebonne were a record of agreed customs allowing for variation, not a written series of demands imposed by threats on an unwilling episcopate.[88] But though in her lifetime she moved with many other lay rulers in her circle and accepted some new reforms, including a measure of freedom of election, this was not enough to satisfy the more extreme exponents of canon law. To say that chapters might elect freely provided they took note of the wishes of lay rulers was not acceptable to reformers like St Bernard or even Henry of Blois, who as churchmen were prepared to propose their own candidates to electors, but wished to exclude lay influence. In many countries a delicately balanced *modus vivendi* had been established. The balance could easily be disturbed in times of civil strife, when the control of churches became a political issue, or during litigation between churchmen over exemption or privilege when an appeal to Rome might lead to the automatic excommunication of royal servants.

If the Empress saw the issues clearly, it was partly because in 1164–1166 she was no longer an active participant; she was on the side-lines of the struggle, better able to see a practicable solution than to bring it about. Henry, bishop of Winchester, who was now an elder statesman, was also generally respected as he urged moderation, but was equally ineffective. It had been different in 1141 when he and Matilda were both in the thick of battle, military and ideological, forced to take quick decisions on day-to-day business, when a wrong move might embroil them in unforeseen difficulties in their own time, and bring down on their heads the vituperation of critics for generations to come. Matilda had too little time in active leadership to learn the difficult art of governing; but in Germany, Rome, England, Anjou and Normandy she gathered experience that enabled her to play the roles of regent, adviser, and transmitter of the English crown with more success than has sometimes been recognised. In this activity, in spite of a quick temper and an occasional error of judgement, her appreciation of how a great many secular prerogatives might be preserved by a realistic and practical acceptance of moderate church reform and increasing papal power was an important element. Leopold Delisle, describing the work of government in Normandy,

[88] Haskins, *Norman Institutions*, 30–8; Orderic, iii. 25–35.

wrote that Geoffrey Plantagenet 'was strongly supported by the intelligence, the activity and the courage of his wife, the Empress Matilda, and to her is due the honour of having prepared the way for the reign of Henry II.'[89] On the ecclesiastical side, her part in enlisting steady support from the church was no less important in ensuring the ultimate victory of the Angevin cause.

[89] L. Delisle, Introduction, *Recueil des Actes de Henri II, roi d'Angleterre et duc de Normandie* (Chartes et Diplômes relatifs à l'Histoire de France, 1909), 139.

MONASTICISM AND SOCIETY IN THE DIOCESE OF YORK 1520–1540

By Claire Cross*

ON TRIAL for his life in the spring of 1537 for his part in the Pilgrimage of Grace Robert Aske from the Tower supplied a retrospective explanation of northen resentment at the dissolution of the monasteries, at that stage still very much in progress and nowhere near completion. Of all the recent changes in religion, he in particular

> grudged against the statute of suppressions, and so did all the country, because the abbeys in the north gave great alms to poor men and laudably served God: in which parts of late days they had small comfort by ghostly teaching. And by the said suppression the service of God is much minished, great number of masses unsaid and consecration of the sacrament now not used in those parts, to the decrease of the faith and spiritual comfort to man's soul, the temple of God ruffed and pulled down, the ornaments and relics of the church irreverently used, tombs of honourable and noble men pulled down and sold, no hospitality now kept in those parts ...
>
> Also the abbeys was one of the beauties of this realm to all men and strangers passing through the same; also all gentlemen much succoured in their needs with money, their younger sons there succoured and in nunneries their daughters brought up in virtue, and also their evidences and money left to the uses of infants in abbeys' hands, always sure there ...

Because of the circumstances in which it was delivered this often quoted lament for the loss of the northern monasteries voiced by an unusually articulate layman might well seem a piece of special pleading. The purpose of this paper is to try to establish what the laity and the secular clergy in the diocese of York thought of their monasteries in the early sixteenth century immediately before they capitulated to the Tudor state.[1]

The York archiepiscopal probate registers, augmented by those for the dean and chapter, the archdeaconry of Richmond, a handful of wills for diocesan peculiars, the archbishops' registers (for the beneficed clergy) and the probate registers of the prerogative court of

* This paper was to have been read on 16 October 1987, but the great storm of 15–16 October prevented the meeting being convened.

[1] *Letters and Papers of Henry VIII*, xii, pt. I no. 901 (2).

Canterbury, provide the only surviving source capable of yielding some idea of northern religious opinion against which Aske's assertions can be tested. Of slightly over five thousand wills made by testators resident in the diocese between 1520 and 1540 just over half contain no mention at all of either monasteries or friaries, and it seems abundantly clear that the majority of northerners owed their allegiance primarily to their parish churches. Around a quarter of these five thousand testators, however, left money to friaries, and approximately an eighth (732 to be precise) to a specified monastic house, a bequest to the one, of course, not excluding an offering to the other. It might well be objected that this result is artificially skewed to minimise secular support for monasticism, since in the five years between 1535 and 1540 with the dissolution in progress it was becoming more and more difficult and eventually impossible for money to be given to friaries and monasteries. However, if only the years 1520 to 1535 are considered, the proportions are not very different: about half the wills relating to these fifteen years make no reference to monasteries or friaries and of the remainder about a third name friaries and a sixth (507) monasteries. An analysis of these bequests to monasteries and to a lesser extent friaries can go some way towards establishing whether the religious houses were perceived by contemporaries to be fulfilling as active a role in northern society as Aske subsequently claimed.[2]

The first perhaps somewhat unexpected fact to emerge from a study of the wills is that northerners looked to a very wide range of monastic institutions, a grand total of one hundred and twenty-one. (This figure does not include friaries which were often alluded to only generically and not by name.) By no means all these religious houses lay within the diocese, which still included the archdeaconry of Richmond as well as the three ridings of Yorkshire and the county of Nottingham. Durham Priory, Newminster Abbey in Northumberland and Whithorn Priory in Wigtownshire all surface in the wills in addition to the more southerly houses of West Dereham in Norfolk, Garendon in Leicestershire and the Charterhouse of Sheen. Well over half of these

[2] The archiepiscopal Probate Registers 9, 10 and 11 in the Borthwick Institute contain the great majority of the wills, that is 4,529 lay wills and 76 clergy wills: there are a further 30 lay wills and 2 clerical wills in the peculiar jurisdictions, most of these printed in *Wills and Administrations from Knaresborough Court Rolls*, i, ed. F. Collins (Surtees Society civ, 1902), and 124 more clergy wills in Archbishop's Registers 27 and 28 and in the Dean and Chapter Probate Register 2 in the York Minster Library. The Dean and Chapter Probate Register 2 and the St Leonard's Hospital Probate Register, also in the Minster Library, provide an additional 84 lay wills made between 1520 and 1540, while the Archdeaconry of Richmond Probate Register (Leeds Archive Office RD/RP 3) has 156 lay wills and 7 clergy wills. The Prerogative Court of Canterbury Registers for the same period (P.R.O. Prob. 11 vols 19–28) yield only a further 7 lay wills and 5 clergy wills of testators primarily resident in the diocese. This gives a total of 5,020 wills.

institutions received only one, two, or at the most five legacies, but there were certain monasteries which appeared far more regularly. The Augustinian priories of Haltemprice, Nostell and Watre, the abbeys of Roche and Whitby and the Cistercian nunnery of Nun Appleton all occurred in between eleven and fifteen wills. The twenty-one most favoured monasteries, each mentioned by between sixteen and forty-one testators, were in rising order of popularity Pontefract Priory, Sawley Abbey, Hull Charterhouse, Marton Priory, Monk Bretton Priory (all named sixteen or seventeen times), Mount Grace Charterhouse, Holy Trinity Priory, York, Meaux Abbey, Bridlington Priory and Swine Nunnery (between twenty-one and twenty-four times), Bolton Priory, Rievaulx Abbey, Kirkstall Abbey, Malton Priory and Kirkham Priory (between twenty-six and thirty times), and, at the very top, Guisborough Priory and Newburgh Priory, St Mary's Abbey, York, Fountains Abbey and Byland Abbey (between thirty-five and forty-one times).

As might well have been predicted testators in their capacity as tenants singled out some of the most important landowners among the religious houses: the great Cistercian abbeys of Byland, Fountains, Rievaulx and Kirkstall together with the very wealthy Benedictine foundation of St Mary's, York, fall into this category, but the prominence of the Augustinian and Gilbertine priories of Marton, Watton, Bridlington, Bolton, Kirkham, Malton, Guisborough and Newburgh must surely be linked to the fact that the conventual churches of these houses also functioned in part as parish churches, as also did the church of Holy Trinity Priory, York. The unexpected popularity of the nunnery of Swine, admittedly the richest of the twenty-three Yorkshire nunneries, can also partly be accounted for by its possession of the parish church of Swine: by far the largest number of bequests the priory received consisted of nominal sums to the prioress for forgotten tithes, though a closer tie is revealed in the will of John Sparke, parson of the Holderness parish of Leven, who left 20 shillings to 'my lady prioresse for recompense of my chargys that I have now in my sekenes put hir to', or in that of a York alderman's widow, Isabel Whitfield, who gave £3 6s. 8d. to her daughter, Dame Margaret, a nun of Swine. These exceptions apart, it seems usually to have been the case that when northern testators felt called upon to include particular religious houses among their beneficiaries they generally did so more because they were their landlords or because they held the appropriation of their parish church rather than because they wished to acknowledge the attraction of the particular form of piety practised there.[3]

[3] Borthwick Institute Prob. Reg. 9 fo. 176r (Sparke); Prob. Reg. 11 pt. I fo. 105r–v (Whitfeld).

If wills can be taken as an accurate guide to their preoccupations in their life-time then a substantial number of northerners agreed with Aske that the saying of masses constituted one of monasteries' most fundamental obligations. Time and again when testators made a bequest to a monastery they acted in the same spirit as Marion Hardy, widow, who gave 20s. to Fountains Abbey in 1530 in return 'for sayng ii trentalles and one messe at the hye alter and to have the belles rong.' Some richer northerners required monasteries to provide considerably more elaborate intercessary services than these. Joan Thurscross, the widow of the very wealthy Hull merchant, Geoffrey Thurscross, in 1523 left the nuns of St Leonard's in her native Grimsby 20s. a year for twelve years towards the finding of a priest, they undertaking to observe her obit for twelve years, and afterwards to pray for her as a sister of the place. In addition to confirming his father's bequests to Fountains Abbey, Sawley Abbey and Bolton Priory Ambrose Pudsey, gentleman, of Bolton by Bowland bestowed £10 each upon Whalley, St Mary's, York, Fountains and Sawley for five trentals and five obits for his soul and his parents' souls with the smaller sum of 50s. for Bolton Priory and £5 for Mount Grace Charterhouse again on condition that the monks sang five trentals for his soul's health.[4]

More humble northerners, too, availed themselves at much less expense of the spiritual services monasteries could perform for them after their deaths. In 1521 Robert Arkesey of Hutton Cranswick left the prior of the house of Watton 26. 8d. 'desiryng hyme that I maye have absolution and be maide a brother of ther religion, and if itt please my forsaid lord prior of Watton to make me a brother, then I wil that the obiter have vis viiid for the cariage of it through the religion.' William Cure, a York alderman, gave the prioress and convent of Moxby 40s. to have the names of himself and his wife entered in their mortilege book. Even more succinctly, and cheaply, William Robinson of Ilkley bequeathed 6s. 8d. to the neighbouring Bolton Priory 'to be brotherryd and my wif sisterd.'[5]

While the overwhelming majority of northern testators asked to be buried in their parish churches, if they could afford it, or otherwise in their parish churchyards, some simultaneously providing for masses in their local monastery or friary, a handful aspired to set up their tombs within a monastic enclosure. Sir Thomas Strangeways, for one, sought burial at Mount Grace. Thomas Atkinson of Ripon wished to

[4] B I Prob. Reg. 9 fo. 115r–v (Hardy), fo. 272r–273r (Thurscross), fo. 214v–215r (Pudsey).
[5] B I Prob. Reg. 9 fo. 187v (Arkesay), fo. 264r (Cure), fo. 154r (Robinson).

lie in the church within the monastery of Our Lady of Fountains; in this case it cannot have been coincidental that one of his sons, Dan Richard Ripon, was a monk of the house. In Hull in 1527 John Cokett chose to be interred not in his parish church but in the Charterhouse. It seems, however, to have been very rare for testators to have contemplated burial in monasteries far from their homes, the only exception being country gentlemen who also possessed a lodging near where their favoured monastery stood. William Emerson of Kirby Underdale in 1533 requested burial in St Mary's Abbey if he died in York: in the same year Anthony Shorton, gentleman, of Boroughbridge was even more specific, seeking to lie by the tomb of Lord Edmund Thornton, the previous abbot. The wish of John Swift of Easington, a village near the extreme tip of the Holderness peninsular, to be buried in the church of the Hull Charterhouse is explained by the fact that his uncle held the office of prior there. Particularly intriguing is the case of Robert Hudson of Campsall in the West Riding who drew up his will in the Cistercian abbey of Newminster in Northumberland: several of the monks witnessed his request to be interred in the abbey church of St Mary where the lord abbot pleased. Perhaps death had caught him unawares on a journey from Yorkshire into Scotland.[6]

Discounting the instances when a religious house had parish responsibilities as at Malton, Bridlington or York where Holy Trinity Priory served the parish of St Nicholas in Micklegate, and where the local inhabitants could legitimately look upon part of the conventual church as their parish church, for lay people to seek burial in a monastic church appears to have been exceptional in the early sixteenth century and Aske seems to have been accurate when he implied that the tombs there were limited to noblemen and gentlemen. In contrast, in those towns where the friars had settled burial in a friary church seems to have been rather more usual and perhaps somewhat less socially exclusive. Between 1520 and 1530 at least five York inhabitants chose to be buried among the friars, Margaret Herynton, for example, requesting to be brought from St Wilfrid's parish besides the Minster to lie along side her husband in the church of the White Friars in Fossgate, another York woman, Agnes More, desiring burial in the Black Friars near her mother, while Thomas Constance, a goldsmith of Colliergate, was also perpetuating a family tradition by seeking interment in the Austin Friars.[7]

[6] B I Prob. Reg. 9 fo. 343v–344r (Strangwayes), fo. 329r (Atkinson), fo. 391r (Cokett); Prob. Reg. 11 pt. I fo. 39v (Emerson), fo. 84v (Shortos); Prob. Reg. 9 fo. 440r–v (Swift), fo. 453v (Hudson).
[7] B I Prob. Reg. 9 fo. 257v (Herynton), fo. 192v (More), fo. 394r–v (Constance).

The will which Sir John Rocliff of Colthorpe made on 6 December 1531 illustrates just how intimate the links between a friary and a gentry family might be. He desired to be buried in the church of the York Grey Friars 'as nighe unto my fader's grave as may convenientlye on hys lyfte syde opon the northe syde of the said churche', specifying that if he died in York his executors should see that the four orders of friars should 'bring my bodye to the Gray Frears churche', while if he died outside the city they were all to meet his body at Holgate and from there follow the coffin to the friary church, every order receiving 6s. 8d. for their labours on the understanding that they said placebo, dirige and mass for his soul. On the day of his sepulchre he wanted his coat armour and his best beast with his horse harness to go next before his body to the Grey Friars and to be offered to God 'at the altare next where I shall bee buryed', after which the Grey Friars were to sing St Gregory's trental for his soul and for all christian souls. The funeral completed, his executors had then to oversee the laying of his grave slab with 'one ymage of the Trinitie sette and fixed in the said throughe stone and one ymage of myself maide kneling undre the said ymage of the Trinitie with one scripture for me in perpetuall remembrance for me within one yeare after the buryall'.

Rocliff's funeral ceremonies could be paralleled in other religious houses many times over: what makes his will exceptional is that he clearly intended his interment to be but the first stage in the continuous commemoration of his family for which he included the most precise instructions. Having conferred upon the convent in perpetuity rents from lands in South Emsall he required a brother of the house every day at eight o'clock to say mass and pray for his soul, for the soul of his father, Brian Rocliff, for Margaret, the testator's wife, for her father's soul, for the souls of the testator's children and his good friends and all christian souls as they were already praying for his father's soul. For celebrating the masses the friars received 20s. with the residue of the rents being used for repairs to the house and were limited to saying the requiem one week at a time so that every friar might have his turn. Each Tuesday Rocliff required the convent to sing the antiphon of Jesu about his grave that they sang on Fridays for his father. When that was done, the friars and convent

bowyng and holdyng downe there hedes with a petuouse voce sing thys verse, '*Nunc, Criste, te petimus, miserere, quesumus, qui venisti redimere perditos, noli dampnari redemptos.*' And anone after that than one of the yong frears sing thys versicle '*Adoramus te, Criste Jhesu, et benedicimus tibi.*' And than all the odre frears to answere, '*Quia per sanctam crucem tuam redemisti mundum.*' And than one of the odre frears to syng '*Oremus*', wyth one collecte according to the antiphone with a perfyte ende of all the frears concludyng, singing 'Amen'. And ymediatlye after the convent to saye thys psalme, '*De profundis*' with the suffrage and these collectes, '*Miserere*', and '*Fidelium*' for my soule and all cristen soules, concludyng with '*Requiescant in pace, Amen.*'[8]

Whereas these wills from the York diocese leave little room for doubt that local monasteries and friaries were performing spiritual services in death, and presumably in life, for a sizeable minority of northerners, Aske's assertion that they were also still providing certain material benefits remains more open to question. One or two of the wills contain hints that some of the richer monasteries may have been assisting 'gentlemen in their needs with money'. Rober Wardrop of Ripon in 1526 ordered his executors to repay the abbot of Jervaulx 20 marks he had borrowed from him. In his will Thomas Esheton, gentleman, of Bessingby in the East Riding recorded that 'I owe to my lord prior of Bridlington of pasche evyn next ensuyng xxs', though this could as well be a reminder of a rent falling due as of a loan proper.[9]

By their very nature inventories are more likely to yield information on the activities of monasteries as money lenders than wills, and unfortunately scarcely any inventories survive for the York diocese in this period. The wills, however, do establish that for certain well placed families monasteries were still offering educational and supervisory facilities, 'their younger sons there succoured, and in nunneries their daughters brought up in virtue'. On his death-bed John Symonson of Helmsley bequeathed his son Robert and his portion to Rievaulx Abbey, his son Richard with his inheritance to the sister abbey of Byland. Similarly in 1521 John Spendley of Kirby Misperton, having left 20s. to the abbot of Rievaulx and 20s. to the convent, went on to ask his honourable lord and gracious master, the abbot of 'Ryvalles', to accept one of his boys and to bring him up out of his part. In the East Riding John Lepyngton wished his son, John, with his portion of £30 to be under the governance of the prior of Bridlington for four years, presumably until he came of age. William Emerson of Kirby Underdale, who had sought burial in St Mary's Abbey in York, made the abbot his supervisor, 'whoo I will besuche to take the portions of my said childeren, Antonye and Margret, and se them governyd by his honorable pleasor and advice at suche tyme convenyent as shall please hym to thynke most necessarye.'[10]

---

[8] B I Prob. Reg. 11 pt. I fo. 181r–182v (Roclyf), printed (with omissions) in *Testamenta Eboracensia*, v, ed. J. Raine (Surtees Society, lxxix, 1884), 319–323.

[9] B I Prob. Reg. 9 fo. 356v (Wardrop), fo. 169v (Esheton).

[10] B I Prob. Reg. 9 fo. 145v (Symonson), fo. 201r (Spendley), fo. 289v (Lepyngton); Prob. Reg. 11 pt. I fo. 39v (Emerson).

Few testators planned the future of their children or grandchildren in quite the same detail as Geoffrey Proctor of Rilston in Craven who instructed his executors 'to make Alicie, my saide son Roberte doughtor, nune at Arthington or elswhere, if she will therto assent, or els to helpe to marye hir with parte of hir fader and moder land as hir moder will was.' It, nevertheless, seems possible that when Richard Dixon gave the prioress of Keldholme custody of his daughter, Joan, and her child's part of £10 he may have intended she should enter religion. In the same way Brian Lorde, merchant, of the parish of St Michael Ousebridge, York, was continuing a family connection with Wilberfoss Priory where his niece, Dame Alice Marshall, was already a professed nun, when he asked his sister, the prioress, to become the guardian of his daughter, Isabel, togehter with her goods.[11]

Rather surprisingly, in his defence of the abbeys Aske did not think of commenting upon the extent to which monasteries were still offering career opportunities for young people in the north, though the probate registers make it abundantly clear that they were fulfilling this role virtually until the end. Both Henry and Margaret Speght of Mick-legate, York, lived to see their son, Richard, enter Holy Trinity in the self-same street. By the time of his mother's death Richard had been elected prior and she entrusted to him the education of her grandson and his nephew, another Richard Speght. Some of these novices certainly came from gentry backgrounds. William Normaval, esquire, of Kildwick by Watton had a sister, Dame Eleanor, a nun in the convent of Nun Appleton, while the daughter of Robert Fairfax, gentleman, of Acaster Malbis, Dame Jane, was a nun at Sinning-thwaite. More often, it seems, at least with male entrants, the religious houses accepted the children of the middling sort in the immediate neighbourhood of the monastery, like Richard Speght. Malton Priory, in particular, took a considerable number of young men from Old and New Malton: George, the son of Lawrence Richardson, draper, of New Malton, was a canon of the priory; similarly the son of Agnes Kellet, widow, of New Malton became a Gilbertine there while John Crawe of Old Malton had a brother, Dan William Rud-stone, almost certainly in the same house where Henry, brother of Robert Walker, again of Old Malton, had also joined the order. The youth of Bridlington, like Thomas the son of Marmaduke and Alice Paiteson, in the same way tended to find places in their Augustinian house. Some Hull inhabitants had forged links with the Lincolnshire priory of Thornton Curtis just across the Humber, where the son of a Hull carver, Harry Passymyer, was a canon as was Dom

---

[11] B I Prob. Reg. 9 fo. 329v–330r (Proctor), fo. 214r (Dicson), fo. 368v (Lorde).

Robert Hull, the brother of Joan Roclif, widow of the Hull merchant William Roclif.[12]

This evidence of predominantly local recruitment applies equally to the great Yorkshire abbeys. Dom William Marshall, abbot of Kirkstall, in 1520 had a brother, Christopher, farming in the Leeds township of Potter Newton. Marmaduke, brother of William Crista-lawe of Coxwold, was a monk in Byland Abbey. The son of John Leyng of Helmsley, Dan Richard Alverton, had been received by Rievaulx Abbey, while Dan Richard Ripon, son of Thomas Atkinson of Ripon, had joined the community at Fountains. In one respect the most interesting of all were the two Cistercian sons of Richard Williamson of Bardsey near Leeds, Dan George and Dan John. When their father made his will in 1521 he left each monk 26s. 8d. to buy a score of sheep, trusting that their respective abbeys of Kirkstall and Revesby in Lincolnshire would allow them the profits of their flocks in their lifetime on the understanding that the sheep reverted to the convents after their death.[13]

These family connections between northern laymen and northern religious houses reinforced economic ties where monasteries in particular areas were often the major local landlord. The economic role of Sawley Abbey seems to have been high among the priorities of Hugh Lawkeland of Giggleswick when having given the abbot 40s. and the convent 26s. 8d. for absolution for himself and his predecessors and for prayers for their souls he went on to appeal to them 'to be good lorde and maisters unto my moder and the childer of William Yveson, my broder.' Richard Gamyll of Bagby in the North Riding bequeathed a filly to the abbot of Byland 'desiryng his lordship for the love of Jhesu and by waye of charitie to be a good and favorable lorde unto my poore wif and my childer.' Similarly Robert Danby of Sutton under Whitestone Cliff presented the abbot of Byland with a colt 'besechyng hym to bee supervysor of thys my laste will, and also to bee good lord to my wyfe and my children.'[14]

Certainly others beside Aske believed that 'money left to the use of infants' was 'always sure' in monastic hands. In 1529, for example, Ralph Aunger of Barwick in Elmet required his executors to put the £40 he had bestowed upon his two daughters and his unborn child into the keeping of some abbey or other safe place until the children came of age or married. Ralph Hopton, esquire, of Armley in the

[12] B I Prob. Reg. 11 pt. I fo. 37r–v (Speghte); Prob. Reg. 9 fo. 133v (Normavale), fo. 400r (Richardson), fo. 402v (Kellet); Prob. Reg. 11 pt. I fo. 69r (Crawe); Prob. Reg. 9 fo. 389v (Walker), fo. 216r (Paiteson), fo. 144r (Passymyer), fo. 170r (Roclyf).
[13] B I Prob. Reg. 9 fo. 106v–107r (Marshall), fo. 250v (Cristalawe); Prob. Reg. 11 pt. I fo. 16v (Leyng); Prob. Reg. 9 fo. 329r (Atkinson), fo. 158v (Williamson).
[14] B I Prob. Reg. 9 fo. 385r (Lawkeland), fo. 400v (Gamyll), fo. 480v (Danby).

parish of Leeds, used his local abbey in a comparable way, instructing his executors to deposit the goods of his son, Christopher, and his daughter, Elizabeth, whose portion amounted to no less than a hundred pounds, in Kirkstall Abbey, secured by an indented bill, until the two children reached maturity.[15]

In his attempt to persuade the Henrician government to allow some religious houses to continue in the north Aske did not distinguish between the services the monasteries performed for the laity and those they extended to the secular clergy, but the wills demonstrate that at least in the diocese of York the secular clergy enjoyed just as close links with religious communities as did their lay counterparts. Of slightly over two hundred wills remaining for the northern secular clergy from between 1520 and 1540 a little under a third include a reference to a monastery, a third to one or more friaries with some containing bequests to both monasteries and friaries. Although very many clergy like the laity chose to have prayers said for their souls in their parish churches, a sizeable minority looked to monasteries and friaries to fulfil this obligation. One of the most fervent upholders of masses for the dead was John Chapman, registrar to the archbishop, who in his will of March 1528 commissioned the celebration of a thousand masses in the city and diocese of York by seculars and regulars, Carthusians and mendicants, naming in particular the charterhouses of Hull, Mount Grace, Beauvale and Coventry, the priors and convents of Guisborough, Hexham and North Ferriby, all the four friaries of York and the Observant Friars of Newcastle. Though restraining his commemoration to trentals and obits, another member of the York Minster circle, John Sheffield, prebendary of St Sepulchre's chapel, also sought the prayers of three northern Charterhouses, in his case those of Mount Grace, Hull and the Isle of Axholme, before going on to make bequests to the nunneries of Stixwould and Greenfield in Lincolnshire. Perhaps men of this stature, both university graduates, were consciously exercising some discrimination between what they considered to be deserving and less deserving religious orders.[16]

Others among the lower clergy also favoured the Carthusians and the Observants. In 1533 Christopher Richardson, one of the priests of the Table in Holy Trinity, Hull, asked to be buried not in his parish church but 'within the west doore directely aganest the hiegh aulter of the churche of the Chartrehouse of Saincte Michaell besydes Kyngestonn upon Hull', paying the prior and convent 10s. for the

---

[15] B I Prob. Reg. 10 fo. 80v–81v (Aunger); Prob. Reg. 11 pt. I fo. 45r–v (Hopton).
[16] B I Prob. Reg. 10 fo. 52v–56r (Chapman); Minster Lib. D & C Prob. Reg. 2 fo. 170v–172r (Sheffeld).

privilege and leaving them five books called 'The Abbot' (almost certainly the five part *Super Libris Decretalium* by Nicholas Tudeschis) and 26s. 8d. to buy a stone to place over his grave with the inscription 'Pray for the sowle of Christofer Richardsone, prest, and all christen sowles, anno domini 153– cum die'. A much humbler cleric, William Coca, chantry priest of Mr Thomas Nelson in Holy Trinity, Micklegate, York, had in his lifetime entered into an agreement with the Hull and Mount Grace Charterhouses: when he died in 1537 he requested that his letters of confraternity be taken back to the respective communities with an additional 20d. each to secure their prayers. A Nottinghamshire rector, Ralph Hedworth, chose to bestow his largesse upon the Observant Friars, setting aside the very substantial sum of £80 to be distributed £20 to the warden of the Observant Friars of Newcastle upon Tyne, £20 to the Grey Friars of Newark upon Trent and the remaining £40 to two other (unspecified) places of their religion at the oversight of the warden of the Newcastle friars to pray for his soul, the souls of John Rayketh and Jane his wife and Dionesse, the testator's sister. One parson, at least, continued to value the friars for their traditional preaching function, though otherwise sermons appear very infrequently in these wills. John Woodward, vicar of Darfield upon Dearne, in 1537 left 6s. 8d. to the doctor of the Grey Friars in Doncaster 'to maike one sermone emonge my perochanes the daye of my buriall, if he maye, or elles as sone as can be after my deceasse'.[17]

While these northern priests, when they turned to monasteries and friaries, concerned themselves primarily with the fate of their souls, some like the laity looked to the religious for other services. In 1528 James Dogeson, vicar of Ampleforth, gave the abbey of Byland 40s. for absolution and committed a relative, John Dogeson, together with a proportion of the testator's goods to the abbot to bring him up at his discretion. Perhaps Dogeson may have envisaged the boy becoming a monk. Other secular clergy disclosed that they had relations already members of monastic communities. Thomas Threpeland, vicar of Christ Church, King's Court, York, in 1529 made his brother, Richard Threpeland, Master of the Hospital at Well in the North Riding, the executor of his will. Dom Guy Oswaldkirk, monk of Rievaulx, may well have been a relation of the parson of Oswaldkirk, Thomas Welburne, who bequeathed him 'some of my bookes suche as he moist desyreth and is moist expedient for hym' in addition to appointing him one of his executors 'if his father abbott will suffre the same'.[18]

[17] B I Archbp. Reg. 28 fo. 175r–v (Richardson); Prob. Reg. 11 pt. I fo. 225r–v (Coca); Archbp. Reg. 27 fo. 160r–161v (Hedworth); Archbp. Reg. 28 fo. 177r–v (Wodewarde).

[18] Minister Lib. D & C Prob. Reg. 2 fo. 145v–146r (Dogeson); B I Archbp. Reg. 27 fo. 164v–165r (Threpeland); Archbp. Reg. 28 fo. 158r–159r (Welburn).

Other secular clergy recognised different obligations which placed them in a monastery's debt. Quite exceptionally in his will of 1521 William Wallas, priest of Bridlington, revealed that he had been helped on the route to ordination by a Yorkshire priory which had provided him with the requisite economic qualification, in gratitude bestowing 20s. upon the house of Watton 'ther as I had my title'. For him at least the granting of a nominal benefice seems to have been something more than a mere formality. In other cases as appropriators monastic houses did in fact offer the means by which some of the secular clergy came to acquire their livings. Thomas Logan, vicar of Hessle and Hull, seems to have regarded the distant priory of Guisborough as no different from any other impropriator, assigning in his will 40s. for delapidations about his vicarage if the prior and convent agreed to the transaction, and if not charging his executors themselves to carry out the repairs. For other clergy, however, the ties appear to have been much more personal. In 1528, for instance, the vicar of Mattersey in Nottinghamshire, John Johnson, gave to the house of St Gilbert in Mattersey 6s. 8d. 'to registre my name as a broder' and 3s. 4d. to the convent at the disposition of the subprior. For Richard Oliver, the incumbent of All Saints, North Street, York, who also lived in near proximity to his priory, the relationship with his monastic patron seems to have been even closer. He requested burial in 1535 not, as would have been customary, in his parish church but in Holy Trinity Priory in Micklegate and left a galley pot to one particular monk, Dan John Kyllingbek, and to the convent in common four books, Cicero's *Epistles* and *Offices*, *Rationale Divinorum* of Guillemus Duranti and a glossed parchment psalter. Oliver clearly felt a kinship with the Triniters.[19]

Perhaps not entirely predictably these northern clerics in the last deade and a half before the dissolution seem to have displayed most interest in nunneries. In 1526 the vicar of Huddersfield, John Hall, asked to be buried in the house of Kirklees before the image of Our Lady of Pity where he instituted an annual obit and gave the prioress and convent the residue of his estate. Thomas Marshall, priest, buried in the Black Friars of Beverley in 1531, obviously knew the members of the community of Nunkeeling intimately, leaving 'to my priores of Nonnekeling xiiis iiiid and a litill blak mare with a stage at hir foot, ... to the suppriorisse xiiis iiiid and a litill blak stagge ambling, and a gold ryng, and to every one of the susters vis viiid, ... to Dame

[19] B I Prob. Reg. 9 fo. 220v (Wallas), and see R. N. Swanson, 'Titles to Orders in Medieval English Episcopal Registers' in *Studies in Medieval History presented to R. H. C. Davis*, ed. H. Mayr-Harting and R. I. Moore (1985), 233–245; B I Archbp. Reg. 28 fo. 178v (Logan); Archbp. Reg. 27 fo. 161r (Johnson); Archbp. Reg. 28 fo. 168r–169r (Olyver).

Isabell Bayn a gowne, ... to Dame Margaret Segwike a gowne, ... to Dame Isabell Mettam a gowne.' He also nominated the prioress and subprioress as his executrices. All these nuns presented themselves before the royal commissioners when they came to extinguish the house in September 1539. As was the case also at Swine, the priory of Wilberfoss held the living of the parish church and when John Watte, priest of Wilberfoss died in 1537, in addition to bequeathing to the prioress and her sisters 6s. 8d. 'for messe and dirige doyng the day of my beryall' he willed 'to Dame Elene Reide, none there, in money iiis iiiid, ... to Dame Agnes Barton my beste coverlet' and the rest of his goods to Mr William Burdon, priest, and Dame Elizabeth Lorde, prioress, to dispose for the health of his soul. Once again all three nuns survived to receive pensions from the state when their convent was supressed two years later.[20]

Other priests, who did not go so far as to make a nunnery their executor, still at this eleventh hour wanted to augment their usually meagre possessions. In addition to establishing an obit at Nun Appleton for which he paid the prioress 16s. and giving 12d. to Dame Joan Gower and 8d. to all the other sisters, John Mylde, the vicar of Masham and Kirkby Malzeard in 1527 presented the prioress with his dole counter and Dame Joan Gower with his 'bede coveryng of newe wark'. After the death of his sister Thomas Welburne, clerk, in 1528 intended that his best side gown and hood together with his mazer should go to the priory of Rosedale, beseeching the prioress 'then being and her susters of there charite' to pray for him, his parents, Robert Alan and Alison his wife, and all christian souls. The vicar of Elvington, William Drymer, in 1532 commissioned masses to be said for his soul at both the nunneries of Moxby and Thicket and gave the prioress of Thicket a further 26. 8d. 'to the pavyng of her closter'. In 1536 William Gurnell, parson of Full Sutton, left 12d. to the lady prioress of Wilberfoss, 8d. to Dame Agnes Barton and 6d. to every other nun and to the priest there to say mass and dirige on the day of his burial, conferring upon Dame Agnes in addition 'my next fedder bedde with a coverlett to the same, a blankett and a payr of sheetes' and upon Dame Ellen Reide a ewe and a lamb.[21]

Standing somewhat apart from the laity in their solicitude for the generally poorly endowed Yorkshire nunneries, northern secular clergy in other respects seem to have mirrored pretty exactly lay

[20] B I Archbp. Reg. 27 fo. 163v (Hall); Prob. Reg. 10 fo. 84r–v (Marshall); *Victoria County History, The County of York*, III (1913), 119–122; B I Prob. Reg. 11 pt. I fo. 229r–v (Watte); *Yorkshire Monasteries, Suppression papers*, ed. J. W. Clay (Yorkshire Archaeological Society, Record Series xlviii, 1912), 166–167.

[21] B I Archbp. Reg. 27 fo. 162r–v (Mylde); Archbp. Reg. 28 fo. 158r–159r (Welburne), fo. 164r–v (Drymer), fo. 174r–v (Gurnell).

attitudes towards the religious life in the early Tudor period. The Carthusians and Observant Friars apart, the secular clergy and the laity do not seem to have expected their monks and nuns to have been living lives of particular austerity, indeed by gifts of pocket money or little luxuries such as better bedding and clothing they were unintentionally tending to undermine the monastic rule. Such developments, however, had a long history and were in no sense new in the sixteenth century. The northern nobility and gentry and even the middle ranks of society expected to receive hospitality and entertainment from their religious houses, and rewarded them accordingly. Besides arranging for prayers to be offered for his soul at the abbeys of Croxton, Kirkstall, Jervaulx, Fountains, Sawley and Cockersand and requesting Master Richard Beverley, Prior of the Black Friars of Lancaster, to preach at his funeral Edward Stanley, Lord Mounteagle, in 1523 thought it not incongruous to confirm in his will the gift of a buck annually to Monk Bretton against Mary Magdalene day which the prior and convent claimed as an old custom from the family.[22]

In the first decades of the sixteenth century the monks of Roche were renowed, or notorious, for their expertise in the hunting field. It is not surprising, therefore, if some of the lower orders of society regarded such communities as in essence little different from the great lay landlords. Certainly for one Yorkshireman, suspected of poaching on his lord's demense, the estates of the abbey of Fountains seemed as much an object of temptation as those of any secular magnate. When he made his will in 1521 George Hardcastle of Pateley Bridge used the occasion to protest his innocence of a crime he thought he stood unjustly accused:

> I desire and prays my lorde of Fountance to be assoled, and he to be agreyd with therfore by my executrix, Katryn, my wife, to doo for me as she semys the best; and I take it oppon of my saul I am not giltye of slayng the buke within my lorde's warrant of Darby, wherfor I am dangerd at Kirkeby.[23]

As counsel for the defence, Robert Aske in 1537 skated over this less acceptable face of northern monasticism. Nevertheless, even the most hostile observer at the time would have found it hard not to concede that whatever their failings religious communities still played a positive part in northern life. With abbots and priors acting as the supervisors of wills and guardians of children and their inheritances, monasteries, nunneries and friaries offering places in religion to local young people, sometimes assisting gentlemen with loans and other

[22] P R O PCC Prob. 11/20 fo. 25 (Stanley).
[23] G. W. O. Woodward, *The Dissolution of the Monasteries* (1966), 144; B I Prob. Reg. 9 fo. 168r (Hardcastle).

facilities expected of banks in more modern periods in addition to performing still highly valued spiritual services for the living and the dead, monasticism in the early sixteenth century appeared to be permanently grafted on to the stock of Yorkshire society. Such was the view of Henry Cawton, one of the last generation of Rievaulx monks, who remembered before the dissolution having read the following verse in a manuscript containing many prophecies which belonged to the abbey:

> Twoe men came riding over Hackney way,
> The one of a blacke horse, the other on a gray;
> The one unto the other did say,
> Loo yonder stood Revess that faire abbay.

'But when he or any other of his fellowes redde it they used to throwe the book away in anger as thinking it impossible ever to come to passe.'[24]

The rank and file of Yorkshire laity seemed as oblivious of the implications of political developments at Westminster as their religious: even in the later 1530s the wills give virtually no indication of future events casting their shadows before. As late as May 1538 Henry Lamley, a Hull draper, made arrangements for his burial before Our Lady in the church of the Austin Friars in the town, paying both houses of friars in Hull 3s. 4d. to bring him to the church and 'do for me after the olde custome', while a York notary, Thomas Water, in September 1539 felt it worthwhile to return his letters of confraternity with bequests of 40s. to the convents of Guisborough and Mount Grace to obtain prayers for his soul. There was one father, though, who rather more accurately read the signs of the times: in the will he made in January 1539 George Norman included a clause enabling his daughter, Isabel, to have her part of his goods, 'if the house be suppresside that she is professid in [Handale Priory], or elles not.' On the whole, therefore, Aske does seem to have been accurately describing the contribution his fellow northerners believed monasticism was still making to local society. Many inhabitants of the diocese of York may have been less conscious than he that 'the abbeys was one of the beauties of this realm for all men and strangers passing through the same' but, judging from their wills, most seem to have agreed that in many very practical ways monasteries and friaries alike both provided succour to the living and offered 'spiritual comfort to man's soul.'[25]

---

[24] W. Dugdale, *Monasticon Anglicanum*, v (1846) 280.
[25] B I Prob. Reg. 11 pt. I fo. 324r–v (Lamley); Minster Lib. D & C Prob. Reg. 2 fo. 188v–190r (Water); B I Prob. Reg. 11 pt. I fo. 363v (Norman).

THE POLITICAL ARTS OF LORD LIVERPOOL

By Boyd Hilton

READ 11 DECEMBER 1987

AFTER her third consecutive election victory in 1987, Margaret
Thatcher chose as her holiday reading Norman Gash's biography of
Lord Liverpool. It was a fitting tribute from one remarkably durable
prime minister to another. No one now thinks of Liverpool as a
mediocrity, let alone an arch one, and the fact that many of his
colleagues were more flamboyant than he was merely adds to his
stature. His achievements as a statesman are emphasised by Gash, who
depicts him as 'one of the great through unacknowledged architects of
the liberal, free trade Victorian state',[1] the first exponent of a public
doctrine which, in both its economic and its moral components, would
be taken up triumphantly by his successors—Peel, Gladstone, and
(it might be argued) Thatcher. His achievements as a politician,
meanwhile, can be measured by the fact that he sustained a fifteen-
year premiership, broken only by his stroke in February 1827, during
a period of extreme social and economic difficulty. This seems all the
more remarkable in view of the fact that the eighteenth century had
seemed to demonstrate that in order to run a stable administration,
a first lord of the treasury needed to be in the House of Commons.

In order to explain his achievement some historians have been
driven to emphasise his personality. In discussing Liverpool's handling
of the awkward cabinet reshuffle of 1821–3, William Brock rightly
describes him as 'peculiarly sensitive to the feelings of others', but
also writes less plausibly about his 'equanimity', his 'amiable' party
management, his 'great tact and great persuasion', 'his powers of
conciliation'.[2] Charles Webster also dilates on Liverpool's 'unfailing
calm and common sense',[3] and the same impression of Liverpool as a
calm, unruffled, 'even tempered' manager of men also survives Gash's
biography. Yet the picture is misleading, since Liverpool was as hyper-
sensitive about his own feelings as he was about those of others,
and often took offence when none had been intended. In 1821 a

---

[1] N. Gash, *Lord Liverpool. The Life and Political Career of Robert Banks Jenkinson 2nd Earl
of Liverpool 1770–1828* (1984), 251–4.
[2] W. R. Brock, *Lord Liverpool and Liberal Toryism 1820 to 1827* (1941: 2nd 1967 edition),
33, 75–6, 170.
[3] C. K. Webster, *The Foreign Policy of Castlereagh 1812–1815. Britain and the Reconstruction
of Europe* (1931), 35.

sympathetic witness, Harriet Arbuthnot, noted that, although 'a most upright, honest, excellent man, conscientiously devoted to the service and to the real good of his country', Liverpool nevertheless possessed a 'disagreeably cold manner and a most querulous, irritable temper, which render it a difficult and unpleasant task to act in public life with him'.[4] Two years later her husband Charles Arbuthnot (who was as devoted to Liverpool as it is possible for a toady to be devoted to anyone) wrote to Huskisson of the prime minister's 'gaucherie': 'He has wounded *you*, and me, and Wallace, and he contrived at first to mortify poor Van[sittart].'[5] Peevish and irritable by nature, nick-named the 'Grand Figitatis', Liverpool admitted that for seventeen years as prime minister he had not been able to open the morning post without a wave of 'anxiety and apprehension' lest it should bring dreadful news. Whatever his secret as a prime minister, it was not that of the cool and calculating unruffler of other men's feathers.

Professors Gash and Brock are, of course, aware of the darker sides to Liverpool's nature, but they are inclined to dismiss them as momentary lapses in a character normally full of aplomb. It is important to stress these darker sides, however, for by emphasising governmental continuity from Liverpool to Gladstone there is a danger of reading the calm seas of Victoria's reign back into the much rougher waters of Liverpool's day. Looking back in 1840, itself not a particularly halcyon date, Sydney Smith recalled as a thing youngsters could not appreciate 'the old-fashioned, orthodox, hand-shaking, bowel-disturbing passion of fear'.[6] Liverpool, who had seen the bastille fall in 1789, only became prime minister after another had been assassinated, and he had to face bomb plots as well as opposition brickbats. He constantly fretted lest hunger or national bankruptcy or a licentious press should spark off a French-style revolution in a country in which the traditional sources of authority seemed to have *lost* their authority, in which bishops might be pelted on sight and most landlords were cordially loathed. In such circumstances, Liverpool's public displays of calm and quiet competence had more to do with tactics than with temperament.

Two questions, one temporal and one spatial, have dominated the historiography of Liverpool's administration. First, did the cabinet reshuffle of 1821–3 cause what Halévy called a 'liberal awakening' or significantly affect in any way the direction of its policies? Second,

---

[4] *The Journal of Mrs Arbuthnot 1820–1832*, ed. F. Bamford and the duke of Wellington (2 vols., 1950), i. 121.

[5] Charles Arbuthnot to Huskisson, Jan. 1823, Huskisson Papers, British Library, Additional MS 38744, fo. 57, quoted in Brock, 171.

[6] Sydney Smith to Bishop Blomfield, 5 Sept. 1840, *The Letters of Sydney Smith*, ed. N. C. Smith (2 vols, Oxford, 1953), ii. 709.

was there any identifiable difference between the policies of so-called 'high' and 'liberal' tories ('so-called' because the terms are not quite contemporary ones)? Both of these questions are legitimate but they are too often intermingled. It is now fashionable to deny that there was a significant change of direction in the early twenties, to say that the improved economic and political climate after 1822 merely enabled the later ministers to do many things which the earlier ministers would have done if they could. There is obviously much truth in this, but it does not follow, as is sometimes supposed, that such continuity proves that there was no significant difference between the policies of high and liberal toryism. This second point might follow if it were the case that high tories were exclusively in charge of policy-making before 1821-3 and liberal tories thereafter, but this demonstrably is not the case. It seems clear in fact that, notwithstanding large tracts of common ground, there were identifiable differences between the two varieties of tory, but it is not the purpose of this essay to examine them. Its central aim is more mundane, to consider once more (for there has been no neglect of the topic by historians) the question of what went on inside Liverpool's administration during 1821-3. This is a political question, and consideration of it reveals the political artistry of one of Britain's most artful prime ministers.

In explaining the element of continuity in policy either side of 1822, historians rely on two arguments. Firstly, and correctly, they point to the fact that the 'new men', Canning, Robinson, Huskisson, and Peel, had all served the ministry, albeit in less exalted capacities, since at least 1814. Secondly, and much less convincingly, they argue that the 'old men' had in fact adumbrated many of the things for which the 'new men' would later take the credit.[7] Thus, in foreign policy Castlereagh's 1820 State Paper is said to have broken with the Holy Alliance and laid the foundations for Canningite isolationism. With respect to penal reform, Mackintosh's committee is said to have set in motion a consensual train of thought on which Peel would capitalise once the immediate post-war threat to law and order had subsided (the inference being that Sidmouth would also have capitalised on it in much the same way). Wallace is said to have paved the way for Huskisson's commercial reforms after 1823, and Vansittart's 1819 budget, providing for some three millions more of direct taxation, is said to have provided the firm financial base from which Robinson's tariff reductions could later proceed. The last example points the obvious danger in this line of interpretation. As chancellor of the

[7] For recent expositions on these lines see N. Gash, *Aristocracy and People. Britain 1815–1865* (1979), 112, 116–17; E.J. Evans, *The Forging of the Modern State. Early Industrial Britain 1783–1870* (1983), 190–1, 198.

exchequer Vansittart was responsible for introducing the 1819 budget to parliament, but that did not make it *his* budget—he was reported to have sobbed all through the crucial meeting to decide it—and certainly he opposed the increase in direct taxation as strongly as he opposed the decision, taken at the same time, to resume cash payments.[8] Vansittart no more controlled the making of financial policy than Spring Rice, Baring, Goulburn, or any other chancellor before Disraeli.[9] 'As to measures', observed a new member of the cabinet, Charles Wynn, in 1823, 'Liverpool must of course give the orders, and [the chancellor] obey.'[10] More generally, however, it can be argued that, as Wynn himself quickly discovered,[11] entering the cabinet did not necessarily bring anyone close to the centre of decision-making. For Liverpool deliberately kept decision-making as far as possible outside the cabinet, and this may have been a secret of his success.

What is immediately striking about Liverpool's administration is that, with respect to decision-making, it was a much more meddlesome and interventionist government than its predecessors. Admittedly it did not have an active social policy, that is it did not do much to control the effects of the Industrial Revolution on the lives of the working classes, for though it tinkered a little with emigration, policing, and combination law, by and large it was left to the whig governments of the 1830s to confront the problems of poverty, public health, factory hours, and the plight of the handloom weavers. Where Liverpool's government was active was in economic policy, for it bombarded the middle classes—whether farmers, merchants, manufacturers, moneyed men, shipowners, or whatever—with a mass of legislation affecting their lives and livelihoods. Paradoxically, where such intervention went toward eliminating or reducing existing monopolies and preferences, ministers often defended it by appealing to the fashionable doctrines of political economy with its goal of *laissez-faire* non-interventionism, but the fact remains that, for those immediately affected, it was itself a form of intervention.

The possibility that Liverpool's goverment might have intervened so much because it wanted to can immediately be discounted. Liverpool and his colleagues wanted nothing more than to leave things

[8] B. Hilton, *Corn, Cash, Commerce. The Economic Policies of the Tory Governments 1815–1830* (Oxford, 1977), 40–8.
[9] Though a case might be made for Sir Charles Wood, chancellor of the exchequer 1846–52. On the chancellorship see H. C. G. Matthew, *Gladstone, 1809–1874* (Oxford, 1986), 110.
[10] Wynn to Buckingham, 20 Jan. 1823, *Memoirs of the Court of George IV, 1820–1830*, ed. R. Grenville, duke of Buckingham and Chandos (2 vols., 1859), i. 411.
[11] Wynn to Buckingham, ?Nov.–Dec. 1822, *Court of George IV*, i. 398.

alone—hence in part their hankering after *laissez-faire*.[12] It is simply that these very reluctant activists were faced with a situation in which activism was unavoidable. Outwardly all ministers paid lipservice to the notion that the different economic sectors were interdependent, that all economic interests stood or fell together, and that special legislation to favour one interest at the expense of others would entail the ruination of them all. It was their way of saying 'no' to the multitude of lobbyists who craved some special favour from the government. Yet it is clear from their private correspondence that Liverpool and his ministers did not believe a word of their public rhetoric, that they instinctively saw only natural division within the country, and habitually looked at issues in terms of interest against interest and of region against region. 'The [Spitalfields] question is not a *national*, but a local one between London and the Country', wrote Liverpool characteristicially.[13] To take another example, the battle over the sugar duties was frequently interpreted as an attempt to transfer 'the profit from one class of home manufacturers to another': that is, from the Yorkshire woollen manufacturers, who largely exported to the West Indies, to the Lancashire cotton manufacturers, who largely exported to the East Indies.[14]

Of course it was inevitable that, as the economy diversified, it should spawn a host of economic pressure groups and commercial lobbies, each one clamouring for government favour. As a sympathetic elder statesman put it, on a whole range of issues 'so many interests are to be conciliated, and so many prejudices to be surmounted'.[15] By and large the government managed to stay aloof from such pleadings, but after 1815 there was one type of economic conflict which it found great difficulty in staying aloof from, and that was the inter-generational conflict which occurred as a result of the transition from a wartime to a peacetime economy. All wars pose the problem of getting 'back to normalcy', and the problems of unemployed soldiers after 1815 and of lost demand in the iron industries are too well known to need enumeration here.[16] But in this particular case the problem was not so much the aggregate effects of the Napoleonic wars on demand or investment or the business cycle, or the rise of one sector

[12] Hilton, *Corn*, 71–5.

[13] Liverpool to Huskisson, 11 April 1824, Huskisson Papers, BL, Add. MS 38745, fo. 234.

[14] Memorandum of 18 Feb. 1823, Huskisson Papers, BL, Add. MS 38761, fos. 95–100.

[15] Grenville to Huskisson, 27 Apr. 1825, Huskisson Papers, BL Add. MS 38746, fos. 186–7.

[16] N. Gash, 'After Waterloo: British society and the legacy of the Napoleonic wars', *T.R.H.S.*, 5th series, xxviii (1978), 145–57.

and the decline of another, as the way in which, within many sectors, the war had divided people by generations. After all, it had been no ordinary war but one which had lasted for twenty-three years and had spawned an entire generation of producers, middlemen, sellers, and buyers. It is often called the first 'total war' because it was fought by economic instruments such as subsidies and blockades as much as by armies and navies. And it also coincided with what some historians regard as a 'take-off', and all must regard as a diversification, of the domestic economy. And so, at the end of the war, there were those who, having been established in their livelihoods before the war, whose livelihoods the war might have disrupted, now shouted 'back to normalcy'! But there were others, a whole generation of others, who had embarked on their livelihoods during the war and for whom the war *was* normalcy. Liverpool's government therefore found itself faced with issues in which it was obliged to take sides, to decide whether it should try to roll back the war and 'return to '93', or whether, by standing aside and refusing to do anything at all, it should endorse and ratify the changed relationships which war had brought about. However it decided, it would of course be assailed by those sections of the community whose interests were prejudiced by its decision.

There are numerous examples of this ministerial dilemma. The landed interest was divided between those landlords and farmers who had taken advantage of wartime prices to cultivate marginal land, and those on more favoured land who had no need of highly protective corn laws. The timber trade was divided between the Baltic merchants, who had dominated before the war, and the Canadian merchants, who had recently usurped their dominance. Because the Baltic supply was cut off in wartime, a special preference had been placed on Canadian timber in order to build up an alternative source of naval supplies. After the war, the Baltic men clamoured for the removal of the preference, since it seemed only fair to them that they should recapture their trade now that the war was over, and in the London merchants' petition of 1820 they raised the banner of free trade, since it suited them in that instance to be free traders. The Canadian merchants protested, on the other hand, that they would never be able to compete with the shorter haul in free trade conditions, and that the government had a duty to safeguard the capital which, for the sake of national security, they had sunk in Canada during the war.[17] Both sides had an honest case, and Liverpool's government had no political or ideological axe to grind in favour of either Canadian or Baltic timber. Canning's rather vague comment, 'I suppose I must vote as my constituents may wish me—that, I take it, will be for

[17] Hilton, *Corn*, 173–5, 190–5.

Canada, versus Norway'—certainly implies that he had no burning commitment on the matter.[18] But though ministers evidently did not feel that the national interest obliged them to take sides, they knew that whichever way they eventually jumped they would offend some eminently decent citiens and render themselves politically unpopular. In the case of timber they managed, after a long struggle, to achieve a compromise, but there was an even more problematic issue, which effected everybody in the same sort of way, and on which compromise was impossible: the currency.

The currency question is sufficiently well understood to require no more than the briefest elaboration here. The *rentier* element in society—and it was this rather than landownership which was the social basis of the Pitt/Liverpool/Peel régime—the *rentier* element, or at least that section of it whose wealth, whether in agriculture or business, had been established before the war, and who had therefore owned money before the war, had seen the value of its money fall since 1797, and thought it only right that the government should resume cash payments after the war at the old par value. On the other hand, those who had started out in business during the war, as a whole generation had done, very often *owed* money because they had, perhaps, borrowed from a country bank or farmed their lands on mortgage, in which case for the government to step in and raise the value of money in order to reverse a depreciation from which they had not benefited, seemed to them to be a gratuitously hostile act of state. Compromise was not possible in this case because virtually no one considered the possibility of returning to the gold standard at a lower value of sterling than had existed before the war. It was a question either of resuming at par or of continuing the restriction indefinitely, and whichever course the government adopted, it was bound to cause grave political offence to thousands of innocent parties.

This essay is only concerned with the political consequences of this generational divide, but it is worth pointing out that beneath the obvious struggle of vested interests, very close to the surface of discussion, and even explicit in the parliamentary debates of 1822, lay an almost philosophical wrangle as to the meaning of 'value' and the status of wartime wealth. Was it 'real', 'legitimate', and 'of sterling worth', or was it 'visionary', 'artificial', 'fictitious', 'speculative', 'shadowy', 'ideal', and 'drunken prosperity'?[19] The inclination of the liberal tories for sound money and free trade had far more to do with

---

[18] Canning to Huskisson, 8 March 1821, Huskisson Papers, BL, Add. MS 38742, fos. 187–97.
[19] Hilton, *Corn*, 96–7; B. Hilton, *The Age of Atonement. The Influence of Evangelicalism on Social and Economic Thought, 1795–1865* (Oxford, 1988), 126–7.

finding a model which would sort out which aspects of economic enterprise fell into which category, which were legitimate and which were fictitious, than with any late nineteenth- or twentieth-century conceptions of economic growth; rather, a model which would ensure economic justice, rewarding toil, thrift, and effort while 'punishing that which is stagnant and corrupt', as Peel put it when discoursing on the 'great machine of society'.[20]

Faced with the problem of having to do endless unpopular things, Liverpool adroitly developed a series of defensive strategies. He was, first of all, a brilliant debater, he and Pitt being regarded by Wellington as the only speakers he had known 'who were quite sure of themselves—who knew exactly what they were going to say'.[21] No one was more adept at 'double-speak'—the obvious example being his declaration in favour of *laissez-faire* in 1812: 'it was undoubtedly true that the less commerce and manufactures were meddled with the more they were likely to prosper'[22]—which to free traders meant that he would tear down tariff barriers just as soon as he could, and to protectionists meant that existing tariff walls should be left alone so that merchants and manufacturers could venture forth in a stable, unchanging context. But Liverpool could not use his debating talents where they were mainly needed, in the lower house where (at least until 1822) the government notoriously lacked the 'gift of the gab', and so he had to resort to tactics of a less obvious kind. What is striking about ministerial correspondence during the Liverpool years is the emphasis on parliamentary tactics, the need to conciliate in disaffected quarters, to catch opponents off their guard, or to hoodwink them as to the government's true intentions. In 1826, for example, ministers debated among themselves whether to agitate the catholic question so as to divert attention from their bill to reduce the corn laws, which was the thing Liverpool had really set his heart on. By comparison, the correspondence of the whig ministers of the 1830s was much more about the ideas behind policy, while that of Peel in the 1840s was much more executive in tone. There need be no surprise in this, for it is often pointed out that 1815–30 was a period when the old eighteenth-century methods of putting business through parliament had been undermined and Victorian reliance on party discipline had not yet developed. It meant that parliament was particularly independent and important, that it acted, in Cookson's words, 'as the

---

[20] B. Hilton, 'Peel: a reappraisal', *Historical Journal*, xxii (1979), 610.
[21] C. K. Webster, *The Foreign Policy of Castlereagh 1815–1822. Britain and the European Alliance* (1925), 14.
[22] Liverpool in House of Lords, 24 July 1812, *Hansard's Parliamentary Debates*, xxiii, 1249.

great decider' of issues to a greater extent probably than before or since.[23]

Parliament *decided*, and so it is not surprising that Liverpool should have practised the art of parliamentary manoeuvre. As early as 1814 Grenville spotted Liverpool's 'system of two distinct sessions—one in which all the money shall be voted in thin houses before Christmas, and another in which all the business shall be done in still thinner houses in the dog-days'.[24] But no doubt all governments behave like this to a greater or lesser extent. More interesting is the way in which Liverpool pursued a conscious—and until 1823 successful—strategy for keeping most of the contentious policy decisions out of the political arena, thereby minimising the political damage and as far as possible escaping the inevitable fall-out from those who were badly affected. This strategy really began in 1816. The previous three years had been dominated by pressure from the landed interest for an increase in the corn law, and select committees had made the necessary recommendation. For a long time Liverpool determined to wash his hands of the matter, and delegated the business to Huskisson, recently appointed a junior minister in charge of woods and forests. Then in February 1815, anxious to prevent too stringent a corn law from being enacted, Liverpool decided that the new bill should be treated as an official measure of the government, and that Robinson, vice-president of the board of trade, should introduce it. Despite some nasty violence from the mob, the ruse broadly worked. Liverpool felt confident that he could now count on the gratitude of the country gentlemen, especially after Waterloo had set the bells ringing. Ministers began the 1816 session, therefore, in a mood of 'unbounded' confidence, assured 'that the Battle would be fought and the triumph gained in discussions on our foreign policy'.[25] The mood turned apprehensive when, on the first substantive vote of the session, both the mover and seconder of the loyal address rebelled against the ministers on a question of the estimates. And shortly afterwards, the government suffered a humiliating defeat over its proposal to continue the wartime property tax, an event which also settled the question, already referred to, of whether the country should attempt a return to a pre-war situation or continue at wartime levels, for without a wartime revenue, retrenchment back towards 1793 was unavoidable. Politically the 1816 scrape led to enormous alarm and despondency in government

[23] J. E. Cookson, *Lord Liverpool's Administration. The Crucial Years 1815–1822* (Edinburgh and London, 1975), 278.

[24] Grenville to Sir John Newport, 17 October 1814, Bodleian Library, Eng. MS Letters, d. 80, fos. 103–6.

[25] Huskisson to Canning, 20 April 1816, Canning Papers, Leeds Public Library MSS., 67/83.

circles, as a result of which Liverpool seems to have decided that never again would he allow his administration to become so exposed. From that moment he sought at all costs to keep *policy* and *politics* in separate compartments, and that meant keeping policy-*makers*, so far as possible, out of such a political arena as the cabinet. Since previous governments had not attempted policy-making in such profusion, this was a less surprising strategy than it might seem to twentieth-century observers.

So the cabinet was stuffed with persons of political or electoral influence, the heads of the many connections which made up the tory coalition, people like Mulgrave, Westmorland, and Bragge Bathurst, whom George IV described as mere 'ornaments'.[26] Once the war was over the cabinet hardly ever met during the recess, and when it did meet its proceedings were often ludicrously unbusinesslike, as Aspinall has shown.[27] Invitations were sent out haphazardly and not everyone might receive one. The prime minister might not bother to attend, or the minister who had summoned the meeting might not attend, in which case none of those present would know what they were there for. There were no agendas or briefings, no minutes, and usually no record of decisions taken. Cabinet dinners were bibulous and, of course, even more chaotic. The cabinet was concerned with all the ceremonial aspects of government, with arranging parliamentary business ('tactics'), and with substantive decision-making in the case of issues which were primarily 'political' in the sense of involving parliamentary difficulty, such as the Six Acts legislated after Peterloo or the Queen Caroline affair. But the cabinet as such was *not* involved in the incessant preparation of important legislation affecting the material lives of the citizenry at large, any more than it was involved in Sidmouth's handling of routine law and order matters by the home department.

As far as possible, Liverpool chose to deal with all such matters in what might be called private and informal meetings, at Walmer Castle or Coombe Wood, his homes during the recess, or at Fife House in Whitehall during parliamentary sessions. In the case of foreign affairs these gatherings might be called an 'inner cabinet', since most of those consulted were also members of the formal cabinet as well: Castlereagh, Canning, Bathurst, Harrowby, and, if he was in the country, Wellington.[28] It was not, however, *the* cabinet, and Castle-

---

[26] George IV's memorandum, Aug. 1827, *The Letters of King George IV 1821–30*, ed. A. Aspinall (3 vols., Cambridge, 1938), iii. 291–2.

[27] A. Aspinall, 'The Cabinet Council, 1783–1835', *Proceedings of the British Academy*, xxxviii (1952), 187–8.

[28] On this 'inner' cabinet see Webster, *Castlereagh 1815–1822*, 15.

reagh would have thought it unduly restrictive to have to discuss in so large a body as the cabinet how he should deal with the latest diplomatic crisis. Webster cites the case in which a few key ministers agreed to the signing in 1815 of a secret treaty with France and Austria against Prussia and Russia without any reference to the cabinet, even though it might have led to war.[29] In fact, such practice was normal. Except on issues of the utmost gravity, the foreign secretary did not feel obliged to share his decision-making with the cabinet, though he would often report to it after the event.

In the case of domestic affairs, many of those involved with the day-to-day business were outside the cabinet. The 'little committee' to which Liverpool once referred as having settled 'all the parliamentary business',[30] seems to have met daily during sessions and frequently enough in the recess. Prominent participants were Castlereagh and Canning; the financial experts Huskisson and Herries; Charles Arbuthnot who, as the nearest thing to a party whip, could best advise on how back-benchers would react to different policies; and, if Ireland was involved, Peel. Most surprising was the occasional involvement, on matters requiring financial expertise, of the man who until 1817 nominally led the opposition, Lord Grenville. Sometimes his participation was clandestine, performed through the offices of the treasury secretary, George Harrison, but on other occasions he attended these private ministerial meetings openly, and was no doubt able to do so in his official capacity as auditor of the exchequer, though this was a near sinecure.

Sometimes, however, an issue was too prominent to be dealt with on the backstairs in this way, in which case Liverpool resorted to the use of select committees, so that controversial policies could be presented as neutral decisions arrived at by all the parties in collusion. Liverpool naturally took good care in handpicking the members of these committees, since he usually knew what answers he wished them to arrive at, but in order to remove responsibility from the government's shoulders it was necessary to include a 'large sprinkling of Opposition', as Huskisson commented about the secret committees appointed in each house of parliament to advise on whether to resume cash payments.[31] The commons committee was even chaired by Robert Peel, a backbench M.P. who was no longer officially connected with the government. It is in fact quite clear that the vital decision to

---

[29] Webster, *Castlereagh 1812–1815*, 374.

[30] Liverpool Papers. BL, Add. MS 38291, fo. 336, quoted in *The Correspondence of Charles Arbuthnot*, ed. A. Aspinall (1941), 19n.

[31] Huskisson to his wife, 3 Feb. 1819, Huskisson Papers, BL, Add. MS 39949, fos. 58–61.

recommend a resumption was taken at Fife House on 3 April when Canning, Huskisson, and Peel, having first suborned Arbuthnot and through him Liverpool, managed to overcome the opposition of Castlereagh, Vansittart, Harrowby, and Bathurst.[32] Liverpool's support was essential, but with it one cabinet minister, one junior minister, and one backbencher could override four cabinet ministers on an issue of the first importance. But though 3 April was the moment of real decision, and it was only necessary afterwards to persuade the secret committees to come up with reports 'on right principles', the decision itself was presented to parliament as one that had been arrived at by the two all-party committees. The cabinet was only informed about the decision on 8 May, that is two days *after* parliament had been presented with the committees' reports, and when Eldon then tried to raise a cry against the proposal, Liverpool was able to brush him off by saying that all the experts in all the parties had already examined the question and had made their minds up. Or, as a lapidary note in Canning's diary puts it: 'Letter from Eldon protesting against the decision: too late.'[33]

In 1820 Liverpool wished to push ahead with tariff reform. In order to pave the way he not only manipulated 'commercial opinion' by encouraging the London merchants to petition, but he also set up select committees of both houses to go through a would-be investigation. To make sure of the right answers, he put the lords committee under the control of the doctrinaire free trader Lansdowne, who was a whig, and he put the commons committee under the control of Thomas Wallace, a junior minister known to be keen on commercial reform, but outside the cabinet and so unconnected with the government *politically*. Liverpool's cunning in the matter of committees was most obvious on the question of the corn laws. In 1820 the backbench squires caused embarrassment by demanding a select committee to inquire into agricultural distress, with the intention that it should recommend an increase in the corn laws. At first this caused gloom in ministerial circles, but then, at Liverpool's instigation, Londonderry suddenly took advantage of a suggestion by a backbench whig in a thin house to move a clause restricting the terms of the inquiry to a technical point concerning the corn trade, thereby emasculating the committee so far as the agricultural protectionists were concerned. Liverpool hoped that the agricultural distress would have lifted before the next session, but it did not, and so in 1821 he had once more to

---

[32] Canning's diary, 2 and 3 April, 10 May, 1819, Canning Papers, 29 D.1.

[33] Liverpool to Eldon, 10 May 1819, *The Public and Private Life of Lord Chancellor Eldon with Selections from his Correspondence*, ed. H. Twiss (3 vols., 1844), ii. 329; Canning's diary, *loc. cit.*

play for time. When the agriculturists demanded another committee, this time with no restriction on subject matter, Liverpool insisted that Huskisson and Ricardo should be on it. Huskisson was a junior minister and therefore *politically* independent of the goverment, and Ricardo was an opposition M.P.; Liverpool inserted them into the committee because he knew full well that they were clever enough to bamboozle the bumpkins and draft a report which would point toward free trade rather than more protection. Londonderry being sympathetic to the landed interest, it was certainly Liverpool who made the decision not to increase the corn laws, yet having done so he was able to shelter behind the all-party committee. When, incidentally, the agriculturists returned to the charge in 1822, demanding from government a more protective corn law as a condition of their continued support, Liverpool's cunning proved equal to the situation. This time, after a third committee had reported perfunctorily, Liverpool at last allowed them to enact a more protective corn law, but he also inserted a clause which stipulated that the new law was not to operate until the price of wheat had reached eighty shillings in the market, something which in 1825 and 1826 he deliberately prevented from happening by Orders in Council to allow bonded wheat out of the warehouses. Canning gave the game away on this last point when in 1827 he described the clause delaying the implementation of the 1822 Act as 'an outwork ... to prevent the body of the law from being ever approached'.[34]

George IV was not correct to say in 1823 that Liverpool's was a 'government of departments',[35] for that underestimates the degree of policy co-ordination which the prime minister exercised. But Wellington was emphatically correct to say in November 1821 that 'ours is not, nor never has been, a *controversial* Cabinet upon any subject',[36] though perhaps he did not properly understand the reason for it, which was that Liverpool had deliberately kept the controversial policy matters, especially those economic policies which affected people's livelihoods, out of its domain. And it must be said that by so doing Liverpool had succeeded remarkably well in keeping his ministry's head above the waters through some very stormy sessions. Of course, by 1822 it was becoming an ever more difficult tactic to maintain. The whigs were furious that they could not properly attack a government which never put its head on the block, so to speak, while more ominously many backbenchers were calling for 'a daring

[34] Hilton, *Corn*, 102–9, 149–56, 269–78.
[35] George IV to Liverpool, 6 Nov. 1823, *The Letters of King George IV 1812–1830* (3 vols., Cambridge, 1938), iii. 39.
[36] Wellington to Fremantle, 3 Dec. 1821, *Memoirs of the Court of George IV*, i. 237.

minister' and were increasingly impatient with what they saw as government by 'Committees of the House of Commons'.[37] But what *really* undermined Liverpool's system was that which is usually taken to be its moment of regeneration—'the turn of the tide', as Gash puts it[38]—the cabinet reshuffle of 1821–3.

Two arguments are usually put forward to explain Liverpool's motives in carrying out this reshuffle. The first, which is correct, is that he needed to energise the political fortunes of his cabinet by increasing its debating strength in the commons to combat the fire-power of Brougham, Tierney, Hume, Burdett, and Mackintosh. The second argument is that he wished to energise the executive strength of his cabinet by admitting those statesmen who showed signs of getting to grips with the practical policy needs of the first industrial nation. Now, if this second argument were correct, it would cast doubt on the view, so far expressed, that Liverpool was anxious to prevent his cabinet from becoming a forum for executive decision-making. And, in fact, it seems clear that parliamentary, not executive, considerations were all important. By 1821, in the aftermath of the Queen Caroline affair, Liverpool was, as he told Charles Bathurst, politically desperate, hated by the king, opposed by the whigs and radicals, and winged by 'a crossfire from Canning, Peel, and the Grenville connexion'.[39] It was to do something about this crossfire that Liverpool set about the work of cabinet reconstruction, which in the event led him to bring in Wynn, Canning, Robinson, Peel, and Huskisson. 'The great and material point to which the Government looked was strength in the House of Commons, and therefore whatever changes would take place in the Cabinet were to be grounded on this consideration alone', is how he put it to a Grenvillite in November 1821,[40] and in the case of the first four of these ministers it is clear that strength in the commons was indeed the main reason for their promotion. Thus it is impossible to suppose that Wynn was taken in to strengthen executive policy-making, or indeed for any other reason than to attract the Grenvilles back into the old Pittite coalition, the price of which was a cabinet seat for Wynn, some loaves and fishes for the kith and kin, and a dukedom for Buckingham. Liverpool had been trying for

[37] Redesdale to Colchester, 4 Jan. 1820, *The Diary and Correspondence of Charles Abbot, Lord Colchester*, ed. Charles, Lord Colchester (3 vols., 1861), iii. 107–8; Fremantle to Buckingham, 9 Feb. 1819, *Memoirs of the Court of England during the Regency, 1811–1820* ed. R. Grenville, duke of Buckingham and Chandos (2 vols., 1856), ii. 301.

[38] Gash, *Liverpool*, 171.

[39] Liverpool to Charles Bathurst, 29 December 1820, Liverpool Papers, BL, Add. MS 38288, fos. 386–8.

[40] W. H. Fremantle's report of a conversation with Lord Liverpool, Nov. 1821, *Court of George IV*, i. 232.

some time to persuade George IV to have Canning back, but it was not until 12 August 1822 that the latter became indispensable. Until then it did not matter much to Liverpool whether Canning came in or went off to be governor general of India, so long as he was not in the Commons and out of office, able to level his crossfire at the treasury bench. After 12 August, which was the day that Londonderry committed suicide, Canning *had* to come in because he was the only man who could lead the commons. From an executive point of view, meaning the nuts and bolts of financial management rather than grand policy-making, Vansittart had been a better chancellor of the exchequer than the lazy Robinson was to be, and he was also a close friend and ally of the prime minister, but he was also a parliamentary laughing stock whereas Robinson was eloquent and popular. Again Londonderry's demise was crucial because he had long acted as Vansittart's 'minder' in the commons, and it was feared that poor Van would not be able to survive without such protection. In Peel's case it would be plausible to argue that admission to cabinet marked the entry of one who would play an important executive role in national affairs, but the fact is that by this time Peel was politically indispensable, the 'coming man' as Canning, whose head at this juncture was constantly over his own shoulder, realised only too well, the spokesman for the 'protestants' who were being increasingly referred to as 'Mr Peel's party'. From a political vantage point alone, Peel had to come in.

And then there was Huskisson. There is not the slightest doubt about his importance from the point of view of policy-making, but it merely made him politically unpopular in many parliamentary circles. In this sense it could be said that he was *too* important to be in Liverpool's cabinet. Since 1814 he had been 'in the habit of daily communication ... on all the interesting matters of Internal Policy',[41] and by 1821 he was in a frustration of self-pity. He felt himself, in his favourite metaphor, to be 'pulling the labouring oar', while all the rest 'are resting on their oars'.[42] 'I have been engaged in rowing the boat while the cabinet ministers sit idle in it—especially Lord Maryborough and Frederick Robinson who sit there like dead weights' (a mordant reference to Vansittart's Dead Weight Annuity Scheme).[43] 'The angry feelings which existed in the [Agricultural] Committee, and which have since expanded themselves through the

---

[41] Liverpool to ?, 21 Nov. 1822, Liverpool Papers, BL, Add. MS 38291, fos. 174–8.
[42] Huskisson to Liverpool, 12 May 1822, Huskisson Papers, BL, Add. MS 38743, fos. 148–51, quoted in *The Huskisson Papers*, ed. L. Melville (1931), 137–9.
[43] E.J. Littleton's diary, 20 Nov. 1821, Hatherton Papers, Staffordshire Record Office, D260/M/F/5/26/5/148–50.

wider sphere of the agricultural part of the House and of the Country, have been concentrated upon me alone.'[44] What he wanted was *either* to swap his sinecure at the woods and forests for an efficient office which would bring him a sort of bureaucratic dignity, *or* to obtain a place in the cabinet and the concomitant political status. At one point, in November 1821, the duke of Wellington took him aside for a man-to-man talk, and told him, with a discrimination worthy of Jane Austen, 'Huskisson, this is more a matter of passion than of feeling with you.'[45] Huskisson was not mollified, and even ventured to compare the Great Duke's fortune with his own: Wellington had 'only to lift up his little finger' and walk into the cabinet while he, on the other hand, had had to put up with 'vague and insincere promises (so far insincere that no effort has been made to give them effect) and empty compliments', no compensation for the 'thankless labour' and 'undivided obloquy' which were his lot.[46] 'It is neither fair towards me, nor for the dignity of the Government, that I should be expected to interfere in the duties and labours which properly belong to responsible and efficient office, while I appear permanently doomed to a situation neither responsible nor official'.[47] When Wynn, who had never contributed anything, was admitted to the cabinet, Huskisson's outrage welled over.

To all this Liverpool replied as soothingly as he could that, while Huskisson's importance was everywhere acknowledged, surely he did not want to force his way into the cabinet, and surely he did not want to offend the king, who was alarmed by the Canningite tide as well as by the size of the cabinet. Would he not agree to be president of the board of trade, with full stipend but without the customary seat in cabinet? Inevitably, Huskisson saw this as a further slight, 'a disparagement to which nothing could induce me to submit', a 'cruel affliction' since 'no man can properly perform those duties out of Cabinet'.[48] At this point Canning wrote to Huskisson, 'L[iverpool] asked me whether you would insist upon Cabinet ... as there would be great objection to it. I asked if on the part of the K(ing]? He

[44] Huskisson to Liverpool, 12 May 1822, Huskisson Papers, BL, Add. MS 38743, fos. 148–51; *Huskisson Papers*, 137–9. It is clear from such comments that Gash is mistaken in describing Huskisson as 'curiously oblivious of his own unpopularity'. Gash, *Liverpool*, 242.

[45] Littleton's diary, 20 Nov. 1821, *loc. cit.*

[46] Huskisson to Liverpool, 14 November 1821, Huskisson Papers, BL, Add. MS 38743, fos. 13–14.

[47] Huskisson to Liverpool, 11 Jan. 1822, Huskisson Papers, BL, Add. MS 38743, fos. 117–20; *Huskisson Papers*, 135.

[48] Huskisson to Canning, November 1822, Huskisson Papers, BL, Add. MS 38743, fo 221; Huskisson to Arbuthnot, 26 December 1822, ibid., fos. 285–6.

said "Yes and elsewhere too".[49] This exchange sent the paranoidal Huskisson off on a further frenzy of speculation as to who it was 'elsewhere' who was intriguing malignly against him. In fact, this was almost certainly a typical piece of verbal cunning on Liverpool's part, in that it was he and no one else who so greatly objected to Huskisson's promotion to the cabinet. George IV told Liverpool on 2 January 1823 that he left the question of a cabinet seat for Huskisson '*entirely* to your decision',[50] and it is quite clear that for the next nine months it was the prime minister, not the king, who kept the door shut. Nor is there any questioning the genuine fury which Huskisson's pretensions aroused in Liverpool, a fury which, given his genuine regard for Huskisson's contribution, can only be explained by his overall desire to keep genuine contributors out of the political lime-light.

Something of the same considerations must have coloured Liverpool's attitude toward Thomas Wallace, vice-president of the board of trade, who had been merrily making his mark under the presidency of the indolent Robinson, but who was 'broken-hearted' at having Huskisson placed over him.[51] He was anxious to be regarded as the ministry's main freer trade protagonist, and considered his claims to the cabinet to be 'full as good as Huskisson's'. Liverpool was genuinely upset at having to thwart Wallace, and did all he could to assuage the wound, but he could not allow Wallace to become too prominent, since Wallace was one of the people he was using to pave the way for what he regarded as essential reforms. Wallace already had an exposed position as chairman of the commons committee on foreign trade, but even more important in Liverpool's view was his leading role on the commission of inquiry into the revenues of Ireland. This was a backstairs inquiry to which Liverpool attached great importance and over which he induced a certain amount of stealth. This letter from Wallace to Herries conveys some of the excitement which Liverpool had instilled into the commissioners:

I write to communicate to you *confidentially* the result of a conversation I had with Lord Liverpool. It is clear that a great deal is

[49] Canning to Huskisson, 3 October 1822, Huskisson papers, BL, Add. MS 38743, fos. 217–20; Brock, *Liverpool and Liberal Toryism*, pp. 163–4.

[50] George IV to Liverpool, 2 Jan. 1823, Huskisson Papers, Add. MS. 38575, fos. 82–3. In November 1823 the king again made it clear that he had sanctioned Huskisson's admission to the cabinet as early as Canning's appointment to the foreign department. George IV to Liverpool, 6 Nov. 1823, *loc. cit.* It was therefore remarkably disingenuous of Liverpool to complain that Huskisson was trying to push his way into the cabinet 'against the wishes of the King and his own friends'. Liverpool to Arbuthnot, 27 Dec. 1822, *Correspondence of Charles Arbuthnot*, 37.

[51] Canning to Liverpool, 18 Jan. 1823, Canning Papers, 70.

expected from us and if we fulfill the intentions and wishes of Government we must be prepared to cut very deep—in fact that we are to be instruments of changing completely the actual system of governing Ireland by Patronage.[52]

There is even some evidence that Huskisson, as well as being envied by Wallace, was himself envious of Wallace's role in Irish and commercial affairs. To accept the presidency of the board of trade without a cabinet seat would mean that 'Wallace will be greater than myself', for 'he is moreover Chairman of that which is now become a kind of Standing Committee of Foreign Trade in the House of Commons, in itself necessarily an instrument of power in his hands'.[53] At all events, Huskisson was far from reconciled by Liverpool's offer of the next cabinet vacancy to occur. During 1823 he took every opportunity that he could to complain about his anomalous position as president without the cabinet. First he objected that several M.P.s connected with the government had opposed the 1823 Spitalfields Bill as a mere 'whim of mine'. Could it be right 'that the important measures, which this Board must be the channel of submitting to the House of Commons, should continue in the management of a President supposed either to bring them forward without the previous sanction of Government, or not to possess sufficient influence to ensure for them the support of its Friends in Parliament'?[54] Although the board of trade was 'so constantly in contact with the feeling and interests which agitate the country at large', without a voice in cabinet it could be no more than a 'Department of Hawkers and Peddlars'. On one occasion he took much pleasure in refusing Liverpool's request that he should attend the cabinet on an *ad hoc* basis to explain to it a particularly complex minute which he had just drafted on the reciprocity of duties act. His attitude was clearly that the cabinet could stew in their own duties: 'I shall leave it to the Cabinet to deal with the whole matter as to them may seem best.'[55] It did not take Liverpool long to realise that Huskisson was going to be even more of a nuisance outside the cabinet than in; and in November 1823 the door was finally opened. From which point, the famed unity of the cabinet was shattered.

Part of the trouble was that, in order to overcome residual feelings

---

[52] Wallace to Herries, 8 Aug. 1821, Herries Papers, British Library, Vol. xxxvi, fos. 105–7).

[53] Huskisson to Ellis, 29 Dec. 1822, Huskisson Papers, BL, Add. MS 38743, fos. 294–8.

[54] Huskisson to Liverpool, 19 June 1823, Huskisson Papers, Add MS 38744 ff. 229–31.

[55] Huskisson to Canning, 25 Oct. 1822 and 25 July 1823, Canning Papers, 67/131, 68/20.

of social inferiority, Huskisson exaggerated the doctrinaire elements of his economic policy. In reality a pragmatic and practical statesman, he liked to show off his cleverness by referring to the terms of trade and the specie flow mechanism, deliberately infuriating the disdainful Eldons and Sidmouths, who were baffled and frightened by political economy. Foreign policy, especially South American policy of course, also proved divisive. Whereas Castlereagh had not regarded the cabinet as a forum for decision-making, the talkative Canning was too spontaneous a person to keep quiet about the current diplomatic state of play. No one was less capable of carrying out Liverpool's strategy of separating policy and politics, for he was a man who saw intrigue in all things, who, as Croker famously said, could not 'take tea without a strategem'. Of course, much business continued to be done in 'inner cabinets' in advance of the real Cabinet, but with Huskisson and Canning in place, all business was now ultimately cabinet business, and the cabinet divided, seriously but not too publicly in 1824, much more seriously in 1825, and in 1826 so seriously that the two sides were simply not on speaking terms. By then Wellington was openly intriguing with foreign ambassadors and the king's physician to undermine the foreign secretary's diplomacy; while this same 'cottage coterie' was caballing with Rothschild and the displaced chancellor, Vansittart, to take advantage of the 1825 stock market crash to put an end to the economic despotism, as high tories like Mrs Arbuthnot thought it to be, of Huskisson and Robinson.[56] The two campaigns were linked, in that these high tories wished to bring England back within the purlieus both of the legitimist diplomatic system centred on Metternich, and the system of international credit centred on Rothschild. The government did not actually break up until 1827, and then it did so ostensibly over a different issue, the catholic question, about which ministers had had little difficulty in agreeing to differ hitherto, but though this gives an impression that Liverpool was an indispensable lynchpin whose removal sundered everything, in truth the rot had set in with the cabinet reshuffle several years before.

During the course of that protracted reshuffle, Bathurst had written to Harrowby that Robinson's appointment as chancellor of the exchequer was 'judicious, as it keeps more in the background *one* of the real objects of the Change, viz. Huskisson's promotion'.[57] This sums up Liverpool's strategy admirably: somehow to satisfy Huskisson without turning him into a political liability. This point can be missed by

[56] *Journal of Mrs Arbuthnot*, ii. 20.
[57] Bathurst to Harrowby, 5 January 1823, Sandon Hall, Harrowby MS 1st series XIV, fo. 123.

historians who are dismissive of Huskisson's feelings of personal disparagement. In his important study of Liverpool's government, John
Cookson writes unsympathetically of Huskisson that 'his was the
classic case of frustrated ambition ... He was beginning to act as if
every man's hand was against him, forgetting that in the cruel world
of politics what others thought of him was vastly more important than
what he thought of himself'. Cookson then quotes Huskisson's outburst
to Canning of 25 October 1822: 'My own impression is ... that
L[iverpool] has some fanciful theory of his own about dividing public
men into two classes—those who are, from the outset, destined to be
drudges—and those who are marked for Cabinet:—and that long ago
He has thrown me into the former class.' Cookson's comment on this
is that 'Neither Canning nor anyone else gave the least encouragement
to this mood of self-pity, Canning himself calling it, though not to
Huskisson's face, out and out "perverseness" '.[58] But that Huskisson,
far from being perverse, was in fact quite correct, seems clear from a
conversation between Liverpool and Canning which Canning had
reported to Huskisson shortly before the latter's outburst. Liverpool's
intention was surely to soothe Huskisson's feelings, but his words had
the opposite effect. Thus Canning reported that while, for personal
reasons, Liverpool would have preferred Vansittart to remain at the
exchequer, he recognised that a change had to be made; in which
case, ideally, he 'would like *you* better in Van[sittart]'s room (if he is
to have any one) than a politician.'[59] It was a hasty, thoughtless, give-
away remark which reveals exactly what was at the heart of the
dispute, which was that Liverpool did not regard Huskisson as a
'politician', but rather as a 'man of business', 'one of the best men of
business in this Country', as Liverpool had put it a few years earlier.[60]

Liverpool's perception of Huskisson's status in public life is easy to
understand, though it was a little old-fashioned. He saw Huskisson as
an eighteenth-century style placeman or 'king's friend', a useful
member of the court and treasury party like his own father, the first
earl. It had been the duty of such people to fulfil important executive
posts and carry out vital functions of government, serving each administration in turn without aspiring to be a 'politicians' or to sit in the
cabinet. In the parliament of 1780 there had been in this category
perhaps forty to fifty members holding efficient government offices,

[58] Huskisson to Canning, 25 October 1822, Huskisson Papers, BL, Add. MS 38743,
fo. 259; Cookson, *Liverpool's Administration*, 386–7. In fact, Canning's reference to Huskisson's perverseness was in respect of a different matter. Canning to Liverpool, 28
December 1822, Canning Papers.
[59] Canning to Huskisson, 3 Oct. 1822, *loc. cit.*
[60] Liverpool to Earl Talbot, 27 May 1818, Liverpool Papers, BL, Add. MS 38272,
fos. 34–7.

about thirty sinecurists, twenty-five more in the court and household, and sixty military or naval commissioners—perhaps 170 in all. As many historians have demonstrated, most of these 'king's friends' had since 1780 been eliminated from parliament by a succession of place acts inspired by Fox, Burke, and Curwen, who objected to a tyrant king having so much obedient lobby fodder. Gradually a process of differentiation had taken place whereby such offices divided into two functional types, parliamentary and political on the one hand, permanent and bureaucratic on the other, a distinction which in the case of under-secretaries was recognised officially in 1831.[61] By that time the permanent officers had been organised so as to form the nucleus of a modern salaried and accountable civil service, with regular office hours, annual holidays, fixed duties, and superannuation benefits, though not yet recruited competitively. However, some fifty of these old 'men of business' had had to remain in parliament, since it was hardly to be expected that aristocratic ministers would be able to master the details of naval victualling, civil list auditing, and other such complex matters. Huskisson was by no means the only public man in the early nineteenth century whose relationship to party was left in an ambiguous position by this trend. George III's madness and the 'waning of the influence of the crown' inevitably meant that junior ministers like him came to see themselves as 'Pitt's young men', or Perceval's, or Liverpool's, rather than as crown servants, which further politicised their outlook. The fact also that since 1783, and except for eighteen months in 1806–7, broadly a single set of men occupied the ministerial benches while another set of men hurled abuse from the opposite side, further cemented these junior ministers' identification with the tory government. Huskisson represented a new breed of career politician who naturally aspired to cabinet rank and who regarded the tory party as the obvious ladder to climb. His claim to political status was, in a sense, recognised just two months after he had been cruelly run over by the *Rocket*, for when the tories finally quit office in November 1830 and the whigs at last succeeded, it was not only the cabinet ministers who changed but also the junior ministers, and once that had happened it was clear to all that such juniors were political appointees who had every right to scramble for a seat in the cabinet. Howick, for example, became under-secretary at the colonial office in 1830, and secretary at war with a seat in the cabinet in 1835.

---

[61] H. Parris, *Constitutional Bureaucracy. The Development of British Public Administration since the Eighteenth Century* (1969); G. E. Aylmer, 'From office-holding to civil service: the genesis of modern bureaucracy', *T.R.H.S.*, 5th series, xxx (1980), 91–108; N. Chester, *The English Administrative System 1780–1870* (Oxford, 1981).

In this context it is instructive to consider how Goderich's ministry fell in January 1828 because of a quarrel between Huskisson and Herries which, Goderich being too feeble to deal with, led the king to send for the duke of Wellington. Now Huskisson and Herries had been quarrelling for all of their professional lives, and it could be argued that their quarrels had been along liberal *versus* high tory lines. When they quarrelled in 1809 they were both insignificant public servants; when they quarrelled in 1819 they were altogether more important but still politically in the shadows; then in 1823 Herries became an M.P. and Secretary to the treasury, while Huskisson stormed the cabinet; and in 1827 they came to occupy the two foremost political offices in the commons, Huskisson as first secretary of state for war and the colonies, Herries as chancellor of the exchequer. If anyone had said in 1809 that within twenty years two such nobodys would quarrel and bring down a government, the prediction would have seemed risible, but that is what happened.

Palmerston is another example of someone who, having served as a junior minister since 1809, suddenly donned a political mantle, Canning's, with his speech on Portugal in 1829, and became foreign secretary a year later. The rise of executive ministers like Huskisson and Palmerston to the political centreground reflects what was perhaps the main facet of politics under Lord Liverpool. The eight-eenth-century system, whereby politics was largely a game played at Westminster, having scant impact on and only intermittently affected by events in the country at large (a Namierite understanding of the period but one which survives subsequent, and in some cases anti-Namierite, research) had broken down, and politics had become inextricably bound up with the material and emotional pre-occupations of the country at large. In this respect it is instructive to compare the constitutional crisis of 1780-4 with that of 1828-32. The former was played against a background of noises off—Wyvill and the association movement, Lord George Gordon, 'public opinion' in the election of 1784—and the importance of these noises must not be underestimated, but it remained to a large extent a palace revolution, settled by political manoeuvre at the centre. In the crisis of 1828-32, however, it is obvious that far more went on than a mere battle between 'ins' and 'outs'. Whatever the reality, and in some respects the outcome proved less dramatic than the anticipation, people certainly *thought* in 1828-32 that, depending on who was in power and so in control of policy—the whigs, or the liberal tories, or the high tories, or the ultra tories—different sections of the community were likely to benefit, both economically and in terms of power and status. Politics were now *real* in the sense that they affected ordinary lives, they might influence the distribution of wealth in a burgeoning economy, or impinge on the cause of reformers against old corruption in church, state, and local government. Liverpool had tried to keep politics insulated from his rapidly changing society, by making the necessary executive adjustments in a non-political way. It had been a heroic attempt but had all too predictably failed, and the reshuffle of 1821–3 had marked the moment of his failure.

It does not follow that, because failure was predictable, the process toward 'real' politics was irreversible. After about 1850, in a context of economic prosperity and relative social harmony, 'equipoise' as it has been called, a broad-based consensus developed with respect to social reform and economic policy. Lawrence Goldman's fascinating study of the National Association for the Promotion of Social Science shows how most of the hard debating and deciding on such important matters could be carried out in a non-parliamentary arena, until the depression of the mid-1880s forced social and economic policy back into politics.[62] The important study by Tim Morgan of Gladstone's first government also shows the importance in such areas of relatively unpoliticised cabinet committees and government departments.[63] Similarly, after 1850 'high' or Westminster politics could be said to have become detached once more from the material concerns of society at large, enabling Maurice Cowling, John Vincent, and Andrew Jones plausibly to depict late-Victorian politics in a Namierite way. There was therefore nothing intrinsically futile in Liverpool's attempt to keep Westminster from social reality, but at a time of great social divisions, which had to be worked out politically, it was an impossible task.

The fact that there was a large measure of continuity in policy-making before and after 1822 does not mean that liberal and high tories must have been substantially the same animals, for the arguments between them raged more or less continuously throughout the period. The ascendancy of the liberals preceded the cabinet reshuffle and was to some extent independent of it, but there is also a subtle sense in which it made the reshuffle necessary. It has been argued elsewhere that high tories adopted a managerial approach to governing, whereas liberal tories saw the state and society in more mechanical or self-regulating terms, and looked rather to set up the right conditions (which as far as possible were *laissez-faire* conditions) for that mechanism to operate.[64] If this distinction is valid, then it follows that

[62] L. Goldman, 'The Social Science Association, 1857–1886: a context for mid-Victorian liberalism', *English Historical Review*, ci (1986), 95–134.

[63] T. D. L. Morgan, 'All for a wise despotism? Robert Lowe and the politics of meritocracy 1852–1873', unpublished Cambridge University Ph.D. (1982), 242–70.

[64] Hilton, 'Peel', *loc. cit.*, 606–8.

the high tory approach to government could function best under the conditions obtaining in the earlier part of Liverpool's ministry. Sidmouth's manipulation of spies and *agents provocateurs*, Castlereagh's congress diplomacy, and Vansittart's accommodations with the great financial houses—all these methods of government required a system in which real decision-making was done as much behind the scenes as possible, rather than 'openly' in cabinet or parliament. In this sense, Peel's early governance of Ireland was high tory *not* because he opposed catholic emancipation as a matter of principle, but because he thought it essential to work 'managerially' through the protestant magistrates, vestries, and police authorities which exercised authority in that country—what Wallace called 'government of Ireland by patronage'. Peel's policy toward Ireland became liberal tory only later when he realised that, in order to secure peace and to safeguard the union, he must create a mechanism for securing social harmony, whether by making ecclesiastical concessions to disaffected catholics or by building up a catholic middle class. And in the same sense it could be argued that Liverpool's failure, as a result of the 1821–3 reshuffle, to keep contentious policy-making out of the political arena, forced him in turn to adopt liberal mechanistic policies, if only so that when they became unpopular he could place the blame on the shoulders of providence instead of on his own.

THE ROYAL HISTORICAL SOCIETY

REPORT OF COUNCIL, SESSION 1987–1988

THE Council of the Royal Historical Society has the honour to present the following report to the Anniversary Meeting.

Council has naturally continued to watch very carefully for any signs that the pursuit of history is being further undermined. It has continued to support both the History at the Universities Defence Group and the campaign for Public Sector History; it has encouraged the Society of Archivists in efforts to protect archive services, especially in the metropolitan areas disturbed by recent local government reforms, and has expressed its strong support for the work of the Standing Conference of National and University Libraries in combatting cuts in library provision. Council feels that in the near future the Society may have to consider acting more directly to gather information on the state of historical education and research if the views of Fellows are to have a decisive influence on policies affecting the profession. Meanwhile Council has discussed at length a response to the University Grants Committee's circular announcing its new 'selectivity exercise'.

The corollary of these defensive actions has been Council's active and material assistance for a variety of new ventures. The increase in the Society's disposable income has made it possible to establish a studentship, the Royal Historical Society Centenary Fellowship, for an initial period of three years at the Institute of Historical Research in London commencing October 1988. It has also been decided to support the development of history in schools and the work of the Young Historian Scheme by awarding annually from 1989 up to ten Young Historian Prizes for achievement in the annual GCSE examination; the adjudication of course-work entries will be carried out by the Education Committee of the Historical Association.

Council has continued its financial help to the Association for History and Computing, and has also been pleased to approve funds from the Robinson Bequest for the active programme of exhibitions and publication mounted by the Director of the Dulwich Picture Gallery. In furtherance of its constant efforts to extend the Society's support for historical research, teaching and education as widely as possible not only at home but outside the United Kingdom, the President with Council's approval wrote personally to 70 scholars abroad inviting them to become Fellows; more than 50 have accepted the invitation.

The Society's publishing programme has moved forward steadily on all fronts. In this connection, Council wishes to record its gratitude to Professor D. M. Palliser for his services as general editor of the *Annual Bibliography of British and Irish History*, and to report that Dr J. J. N. Palmer and Dr B. A. English have accepted its invitation to succeed him as joint editors. The proposal, mentioned in last year's Report, for a series of *Bibliographies of European History* was endorsed by Council on the recommendation of its working party, and soundings are now being made in pursuit of editors and funds.

The year has also seen further reorganisation of the Society's Special Collection of rare books, and approval by Council of a continuing programme for the conservation of these volumes. The Society's Office has been substantially re-equipped in the manner of a computer age; this has already proved of considerable advantage in the conduct of the routine administration, and further benefits to the Society are anticipated. Every possible effort is being made to increase the numbers of those attending the Society's meetings. To that end and for the enhancement of the Society's Transactions, Council has decided to hold a special one-day conference in September 1989, and is considering the possibility of holding further such meetings outside London. Council also hopes to commemorate in an appropriate fashion the centenary in July 1989 of the Society's Royal Charter.

Council was delighted to receive the news both of Professor P. Collinson's appointment as Regius Professor of Modern History at Cambridge and of Professor C. S. R. Russell's translation to the House of Lords, and had pleasure in noting the conferment of knighthood upon Dr Keith Thomas as well as the election of Professor G. Duby to the Académie Française.

An evening party was held for members and guests in the Housman Room at University College London on Wednesday, 1 July 1987. 179 acceptances to invitations were received, and it was as usual well-attended.

At the Anniversary Meeting on 20 November 1987 a proposal to revise the By-laws defining the category of Retired Fellow was adopted, and the existing Officers of the Society were re-elected.

Council was subsequently delighted to learn of Professor R. M. Goode's election to the bar, but regrets that this has necessitated his resignation from the position of Honorary Solicitor with the Society. His advice, notably in the negotiation of new premises for the Society, has placed the Society in his debt. The search for a successor is in progress.

Council also accepted with great regret the early retirement of Mrs Jean Chapman, who had served the Society with great distinction as its Executive Secretary for 14 years; an informal presentation was made to her after the Council Meeting on 4 March 1988. Mrs J. N.

McCarthy was appointed to fill the vacancy thus caused.

The representation of the Society upon various bodies was as follows: Professor F. M. L. Thompson and Mr A. T. Milne on the Joint Anglo-American Committee exercising a general supervision over the production of the *Bibliographies of British History*; Professor G. W. S. Barrow, Mr M. Roper and Professor P. H. Sawyer on the Joint Committee of the Society and the British Academy established to prepare an edition of Anglo-Saxon charters; Professor E. B. Fryde on a committee to regulate British co-operation in the preparation of a new repertory of medieval sources to replace Potthast's *Bibliotheca Historica Medii Aevi*; Professor H. R. Loyn on a committee to promote the publication of photographic records of the more significant collections of British Coins; Professor P. Lasko on the Advisory Council of the reviewing Committee on the Export of Works of Art; Professor R. C. Floud and Professor W. A. Speck on the British National Committee of the International Historical Congress; Dr G. H. Martin on the Council of the British Records Association; Mr M. R. D. Foot on the Committee to advise the publishers of *The Annual Register*; Professor K. Cameron on the Trust for Lincolnshire Archaeology; Professor C. J. Holdsworth and, since March, Professor W. Doyle on the History at the Universities Defence Group; Mr G. C. F. Forster nominated by the Society to the Council of the British Association for Local History; and Dr A. I. Doyle on the Anthony Panizzi Foundation. Council received reports from its representatives.

Professor Glanmor Williams represents the Society on the Court of the University College of Swansea, Professor A. L. Brown on the University Conference of Stirling University; and Professor C. N. L. Brooke on the British Sub-Commission of the Commission International d'Histoire Ecclésiastique Comparée. Professor W. N. Medlicott represented the Society on the Court of the University of Exeter.

The Vice-Presidents retiring under By-law XVI were Professor P. Collinson, FBA and Professor P. Smith. Miss Valerie Cromwell and Professor P. J. Marshall were elected to replace them. The members of Council retiring under By-law XIX were Miss Valerie Cromwell, Professor P. J. Marshall and Mr P. A. Slack. Dr J. R. Dinwiddy, Professor W. Doyle, Professor R. A. Griffiths and Dr Gillian Sutherland were elected to fill the vacancies.

Messrs Davis, Watson and Co., were appointed auditors for the year 1987–8 under By-law XXVIII.

Publications and Papers read

Transactions, Fifth Series, Volume 38, and *Correspondence of Swedish Ambassadors in England*, (Camden, Fourth Series, Volume 36) went to press during the session and are due to be published in November 1988. The following works were published during the session: *The Short Parliament (1640) Diary of Sir Thomas Aston*, edited by Judith D. Maltby; and five volumes in the STUDIES IN HISTORY series: *The Territorial Army, 1907–1940* by Peter Dennis (volume 51); *The Jews in Palestine, 1800–1882* by Tudor Parfitt (volume 52); *Wales in the Reign of James I* by G. Dyfnallt Owen (volume 53); *James Bryce's 'American Commonwealth', The Anglo-American Background*, by Hugh Tulloch (volume 54); *Imperial Reaction: The Imperial Aulic Council and Imperial Politics in the Reign of Charles VI*, by Michael Hughes (volume 55); *Sir Robert Heath, 1575–1649*.

At the ordinary meetings of the Society the following papers were read:

'Lord Liverpool: the art of politics and the practice of government', by Dr Boyd Hilton (11 December 1987).

'Burial and Status in the Early Medieval West' by Dr Edward James (29 January 1987).

'The Hapsburgs and the Hungarian Problem, 1790–1848', by Dr R. J. W. Evans (4 March 1988).

'Censorship, propaganda and public opinion: the case of the Katyn graves, 1943' by Mr P. M. H. Bell (22 April 1988).

'The Royal Historical Society and late-Victorian Historiography' by Professor J. W. Burrow (6 July 1988: Prothero lecture).

The havoc caused in southern England by the great storm of 15–16 October 1987 unfortunately prevented Professor Claire Cross from reading her paper 'Monasticism and Society in the Diocese of York, 1520–1540'; this is nevertheless to appear in the *Transactions*.

At the Anniversary Meeting on 20 November 1987, the President, Dr G. E. Aylmer, delivered an address on 'Collective mentalities in mid-seventeenth-century England: III: Varieties of Radicalism'.

The Whitfield Prize for 1987 was awarded to Dr Kevin Sharpe for his book *Criticism and Compliment: The politics of literature in the England of Charles I* (CUP).

The Alexander Prize for 1988 was awarded to R. A. W. Rex, M.A., for his essay *The English Campaign against Luther in the 1520s*, which was read to the Society on 20 May 1988.

Membership

Council records with regret the deaths of 24 Fellows. Among these Council would mention especially Mr C. E. Blunt, who served on the Finance Committee for many years to the great benefit of the Society,

Professor C. R. Cheney, an Honorary Vice-President, Professor F. J. Fisher, a former Vice-President, and Professor W. N. Medlicott, a former member of Council. The resignations of 2 Fellows, and 10 Subscribing Libraries were received. 4 Fellows, 2 Associates and 2 Libraries were removed from the roll for non-payment of subscription. Professor K. Inglis was elected a Corresponding Fellow. In addition to the 53 overseas scholars who accepted the President's invitation to become Fellows of the Society, a further 67 Fellows and 5 Associates were elected and 2 Libraries were admitted. 13 Fellows transferred to the Category of Retired Fellow. The membership of the Society on 30 June 1988 comprised 1750 Fellows (including 63 Life Fellows and 114 Retired Fellows), 40 Corresponding Fellows, 149 Associates and 697 Subscribing Libraries (1649, 39, 147 and 707 respectively on 30 June 1987). The Society exchanged publications with 15 Societies, British and foreign.

Finance

The format of the annual accounts for the year ending 30 June 1988 has been modified, and it is hoped that this has produced greater clarity in the presentation of information. It will be noted that the excess of income over expenditure for the year ending 30 June 1988 is £36,110, a considerable increase since the previous year (£8,335). This improvement in the financial position of the Society is more apparent than real, reflecting an over-provision for publications in the year ending 30 June 1987. This reduced the surplus for 1986/7, and increased it for 1987/8. It should also be noted that the new expenditure upon which Council has resolved as a result of the merging of the Sinking and General Funds has not yet started to appear. The income for the year ending 30 June 1988 has consequently been augmented by the merger of the two Funds, without expenditure yet being incurred.

ROYAL HISTORICAL SOCIETY

Balance Sheet as at 30th June 1988

	Notes	1988 £	1988 £	1987 £	1987 £
Fixed Assets	2		3,864		
Investments	3		596,198		508,988
Current Assets					
Stocks	1(c)	3,113		947	
Debtors	4	11,196		11,670	
Cash at Bank and in Hand	5	38,490		51,245	
		52,799		63,862	
Creditors: Amounts falling due within one year	6	39,898		63,621	
Net Current Assets			12,901		241
			612,963		509,229
Represented By:					
General Fund			564,121		461,740
Miss E. M. Robinson Bequest			26,539		24,520
A. S. Whitfield Prize Fund			13,452		13,064
Studies in History			8,851		9,905
			612,963		509,229

ROYAL HISTORICAL SOCIETY

Income and Expenditure Account for the Year Ended 30th June 1988

GENERAL FUND

	Notes	1988 £	1988 £	1987 £	1987 £
INCOME					
Subscriptions.	7		42,582		40,2
Investment income			50,551		45,2
Royalties and reproduction fees.			469		
Donations and sundry income			927		1,2
			94,529		87,0
EXPENDITURE					
SECRETARIAL AND ADMINISTRATIVE					
Salaries, pensions and national insurance		22,034		17,618	
Printing and stationery		3,495		3,704	
Postage and telephone		1,963		2,337	
Audit and accountancy		2,875		1,265	
Insurance .		357		301	
Meetings and travel.		2,992		2,335	
Repairs and renewals		1,415		2,500	
Depreciation	1(b)	1,163		—	
			36,294		30,0
PUBLICATIONS					
Literary director's expenses		225		240	
Publishing costs for the year .	8(a)	(942)		16,541	
Provisions for publications in progress .	8(b)	24,000		31,300	
Other publication costs .	8(c)	(575)		231	
Scottish Texts and Calendars.		—		8,977	
Sales of publications.		(4,393)		(11,286)	
			18,315		46,0
LIBRARY AND ARCHIVES	1(d)				
Purchase of books and publications		936		733	
Binding		590		792	
Library assistance		—		62	
			1,526		1,5
OTHER CHARGES					
Alexander prize.		384		132	
Prothero lecture		100		100	
Grants		1,000		700	
Donations and sundry expenses		300		134	
A level prizes		500		500	
			2,284		1,5
CONFERENCE					
Domesday conference expenditure.		—		10,250	
Domesday conference income.		—		(10,167)	
			—		
			58,419		79,2
Excess of income over expenditure.			36,110		8,3
Surplus on sale of investments			66,271		49,1
			102,381		57,4
Transfer from Miss E. M. Robinson Bequest			—		2,3
			102,381		59,8
Balance brought forward.			461,740		401,8
Balance carried forward .			564,121		461,7

SPECIAL FUNDS

		1988		1987	
	£	£	£	£	
MISS E. M. ROBINSON BEQUEST					
INCOME					
Investment income		1,612		2,395	
Surplus on sale of investments		907		3,057	
		2,519		5,452	
EXPENDITURE.					
Grant to Dulwich Picture Gallery.		500		—	
Excess of income over expenditure for the year.		2,019		5,452	
Transfer to General Fund		—		(2,395)	
		2,019		3,057	
Balance brought forward		24,520		21,463	
Balance carried forward.		26,539		24,520	
S. WHITFIELD PRIZE FUND					
INCOME					
Investment income.		1,215		1,452	
EXPENDITURE					
Prize awarded.	600		600		
Advertisement.	227	827	132	732	
Excess of income over expenditure for the year.		388		720	
Balance brought forward.		13,064		12,344	
Balance carried forward.		13,452		13,064	
STUDIES IN HISTORY					
INCOME					
Royalties.		1,631		3,226	
Investment income.		746		887	
		2,377		4,113	
EXPENDITURE					
Honorarium	2,750		2,750		
Editor's expenses	681		574		
Review copies.	—		188		
Ex gratia payments.	—		200		
		3,431		3,712	
Excess of expenditure over income for the year.		(1,054)		401	
Balance brought forward.		9,905		9,504	
		8,851		9,905	

179

ROYAL HISTORICAL SOCIETY

STATEMENT OF SOURCE AND APPLICATION OF FUNDS FOR THE YEAR ENDED 30TH JUNE 1988

	1988 £	1988 £	1987 £	1987 £
SOURCE OF FUNDS				
Excess of income over expenditure for the year				
General fund				
Miss E. M. Robinson Bequest.		102,381		57,
A. S. Whitfield prize fund		2,019		5,
Studies in history fund		388		
		(1,054)		
		103,734		64,
Adjustment for items not involving the movement of funds				
Depreciation	1,163		—	
Surplus on sale of investments	(67,178)		(52,216)	
		(66,015)		(52,
Total generated from operations		37,719		11,
Funds from other courses				
Sale of investments		41,618		91,
		79,337		102,
APPLICATION OF FUNDS				
Purchase of fixed assets	5,027		—	
Purchase of investments	61,650		80,473	
		66,677		80,
		12,660		22,
INCREASE/(DECREASE) IN WORKING CAPITAL				
Stock		2,166		(4,
Debtors		(474)		(6,
Creditors		23,723		15,5
Liquid funds		(12,755)		17,0
		12,660		22,4

ACCOUNTING POLICIES

) *Basis of accounting*
These accounts have been prepared under the historical cost convention.

a) *Depreciation*
Depreciation is calculated by reference to the cost of fixed assets using a straight line basis at rates considered appropriate having regard to the expected lives of the fixed assets.
The annual rates of depreciation in use are:

Furniture and equipment	10%
Computer equipment	25%

Prior to 1st July 1987 the full cost of fixed assets was written off to General Fund in the year of purchase.

c) *Stocks*
Stock is valued at the lower of cost and net realisable value.

d) *Library and archives*
The cost of additions to the library and archives is written off in the year of purchase.

FIXED ASSETS

	Computer Equipment	Furniture and Equipment	Total
	£	£	£
Cost			
Additions during year	4,407	620	5,027
Disposals during year	—		
At 30th June 1988	4,407	620	5,027
Depreciation			
Charge for year	1,101	62	1,163
At 30th June 1988	1,101	62	1,163
Net book value			
At 30th June 1988	3,306	558	3,864
At 30th June 1987	—	—	—

The cost of additions to the library and archives is written off in the year of purchase.
Prior to 1st July 1987 the cost of furniture and equipment was written off in the year of purchase. Items acquired before that date are not reflected in the above figures.

INVESTMENTS

	1988	1987
	£	£
Quoted securities at cost	512,735	447,410
(market value £1,028,349; 1987 £1,270,452)		
Money at call	73,463	41,578
Short term deposit	10,000	20,000
	596,198	508,988

4. Debtors

	1988 £	19
Sundry debtors	9,595	10
Prepayments	1,601	
	11,196	11

5. Cash at bank and in hand

	1988 £	19 £
Deposit accounts	28,475	4
Current accounts	9,995	7
Cash in hand	20	
	38,490	51

6. Creditors

	1988 £	19 £
Sundry creditors	7,202	
Subscriptions received in advance	7,117	6
Accruals	1,580	
Provision for publications	24,000	55
	39,898	63

7. Subscriptions

	1988 £	19 £
Current subscriptions	38,484	36
Subscriptions arrears received	2,238	1
Income tax recovered on covenanted subscriptions	1,860	1
	42,582	40

8. Publications
   (a) Publishing costs for the year £

Transactions, fifth series	Vol. 37	11,394
Camden, fourth series	Vol. 33	3,373
	Vol. 34	15,089
	Vol. 35	10,684
Guides and handbooks	No. 2	918
	No. 15	8,950
		50,408
Less: Provision brought forward		(51,350)
		(942)

   (b) Provision for publications in progress

Transactions, fifth series	Vol. 38	12,500
Camden, fourth series	Vol. 36	11,500
		24,000

   (c) Other publication costs

Annual bibliography	1,279
Less: Royalties received	1,854
	(575)

G. E. AYLMER, *President*
M. J. DAUNTON, *Treasurer*

We have audited the accounts on pages 177 to 182 in accordance with approved Auditing Standards.
In our opinion the accounts, which have been prepared under the historical cost condition, give a true an
fair view of the Society's affairs at 30th June 1988 and of its surplus and source and application of funds for t
year then ended.

118, SOUTH STREET, DORKING
6th September, 1988

DAVIES, WATSON & C
Chartered Accountan

THE DAVID BERRY ESSAY TRUST

Balance Sheet as at 30th June 1988

	1988 £	1988 £	1987 £	1987 £
⸰STMENTS				
3.63 shares in the Charities Official Investment Fund		530		530
⸰arket value £2,007; 1987 £2,450)				
⸰ENT ASSETS				
⸰sh at bank				
⸰eposit account .	2,383		2,053	
⸰urrent account .	1		1	
	2,384		2,054	
⸰EDITORS: Accounts falling due within one year	227		—	
⸰CURRENT ASSETS .		2,157		2,054
		2,687		2,584
⸰esented by:				
⸰mulated fund .		2,687		2,584

⸰COME AND Expenditure Account for the Year Ended 30th June 1988

	1988 £	1987 £
⸰ME		
⸰vidends	240	223
⸰terest .	90	98
	330	321
⸰ENDITURE		
⸰dvertisement	227	—
⸰xcess of income over expenditure for the year	103	321
⸰alance brought forward	2,584	2,263
⸰alance carried forward	2,687	2,584

late David Berry, by his Will dated 23 April 1926, left £1,000 to provide in every three years a gold medal prize money for the best essay on the Earl of Bothwell or, at the discretion of the Trustees, on Scottish ⸰ory of the James Stuarts I to VI, in memory of his father the late Rev. David Berry.

⸰he Trust is regulated by a scheme sanctioned by the Chancery Division of the High Court of Justice dated ⸰anuary 1930, and made in action 1927 A 1233 David Anderson Berry deceased, Hunter and Another V ⸰ertson and Another and since modified by an order of the Charity Commissioners made on 11 January ⸰8 removing the necessity to provide a medal.

⸰he Royal Historical Society is now the Trustee. The investment held on Capital Account consists of 634 ⸰arities Official Investment Fund shares (Market Value £2,630; 1987 £3,213).

⸰he Trustee will in every second year of the three year period advertise inviting essays.

⸰/e have audited the accounts on this page in accordance with approved Auditing Standards. ⸰n our opinion the accounts, which have been prepared under the historical cost condition, give a true and ⸰ view of the trust's affairs at 30th June 1988 and of its surplus for the year then ended and comply with the ⸰visions of the trust deed.

⸰, South Street, Dorking
September, 1988

DAVIES, WATSON & CO.
Chartered Accountants

ALEXANDER PRIZE

The Alexander Prize was established in 1897 by L. C. Alexander, F.R.Hist.S. It consists of a silver medal and £100 awarded annually for an essay upon some historical subject. Candidates may select their own subject provided such subject has been previously submitted to and approved by the Literary Director. The essay must be a genuine work of original research, not hitherto published, and one which has not been awarded any other prize. It must not exceed 6,000 words in length and must be sent in on or before 1 November of any year. The detailed regulations should be obtained in advance from the Secretary. Candidates must be under the age of 30.

LIST OF ALEXANDER PRIZE ESSAYISTS (1898-1986)[1]

1898. F. Hermia Durham ('The relations of the Crown to trade under James I').

1899. W. F. Lord, BA ('The development of political parties during the reign of Queen Anne').

1901. Laura M. Roberts ('The Peace of Lunéville').

1902. V. B. Redstone ('The social condition of England during the Wars of the Roses').

1903. Rose Graham ('The intellectual influence of English monasticism between the tenth and the twelfth centuries').

1904. Enid W. G. Routh ('The balance of power in the seventeenth century').

1905. W. A. P. Mason, MA ('The beginnings of the Cistercian Order').

1906. Rachel R. Reid, MA ('The Rebellion of the Earls, 1569').

1908. Kate Hotblack ('The Peace of Paris, 1763').

1909. Nellie Nield, MA ('The social and economic condition of the unfree classes in England in the twelfth and thirteenth centuries').

1912. H. G. Richardson ('The parish clergy of the thirteenth and fourteenth centuries').

1917. Isobel D. Thornely, BA ('The treason legislation of 1531-1534').

1918. T. F. T. Plucknett, BA ('The place of the Council in the fifteenth century').

1919. Edna F. White, MA ('The jurisdiction of the Privy Council under the Tudors').

1920. J. E. Neale, MA ('The Commons Journals of the Tudor Period').

1922. Eveline C. Martin ('The English establishments on the Gold Coast in the second half of the eighteenth century').

1923. E. W. Hensman, MA ('The Civil War of 1648 in the east midlands').

1924. Grace Stretton, BA ('Some aspects of mediæval travel').

1925. F. A. Mace, MA ('Devonshire ports in the fourteenth and fifteenth centuries').

[1] No award was made in 1900, 1907, 1910, 1911, 1913, 1914, 1921, 1946, 1948, 1956, 1969, 1975, 1977, and 1987. The Prize Essays for 1909 and 1919 were not published in the *Transactions*. No Essays were submitted in 1915, 1916 and 1943.

1926. Marian J. Tooley, MA ('The authorship of the *Defensor Pacis*').

1927. W. A. Pantin, BA ('Chapters of the English Black Monks, 1215–1540').

1928. Gladys A. Thornton, BA, PhD ('A study in the history of Clare, Suffolk, with special reference to its development as a borough').

1929. F. S. Rodkey, AM, PhD ('Lord Palmerston's policy for the rejuvenation of Turkey, 1839–47').

1930. A. A. Ettinger, DPhil ('The proposed Anglo-Franco-American Treaty of 1852 to guarantee Cuba to Spain').

1931. Kathleen A. Walpole, MA ('The humanitarian movement of the early nineteenth century to remedy abuses on emigrant vessels to America').

1932. Dorothy M. Brodie, BA ('Edmund Dudley, minister of Henry VII').

1933. R. W. Southern, BA ('Ranulf Flambard and early Anglo-Norman administration').

1934. S. B. Chrimes, MA, PhD ('Sir John Fortescue and his theory of dominion').

1935. S. T. Bindoff, MA ('The unreformed diplomatic service, 1812–60').

1936. Rosamund J. Mitchell, MA, BLitt ('English students at Padua, 1460–1475').

1937. C. H. Philips, BA ('The East India Company "Interest", and the English Government, 1783–4').

1938. H. E. I. Philips, BA ('The last years of the Court of Star Chamber, 1630–41').

1939. Hilda P. Grieve, BA ('The deprived married clergy in Essex, 1553–61').

1940. R. Somerville, MA ('The Duchy of Lancaster Council and Court of Duchy Chamber').

1941. R. A. L. Smith, MA, PhD ('The *Regimen Scaccarii* in English monasteries').

1942. F. L. Carsten, DPhil ('Medieval democracy in the Brandenburg towns and its defeat in the fifteenth century').

1944. Rev. E. W. Kemp, BD ('Pope Alexander III and the canonization of saints').

1945. Helen Suggett, BLitt ('The use of French in England in the later middle ages').

1947. June Milne, BA ('The diplomacy of John Robinson at the court of Charles XII of Sweden, 1697–1709').

1949. Ethel Drus, MA ('The attitude of the Colonial Office to the annexation of Fiji').

1950. Doreen J. Milne, MA, PhD ('The results of the Rye House Plot, and their influence upon the Revolution of 1688').

1951. R. G. Davies, BA ('The origins of the commission system in the West India trade').

1952. G. W. S. Barrow, BLitt ('Scottish rulers and the religious orders, 1070–1153').

1953. W. E. Minchinton, BSc(Econ) ('Bristol—metropolis of the west in the eighteenth century').

1954. Rev. L. Boyle, OP ('The *Oculus Sacerdotis* and some other works of William of Pagula').

1955. G. F. E. Rudé, MA, PhD ('The Gordon riots: a study of the rioters and their victims').

1957. R. F. Hunnisett, MA, DPhil ('The origins of the office of Coroner').

1958. Thomas G. Barnes, AB, DPhil ('County politics and a puritan *cause célèbre*: Somerset churchales, 1633').

1959. Alan Harding, BLitt ('The origins and early history of the Keeper of the Peace').

1960. Gwyn A. Williams, MA, PhD ('London and Edward I').

1961. M. H. Keen, BA ('Treason trials under the law of arms').

1962. G. W. Monger, MA, PhD ('The end of isolation: Britain, Germany and Japan, 1900–1902').

1963. J. S. Moore, BA ('The Domesday teamland: a reconsideration').

1964. M. Kelly, PhD ('The submission of the clergy').

1965. J. J. N. Palmer, BLitt ('Anglo-French negotiations, 1390–1396').

1966. M. T. Clanchy, MA, PhD ('The Franchise of Return of Writs').

1967. R. Lovatt, MA, DPhil, PhD ('The *Imitation of Christ* in late medieval England').

1968. M. G. A. Vale, MA, DPhil ('The last years of English Gascony, 1451–1453').

1970. Mrs Margaret Bowker, MA, BLitt ('The Commons Supplication against the Ordinaries in the light of some Archidiaconal Acta').

1971. C. Thompson, MA ('The origins of the politics of the Parliamentary middle groups, 1625–1629').

1972. I. d'Alton, BA ('Southern Irish Unionism: A study of Cork City and County Unionists, 1884–1914').

1973. C. J. Kitching, BA, PhD ('The quest for concealed lands in the reign of Elizabeth I').

1974. H. Tomlinson, BA ('Place and Profit: an Examination of the Ordnance Office, 1660–1714').

1976. B. Bradshaw, MA, BD ('Cromwellian reform and the origins of the Kildare rebellion, 1533–34').

1978. C. J. Ford, BA ('Piracy or Policy: The Crisis in the Channel, 1400–1403').

1979. P. Dewey, BA, PhD ('Food Production and Policy in the United Kingdom, 1914–1918').

1980. Ann L. Hughes, BA, PhD ('Militancy and Localism: Warwickshire Politics and Westminster Politics, 1643–1647').

1981. C. J. Tyerman, MA ('Marino Sanudo Torsello and the Lost Crusade. Lobbying in the Fourteenth Century').

1982. E. Powell, BA, DPhil ('Arbitration and the Law in England in the Late Middle Ages').

1983. A. G. Rosser, MA ('The essence of medieval urban communities: the vill of Westminster 1200–1540').

1984. N. L. Ramsay, MA, LLB ('Retained Legal Counsel, c. 1275–1475').

1985. George S. Garnett, MA ('Coronation and Propaganda: Some Implications of the Norman Claim to the Throne of England in 1066').

1986. C. J. Given-Wilson ('The King and the Gentry in Fourteenth-Century England').

1988. R. A. W. Rex, MA (The English Campaign against Luther in the 1520s).

DAVID BERRY PRIZE

The David Berry Prize was established in 1929 by David Anderson-Berry in memory of his father, the Reverend David Berry. It consists of a money prize awarded every three years for Scottish history. Candidates may select any subject dealing with Scottish history within the reigns of James I to James VI inclusive, provided such subject has been previously submitted to and approved by the Council of the Royal Historical Society. The essay must be a genuine work of original research not hitherto published, and one which has not been awarded any other prize. The essay should be between 6,000 and 10,000 words, excluding footnotes and appendices. It must be sent in on or before 31 October 1988.

LIST OF DAVID BERRY PRIZE ESSAYISTS (1937–85)[1]

1937. G. Donaldson, MA ('The polity of the Scottish Reformed Church c. 1460–1580, and the rise of the Presbyterian movement').

1943. Rev. Prof. A. F. Scott Pearson, DTh, DLitt ('Anglo-Scottish religious relations, 1400–1600').

1949. T. Bedford Franklin, MA, FRSE ('Monastic agriculture in Scotland, 1440–1600').

1955. W. A. McNeill, MA ('"Estaytt" of the king's rents and pensions, 1621').

1958. Prof. Maurice Lee, PhD ('Maitland of Thirlestane and the foundation of the Stewart despotism in Scotland').

1964. M. H. Merriman ('Scottish collaborators with England during the Anglo-Scottish war, 1543–1550').

1967. Miss M. H. B. Sanderson ('Catholic recusancy in Scotland in the sixteenth century').

1970. Athol Murray, MA, LLB, PhD ('The Comptroller, 1425–1610').

1973. J. Kirk, MA, PhD ('Who were the Melvillians: A study in the Personnel and Background of the Presbyterian Movement in late Sixteenth-century Scotland').

1976. A. Grant, BA, DPhil ('The Development of the Scottish Peerage').

1985. Rev. G. Mark Dilworth ('The Commendator System in Scotland').

[1] No essays were submitted in 1940 and 1979. No award was made in 1946, 1952, 1961 and 1982.

WHITFIELD PRIZE

The Whitfield Prize was established by Council in 1976 as a money prize of £400 out of the bequest of the late Professor Archibald Stenton Whitfield: in May 1981 Council increased the prize to £600. Until 1982 the prize was awarded annually to the STUDIES IN HISTORY series. From 1983 the prize, value £600, will be awarded annually to the best work of English or Welsh history by an author under 40 years of age, published in the United Kingdom. The award will be made by Council in the Spring of each year in respect of works published in the preceding calendar year. Authors or publishers should send two copies (non-returnable) of a book eligible for the competition to the Society to arrive not later than 31 December of the year of publication.

LIST OF WHITFIELD PRIZE WINNERS (1977–1987)

1977. K. D. Brown, MA, PhD (*John Burns*).
1978. Marie Axton, MA, PhD (*The Queen's Two Bodies: Drama and the Elizabethan Succession*).
1979. Patricia Crawford, MA, PhD (*Denzil Holles, 1598–1680: A study of his Political Career*).
1980. D. L. Rydz (*The Parliamentary Agents: A History*).
1981. Scott M. Harrison (*The Pilgrimage of Grace in the Lake Counties 1536–7*).
1982. Norman L. Jones (*Faith by Statute: Parliament and the Settlement of Religion 1559*).
1983. Peter Clark (*The English Alehouse: A social history 1200–1830*).
1984. David Hempton, BA, PhD (*Methodism and Politics in British Society 1750–1850*).
1985. K. D. M. Snell, MA, PhD (*Annals of the Labouring Poor*).
1986. Diarmaid MacCulloch, MA, PhD, FSA (*Suffolk and the Tudors: Politics and Religion in an English County 1500–1600*).
1987. Kevin M. Sharpe, MA, DPhil (*Criticism and Compliment: The politics of literature in the England of Charles I*).

THE ROYAL HISTORICAL SOCIETY

(INCORPORATED BY ROYAL CHARTER)

OFFICERS AND COUNCIL—1988

Patron
HER MAJESTY THE QUEEN

President
G. E. AYLMER, MA, DPhil, FBA

Honorary Vice-Presidents

Professor J. H. Burns, MA, PhD
Professor A. G. Dickens, CMG, MA, DLit, DLitt, LittD, FBA, FSA
Professor G. Donaldson MA, PhD, DLitt, DLitt, FRSE, FBA
Sir Geoffrey Elton, MA, PhD, LittD, DLitt, DLitt, DLit, FBA
Professor P. Grierson, MA, LittD, FBA, FSA
Sir John Habakkuk, MA, FBA
Professor Sir Keith Hancock, KBE, MA, DLitt, FBA
Professor D. Hay, MA, DLitt, FBA, FRSE, Dr h.c. Tours
Professor J. C. Holt, MA, DPhil, DLitt, FBA, FSA
Professor R. A. Humphreys, OBE, MA, PhD, DLitt, LittD, DLitt, DUniv
Miss K. Major, MA, BLitt, LittD, FBA, FSA
Professor D. B. Quinn, MA, PhD, DLit, DLitt, DLitt, DLitt, LLD, DHL,
    Hon FBA
The Hon. Sir Steven Runciman, CH, MA, DPhil, LLD, LittD, DLitt, LitD,
    DD, DHL, FBA, FSA
Sir Richard Southern, MA, DLitt, LittD, DLitt, FBA
Professor C. H. Wilson, CBE, MA, LittD, DLitt, DLitt, DLitt, FBA

Vice-Presidents

G. H. Martin, CBE, MA, DPhil
Professor K. G. Robbins, MA, DPhil, DLitt
Professor R. B. Dobson, MA, DPhil
Professor G. S. Holmes, MA, DLitt, FBA
Miss B. Harvey, MA, BLitt, FBA
Professor W. R. Ward, DPhil
Miss V. Cromwell, MA
Professor P. J. Marshall, MA, DPhil

STANDING COMMITTEES 1988

Finance Committee

PROFESSOR OLIVE ANDERSON
MISS V. CROMWELL
P. J. C. FIRTH
PROFESSOR R. C. FLOUD
DR. G. H. MARTIN, CBE
PROFESSOR B. E. SUPPLE, PhD, MA
And the Officers

Publications Committee

PROFESSOR D. E. D. BEALES
C. R. ELRINGTON, MA, FSA
MISS B. HARVEY, FBA
PROFESSOR M. A. JONES, MA, DPhil
PROFESSOR D. M. PALLISER
PROFESSOR C. S. R. RUSSELL
PROFESSOR W. A. SPECK
DR. GILLIAN SUTHERLAND
And the Officers

Library Committee

PROFESSOR OLIVE ANDERSON
DR J. R. DINWIDDY
PROFESSOR P. J. MARSHALL
PROFESSOR C. S. R. RUSSELL
And the Officers

LIST OF FELLOWS OF THE
ROYAL HISTORICAL SOCIETY

Names of Officers and Honorary Vice-Presidents are printed in capitals.
Those marked* have compounded for their annual subscriptions.

Abramsky, Professor Chimen A., MA, Dept of Hebrew and Jewish Studies, University College London, Gower Street, London WC1E 6BT.

Abulafia, D. S. H., MA, PhD, Gonville and Caius College, Cambridge CB2 1TA.

Acton, E. D. J., PhD, School of History, The University, P.O. Box 147, Liverpool L69 3BX.

Adair, Professor J. E., MA, PhD, Newlands Cottage, 41 Pewley Hill, Guildford, Surrey.

Adam, Professor R. J., MA, Easter Wayside, Hepburn Gardens, St Andrews KY16 9LP.

Adams, Professor Ralph J. Q., PhD, Dept of History, Texas A & M University, College Station, Texas 77843-4236, U.S.A.

Adams, S. L., BA, MA, DPhil, 4 North East Circus Place, Edinburgh EH3 6SP.

Adamthwaite, Professor A.P., BA, PhD, 780 King Lane, Leeds LS17 7AU.

Addison, P., MA, DPhil, Dept of History, The University, William Robertson Building, George Square, Edinburgh EH8 9JY.

Ailes, A., MA, 24 Donnington Gardens, Reading, Berkshire RG1 5LY.

Akenson, D. H., BA, PhD, Dept of History, Queen's University, Kingston, Ontario, Canada, K7L 3N6.

Akrigg, Professor G. P. V., BA, PhD, FRSC, 8-2575 Tolmie Street, Vancouver, B.C., Canada, V6R 4M1.

Alcock, Professor L., MA, FSA, 29 Hamilton Drive, Glasgow G12 8DN.

Alder, G. J., BA, PhD, Dept of History, The University, Whiteknights, Reading RG6 2AA.

Alderman, G., MA, DPhil, 172 Colindeep Lane, London NW9 6EA.

Allan, D. G. C., MSc(Econ), PhD, c/o Royal Society of Arts, John Adam Street, London WC2N 6EZ.

Allen, D. F., BA, PhD, School of History, The University, P.O. Box 363, Birmingham B15 2TT.

Allen, D. H., BA, PhD, 105 Tuddenham Avenue, Ipswich, Suffolk IP4 2HG.

Allmand, C. T., MA, DPhil, FSA, 111 Menlove Avenue, Liverpool L18 3HP.

Alsop, J. D., BA, MA, PhD, Dept of History, McMaster University, 1280 Main Street West, Hamilton, Ontario, Canada L8S 4L9.

Altholz, Professor J., PhD, Dept of History, University of Minnesota, 614 Social Sciences Building, Minneapolis, Minn. 55455, U.S.A.

Altschul, Professor M., PhD, Case Western Reserve University, Cleveland, Ohio 44106, U.S.A.

Ambler, R. W., PhD, 37 Cumberland Avenue, Grimsby, South Humberside DN32 0BT.

Anderson, Professor M. S., MA, PhD, 45 Cholmeley Crescent, London N6 5EX.

Anderson, Professor Olive, MA, BLitt, Dept of History, Westfield College, London NW3 7ST.

Anderson, R. D., MA, DPhil, 7 North West Circus Place, Edinburgh EH3 6ST.

Anderson, Miss S. P., MA, BLitt, 17-19 Chilworth Street, London W2 3QU.

Andrew, C. M., MA, PhD, Corpus Christi College, Cambridge CB2 1RH.

Anglesey, The Most Hon., The Marquess of, FSA, FRSL, Plas-Newydd, Llanfairpwll, Anglesey LL61 6DZ.

Anglo, Professor S., BA, PhD, FSA, 59 Green Ridge, Withdean, Brighton BN1 5LU.

Angold, M. J., BA, DPhil, 17 Morningside Park, Edinburgh EH10 5HD.

Annan, Lord, OBE, MA, DLitt, DUniv, 16 St John's Wood Road, London NW8 8RE.

Annis, P. G. W.. BA, 65 Longlands Road, Sidcup, Kent DA15 7LQ.

Appleby, J. S.. Little Pitchbury, Brick Kiln Lane, Great Horkesley, Colchester, Essex CO6 4EU.

Armstrong, Miss A. M.. BA, 7 Vale Court, Mallord Street, London SW3.

Armstrong, C. A. J., MA, FSA, Gayhurst, Lincombe Lane, Boars Hill, Oxford OX1 5DZ.

Armstrong, Professor F. H., PhD, Dept of History, University of Western Ontario, London, Ontario, Canada N6A 3K7.

Armstrong, W. A., BA, PhD, Eliot College, The University, Canterbury, Kent CT2 7NS.

Arnstein, Professor W. L., PhD, Dept of History, University of Illinois at Urbana-Champaign, 309 Gregory Hall, Urbana, Ill. 61801, U.S.A.

Artibise, Professor Alan F. J., PhD, Community and Regional Planning, University of British Columbia, 6333 Memorial Road, Vancouver, B. C., Canada, V6T 1W5.

Ash, Marinell, BA, MA, PhD, 42 Woodburn Terrace, Edinburgh EH10 4ST.

Ashton, Professor R., PhD, The Manor House, Brundall, near Norwich NOR 86Z.

Ashworth, J., BA, MLitt, DPhil, School of English and American Studies, University of East Anglia, Norwich NR4 7TJ.

Ashworth, Professor W., BSc(Econ), PhD, Flat 14, Wells Court, Wells Road, Ilkley, W. Yorks. LS29 9LG.

Asquith, Ivon, BA, PhD, 19 Vicarage Lane, New Hinksey, Oxford OX1 4RQ.

Aston, Margaret E., MA, DPhil, Castle House, Chipping, Ongar, Essex.

Austin, The Rev. Canon, M. R. BD, MA, PhD, 22 Marlock Close, Fiskerton, Nr Southwell, Notts. NG25 0UB.

Axelson, Professor E. V., DLitt, Box 15, Constantia, 7848, S. Africa.

*Aydelotte, Professor W. O., PhD, State University of Iowa, Iowa City, Iowa, U.S.A.

AYLMER, G. E., MA, DPhil, FBA, (*President*), St Peter's College, Oxford OX1 2DL.

Bahlman, Professor Dudley W. R., MA, PhD, Dept of History, Williams College, Williamstown, Mass. 01267, U.S.A.

Bailie, The Rev. W. D., MA, BD, PhD, DD, 45 Morpra Drive, Saintfield, Co. Down, N. Ireland.

Bailyn, Professor B., MA, PhD, LittD, LHD, Widener J, Harvard University, Cambridge, Mass. 02138, U.S.A.

Baines, A. H. J., PhD, MA, LLB, FSA, FRSA, FSS, Finmere, 90 Eskdale Avenue, Chesham, Bucks. HP5 3AY.

Baker, D., BSc, PhD, MA, BLitt, 21 Valenciennes Road, Sittingbourne, Kent, ME10 1EN.

Baker, J. H., LLD, FBA, St Catharine's College, Cambridge CB2 1RL.

Baker, L. G. D., MA, BLitt, 5 Allendale, Southwater, Horsham, West Sussex RH13 7UE.

Baker, T. F. T., BA, Camden Lodge, 50 Hastings Road, Pembury, Kent.

Ball, A. W., BA, 71 Cassiobury Park Avenue, Watford, Herts. WD1 7LD.

Ballhatchet, Professor K. A., MA, PhD, 12 Park Lane, Richmond, Surrey TW9 2RA.

Banks, Professor J. A., MA, Dept of Sociology, The University, Leicester LE1 7RH.

Barber, M. C., BA, PhD, Dept of History, The University, Whiteknights, Reading, Berks. RG6 2AA.

Barber, R. W., MA, PhD, FSA, Stangrove Hall, Alderton, near Woodbridge, Suffolk IP12 3BL.

Barker, A. J., BA, MA, PhD, Dept of History, University of Western Australia, Nedlands, Western Australia 6009.

Barker, Professor T. C., MA, PhD, Minsen Dane, Brogdale Road, Faversham, Kent.

Barkley, Professor the Rev. J. M., MA, DD, 2 College Park, Belfast, N. Ireland.

*Barlow, Professor F., MA, DPhil, FBA, Middle Court Hall, Kenton, Exeter.

Barnard, T. C., MA, DPhil, Hertford College, Oxford OX1 3BW.

Barnes, Miss P. M., PhD, 6 Kings Yard, Kings Ride, Ascot, Berks. SL5 8AH.

Barnett, Correlli, MA, Catbridge House, Rast Carleton, Norwich, Norfolk.

Barratt, Miss D. M., DPhil, The Corner House, Hampton Poyle, Kidlington, Oxford.

Barratt, Professor G. R. de V., PhD, 197 Belmont Avenue, Ottawa, Canada K1S OV7.

Barron, Mrs C. M., MA, PhD, 35 Rochester Road, London NW1.

Barrow, Professor G. W. S., MA, BLitt, DLitt, FBA, FRSE, 12a Lauder Road, Edinburgh EH9 2EL.

Bartlett, Professor C. J., PhD, Dept of Modern History, The University, Dundee DD1 4HN.

Bartlett, Professor R. J. MA, DPhil, Dept of History, University of Chicago, 1126 East 59th Street, Chicago, Illinois 60637, U.S.A.

Bates, D., PhD, Dept of History, University College, P.O. Box 78, Cardiff CF1 1XL.

Batho, Professor G. R., MA, Fivestones, 3 Archery Rise, Durham DH1 4LA.

Baugh, Professor Daniel A., PhD, Dept of History, McGraw Hall, Cornell University, Ithaca, N.Y. 14853, U.S.A.

Baxter, Professor S. B., PhD, 608 Morgan Creek Road, Chapel Hill, N.C. 27514, U.S.A.

Baylen, Professor J. O., MA, PhD, 45 Saffron Court, Compton Place Road, Eastbourne, E. Sussex, BN21 1DY.

Beachey, Professor R. W., BA, PhD, 1 Rookwood, De La Warr Road, Milford-on-Sea, Hampshire.

Beales, Professor D. E. D., MA, PhD, LittD, Sidney Sussex College, Cambridge CB2 3HU.

Bealey, Professor F., BSc(Econ), Dept of Politics, The University, Taylor Building, Old Aberdeen AB9 2UB.

Bean, Professor J. M. W., MA, DPhil, 622 Fayerweather Hall, Columbia University, New York, N.Y. 10027, U.S.A.

Beardwood, Miss Alice, BA, BLitt, DPhil, 415 Miller's Lane, Wynnewood, Pa, U.S.A.

Beasley, Professor W. G., PhD, FBA, 172 Hampton Road, Twickenham, Middlesex TW2 5NJ.

Beattie, Professor J. M., PhD, Dept of History, University of Toronto, Toronto Canada, M5S 1A1.

Beauroy, Dr Jacques M., 15 Avenue Marie-Amélie, Chantilly, France 60500.

Bebbington, D. W., MA, PhD, 5 Pullar Avenue, Bridge of Allan, Stirling FK9 4TB.

Beckerman, John S., PhD, 225 Washington Avenue, Hamden, Ct. 06518, U.S.A.

Beckett, I. F. W., BA, PhD, Cottesloe House, The Dene, Hindon, Wiltshire SP3 6EE.

Beckett, Professor J. C., MA, 19 Wellington Park Terrace, Belfast 9, N. Ireland.

Beckett, J. V., BA, PhD, Dept of History, The University, Nottingham NG7 2RD.

Bedarida, Professor F., 13 rue Jacob, Paris 75006, France.

Beddard, R. A., MA, DPhil, Oriel College, Oxford OX1 4EW.

*Beer, E. S. de, CBE, MA, DLitt, FBA, FSA, Stoke House, Stoke Hammond MK17 9BN.

Beer, Professor Samuel H., PhD, Faculty of Arts & Sciences, Harvard University, Littauer Center G-15, Cambridge, Mass. 02138, U.S.A.

Belchem, J. C., BA, DPhil, Dept of History, The University, 8 Abercromby Square, Liverpool L69 3BX.

Bell, A., Rhodes House Library, Oxford OX2 7RU.

Bell, P. M. H., BA, BLitt, School of History, The University, P.O. Box 147, Liverpool L69 3BX.

Bellenger, Dominic T. J. A., MA, PhD, Downside Abbey, Stratton-on-the-Fosse, Bath BA3 4RH.

Beloff, Lord, DLitt, FBA, Flat No. 9, 22 Lewes Crescent, Brighton BN2 1GB.

Benedikz, B. S., MA, PhD, Main Library, University of Birmingham, P.O. Box 363, Birmingham B15 2TT.

Bennett, M. J., BA, PhD, History Dept, University of Tasmania, Box 252C, G.P.O., Hobart, Tasmania 7001, Australia.

Benson, Professor J., BA, MA, PhD, The Polytechnic, Wolverhampton, West Midlands, WV1 1LY.

Bentley, M., BA, PhD, Dept of History, The University, Sheffield S10 2TN.

Berghahn, Professor V. R., MA, PhD, Dept of History, University of Warwick, Coventry CV4 7AL.

Bergin, J., MA, PhD, Dept of History, The University, Manchester M13 9PL.

Bernard, G. W., MA, DPhil, 92 Bassett Green Village, Southampton.

Bhila, Professor H. H. K., BA, MA, PhD, Parliament of Zimbabwe, Box 8055, Causeway, Harare, Zimbabwe.

Biddiss, Professor M. D., MA, PhD, Dept of History, The University, Whiteknights, Reading RG6 2AA.

Bidwell, Brigadier R. G. S., OBE, 8 Chapel Lane, Wickham Market, Wood-bridge, Suffolk IP13 0SD.

Bill, E. G. W., MA, DLitt, Lambeth Palace Library, London SE1.

Biller, P. P. A., MA, DPhil, Dept of History, The University, Heslington, York YO1 5DD.

Binfield, J. C. G., MA, PhD, 22 Whiteley Wood Road, Sheffield S11 7FE.

Birch, A., MA, PhD, University of Hong Kong, Hong Kong.

Birke, Professor A. M., DPhil, DPhil-Habil, German Historical Institute, 17 Bloomsbury Square, London WC1A 2LP.

Bishop, A. S., BA, PhD, 44 North Acre, Banstead, Surrey SM7 2EG.

Bishop, T. A. M., MA, 16 Highbury Road, London SW19 7PR.

Black, Professor Eugene C., PhD, Dept of History, Brandeis University, Waltham, Mass. 02154, U.S.A.

Black, J. M. PhD, 3 Roseworth Crescent, Gosforth, Newcastle NE3 1NR.

Black, R. D., BA PhD, School of History, The University, Leeds LS2 9JT.

Blackbourn, D., MA, PhD, Dept of History, Birkbeck College, Malet Street, London WC1E 7HX.

Blackwood, B. G., BA, BLitt, DPhil, 4 Knights Close, Felixstowe, Suffolk IP11 9NU.

Blake, E. O., MA, PhD, Roselands, Moorhill Road, Westend, Southampton SO3 3AW.

Blake, Lord, MA, FBA, Riverview House, Brundall, Norwich NR13 5LA.

Blakemore, H., PhD, 43 Fitzjohn Avenue, Barnet, Herts, EN5 2HN.

*Blakey, Professor R. G., PhD, c/o Mr Raymond Shove, Order Dept, Library, University of Minnesota, Minneapolis 14, Minn., U.S.A.

Blanning, T. W. C., MA, PhD, Sidney Sussex College, Cambridge CB2 3HU.

Blewett, Hon Dr N., BA, DipEd, MA, DPhil, 68 Barnard Street, North Adelaide, South Australia 5006.

Blinkhorn, RM., BA, AM, DPhil, Dept of History, The University, Bailrigg, Lancaster LA1 4YG.

Blomfield, Mrs K., 8 Elmdene Court, Constitution Hill, Woking, Surrey GU22 7SA.

Board, Mrs Beryl A., The Old School House, Stow Maries, Chelmsford, Essex CM3 6SL.

*Bolsover, G. H., OBE, MA, PhD, 7 Devonshire Road, Hatch End, Middle-sex HA5 4LY.

Bolton, Brenda, M., BA, Dept of History, Westfield College, Kidderpore Avenue, London NW3 7ST.

Bolton, Professor G. C., MA, DPhil, Dept of History, Murdoch University, Murdoch, W. Australia 6150.

Bolton, J. L. BA, BLitt, Dept of History, Queen Mary College, Mile End Road, London E1 4NS.

Bond, Professor B. J., BA, MA, Dept of War Studies, King's College, Strand, London WC2R 2LS.

Bonney, Professor R. J., MA. DPhil, Dept of History, The University, Leicester LE1 7RH.

Booker, J. M. L., BA, MLitt, DPhil, Braxted Place, Little Braxted, Witham, Essex CM8 3LD.

Boon, G. C., BA, FSA, FRNS, National Museum of Wales, Cardiff CF1 3NP.

Borrie, M. A. F., BA, The British Library, Dept of Manuscripts, Great Russell Street, London WC1B 3DG.

Bossy, Professor J. A., MA, PhD, Dept of History, University of York, Heslington, York YO1 5DD.

Bottigheimer, Professor Karl S., Dept of History, State University of New York, Stony Brook, Long Island, N.Y., U.S.A.

Bourne, J. M., BA, PhD., 33 St. John's Road, Selly Park, Birmingham B29 7EP.

Bourne, Professor K., BA, PhD, FBA, London School of Economics, Houghton Street, Aldwych, London WC2A 2AE.

Bowker, Mrs M., MA, BLitt, 14 Bowers Croft, Cambridge CB1 4RP.

Bowyer, M. J. F., 32 Netherhall Way, Cambridge.

*Boxer, Professor C. R., DLitt, FBA, Ringshall End, Little Gaddesden, Berkhamsted, Herts.

Boyce, D. G., BA, PhD, Dept of Political Theory and Government, University College of Swansea, Swansea SA2 8PP.

Boyle, T., Cert.Ed, BA, MPhil, Jersey Cottage, Mark Beech, Edenbridge, Kent TN8 5NS.

Boynton, L. O. J., MA, DPhil, FSA, Dept of History, Westfield College, London NW3 7ST.

Brading, D. A., MA, PhD, 28 Storey Way, Cambridge.

Bradshaw, Rev. B., MA, BD, PhD, Queens' College, Cambridge CB3 9ET.

Brake, Rev. G. Thompson, 61 Westwood Gardens, Hadleigh, Benfleet, Essex SS7 2SH.

Brand, P. A., MA, DPhil, 155 Kennington Road, London SE11.

Brandon, P. F., BA, PhD, Greensleeves, 8 St Julian's Lane, Shoreham-by-Sea, Sussex BN4 6YS.

Bray, Jennifer R., MA, PhD, 99 Benthall Road, London N16.

Breck, Professor A. D., MA, PhD, LHD, DLitt, University of Denver, Denver, Colorado 80210, U.S.A.

Breen, Professor T. H., PhD, Dept of History, North Western University, Evanston, Illinois 60208, U.S.A.

Brentano, Professor R., DPhil, University of California, Berkeley 4, Calif., U.S.A.

Brett, M., MA, DPhil, Robinson College, Cambridge CB3 9AN.

Breuilly, J. J., BA, DPhil, Dept of History, The University, Manchester M13 9PL.

Bridge, C. R., BA, PhD, Institute of Commonwealth Studies, 27-28 Russell Square, London WC1B 5DS.

Bridge, F. R., PhD, The Poplars, Rodley Lane, Rodley, Leeds.

Bridges, R. C., BA, PhD, Dept of History, University of Aberdeen, King's College, Aberdeen AB9 2UB.

Brigden, Susan, BA, PhD, MA, Lincoln College Oxford, OX1 3DR.

Briggs, Lord, BSc(Econ), MA, DLitt, FBA, Worcester College, Oxford OX1 2HB.

Briggs, J. H. Y., MA, Dept of History, The University, Keele, Staffs. ST5 5BG.

Briggs, R., MA, All Souls College, Oxford OX1 4AL.

Britnell, R. H., MA, PhD, Dept. of History, The University, 43-46 North Bailey, Durham, DH1 3EX.

Broad, J., BA, DPhil, Dept of History, Polytechnic of North London, Prince of Wales Road, London NW5 3LB.

Broadhead, P. J., BA, PhD, Dept of History, Goldsmiths' College, Lewisham Way, London SE14 6NW.

Brock, M. G., MA, Nuffield College, Oxford OX1 1NF.

Brock, Professor W. R., MA, PhD, 49 Barton Road, Cambridge CB3 9LG.

Brocklesby, R., BA, The Elms, North Eastern Road, Thorne, Doncaster, S. Yorks. DN8 4AS.

Brogan, D. H. V., MA, Dept of History, University of Essex, Wivenhoe Park, Colchester CO4 3SQ.

*Brooke, Professor C. N. L., MA, LittD, FBA, FSA, Faculty of History, West Road, Cambridge CB3 9EF.

Brooke, Mrs R. B., MA, PhD, c/o Faculty of History, West Road, Cambridge CB3 9EF.

Brooks, C. W., AB, DPhil, Dept of History, The University, 43 North Bailey, Durham, DH1 3EX.

Brooks, Professor N. P., MA, DPhil, Dept of Medieval History, The University, Birmingham B15 2TT.

Brown, Professor A. L., MA, DPhil, Dept of History, The University, Glasgow G12 8QQ.

Brown, The Rev. A. W. G., BA, BD, PhD, The Manse, 28 Quay Road, Ballycastle, Co. Antrin BT54 6BH.

Brown, G. S., PhD, 1720 Hanover Road, Ann Arbor, Mich. 48103, U.S.A.

Brown, Judith M., MA, PhD, 8 The Downs, Cheadle, Cheshire SK8 1JL.

Brown, K. D., BA, MA, PhD, Dept of Economic and Social History, The Queen's University, Belfast BT7 1NN, N. Ireland.

Brown, Professor M. J., MA, PhD, 350 South Candler Street, Decatur, Georgia 30030, U.S.A.

Brown, P. D., MA, 18 Davenant Road, Oxford OX2 8BX.

Brown, P. R. L., MA, FBA, Hillslope, Pullen's Lane, Oxford.

Brown, R. A., MA, DPhil, DLitt, FSA, King's College, Strand, London WC2R 2LS.

Brown, T. S., MA, PhD, Dept of History, The University, William Robertson Building, 50 George Square, Edinburgh, EH8 9JY.

Brown, Professor Wallace, PhD, Dept of History, University of New Brunswick, P.O. Box 4400, Fredericton, NB., Canada E3B 5AE.

Bruce, J. M., ISO, MA, FRAeS, 51 Chiltern Drive, Barton-on-Sea, New Milton, Hants. BH25 7JZ.

Brundage, Professor J. A., Dept of History, University of Wisconsin at Milwaukee, Milwaukee, Wisconsin, U.S.A.

Bryson, Professor W. Hamilton, School of Law, University of Richmond, Richmond, Va. 23173, U.S.A.

Buchanan, R. A., MA, PhD, School of Humanities and Social Sciences, The University, Claverton Down, Bath BA2 7AY.

Buckland, P. J. B., MA, PhD, 6 Rosefield Road, Liverpool L25 8TF.

Bueno de Mesquita, D. M., MA, PhD, 283 Woodstock Road, Oxford OX2 7NY.

Buisseret, Professor D. J., MA, PhD, The Newberry Library, 60 West Walton Street, Chicago, Ill. 60610, U.S.A.

Bullock, Lord, MA, DLitt, FBA, St Catherine's College, Oxford OX1 3UJ.

Bullock-Davies, Constance, BA, PhD, Dept of Classics, University College of North Wales, Bangor, Gwynedd LL57 2DG.

Bullough, Professor D. A., MA, FSA, Dept of Mediaeval History, The University, 71 South Street, St Andrews, Fife KY16 9AJ.

Bumsted, Professor J. M., PhD, St John's College, University of Manitoba, Winnipeg, Mb., Canada R3T 2MS.

Burke, U. P., MA, Emmanuel College, Cambridge CB2 3AP.

Burleigh, M., BA, PhD, Dept of History, Queen Mary College, Mile End Road, London E1 4NS.

BURNS, Professor J. H., MA, PhD, 6 Chiltern House, Hillcrest Road, London W5 1HL.

Burroughs, P., PhD, Dept of History, Dalhousie University, Halifax, Nova Scotia, Canada B3H 3J5.
Burrow, Professor J. W., MA., PhD, Sussex University, Falmer, Brighton BN1 9QX.
Butler, R. D'O., CMG, MA, DLitt, All Souls College, Oxford OX1 4AL.
Byerly, Professor B. F., BA, MA, PhD, Dept of History, University of Northern Colorado, Greeley, Colorado 80631, U.S.A.
Bythell, D., MA, DPhil, Dept of History, University of Durham, 43/46 North Bailey, Durham DH1 3EX.

Cabaniss, Professor J. A., PhD, University of Mississippi, Box No. 253, University, Mississippi 38677, U.S.A.
Callahan, Professor Raymond, PhD, Dept of History, University of Delaware, Newark, Delaware 19716, U.S.A.
Callahan, Professor Thomas, Jr., PhD, Dept of History, Rider College, Lawrenceville, N.J. 08648, U.S.A.
Calvert, Brigadier J. M. (ret.), DSO, MA, MICE, 33a Mill Hill Close, Haywards Heath, Sussex.
Calvert, Professor P. A. R., MA, PhD, AM, Dept of Politics, University of Southampton, Highfield, Southampton SO9 5NH.
Cameron, A., BA, 6 Braid Crescent, Morningside, Edinburgh EH10 6AU.
Cameron, Professor J. K., MA, BD, PhD, St Mary's College, University of St Andrews, Fife KY16 9JU.
Cameron, Professor K., PhD, FBA, Dept of English, The University, Nottingham NG7 2RD.
Campbell, Professor A. E., MA, PhD, 3 Belbroughton Road, Oxford, OX2 6UZ.
Campbell, J., MA, FBA, Worcester College, Oxford OX1 2HB.
*Campbell, Professor Mildred L., PhD, Vassar College, Poughkeepsie, N.Y., U.S.A.
Campbell, Professor R. H., MA, PhD, Craig, Glenluce, Newton Stewart, Wigtownshire DG8 0NR.
Cannadine, D. N., BA, DPhil, Christ's College, Cambridge CB2 3BU.
Canning, J. P., MA, PhD, Dept of History, University College of North Wales, Bangor, Gwynedd LL57 2DG.
Cannon, Professor J. A., CBE, MA, PhD, Dept of History, The University, Newcastle upon Tyne NE1 7RU.
Canny, Professor N. P., MA, PhD, Dept of History, University College, Galway, Ireland.
Cant, R. G., MA, DLitt, 3 Kinburn Place, St Andrews, Fife KY16 9DT.
Cantor, Professor N. F., PhD, Dept of History, New York University, 19 University Place, New York, N.Y. 10003, U.S.A.
Capp, B. S., MA, DPhil, Dept of History, University of Warwick, Coventry, Warwickshire CV4 7AL.
Carey, P. B. R., DPhil, Trinity College, Oxford OX1 3BH.
*Carlson, Leland H., PhD, Huntington Library, San Marino, California 91108, U.S.A.
Carlton, Professor Charles, Dept of History, North Carolina State University, Raleigh, N.C. 27607, U.S.A.
Carman, W. Y., FSA, 94 Mulgrave Road, Sutton, Surrey.
Carpenter, D. A., MA, DPhil, Dept of History, Queen Mary College, Mile End Road, London E1 4NS.
Carpenter, M. Christine, MA, PhD, New Hall, Cambridge CB3 0DF.

Carr, A. D., MA, PhD, Dept of Welsh History, University College of North Wales, Bangor, Gwynedd LL57 2DG.

Carr, Sir Raymond, MA, FBA, Burch, North Molton, South Molton, EX36 3JU.

Carr, W., PhD, 22 Southbourne Road, Sheffield S10 2QN.

Carrington, Miss Dorothy, 3 Rue Emmanuel Arene, 20 Ajaccio, Corsica.

Carter, Jennifer J., BA, PhD, The Old Schoolhouse, Glenbuchat, Strathdon, Aberdeenshire AB3 8TT.

Carwardine, R. J., MA, DPhil, Dept of History, The University, Sheffield S10 2TN.

Casey, J., BA, PhD, School of Modern Languages and European History, University of East Anglia, Norwich NR4 7TJ.

Cassels, Professor Alan, MA, PhD, Dept of History, McMaster University, Hamilton, Ontario, Canada L8S 4L9.

Catto, R. J. A. I., MA, Oriel College, Oxford OX1 4EW.

Cazel, Professor Fred A., Jr., Dept of History, University of Connecticut, Storrs, Conn. 06268, U.S.A.

Cell, Professor J. W., PhD, Dept of History, Duke University, Durham, NC 27706, U.S.A.

Chadwick, Professor W. O., OM, KBE, DD, DLitt, FBA, Selwyn Lodge, Cambridge CB3 9DQ.

Challis, C. E., MA, PhD, 14 Ashwood Villas, Headingley, Leeds 6.

Chalmers, C. D., Public Record Office, Ruskin Avenue, Kew, Richmond, Surrey TW9 4DU.

Chamberlain, Muriel E., MA. DPhil, Dept of History, University College of Swansea, Singleton Park, Swansea SA2 7BR.

Chambers, D. S., MA, DPhil, Warburg Institute, Woburn Square, London WC1H 0AB.

Chandaman, Professor C. D., BA, PhD, 23 Bellamy Close, Ickenham, Uxbridge UB10 8SJ.

Chandler, D. G., MA, Hindford, Monteagle Lane, Yateley, Camberley, Surrey.

Chaplais, P., PhD, FBA, FSA, Lew Lodge, Lew, Oxford OX8 2BE.

Chapman, Professor R.A., BA, MA, PhD, FBIM, Dept of Politics, The University, 48 Old Elvet, Durham, DH1 3LZ.

Charles-Edwards, T. M., DPhil, Corpus Christi College, Oxford OX1 4JF.

Charmley, J., MA, DPhil, School of English and American Studies, University of East Anglia, Norwich NR4 7TJ.

Chaudhuri, Professor Kirti Narayan, BA, PhD, History Department, S.O.A.S., University of London, Malet Street, London WC1E 7HD.

Cheney, Mrs Mary, MA, 17 Westberry Court, Grange Road, Cambridge CB3 9BG.

Cherry, John, MA, 58 Lancaster Road, London N4.

Chibnall, Mrs Marjorie, MA, DPhil, FBA, 7 Croftgate, Fulbrooke Road, Cambridge CB3 9EG.

Child, C. J., OBE, MA, PhD, 94 Westhall Road, Warlingham, Surrey CR3 9HB.

Childs, J. C. R., BA, PhD, School of History, The University, Leeds LS2 9JT.

Childs, Wendy R., MA, PhD, School of History, The University, Leeds LS2 9JT.

Chitnis, Anand Chidamber, BA, MA, PhD, Dept of History, The University, Stirling FK9 4LA.

Christiansen, E., New College, Oxford OX1 3BN.

Christianson, Assoc. Professor P. K., PhD, Dept of History, Queen's University, Kingston, Ontario K7L 3N6, Canada.

Christie, Professor I. R., MA, FBA, 10 Green Lane, Croxley Green, Herts. WD3 3HR.

Church, Professor R. A., BA, PhD, School of Social Studies, University of East Anglia, Norwich NOR 88C.

Cirket, A. F., 71 Curlew Crescent, Bedford.

Clanchy, M. T., MA, PhD, FSA, 28 Hillfield Road, London NW6 1PZ.

Clark, A. E., MA, 32 Durham Avenue, Thornton Cleveleys, Blackpool FY5 2DP.

Clark, D. S. T., BA, PhD, Dept of History, University College of Swansea, Swansea SA2 8PP.

Clark, J. C. D., MA, PhD, All Souls College, Oxford OX1 4AL.

Clark, P. A., MA, Dept of Economic and Social History, The University, Leicester LE1 7RH.

Clarke, Howard B., BA, PhD, Room K104, Arts-Commerce-Law Building, University College, Dublin 4, Ireland.

Clarke, P. F., MA, PhD, St John's College, Cambridge CB2 1TP.

Clementi, Miss D., MA, DPhil, Flat 7, 43 Rutland Gate, London SW7 1BP.

Clemoes, Professor P. A. M., BA, PhD, Emmanuel College, Cambridge CB2 3AP.

Cliffe, J. T., BA, PhD, 263 Staines Road, Twickenham, Middx. TW2 5AY.

Clive, Professor J. L., PhD, 38 Fernald Drive, Cambridge, Mass. 02138, U.S.A.

Clough, C. H., MA, DPhil, FSA, School of History, The University, P.O. Box 147, Liverpool L69 3BX.

Cobb, H. S., MA, FSA, 1 Child's Way, London NW11.

Cobban, A. B., MA, PhD, School of History, The University, P.O. Box 147, Liverpool L69 3BX.

Cockburn, Professor J. S., LLB, LLM, PhD, History Dept, University of Maryland, College Park, Maryland 20742, U.S.A.

Cocks, E. J., MA, Middle Lodge, Ardingly, Haywards Heath, Sussex RH17 6TS.

Cohn, H. J., MA, DPhil, Dept of History, University of Warwick, Coventry CV4 7AL.

Cohn, Professor N. R. C., MA, DLitt, FBA, Orchard Cottage, Wood End, Ardeley, Herts. SG2 7AZ.

Cole, Maija J., BA, MA, PhD, 117 Glen Parkway, Hamden, Conn. 06517, U.S.A.

Coleman, B. I., MA, PhD, Dept of History, The University, Exeter EX4 4QH.

Coleman, C. H. D., MA, Dept of History, University College London, Gower Street, London WC1E 6BT.

Coleman, Professor D. C., BSc(Econ.), PhD, LittD, FBA, Over Hall, Cavendish, Sudbury, Suffolk.

Coleman, Professor F. L., MA, PhD, Dept of Economics & Economic History, Rhodes University, P.O. Box 94, Grahamstown 6140, S. Africa.

Colley, Professor Linda J., BA, MA, PhD, Dept of History, Yale University, PO Box 1504A, Yale Station, New Haven, Connecticut 06520-7425, U.S.A.

Collier, W. O., MA, FSA, 34 Berwyn Road, Richmond, Surrey.

Collinge, J. M., BA, 36 Monks Road, Enfield, Middlesex EN2 8BH.

Collini, S. A., MA, PhD, Dept of History, The University, Falmer, Brighton, Sussex BN1 9QX.

Collins, B. W., MA, PhD, Dept of Modern History, The University, Glasgow G12 8QQ.

Collins, Mrs I., MA, BLitt, School of History, The University, P.O. Box 147, Liverpool L69 3BX.

Collinson, Professor P., MA, PhD, FBA, Dept of History, The University, Sheffield ST10 2TN.

Colvin, H. M., CBE, MA, FBA, St John's College, Oxford OX1 3JP.

Colyer, R. J., BSc, PhD, Inst. of Rural Sciences, University College of Wales, Aberystwyth, Dyfed.

Congreve, A. L., MA, FSA, Galleons Lap, Sissinghurst, Kent TN17 2JG.

Connell-Smith, Professor G. E., PhD, 7 Braids Walk, Kirkella, Hull, Yorks. HU10 7PA.

Connolly, Sean J., BA, DPhil, Dept of History, University of Ulster, Coleraine, Northern Ireland BT52 1SA.

Constantine, S., BA, DPhil, Dept of History, The University, Bailrigg, Lancaster LA1 4YG.

Contamine, Professor P., DèsL., 12 Villa Croix-Nivert, 75015 Paris, France.

Conway, Professor A. A., MA, University of Canterbury, Christchurch 1, New Zealand.

Conway, S. R., BA, PhD, The Bentham Project, Dept of History, University College London, London WC1E 6BT.

Cook, C. P., MA, DPhil, Dept of History, The Polytechnic of North London, Prince of Wales Road, London NW5 3LB.

Cooke, Professor, J. J., PhD., Dept of History, University of Mississippi, College of Liberal Arts, University, Miss. 38677, U.S.A.

Coolidge, Professor R. T., MA, BLitt, History Dept, Loyola Campus, Concordia University, 7141 Sherbrooke Street West, Montreal, Quebec Canada H4B 1R6.

Cooper, Janet M., MA, PhD, 7 Stonepath Drive, Hatfield Peverel, Chelmsford CM3 2LG.

Cope, Professor Esther S., PhD, Dept of History, Univ. of Nebraska, Lincoln, Neb. 68508, U.S.A.

Copley, A. R.H., MA, MPhil, Rutherford College, The University, Canterbury, Kent CT2 7NX.

Corfield, Penelope J., MA, PhD, Dept of History, Royal Holloway and Bedford New College, Egham, Surrey TW20 0EX.

Cornell, Professor Paul G., PhD, 202 Laurier Place, Waterloo, Ontario, Canada N2L 1K8.

Corner, D. J., BA, Dept of History, St Salvator's College, The University, St Andrews, Fife KY16 9AJ.

Cornford, Professor J. P., MA, The Brick House, Wicken Bonhunt, Saffron Walden, Essex CB11 3UG.

Cornwall, J. C. K., MA, 1 Orchard Close, Copford Green, Colchester, Essex.

Corson, J. C., MA, PhD, Mossrig, Lilliesleaf, Melrose, Roxburghshire.

Cosgrove, A. J., BA, PhD, Dept of Medieval History, University College, Dublin 4, Ireland.

Coss, P. R., BA, PhD, 20 Whitebridge Close, Whitebridge Grove, Gosforth, Newcastle upon Tyne NE3 2DN.

Costeloe, Professor M. P., BA, PhD, Dept of Hispanic and Latin American Studies, The University, 83 Woodland Road, Bristol BS8 1RJ.

Countryman, E. F., PhD, Dept of History, University of Warwick, Coventry CV4 7AL.

Cowan, I. B., MA, PhD, Dept of History, University of Glasgow, Glasgow G12 8QQ.

Coward, B., BA, PhD, Dept of History, Birkbeck College, Malet Street, London WC1E 7HX.

Cowdrey, Rev. H. E. J., MA, St Edmund Hall, Oxford OX1 4AR.

Cowie, Rev. L. W., MA, PhD, 38 Stratton Road, Merton Park, London SW19 3JG.

Cowley, F. G., PhD, 17 Brookvale Road, West Cross, Swansea, W. Glam.

Cox, D. C., BA, PhD, 12 Oakfield Road, Copthorne, Shrewsbury SY3 8AA.

Craig, R. S., BSc(Econ), The Anchorage, Bay Hill, St Margarets Bay, nr Dover, Kent CT15 6DU.

Cramp, Professor Rosemary, MA, BLitt, FSA, Department of Archaeology, 46 Saddler Street, Durham DH1 3NU.

Crampton, R. J., BA, PhD, Rutherford College, The University, Canterbury, Kent CT2 7NP.

Cranfield, L. R., Lot 2, Selby Avenue, Warrandyte, Victoria, Australia 3113.

Craton, Professor M. J., BA, MA, PhD, Dept of History, University of Waterloo, Waterloo, Ontario, Canada N2L 3G1.

Crawford, Patricia M., BA, MA, PhD, Dept of History, University of Western Australia, Nedlands, Western Australia 6009.

*Crawley, C. W., MA, 1 Madingley Road, Cambridge.

Cremona, His Hon Chief Justice Professor J. J., KM, DLitt, PhD, LLD, DrJur, 5 Victoria Gardens, Sliema, Malta.

Cressy, D. A., 231 West Sixth Street, Claremont, Calif. 91711, U.S.A.

Crimmin, Patricia K., MPhil, BA, Dept of History, Royal Holloway and Bedford New College, Egham Hill, Egham, Surrey TW20 0EX.

Crisp, Professor Olga, BA, PhD, 'Zarya', 1 Milbrook, Esher, Surrey.

Croft, Pauline, MA, DPhil, Dept of History, Royal Holloway and Bedford New College, Egham Hill, Egham, Surrey TW20 0EX.

Crombie, A. C., BSc, MA, PhD, Trinity College, Oxford OX1 3BH.

Cromwell, Miss V., MA, Arts Building, University of Sussex, Brighton, Sussex BN1 9QN.

Crook, D., MA, PhD, Public Record Office, Chancery Lane, London WC2A 1LR.

Crosby, Professor T. L., Dept of History, Wheaton College, Norton, Mass., 02766 USA.

Cross, Professor Claire, MA, PhD, Dept of History, The University, York YO1 5DD.

Crossick, G. J., MA, PhD, Dept of History, University of Essex, Wivenhoe Park, Colchester CO4 3SQ.

Crouch, D. B., PhD, 17c St Johns Grove, Archway, London N19 5RW.

Crowder, Professor C. M. D., DPhil, Queen's University, Kingston, Ontario, Canada K7L 3N6.

Crowder, Professor M., MA, Dept of History, University of Botswana, P.B. 0022, Gaborone, Botswana.

Crowe, Miss S. E., MA, PhD, 112 Staunton Road, Headington, Oxford.

Crozier, A. J., BA, MA, PhD, Bro Wen, 85 Upper Garth Road, Bangor, Gwynedd LL57 2SS.

Cruickshank, C. G., MA, DPhil, 15 McKay Road, Wimbledon Common, London SW20.

Cruickshanks, Eveline G., PhD, 46 Goodwood Court, Devonshire Street, London W1N 1SL.

Cumming, Professor A., MA, DipMA, PGCE, PhD, Centre for Education Studies, University of New England, Armidale, Australia 2351.

Cumming, I., MEd, PhD, 672a South Titirangi Road, Titirangi, Auckland, New Zealand.

Cummins, Professor J. S., PhD, University College London, Gower Street, London WC1E 6BT.

Cumpston, Miss I. M., MA, DPhil, 18 Fuller Street, Deakin, Canberra 2600, Australia.

Cunliffe, Professor M. F., MA, BLitt, DHL, Room 102, T Building, George Washington University, 2110 G. Street N.W., Washington, D.C., 20052, U.S.A.

Cunningham, Professor A. B., MA, PhD, Simon Fraser University, Burnaby 2, B.C., Canada.

Currie, C. R. J., MA, DPhil, Institute of Historical Research, Senate House, Malet Street, London WC1E 7HU.

Currie, R., MA, DPhil, Wadham College, Oxford OX1 3PN.

Curry, Anne E., BA, MA, PhD, 5 Melrose Avenue, Reading, Berkshire RG6 2BN.

Curtis, Professor L. Perry, Jr, PhD, Dept of History, Brown University, Providence, R.I. 02912, U.S.A.

*Cuttino, G. P., DPhil, FBA, FSA, 1270 University Dr. N. E., Atlanta, Ga. 30306, U.S.A.

Cuttler, S. H., BPhil, DPhil, 5051 Clanranald #302, Montreal, Quebec, Canada H3X 2S3.

*Dacre, Lord, MA, FBA, Peterhouse, Cambridge CB2 1RD.

Dakin, Professor D., MA, PhD, 20 School Road, Apperley, Gloucester GL19 4DJ.

Das Gupta, A., MA, PhD, National Library, Belvedere, Calcutta, India 700027.

DAUNTON, M. J., BA, PhD (Hon. Treasurer), Dept of History, University College London, Gower Street, London WC1E 6BT.

Davenport, Professor T. R. H., MA, PhD, Dept of History, Rhodes University, P.O. Box 94, Grahamstown 6140, South Africa.

Davenport-Hines, R. P. T., PhD, BA, 51 Elsham Road, London W14 8HD.

Davidson, R., MA, PhD, Dept of Economic and Social History, The University, 50 George Square, Edinburgh EH8 9JY.

Davies, C. S. L., MA, DPhil, Wadham College, Oxford OX1 3PN.

Davies, Canon E. T., BA, MA, 11 Tŷ Brith Gardens, Usk, Gwent.

Davies, I. N. R., MA, DPhil, 22 Rowland Close, Wolvercote, Oxford.

Davies, P. N., MA, PhD, Cmar, Croft Drive, Caldy, Wirral, Merseyside.

Davies, R. G., MA, PhD, Dept of History, The Victoria University of Manchester, Oxford Road, Manchester M13 9PL.

Davies, Professor R. R., BA, DPhil, University College of Wales, Dept of History, 1 Laura Place, Aberystwyth SY23 2AU.

Davies, Professor Wendy, BA, PhD, Dept of History, University College London, Gower Street, London WC1E 6BT.

*Davis, G. R. C., CBE, MA, DPhil, FSA, 214 Somerset Road, London SW19 5JE.

Davis, J. A., MA, DPhil, Dept of History, University of Warwick, Coventry CV4 7AL.

Davis, Professor J. C., Dept of History, Massey University, Palmerston North, New Zealand.

Davis, Professor R. H. C., MA, FBA, FSA, 349 Banbury Road, Oxford OX2 7PL.

Davis, Professor Richard W., Dept of History, Washington University, St Louis, Missouri 63130, U.S.A.

*Dawe, D. A., 46 Green Lane, Purley, Surrey.

Deane, Professor Phyllis M., MA, 4 Stukeley Close, Cambridge CB3 9LT.

*Deeley, Miss A. P., MA, 41 Linden Road, Bicester, Oxford.

de Hamel, C. F. R., BA, DPhil, FSA, Chase House, Perry's Chase, Greenstead Road, Ongar, Essex CM5 9LA.

de la Mare, Miss A. C., MA, PhD, Bodleian Library, Oxford.

Denham, E. W., MA, 4 The Ridge, 89 Green Lane, Northwood, Middx. HA6 1AE.

Dennis, P. J., MA, PhD, Dept of History, University College, University of New South Wales, Australian Defence Force Academy, Campbell, A.C.T. 2600, Australia.

Denton, J. H., BA, PhD, Dept of History, The University, Manchester M13 9PL.

Devine, T. M., BA, Viewfield Cottage, 55 Burnbank Road, Hamilton, Strathclyde Region.

Dewey, P. E., BA, PhD, Dept of History, Royal Holloway and Bedford New College, Egham Hill, Egham, Surrey TW20 0EX.

DICKENS, Professor A. G., CMG, MA, DLit, DLitt, LittD, FBA, FSA, Institute of Historical Research, University of London, Senate House, London WC1E 7HU.

Dickinson, Professor H. T., BA, MA, PhD, Dept of Modern History, The University, Edinburgh EH8 9YL.

Dickinson, Rev. J. C., MA, DLitt, FSA, Yew Tree Cottage, Barngarth, Cartmel, South Cumbria.

Dickson, P. G. M., MA, DPhil, St Catherine's College, Oxford, OX1 3UJ.

Dilks, Professor D. N., BA, Dept of International History, The University, Leeds LS2 9JT.

Dilworth, Rev. G. M., OSB, MA, PhD, Scottish Catholic Archives, Columba House, 16 Drummond Place, Edinburgh EH3 6PL.

Dinwiddy, J. R., PhD, Dept of History, Royal Holloway and Bedford New College, Egham Hill, Egham, Surrey TW20 0EX.

Ditchfield, G. McC, BA, PhD, Darwin College, University of Kent, Canterbury, Kent CT2 7NY.

Dobson, Professor R. B., MA, DPhil, Dept of History, The University, Heslington, York YO1 5DD.

Dockrill, M. L., MA, BSc(Econ), PhD, Dept of History, King's College London, Strand, London WC2R 2LS.

*Dodwell, Miss B., MA, The University, Reading RG6 2AH.

Dodwell, Professor C. R., MA, PhD, FSA, History of Art Department, The University, Manchester M13 9PL.

Don Peter, The Rt Revd Monsignor W. L. A., MA, PhD, Aquinas University College, Colombo 8, Sri Lanka.

Donahue, Professor Charles, Jr, AB, LLB, Dept of Law, Harvard University, Cambridge, Mass. 02138, U.S.A.

*DONALDSON, Professor G., MA, PhD, DLitt, DLitt, FRSE, FBA, 6 Pan Ha', Dysart, Fife KY1 2TL.

Donaldson, Professor P. S., MA, PhD, Dept of Humanities, 14n-422, Massachusetts Institute of Technology, Cambridge, Mass. 02139, U.S.A.

*Donaldson-Hudson, Miss R., BA, (address unknown).

Donoughue, Lord, MA, DPhil, 7 Brookfield Park, London NW5 1ES.

Dore, R. N., MA, Holmrook, 19 Chapel Lane, Hale Barns, Altrincham, Cheshire WA15 0AB.

Dow, Frances D., MA, DPhil, Dept of History, University of Edinburgh, George Square, Edinburgh EH8 9JY.

Downer, L. J., MA, BA, LLB, 29 Roebuck Street, Red Hill, Canberra, Australia 2601.

Doyle, A. I., MA, PhD, University College, The Castle, Durham.

Doyle, Professor W., MA, DPhil, DrHC, Dept of History, The University, 13-15 Woodland Road, Bristol BS8 1TB.

Driver, J. T., MA, BLitt, PhD, 25 Abbot's Grange, Chester CH2 1AJ.

*Drus, Miss E., MA, 18 Brampton Tower, Bassett Avenue, Southampton SO1 7FB.

Duckham, Professor B. F., MA, Dept of History, St David's University College, Lampeter, Dyfed SA48 7ED.

Duffy, Michael, MA, DPhil, Dept of History and Archaeology, The University, Queen's Drive, Exeter EX4 4QH.

Duggan, Anne J., BA, PhD, Dept of History, Queen Mary College, Mile End Road, London E1 4NS.

Duggan, C., PhD, Dept of History, King's College London, Strand, London WC2R 2LS.

Dugmore, The Rev. Professor C. W., DD, Thame Cottage, The Street, Puttenham, Guildford, Surrey GU3 1AT.

Duke, A. C., MA, Dept of History, The University, Southampton SO9 5NH.

Dumville, D. N., MA, PhD, Dept of Anglo-Saxon, Norse and Celtic, University of Cambridge, 9 West Road, Cambridge CB3 9DP.

Dunbabin, Jean H., MA, DPhil, St Anne's College, Oxford OX2 6HS.

Dunbabin, J. P. D., MA, St Edmund Hall, Oxford OX1 4AR.

Duncan, Professor A. A. M., MA, Dept of History, The University, 9 University Gardens, Glasgow G12 8QQ.

Dunn, Professor R. S., PhD, Dept of History, The College, University of Pennsylvania, Philadelphia, 19104, Pa., U.S.A.

Dunning, R. W., BA, PhD, FSA, Musgrove Manor East, Barton Close, Taunton TA1 4RU.

Durack, Mrs I. A., MA, PhD, University of Western Australia, Nedlands, Western Australia 6009.

Durey, M. J., BA, DPhil, School of Social Inquiry, Murdoch University, Perth 6150, Western Australia.

Durie, A. J., MA, PhD, Dept of Economic History, Edward Wright Building, The University, Aberdeen AB9 2TY.

Durkan, J., MA, PhD, DLitt, Dept of Scottish History, The University, Glasgow G12 8QH.

Durston, C. G., MA, PhD, 49 Percy Street, Oxford.

Dusinberre, W. W., PhD, Dept of History, University of Warwick, Coventry CV4 7AL.

Dutton, D. J., BA, PhD, School of History, The University, P.O. Box 147, Liverpool L69 3BX.

Dyer, C. C., BA, PhD, School of History, The University, P.O. Box 363, Birmingham B15 2TT.

Dykes, D. W., MA, Cherry Grove, Welsh St Donats, nr Cowbridge, Glam. CF7 7SS.

Dyson, Professor K. H. F., BSc(Econ), MSc(Econ), PhD, Undergraduate School of European Studies, The University, Bradford BD7 1DP.

Earle, P., BSc(Econ), PhD, Dept of Economic History, London School of Economics, Houghton Street, London WC2A 2AE.

Eastwood, Rev. C. C., PhD, Heathview, Monks Lane, Audlem, Cheshire SW3 0HP.

Eckles, Professor R. B., PhD, Apt 2, 251 Brahan Blvd., San Antonio, Texas 78215, U.S.A.

Edbury, P. W., MA, PhD, Dept of History, University College, P.O. Box 78, Cardiff CF1 1XL.

Eddy, Rev. J. J., BA, DPhil, History Dept, The Research School of Social Sciences, The Australian National University, GPO Box 4, Canberra, A.C.T. 2601, Australia.

Ede, J. R., CB, MA, Palfreys, East Street, Drayton, Langport, Somerset TA10 0JZ.

Edmonds, Professor E. L., MA, PhD, University of Prince Edward Island, Charlottetown, Prince Edward Island, Canada.

Edwards, F. O., SJ, BA, FSA, 114 Mount Street, London W1Y 6AH.

Edwards, J. H., MA, DPhil, School of History, The University, P.O. Box 363, Birmingham B15 2TT.

Edwards, O. D., BA, Dept of History, William Robertson Building, The University, George Square, Edinburgh EH8 9YL.

Edwards, Professor R. W. D., MA, PhD, DLitt, 21 Brendan Road, Donnybrook, Dublin 4, Ireland.

Ehrman, J. P. W., MA, FBA, FSA, The Mead Barns, Taynton, Nr Burford, Oxfordshire OX8 5UH.

Eisenstein, Professor Elizabeth L., PhD, 82 Kalorama Circle N.W., Washington D.C. 20008, U.S.A.

Eldridge, C. C., PhD, Dept of History, Saint David's University College, Lampeter, Dyfed SA48 7ED.

Eley, G. H., BA, DPhil, MA, MA, Dept of History, University of Michigan, Ann Arbor, Michigan 48109, U.S.A.

Elliott, Professor J. H., MA, PhD, FBA, The Institute for Advanced Studies, Princeton, New Jersey 08540, U.S.A.

Elliott, Marianne, BA, DPhil, Dept of History, The University, P.O. Box 147, Liverpool L69 3BX.

Ellis, G. J., MA, DPhil, Hertford College, Oxford OX1 3BW.

Ellis, R. H., MA, FSA, Cloth Hill, 6 The Mount, London NW3.

Ellis, S. G., BA, MA, PhD, Dept of History, University College, Galway, Ireland.

Ellsworth, Professor Edward W., AB, AM, PhD, 27 Englewood Avenue, Brookline, Mass. 02146, U.S.A.

Ellul, M., BArch, DipArch, 'Pauline', 55 Old Railway Road, Birkirkara, Malta.

Elrington, C. R., MA, FSA, Institute of Historical Research, Senate House, Malet Street, London WC1E 7HU.

ELTON, Professor Sir Geoffrey, MA, PhD, LittD, DLitt, DLitt, DLit, FBA, 30 Millington Road, Cambridge CB3 9HP.

Elvin, L., FSA, FRSA, 10 Almond Avenue, Swanpool, Lincoln LN6 0HB.

*Emmison, F. G., MBE, PhD, DUniv, FSA, 8 Coppins Close, Chelmsford, Essex CM2 6AY.

Emsley, C., BA, MLitt, Arts Faculty, The Open University, Walton Hall, Milton Keynes MK7 6AA.

Emy, Professor H. V., PhD, Dept of Politics, Monash University, Wellington Road, Clayton, Melbourne 3146, Australia.

English, Barbara A., MA, PhD, FSA, Centre of Regional and Local History, Loten Building, The University, Hull, HU6 7RX.

Erickson, Charlotte, J., PhD, 8 High Street, Chesterton, Cambridge CB4 1NG.

*Erith, E. J., Shurlock House, Shurlock Row, Berkshire.

Erskine, Mrs A. M., MA, BLitt, FSA, 44 Birchy Barton Hill, Exeter EX1 3EX.

Evans, Mrs A. K. B., PhD, FSA, White Lodge, 25 Knighton Grange Road, Leicester LE2 2LF.

Evans, E. J., MA, PhD, Dept of History, Furness College, University of Lancaster, Bailrigg, Lancaster LA1 4YG.

Evans, Gillian R., PhD, Sidney Sussex College, Cambridge CB2 3HU.

Evans, R. J., MA, DPhil, School of European Studies, University of East Anglia, Norwich NR4 7TJ.

Evans, R. J. W., MA, PhD, FBA, Brasenose College, Oxford OX1 4AJ.

Everitt, Professor A. M., MA, PhD, The University, Leicester LE1 7RH.

Eyck, Professor U. F. J., MA, BLitt, Dept of History, University of Calgary, 2500 University Drive NW, Calgary, Alberta, Canada T2N IN4.

Fage, Professor J. D., MA, PhD, Centre of West African Studies, The University, Birmingham B15 2TT.

Fairs, G. L., MA, Thornton House, Bear Street, Hay-on-Wye, Hereford HR3 5AN.

Falkus, M. E., BSc(Econ), Dept of History, London School of Economics, Houghton Street, London WC2A 2AE.

Farmer, D. F. H., BLitt, FSA, The University, Reading RG6 2AH.

Farr, M. W., MA, FSA, 12 Emscote Road, Warwick.

Fell, Professor C. E., MA, Dept of English, The University, Nottingham NG7 2RD.

Fellows-Jensen, Gillian M., BA, PhD, Københavns Universitets, Institut For Navneforskning, Njalsgade 80, DK-2300 København S, Denmark.

Fenlon, Rev. D. B., BA, PhD, Oscott College, Chester Road, Sutton Coldfield, West Midlands, B73 5AA.

Fenn, Rev. R. W. D., MA, BD, FSAScot, The Ditch, Bradnor View, Kington, Herefordshire.

Fennell, Professor J., MA, PhD, 8 Canterbury Road, Oxford OX2 6LU.

Ferguson, Professor A. B., PhD, Dept of History, Duke University, 6727 College Station, Durham, N.C. 27708, U.S.A.

Fernandez-Armesto, F. F. R., DPhil, River View, Headington Hill, Oxford.

Feuchtwanger, E. J., MA, PhD, Highfield House, Dean Sparsholt, nr Winchester, Hants.

Fieldhouse, Professor D. K., MA, Jesus College, Cambridge CB5 8BL.

Finer, Professor S. E., MA, All Souls College, Oxford OX1 4AL.

Fines, J., MA, PhD, 119 Parklands Road, Chichester.

Finlayson, G. B. A. M., MA, BLitt, 11 Burnhead Road, Glasgow G43 2SU.

Fisher, Professor Alan W., PhD, Dept of History, Michigan State University, East Lansing, Michigan 48824, U.S.A.

Fisher, D. J. V., MA, Jesus College, Cambridge CB3 9AD.

Fisher, H. E. Stephen, BSc, PhD, Dept of History, The University, Amory Building, Rennes Drive, Exeter EX4 4RJ.

Fisher, J. R., BA, MPhil, PhD, School of History, The University, P.O. Box 147, Liverpool L69 3BX.

Fisher, R. M., MA, PhD, Dept of History, University of Queensland, St Lucia, Queensland, Australia 4067.

Fisher, Professor S. N., PhD, 6000 Riverside Drive, B333, Dublin, Ohio 43017-1494, U.S.A.

Fishwick, Professor D., BA, MA, DLitt, Dept of Classics, Humanities Centre, University of Alberta, Edmonton, Alberta, Canada T6G 2E6.

Fitch, Dr M. F. B., FSA, 37 Avenue de Montoie, 1007 Lausanne, Switzerland.

Fitzpatrick, M. H., PhD, 'Garreg-Wen', Bronant, Aberystwyth, Dyfed SY23 4TQ.

Fletcher, Professor A. J., MA, Dept of History, University of Durham, 43/46 North Bailey, Durham, DH1 3EX.

*Fletcher, The Rt Hon. The Lord, PC, BA, LLD, FSA, 51 Charlbury Road, North Oxford OX2 6UX.

Fletcher, R. A., MA, Dept of History, The University, York YO1 5DD.

Flint, Professor J. E., MA, PhD, Dalhousie University, Halifax, Nova Scotia, Canada B3H 3J5.

Flint, Valerie I. J., MA, DPhil, Dept of History, The University, Private Bag, Auckland, New Zealand.

Floud, Professor R. C., MA, DPhil, Dept of History, Birkbeck College, Malet Street, London WC1E 7HX.

Fogel, Professor Robert W., PhD, Center for Population Economics, University of Chicago, 1101 East 58th Street, Chicago, Illinois 60637, U.S.A.

Foot, M. R. D., MA, BLitt, 45 Countess Road, London NW5 2XH.

Forbes, D., MA, 18 Thornton Close, Girton, Cambridge CB3 0NQ.

Forbes, Thomas R., BA, PhD, FSA, 86 Ford Street, Hamden, Conn. 06517, U.S.A.

Ford, W. K., BA, 48 Harlands Road, Haywards Heath, West Sussex RH16 1LS.

Forster, G. C. F., BA, FSA, School of History, The University, Leeds LS2 9JT.

Foster, Professor Elizabeth R., AM, PhD, 205 Strafford Avenue, Wayne, Pa. 19087, U.S.A.

Foster, R. F., MA, PhD, Dept of History, Birkbeck College, Malet Street, London WC1E 7HX.

Fowler, Professor K. A., BA, PhD, 2 Nelson Street, Edinburgh 3.

Fowler, Professer P. J., MA, PhD, Dept of Archaeology, The University, Newcastle upon Tyne NE1 7RU.

Fox, J. P., BSc(Econ), MSc(Econ), PhD, 98 Baring Road, London SE12 0PT.

Fox, L., OBE, DL, LHD, MA, FSA, FRSL, Silver Birches, 27 Welcombe Road, Stratford-upon-Avon, Warwickshire.

Fox, R., MA, DPhil, Science Museum Library, South Kensington, London SW7 5NH.

Frame, R. F., MA, PhD, Dept of History, The University, 43 North Bailey, Durham DH1 3HP.

Franklin, M. J., MA, PhD, Wolfson College, Cambridge CB3 9BB.

Franklin, R. M., The Corner House, Eton College, Windsor, Berkshire SL4 6DB.

Fraser, Lady Antonia, 52 Campden Hill Square, London W8.

*Fraser, Miss C. M., PhD, 39 King Edward Road, Tynemouth, Tyne and Wear NE30 2RW.

Fraser, D., BA, MA, PhD, 117 Alwoodley Lane, Leeds, LS17 7PN.

Fraser, Professor Peter, MA, PhD, The Priory, Old Mill Lane, Marnhull, Dorset DT10 1JX.

Freeden, M. S., DPhil, Mansfield College, Oxford OX1 3TF.

French, D. W., BA, PhD, Dept of History, University College London, Gower Street, London WC1E 6BT.

Frend, Professor W. H. C., MA, DPhil, DD, FBA, FRSE, FSA, The Rectory, Barnwell, nr Peterborough, Northants. PE8 5PG.

Fritz, Professor Paul S., BA, MA, PhD, Dept of History, McMaster University, Hamilton, Ontario, Canada.

Frost, A. J., BA, MA, MA, PhD, Dept of History, La Trobe University, Bundoora, Victoria 3083, Australia.

Fryde, Professor E. B., DPhil, Preswylfa, Trinity Road, Aberystwyth, Dyfed.

Fryde, Natalie M., BA, DrPhil, Schloss Grünsberg, D-8503 Altdorf, Germany.

*Fryer, Professor C. E., MA, PhD (address unknown).

Fryer, Professor W. R., BLitt, MA, 68 Grove Avenue, Chilwell, Beeston, Nottingham NG9 4DX.

Frykenberg, Professor R. E., MA, PhD, 1840 Chadbourne Avenue, Madison, Wis. 53705, U.S.A.

Fuidge, Miss N. M., Flat 3, 17 Cleve Road, London NW6 3RR.

Fulbrook, Mary J. A., MA, AM, PhD, Dept of German, University College London, Gower Street, London WC1E 6BT.

*Furber, Professor H., MA, PhD, c/o History Department, University of Pennsylvania, Philadelphia 4, Pa., U.S.A.

Fussell, G. E., DLitt, 3 Nightingale Road, Horsham, West Sussex RH12 2NW.

Fyrth, H. J., BSc(Econ), 72 College Road, Dulwich, London SE21.

Gabriel, Professor A. L., PhD, FMAA, CFIF, CFBA, P.O. Box 578, University of Notre Dame, Notre Dame, Indiana 46556, U.S.A.

*Galbraith, Professor J. S., BS, MA, PhD, Dept of History C-004, University of California, San Diego, La Jolla, Calif. 92093, U.S.A.

Gale, Professor H. P. P., OBE, PhD, 38 Brookwood Avenue, London SW13.

Gale, W. K. V., 19 Ednam Road, Goldthorn Park, Wolverhampton WV4 5BL.

Gann, L. H., MA, BLitt, DPhil, Hoover Institution, Stanford University, Stanford, Calif. 94305, U.S.A.

Garnett, G., MA, St John's College, Cambridge CB2 1TP.

Gash, Professor N., MA, BLitt, FBA, Old Gatehouse, Portway, Langport, Somerset TA10 0NQ.

Gaskell, S. M., MA, PhD, 4 Lings Coppice, Croxted Road, Dulwich, London SE21 8SY.

Gee, E. A., MA, DPhil, FSA, 28 Trentholme Drive, The Mount, York YO2 2DG.

Geggus, D. P., MA, DPhil, Dept of History, University of Florida, Gainesville, Florida 32611, U.S.A.

Genet, J.-Ph., Agrégé d'Histoire, 147 Avenue Parmentier, Paris 75010, France.

Gentles, Professor I., BA, MA, PhD, Dept of History, Glendon College, 2275 Bayview Avenue, Toronto, Canada M4N 3M6.

Gerlach, Professor D. R., MA, PhD, University of Akron, Akron, Ohio 44325, U.S.A.

Gibbs, G. C., MA, Dept of History, Birkbeck College, Malet Street, London WC1E 7HX.

Gibbs, Professor N. H., MA, DPhil, All Souls College, Oxford OX1 4AL.

Gibson, J. S. W., FSA, Harts Cottage, Church Hanborough, Oxford OX7 2AB.

Gibson, Margaret T., MA, DPhil, School of History, The University, P.O. Box 147, Liverpool L69 3 BX.

Gifford, Miss D. H., PhD, FSA, 1 Pondtail Road, Fleet, nr Aldershot, Hants. GU13 9JW.

Gilbert, Professor Bentley B., PhD, Dept of History, University of Illinois at Chicago Circle, Box 4348, Chicago, Ill. 60680, U.S.A.

Gildea, R. N., MA, DPhil, Merton College, Oxford OX1 4JD.

Gilkes, R. K., MA, 75 Fouracre Road, Downend, Bristol.

Gilley, S. W., BA, DPhil, Dept of Theology, University of Durham, Abbey House, Palace Green, Durham DH1 3RS.

Gillingham, J. B., MA, London School of Economics, Houghton Street, Aldwych, London WC2A 2AE.

Ginter, Professor D. E., AM, PhD, Dept of History, Sir George Williams University, Montreal 107, Canada.

de Giorgi, Roger, Development House, Floriana, Malta.

Girtin, T., MA, Butter Field House, Church Street, Old Isleworth, Middx.

Gleave, Group Capt. T. P., CBE, RAF (ret.), Willow Bank, River Gardens. Bray-on-Thames, Berks. SL6 2BJ.

*Glover, Professor R. G., MA, PhD, 2937 Tudor Avenue, Victoria, B.C. Canada V8N IM2.

*Godber, Miss A. J., MA, FSA, Mill Lane Cottage, Willington, Bedford.

*Godfrey, Professor J. L., MA, PhD, 231 Hillcrest Circle, Chapel Hill, N.C., U.S.A.

Goldie, Mark, MA, PhD, Churchill College, Cambridge CB3 0DS.

Golding, B. J., MA, DPhil, Dept of History, The University, Highfield, Southampton SO9 5NH.

Goldsmith, Professor M. M., PhD, Dept of Politics, University of Exeter, Exeter EX4 4RJ.

Goldsworthy, D. J. BA, BPhil, DPhil, Dept of Politics, Monash University, Clayton, Victoria 3168, Australia.

Gollin, Professor A., DLitt, Dept of History, University of California, Santa Barbara, Calif. 93106, U.S.A.

Gooch, John, BA, PhD, Dept of History, The University, Bailrigg, Lancaster LA1 4YG.

Goodman, A. E., MA, BLitt, Dept of Medieval History, The University, Edinburgh EH8 9YL.

Goodspeed, Professor D. J., BA, 164 Victoria Street, Niagara-on-the-Lake, Ontario, Canada.

*Gopal, Professor S., MA, DPhil, 30 Edward Elliot Road, Mylapore, Madras, India.

Gordon, Professor P., BSc(Econ), MSc(Econ), PhD, 241 Kenton Road, Kenton, Harrow HA3 0HJ.

Goring, J. J., MA, PhD, 31 Houndean Rise, Lewes, East Sussex BN7 1EQ.

Gorton, L. J., MA, 41 West Hill Avenue, Epsom, Surrey.

Gosden, Professor P. H. J. H. MA, PhD, School of Education, The University, Leeds LS2 9JT.

Gough, Professor Barry M., PhD, History Dept, Wilfrid Laurier University, Waterloo, Ontario, Canada N2L 3C5.

Gowing, Professor Margaret, CBE, MA, DLitt, BSc(Econ), FBA, Linacre College, Oxford OX1 1SY.

Graham-Campbell, J. A., MA, PhD, FSA, Dept of History, University College London, Gower Street, London WC1E 6BT.

Gransden, Antonia, MA, PhD, DLitt, FSA, Dept of History, The University, University Park, Nottingham NG7 2RD.

Grant, A., BA, DPhil, Dept of History, The University, Bailrigg, Lancaster LA1 4YG.

Grattan-Kane, P., 12 St John's Close, Helston, Cornwall.

Graves, Professor Edgar B., PhD, LLD, LHD, 318 College Hill Road, Clinton, New York 13323, USA.

Gray, Canon D. C., PhD, MPhil, 1 Little Cloister, Westminster Abbey, London SW1P 3PL.

Gray, Professor J. R., MA, PhD, School of Oriental and African Studies, University of London, London WC1E 7HP.

Gray, J. W., MA, Dept of Modern History, The Queen's University, Belfast BT7 1NN, N. Ireland.

Gray, Miss M., MA, BLitt, 68 Dorchester Road, Garstang, Preston PR3 1HH.

Greatrex, Professor Joan G, MA, The Highlands, Great Donard, Symonds Yat, Herefordshire, HR9 6DY.

Greaves, Professor Richard L., PhD, 910 Shadowlawn Drive, Tallahassee, Florida 32312, U.S.A.

Greaves, Mrs R. L., PhD, 1920 Hillview Road, Lawrence, Kansas 66044, U.S.A.

Green, I. M., MA, DPhil, Dept of Modern History, The Queen's University, Belfast BT7 1NN, N. Ireland.

Green, Judith A., BA, DPhil, Dept of Modern History, The Queen's University, Belfast BT7 1NN, N. Ireland.

Green, Professor Thomas A., BA, PhD, JD, Legal Research Building, University of Michigan Law School, Ann Arbor, Michigan 48109, U.S.A.

Green, Rev. V. H. H., MA, DD, Lincoln College, Oxford OX1 3DR.

Green, Professor W. A., PhD, Dept of History, Holy Cross College, Worcester, Mass. 01610, U.S.A.

Greene, Professor Jack P., Dept of History, The Johns Hopkins University, Baltimore, Md. 21218, U.S.A.

Greengrass, M., MA, DPhil, Dept of History, The University, Sheffield S10 2TN.

Greenhill, B. J., CB, CMG, DPh, FSA, West Boetheric Farmhouse, St Dominic, Saltash, Cornwall PL12 6SZ.

Greenslade, M. W., JP, MA, FSA, 20 Garth Road, Stafford ST17 9JD.

Greenway, D. E., MA, PhD, Institute of Historical Research, Senate House, Malet Street, London WC1E 7HU.

Gregg, E., MA, PhD, Dept of History, University of South Carolina, Columbia, S.C. 29208, U.S.A.

Grenville, Professor J. A. S., PhD, School of History, University of Birmingham, P.O. Box 363, Birmingham B15 2TT.

Gresham, C. A., BA, DLitt, FSA, Bryn-y-deryn, Criccieth, Gwynedd LL52 0HR.

GRIERSON, Professor P., MA, LittD, FBA, FSA, Gonville and Caius College, Cambridge CB2 1TA.

Grieve, Miss H. E. P., BA, 153 New London Road, Chelmsford, Essex.

Griffiths, Professor R. A., PhD, University College, Singleton Park, Swansea SA2 8PP.

Grimble, I., MA, PhD, 7 Seaforth Lodge, London SW13.

Grisbrooke, W. J., MA, Jokers, Bailey Street, Castle Acre, King's Lynn, Norfolk PE32 2AG.

*Griscom, Rev. Acton, MA (address unknown).

Gruner, Professor Wolf D., DrPhil, DrPhil. Habil, Pralleweg 7, 2000 Hamburg 67 (Volksdorf), West Germany.

Gupta, Professor P. S., MA, DPhil, E-75 Masjid Moth, New Delhi, 110048, India.

Guth, Professor D. J., Faculty of Law, University of British Columbia, Vancouver, B.C., Canada V6T 1Y1.

Guy, J. A., PhD, Dept of History, The University, Wills Memorial Building, Queens Road, Bristol BS8 1RJ.

HABAKKUK, Sir John (H.), MA, DLitt, FBA, Jesus College, Oxford OX1, 3DW.

Haber, Professor F. C., PhD, 3110 Wisconsin Avenue NW, #904, Washington, D.C. 20016, U.S.A.

Hackett, Rev. M. B., OSA, BA, PhD, Curia Generalizia Agostiniana, Via del S. Uffizio 25, 00193 Rome, Italy.

Hackmann, Willem D., DPhil, Museum of the History of Science, University of Oxford, Broad Street, Oxford OX1 3AZ.

Haddock, B. A., BA, DPhil, Dept of Political Theory and Government, The University, Singleton Park, Swansea, SA2 8PP.

Haffenden, P. S., PhD, 4 Upper Dukes Drive, Meads, Eastbourne, East Sussex BN20 7XT.

Haigh, C. A., MA, PhD, Christ Church, Oxford OX1 1DP.

Haight, Mrs M. Jackson, PhD, 3 Wolger Road, Mosman, N.S.W. 2088, Australia.

Haines, R. M., MA, MLitt, DPhil, FSA, 20 Luttrell Avenue, London SW15 6PF.

Hainsworth, D. R., MA, PhD, Dept of History, University of Adelaide, North Terrace, Adelaide, South Australia 5001.

Hair, Professor P. E. H., MA, DPhil, School of History, The University, P.O. Box 147, Liverpool L69 3BX.

Hale, Professor J. R., MA, FBA, FSA, Dept of History, University College London, Gower Street, London WC1E 6BT.

Haley, Professor K. H. D., MA, BLitt, 15 Haugh Lane, Sheffield S11 9SA.

Hall, Professor Emeritus A. R., MA, PhD, DLitt, FBA, 14 Ball Lane, Tackley, Oxford OX5 3AG.

Hall, B., MA, PhD, FSA, DD (Hon.), 2 Newton House, Newton St Cyres, Devon EX5 5BL.

Hallam, Elizabeth M., BA, PhD, Public Record Office, Chancery Lane, London WC2A 1LR.

Hallam, Professor H. E., MA, PhD, University of Western Australia, Nedlands 6009, Western Australia.

Hamer, Professor D. A., MA, DPhil, History Dept, Victoria University of Wellington, Private Bag, Wellington, New Zealand.

Hamilton, B., BA, PhD, Dept of History, The University, Nottingham NG7 2RD.

Hammersley, G. F., BA, PhD, Dept of History, University of Edinburgh, William Robertson Building, George Square, Edinburgh EH8 9JY.

Hamnett, B. R., BA, MA, PhD, Dept of History, University of Strathclyde, McLance Building, 16 Richmond Street, Glasgow G1 1QX.

Hampson, Professor N., MA, Ddel'U, 305 Hull Road, York YO1 3LB.

Hand, Professor G. J., MA, DPhil, Faculty of Law, University of Birmingham, P.O. Box 363, Birmingham B15 2TT.

Handford, M. A., MA, MSc, 6 Spa Lane, Hinckley, Leicester LE10 1JB.

Hanham, H. J., MA, PhD, The Croft, Bailrigg Lane, Bailrigg, Lancaster LA1 4XP.

Harcourt, Freda, PhD, Dept of History, Queen Mary College, Mile End Road, London E1 4NS.

Harding, Professor A., MA, BLitt, School of History, The University, P.O. Box 147, Liverpool L69 3BX.

Harding, The Hon. Mr Justice H. W., BA, LLD, FSA, 39 Annunciation Street, Sliema, Malta.

Haren, M. J., DPhil, 5 Marley Lawn, Dublin 16, Ireland.

Harfield, Major A. G., BEM, 19 Grove Road, Barton-on-Sea, Hampshire BH25 7DJ.

Hargreaves, Professor J. D., MA, 'Balcluain', Raemoir Road, Banchory, Kincardineshire.

Harkness, Professor D. W., MA, PhD, Dept of Irish History, The Queen's University, Belfast BT7 1NN, N. Ireland.

Harman, Rev. L. W., 72 Westmount Road, London SE9.

Harper Marjory-Ann D., MA, PhD, Silverdale, Disblair, Newmachar, Aberdeen AB5 0RN.

Harper-Bill, C., BA, PhD, 15 Cusack Close, Strawberry Hill, Twickenham, Middlesex.

Harris, G. G., MA, 4 Lancaster Drive, London NW3.

Harris, Mrs J. F., BA, PhD, 30 Charlbury Road, Oxford OX1 3UJ.

Harris, Professor J. R., MA, PhD, Dept of History, The University, P.O. Box 363, Birmingham B15 2TT.

Harrison, B. H., MA, DPhil, Corpus Christi College, Oxford OX1 4JF.

Harrison, C. J., BA, PhD, Dept of History, The University, Keele, Staffs. ST5 5BG.

Harrison, Professor Royden, MA, DPhil, 4 Wilton Place, Sheffield S10 2BT.

Harriss, G. L., MA, DPhil, FSA, Magdalen College, Oxford OX1 4AU.

Hart, C. J. R., MA, MB, DLitt, Goldthorns, Stilton, Cambs. PE7 3RH.

Harte, N. B., BSc(Econ), Dept of History, University College London, Gower Street, London WC1E 6BT.

Hartley, T. E., BA, PhD, Dept of History, The University, Leicester LE1 7RH.

Harvey, Miss B. F., MA, BLitt, FBA, Somerville College, Oxford OX2 6HD.

Harvey, Margaret M., MA, DPhil, St Aidan's College, Durham DH1 3LJ.

Harvey, Professor P. D. A., MA, DPhil, FSA, Dept of History, The University, 43/46 North Bailey, Durham DH1 3EX.

Harvey, Sally P. J., MA, PhD, Swanborough Manor, Swanborough, Lewes, E. Sussex BN7 3PF.

Haskell, Professor F. J., MA, FBA, Trinity College, Oxford OX1 3BH.

Haskins, Professor G. L., AB, LLB, JD, MA, University of Pennsylvania, The Law School, 3400 Chestnut Street, Philadelphia, Pa. 19104 U.S.A.

Haslam, Group Captain E. B., MA, RAF (retd), 27 Denton Road, Wokingham, Berks. RG11 2DX.

Haslam, Jonathan G., BSc(Econ), MLitt, PhD, 1610c Beekman Place NW, Washington, D.C., 20009, U.S.A.

Hasler, Peter W., BA, MA, History of Parliament Trust, Institute of Historical Research, 34 Tavistock Square, London WC1H 9EZ.

Hassall, W. O., MA, DPhil, FSA, The Manor House, 26 High Street, Wheatley, Oxford OX9 1XX.

Hast, Adele, PhD, 210 Fourth Street, Wilmette, Illinois 60091, U.S.A.

Hatcher, M. J., BSc(Econ), PhD, Corpus Christi College, Cambridge CB2 1RH.

Hatley, V. A., BA, ALA, 6 The Crescent, Northampton NN1 4SB.

Hatton, Professor Ragnhild M., PhD, Cand.Mag(Oslo), Dr.h.c., 49 Campden Street, London W8.

Havighurst, Professor A. F., MA, PhD, 11 Blake Field, Amherst, Mass. 01002, U.S.A.

Havinden, M. A., MA, BLitt, Dept of Economic History, Amory Building, The University, Exeter EX4 4QH.

Havran, Professor M. J., MA, PhD, Corcoran Dept of History, Randall Hall, University of Virginia, Charlottesville, Va. 22903, U.S.A.

Hawke, Professor G. R., BA, BCom, DPhil, Dept of History, Victoria, University of Wellington, Private Bag, Wellington, New Zealand.

HAY, Professor D., MA, DLitt, FBA, FRSE, Dr. h.c. Tours, 31 Fountainville Road, Edinburgh EH9 2LN.

Hayes, P. M., MA, DPhil, Keble College, Oxford OX1 3PG.

Hayter, A. J., BA, PhD, Chase House, Mursley, N. Bucks. MK17 0RT.

Hayton, D. W., BA, DPhil, 8 Baker Street, Ampthill, Bedford MK45 2QE.

Hazlehurst, Cameron, BA, DPhil, FRSL, 8 Hunter Street, Yarralumla, A.C.T. 2600, Australia.

Heal, Mrs Felicity, PhD, Jesus College, Oxford OX1 3DW.

Hearder, Professor H., BA, PhD, Dept of History, University College, P.O. Box 78, Cardiff CF1 1XL.

Heath, P., MA, Dept of History, The University Hull HU6 7RX.

Heathcote, T. A., BA, PhD, Cheyne Cottage, Birch Drive, Hawley, Camberley, Surrey.

Heesom, A. J., MA, Dept of History, The University, 43 North Bailey, Durham DH1 3HP.

Hellmuth, Eckhart H., PhD, German Historical Institute, 17 Bloomsbury Square, London WC1A 2LP.

Helmholz, R. H., PhD, LLB, The Law School, University of Chicago, 1111 East 60th Street, Chicago, Ill. 60637, U.S.A.

Hembry, Mrs P. M., BA, PhD, Pleasant Cottage, Crockerton, Warminster, Wilts. BA12 8AJ.

Hempton, D. N., BA, PhD, Dept of Modern History, The Queen's University, Belfast, BT7 1NN, N. Ireland.

Hendy, M. F., MA, 29 Roberts Road, Cambridge, Mass. 02138, U.S.A.

Henning, Professor B. D., PhD, History of Parliament, 34 Tavistock Square, London WC1H 9EZ.

Hennock, Professor E. P., MA, PhD, School of History, University of Liverpool, P.O. Box 147, Liverpool L69 3BX.

Henstock, A. J. M., BA, Nottinghamshire Record Office, County House, Nottingham NG1 1HR.

Heppell, Muriel, BA, MA, PhD, 97 Eton Place, Eton College Road, London NW3 2DB.

Herde, Professor Peter, PhD, Cranachstr. 7, D 8755 Alzenau, F.R. of Germany.

Herrup, Cynthia B., PhD, MA, BSJ, Dept of History, 6727 College Station, Duke University, Durham, N.C. 27708, U.S.A.

Hexter, Professor J. H., PhD, Dept of History, Washington University, St Louis, Missouri, U.S.A.

Hey, D. G., MA, PhD, Division of Continuing Education, The University, Sheffield S10 2TN.

Hicks, M. A., BA, MA, DPhil, Dept of History, King Alfred's College, Winchester Hampshire, SO22 4NR.

Higham, R. A., BA, PhD, Dept of History and Archaeology, University of Exeter, Queen's Building, Queen's Drive, Exeter.

Highfield, J. R. L., MA, DPhil, Merton College, Oxford OX1 4JD.

Higman, Professor B. W. C., PhD, Dept of History, University of the West Indies, Mona, Kingston 7, Jamaica.

Hill, B. W., BA, PhD, School of English and American Studies, University of East Anglia, University Plain, Norwich NR4 7TJ.

Hill, J. E. C., MA, DLitt, FBA, Woodway, Sibford Ferris, nr Banbury, Oxfordshire OX15 5RA.

Hill, Professor L. M., AB, MA, PhD, 5066 Berean Lane, Irvine, Calif. 92664, U.S.A.

*Hill, Miss M. C., MA, Crab End, Brevel Terrace, Charlton Kings, Cheltenham, Glos.

*Hill, Professor Rosalind M. T., MA, BLitt, FSA, Westfield College, Kidderpore Avenue, London NW3 7ST.

Hilton, A. J. Boyd, MA, DPhil, 1 Carlyle Road, Cambridge CB4 3DN.

Hilton, Professor R. H., DPhil, FBA, University of Birmingham, P.O. Box 363, Birmingham B15 2TT.

Himmelfarb, Professor Gertrude, PhD, The City University of New York, Graduate Center, 33 West 42 St, New York, N.Y. 10036, U.S.A.

Hind, R. J., BA, PhD, Dept of History, University of Sydney, Sydney, N.S.W. 2006, Australia.

*Hinsley, Professor F. H., OBE, MA, St John's College, Cambridge CB2 1TP.

Hirst, Professor D. M., PhD, Dept of History, Washington University, St Louis, Missouri, U.S.A.

Hoak, Professor Dale E., PhD, Dept of History, College of William and Mary, Williamsburg, Virginia 23185, U.S.A.

*Hodgett, G. A. J., MA, FSA, King's College London, Strand, London WC2R 2LS.

Holderness, B. A., MA, PhD, School of Economic and Social Studies, University of East Anglia, Norwich NR4 7TJ.

Holdsworth, Professor C. J., MA, PhD, FSA, 5 Pennsylvania Park, Exeter EX4 6HD.

Hollaender, A. E. J., PhD, FSA, 119 Narbonne Avenue, South Side, Clapham Common, London SW4 9LQ.

Hollis, Patricia, MA. DPhil, 30 Park Lane, Norwich NOR 4TF.

Hollister, Professor C. Warren, MA, PhD, University of California, Santa Barbara, Calif. 93106, U.S.A.

Holmes, Professor Clive A., MA, PhD, Dept of History, McGraw Hall, Cornell University, N.Y. 14853, U.S.A.

Holmes, G. A., MA, PhD, Highmoor House, Weald, Bampton, Oxon. OX8 2HY.

Holmes, Professor G. S., MA, DLitt, FBA, Tatham House, Burton-in-Lonsdale, Carnforth, Lancs.

Holroyd, M. de C. F., 85 St Mark's Road, London W10.

HOLT, Professor J. C., MA, DPhil, DLitt, FBA, FSA, Fitzwilliam College, Cambridge CB3 0DG.

Holt, Professor P. M., MA, DLitt, FBA, Dryden Spinney, South End, Kirtlington, Oxford OX5 3HG.

Holt, The Rev. T. G., SJ, MA, FSA, 114 Mount Street, London W1Y 6AH.

Honey, Professor, J. R. de S., MA, DPhil, 5 Woods Close, Oadby, Leicester LE2 4FJ.

Hopkin, D. R., BA, PhD, Maesgwyn, Llangawsai, Aberystwyth, Dyfed.

Hopkins, E., MA, PhD, 77 Stevens Road, Stourbridge, West Midlands DY9 0XW.

Hoppen, K. T., MA, PhD, Dept of History, The University, Hull HU6 7RX.

Hoppit, J., MA, PhD, Dept of History, University College London, Gower Street, London WC1E 6BT.

Horrox, Rosemary E., MA, PhD, 61-3 High Street, Cottenham, Cambridge CB4 4SA.

Horton, A.V.M., BA, MA, PhD, 4 Birch Lea, East Leake, Loughborough LE12 6LA.

Horwitz, Professor H. G., BA, DPhil, Dept of History, University of Iowa, Iowa City, Iowa 52242, U.S.A.

Houlbrooke, R. A., MA, DPhil, Faculty of Letters and Social Sciences, The University, White Knights, Reading RG6 2AH.

Housley, N. J., MA, PhD, Dept of History, The University, Leicester, LE1 7RH.

*Howard, C. H. D., MA, 15 Sunnydale Gardens, London NW7 3PD.

*Howard, Sir Michael, CBE, MC, DLitt, FBA, Oriel College, Oxford OX1 4EW.

Howarth, Mrs J. H., MA, St Hilda's College, Oxford OX4 1DY.

Howat, G. M. D., MA, MLitt, Old School House, North Moreton, Didcot, Oxfordshire OX11 9BA.

Howell, Miss M. E., MA, PhD, 10 Blenheim Drive, Oxford OX2 8DG.

Howell, P. A., MA., PhD, School of Social Sciences, The Flinders University of South Australia, Bedford Park, South Australia 5042.

Howell, Professor R., MA, DPhil, Dept of History, Bowdoin College, Brunswick, Maine 04011, U.S.A.

Howells, B. E., MA, Whitehill, Cwm Ann, Lampeter, Dyfed.

Hoyle, R. W., BA, DPhil, 13 Parker St., Oxford OX4 1TD.

Hudson, Miss A., MA, DPhil, Lady Margaret Hall, Oxford OX2 6QA.

Hudson, T. P., MA, PhD, 23 Glenwood Avenue, Bognor Regis, West Sussex, PO22 8BT.

Hufton, Professor Olwen H., BA, PhD, 40 Shinfield Road, Reading, Berks.

Hughes, J. Q., MC, MA, BArch, PhD, Dip. Civic Design, 10a Fulwood Park, Liverpool L17 5AH.

Hull, F., BA, PhD, 135 Ashford Road, Bearsted, Maidstone ME14 4BT.

HUMPHREYS, Professor R. A., OBE, MA, PhD, DLitt, LittD, DLitt, DUniv, 5 St James's Close, Prince Albert Road, London NW8 7LG.

Hunnisett, R. F., MA, DPhil, 23 Byron Gardens, Sutton, Surrey SM1 3QG.

Hunt, K. S., PhD, MA, Rhodes University Grahamstown 6140, South Africa.

Hurst, M. C., MA, St John's College, Oxford OX1 3JP.

Hurt, J. S., BA, BSc(Econ), PhD, Sutton House, Madeira Lane, Freshwater, Isle of Wight PO40 9SP.

*Hussey, Professor Joan M., MA, BLitt, PhD, FSA, Royal Holloway and Bedford New College, Egham Hill, Egham, Surrey TW20 0EX.

Hutchinson, J. H., 182 Burton Stone Lane, York YO3 6DF.

Hutton, R. E., BA, DPhil, Dept of History, The University, Wills Memorial Building, Queen's Road, Bristol BS8 1RJ.

Hyams, P. R., MA, DPhil, Pembroke College, Oxford OX1 1DW.
*Hyde, H. Montgomery, MA, DLit, Westwell House, Tenterden, Kent.

Ingham, Professor K., OBE, MA, MA, DPhil, The Woodlands, 94 West Town Lane, Bristol BS4 5DZ.
Ingram Ellis, Professor E. R., MA, PhD, Dept of History, Simon Fraser University, Burnaby, B.C, Canada V5A IS6.
Inkster, Ian, PhD, Dept of Economic History, University of New South Wales, P.O. Box 1, Kensington, N.S.W., Australia 2033.
Israel, Professor J. I., MA, DPhil, Dept of History, University College London, Gower Street, London WC1E 6BT.
Ives, E. W., PhD, 214 Myton Road, Warwick.

Jack, Professor R. I., MA, PhD, University of Sydney, Sydney, N.S.W., Australia.
Jack, Mrs S. M., MA, BLitt, University of Sydney, Sydney, N.S.W., Australia.
Jackman, Professor S. W., PhD, FSA, 1065 Deal Street, Victoria, British Columbia, Canada.
Jackson, J. T., PhD, Dept of History, University College of Swansea, Singleton Park, Swansea SA2 7BR.
Jackson, P., MA, PhD, Dept of History, The University, Keele, Staffs. ST5 5BG.
Jacob, Professor Margaret C., Office of the Dean, Lang College, New School for Social Research, 66 West 12th Street, New York, N.Y. 10071, U.S.A.
Jagger, Rev. P. J., MA, MPhil, PhD, St Deiniol's Library, Hawarden, Deeside, Clwyd CH5 3DF.
Jalland, Patricia, PhD, MA, BA, School of Social Inquiry, Murdoch University, Murdoch, Western Australia 6150.
James, Edward, MA, DPhil, FSA, Dept of History, The University, Heslington, York YO1 5DD.
James, M. E., MA, Middlecote, Stonesfield, Oxon. OX7 2PU.
James, R. Rhodes, MP, MA, FRSL, The Stone House, Great Gransden, nr Sandy, Beds.
James, Thomas B., MA, PhD, 35 Alresford Road, Winchester SO23 8HG.
Jarrett, J. D., 58 Beaconsfield Road, London SE3 7LG.
Jeffery, K. J., MA, PhD, Dept of History, University of Ulster, Shore Road, Newtownabbey, Co. Antrim, N. Ireland BT37 0QB.
Jenkins, Professor B. A., PhD, 133 Lorne, Lennoxville, Quebec, Canada.
Jenkins, Professor D., MA, LLM, LittD, Dept of Law, University College of Wales, Adeilad Hugh Owen, Penglais, Aberystwyth SY23 3DY.
Jeremy, D. J., BA, MLitt, PhD, Heatherbank, 2 Old Hall Drive, Whaley Bridge, nr. Stockport, Cheshire SK12 7HF.
Jewell, Miss H. M., MA, PhD, School of History, The University, P.O. Box 147, Liverpool L69 3BX.
Johnson, D. J., BA, 41 Cranes Park Avenue, Surbiton, Surrey.
Johnson, Professor D. W. J., BA, BLitt, Dept of History, University College London, Gower Street, London WC1E 6BT.
*Johnson, J. H., MA, Whitehorns, Cedar Avenue, Chelmsford, Essex.
Johnson, P. A., MA, DPhil, Dept of Economic History, London School of Economics, Houghton Street, London WC2A 2AE.
Johnston, Professor Edith M., MA, PhD, Dept of History, Macquarie Univ., North Ryde, N.S.W. 2113, Australia.

Johnston, Professor S. H. F., MA, Fronhyfryd, Llanbadarn Road, Aberystwyth, Dyfed.

Jones, C. D. H., BA, DPhil, Dept of History and Archaeology, The University, The Queen's Drive, Exeter EX4 4QH.

Jones, Clyve, MA, MLitt, 41 St Catherines Court, London W4 1LB.

Jones, D. J. V., BA, PhD, Dept of History, University College of Swansea, Singleton Park, Swansea SA2 8PP.

Jones, Dwyryd W., MA, DPhil, Dept of History, The University, Heslington, York YO1 5DD.

Jones, Revd F., BA, MSc, PhD, 4a Castlemain Avenue, Southbourne, Bournemouth BH6 5EH.

Jones, G. A., MA, PhD, Monks Court, Deddington, Oxford OX5 4TE.

Jones, G. E., MA, PhD, MEd, 130 Pennard Drive, Pennard, Gower, West Glamorgan.

Jones, Professor G. Hilton, PhD, Dept of History, Eastern Illinois University, Charleston, Ill. 61920, U.S.A.

Jones, Professor G. W., BA, MA, DPhil, Dept of Government, London School of Economics, Houghton Street, London WC2A 2AE.

Jones, H. E., MA, DPhil, Flat 3, 115-117 Highlever Road, London W10 6PW.

Jones, Professor I.G., MA, DLitt, 12 Laura Place, Aberystwyth, Dyfed SY23 3DY.

Jones, J. D., MA, PhD, Woodlands Cottage, Marvel Lane, Newport, Isle of Wight PO30 3DT.

Jones, Professor J. R., MA, PhD, School of English and American Studies, University of East Anglia, Norwich NOR 30A.

Jones, Professor M. A., MA, DPhil, Dept of History, University College London, Gower Street, London WC1E 6BT.

Jones, Mrs Marian H., MA, Glwysgoed, Caradog Road, Aberystwyth, Dyfed.

Jones, M. C. E., MA, DPhil, FSA, Dept of History, The University, Nottingham NG7 2 RD.

Jones, The Venerable O. W., MA, 10 Camden Crescent, Brecon, Powys LD3 7BY.

Jones, P. J., DPhil, FBA, Brasenose College, Oxford OX1 4AJ.

Jones, Professor W. J., PhD, DLitt, FRSC, Dept of History, The University of Alberta, Edmonton, Canada T6G 2H4.

Jones-Parry, Sir Ernest, MA, PhD, Flat 3, 34 Sussex Square, Brighton, Sussex BN2 5AD.

Judd, D. O., BA, PhD, Dept of History and Philosophy, Polytechnic of North London, Prince of Wales Road, London NW6.

Judson, Professor Margaret A., PhD, 8 Redcliffe Avenue, Highland Park, N.J. 08904, U.S.A.

Judt, T. R., St Anne's College, Oxford OX2 6HS.

Jukes, Rev. H. A. Ll., MA, STh, St Catherines, 1 St Mary's Court, Ely, Cambs. CB7 4HQ.

Jupp, P. J., BA, PhD, 42 Osborne Park, Belfast, N. Ireland BT9 6JN.

Kaeuper, Professor R. W., MA, PhD, 151 Village Lane, Rochester, New York 14610, U.S.A.

Kamen, H. A. F., MA, DPhil, Dept of History, The University of Warwick, Coventry CV4 7AL.

Kanya-Forstner, A. S., PhD, Dept of History, York University, 4700 Keele Street, Downsview, Ontario, Canada M3J 1P3.

Kapelle, Asst. Professor, William E., PhD, History Department, Brandeis University, Waltham, Mass. 00254, U.S.A.

Kealey, Professor Gregory S., PhD, Dept of History, Memorial University of Newfoundland, St John's, Newfoundland. Canada A1C 5S7.

Kedward, H. R., MA, MPhil, 137 Waldegrave Road, Brighton BN1 6GJ.

Keefe, Professor Thomas K., BA, PhD, Dept of History, Appalachian State University, Boone, N.C. 28608, U.S.A.

Keegan, J. D. P., MA, The Manor House, Kilmington, nr. Warminster, Wilts. BA12 6RD.

Keeler, Mrs Mary F., PhD, 302 West 12th Street, Frederick, Maryland 21701, U.S.A.

Keen, L. J., MPhil, Dip Archaeol, FSA, 7 Church Street, Dorchester, Dorset.

Keen, M. H. MA, DPhil, Balliol College, Oxford OX1 3BJ.

Keene, D. J., MA, DPhil, 162 Erlanger Road, Telegraph Hill, London SE14 5TJ.

Kellas, J. G., MA, PhD, Dept of Politics, Glasgow University, Adam Smith Building, Glasgow G12 8RT.

Kellaway, C. W., MA, FSA, 18 Canonbury Square, London N1.

Kelly, Professor T., MA, PhD, FLA, Oak Leaf House, Ambleside Road, Keswick, Cumbria CA12 4DL.

Kemp, Miss B., MA, FSA, St Hugh's College, Oxford OX2 6LE.

Kemp, B. R., BA, PhD, 12 Redhatch Drive, Earley, Reading, Berks.

Kemp, The Right Rev. E. W., DD, The Lord Bishop of Chichester, The Palace, Chichester, Sussex PO19 1PY.

Kemp, Lt-Commander P. K., RN, Malcolm's, 51 Market Hill, Maldon, Essex.

Kendle, Professor J. E., PhD, St John's College, University of Manitoba, Winnipeg, Manitoba, Canada R3T 2MS.

Kennedy, J., MA, 14 Poolfield Avenue, Newcastle-under-Lyme, Staffs. ST5 2NL.

Kennedy, Professor P. M., BA, DPhil, Dept of History, Yale University, 237 Hall of Graduate Studies, New Haven, Conn. 06520, U.S.A.

Kent, Professor C. A., DPhil, Dept of History, University of Saskatchewan, Saskatoon, Sask. Canada S7N 0WO.

Kent, Professor J. H. S., MA, PhD, Dept of Theology, University of Bristol, Senate House, Bristol BS8 1TH.

Kent, Miss M. R., PhD, BA, BA, School of Social Sciences, Deakin University, Geelong, Victoria, Australia 3217.

Kenyon, Professor J. P., PhD, Dept of History, University of Kansas, 3001, Wescoe Hall, Lawrence, Kansas 66045-2130, U.S.A.

Kenyon, J. R., BA, ALA, The Library, National Museum of Wales, Cardiff CF1 3NP.

Kerridge, Professor E. W. J., PhD, 2 Bishops Court, off Church Road, Broughton, Chester CH4 0QZ.

Kettle, Miss A. J., MA, FSA, Dept of Mediaeval History, The University, 71 South Street, St Andrews, Fife KY16 9AL.

Keynes, S. D., MA, PhD, Trinity College, Cambridge CB2 1TQ.

Kiernan, Professor V. G., MA, 'Woodcroft', Lauder Road, Stow, Galashiels, Scotland TD1 2QW.

*Kimball, Miss E. G., BLitt, PhD, 200 Leeder Hill Drive, Apt 640, Hamden, Conn. 06517, U.S.A.

King, Professor E. B., PhD, Dept of History, The University of the South, Box 1234, Sewanee, Tennessee 37375, U.S.A.

King, E. J., MA, PhD, Dept of History, The University, Sheffield S10 2TN.

King, P. D., BA, PhD, Dept of History, Furness College, The University, Bailrigg, Lancaster LA1 4YG.

Kirby, D. P., MA, PhD, Manoraven, Llanon, Dyfed.

Kirby, J. L., MA, FSA, 209 Covington Way, Streatham, London SW16 3BY.

Kirby, M. W., BA, PhD, Dept of Economics, Gillow House, The University, Lancaster LA1 4YX.

Kirk, J., MA, PhD, DLitt, Dept of Scottish History, University of Glasgow, Glasgow G12 8QQ.

Kirk, Linda M., MA, PhD, Dept of History, The University, Sheffield S10 2TN.

Kirk-Greene, A. H. M., MBE, MA, St Antony's College, Oxford OX2 6JF.

Kishlansky, Professor Mark, Dept of History, University of Chicago, 1126 East 59th Street, Chicago, Illinois 60637, U.S.A.

Kitchen, Professor Martin, BA, PhD, Dept of History, Simon Fraser University, Burnaby, B.C. Canada V5A 1S6.

Kitching, C. J., BA, PhD, FSA, 11 Creighton Road, London NW6 6EE.

Klibansky, Professor R., MA, PhD, DPhil, FRSC, 608 Leacock Building, McGill University, P.O. Box 6070, Station A, Montreal, Quebec, Canada H3C 3G1.

Knafla, Professor L. A., MA, PhD, Dept of History, University of Calgary, Alberta, Canada.

Knecht, Professor R. J., MA, DLitt, 79 Reddings Road, Moseley, Birmingham B13 8LP.

Knight R. J. B., MA, PhD, 133 Coleraine Road, London SE3 7NT.

Knowles, C. H., PhD, Dept of History, University College, P.O. Box 78, Cardiff CF1 1XL.

Knox, B. A., BA, BPhil, Dept of History, Monash University, Clayton, Victoria, 3168, Australia.

Koch, Hannsjoachim W., BA, DPhil, Dept of History, The University, Heslington, York YO1 5DD.

Kochan, L. E., MA, PhD, 237 Woodstock Road, Oxford OX2 7AD.

Koenigsberger, Dorothy M. M., BA, PhD, 41a Lancaster Grove, London NW3.

Koenigsberger, Professor H. G., MA, PhD, 41a Lancaster Grove, London NW3.

Kohl, Professor Benjamin G., AB, MA, PhD, Dept of History, Vassar College, Poughkeepsie, New York, 12601, U.S.A.

Kollar, Professor Rene M., BA, MDiv, MA, PhD, St Vincent Archabbey, Latrobe, Pa. 15650, U.S.A.

Korr, Charles P., MA, PhD, College of Arts and Sciences, Dept of History, University of Missouri, 8001 Natural Bridge Road, St Louis, Missouri 63121, U.S.A.

Kossmann, Professor E. H., DLitt, Rijksuniversiteit te Groningen, Groningen, The Netherlands.

Kouri, Professor E. I., PhD, Clare Hall, Cambridge CB3 9AL.

Kubicek, Professor R. V., BEd, MA, PhD, Dept of History, University of British Columbia, Vancouver, B. C., Canada V6T 1W5.

Lake, P., BA, PhD, Dept of History, Royal Holloway and Bedford New College, Egham Hill, Egham, Surrey TW20 0EX.

Lambert, The Hon. Margaret, CMG, PhD. 39 Thornhill Road, Barnsbury Square, London N1 1JS.

Lambert, W. R., BA, PhD, 36 Five Mile Drive, Oxford OX2 8HR.

Lamont, W. M., PhD, Manor House, Keighton Road, Denton, Newhaven, Sussex BN9 0AB.

Lander, J. R., MA, MLitt, FRSC, 5 Canonbury Place, London, N1 2NQ.

Landes, Professor D. S., PhD, Widener U, Harvard University, Cambridge, Mass. 02138, U.S.A.

Landon, Professor M. de L., MA, PhD, Dept of History, The University, Mississippi 38677 U.S.A.

Langford, P., MA, DPhil, Lincoln College, Oxford OX1 3DR.

Langhorne, R. T. B., MA, 15 Madingley Road, Cambridge.

Lannon, Frances, MA, DPhil, Lady Margaret Hall, Oxford OX2 6QA.

Lapidge, M., BA, MA, PhD, Dept of Anglo-Saxon, Norse and Celtic, University of Cambridge, 9 West Road, Cambridge CB3 9DP.

Larkin, Professor M. J. M., MA, PhD, Dept of History, The University, George Square, Edinburgh EH8 9JY.

Larner, J. P., MA, Dept of History, The University, Glasgow G12 8QQ.

Lasko, Professor P. E., BA, FSA, 53 Montagu Square, London W1H 1TH.

Latham, R. C., CBE, MA, FBA, Magdalene College, Cambridge CB3 0AG.

Law, J. E., MA, DPhil, Dept of History, University College of Swansea, Swansea SA2 8PP.

Lawrence, Professor C. H., MA, DPhil, Royal Holloway and Bedford New College, Egham Hill, Egham, Surrey TW20 0EX.

Laws, Captain W. F., BA, MLitt, 23 Marlborough Road, St. Leonards, Exeter EX2 4TJ.

Lead, P., MA, 11 Morland Close, Stone, Staffs. ST15 0DA.

Le Cordeur, Professor Basil A., MA, PhD, Dept of History, University of Cape Town, Rondebosch 7700, Republic of South Africa.

Leddy, J. F., MA, BLitt, DPhil, University of Windsor, Windsor, Ontario, Canada.

Lee, Professor J. M., MA, BLitt, Dept of Politics, The University, 12 Priory Road, Bristol BS8 1TU.

Lehmann, Professor H., DPhil, c/o German Historical Institute, 1759 R.St.N.W., Washington D.C., 20009, U.S.A.

Lehmann, Professor J. H., PhD, De Paul University, 25e Jackson Blvd., Chicago, Illinois 60604, U.S.A.

Lehmberg, Professor S. E., PhD, Dept of History, University of Minnesota, Minneapolis, Minn. 55455, U.S.A.

Leinster-Mackay, D. P., MA, MEd, PhD, Dept of Education, University of Western Australia, Nedlands, Western Australia 6009.

Lenman, B. P., MA, LittD, Dept of Modern History, University of St Andrews, St Andrews, Fife KY16 9AL.

Lentin, A., MA, PhD, 57 Maids Causeway, Cambridge CB5 8DE.

Leslie, Professor R. F., BA, PhD, Market House, Church Street, Charlbury, Oxford OX7 3PP.

Lester, Professor M., PhD, Dept of History, Davidson College, Davidson, N.C. 28036, U.S.A.

Levine, Professor Joseph M., Dept of History, Syracuse University, Syracuse, New York 13210, U.S.A.

Levine, Professor Mortimer, PhD, 529 Woodhaven Drive, Morgantown, West Va. 26505, U.S.A.

Levy, Professor F. J., PhD, University of Washington, Seattle, Wash. 98195, U.S.A.

Lewis, Professor A. R., MA, PhD, History Dept, University of Massachusetts, Amherst, Mass. 01003, U.S.A.

Lewis, Professor B., PhD, FBA, Near Eastern Studies Dept, Jones Hall, The University, Princeton, N.J. 08540, U.S.A.

Lewis, C. W., BA, FSA, University College, P.O. Box 78, Cardiff CF1 1XL.

Lewis, Professor G., MA, DPhil, Dept of History, University of Warwick, Coventry CV4 7AL.

Lewis, P. S., MA, All Souls College, Oxford OX1 4AL.

Lewis, R. A., PhD, Y Berth Glyd, Siliwen Road, Bangor, Gwynedd LL57 2BS.

Lewis, R. Gillian, St Annes College, Oxford OX2 6HS.

Leyser, Professor K., TD, MA, FBA, FSA, All Souls College, Oxford OX1 4AL.

Liddell, W. H., BA, MA, Dept of Extra-Mural Studies, University of London, 26 Russell Square London WX1B 5DG.

Liddle, Peter H., BA, MLitt, 'Dipity Cottage', 20 Lime Street, Waldridge Fell, nr Chester-le-Street, Co. Durham.

Lieu, Samuel N. C., BA, MA, DPhil, 2a Dickinson Square, Croxley Green, Rickmansworth, Herts. WD3 3EZ.

Lindley, K. J., BA, MA, PhD, Dept of History, New University of Ulster, Coleraine, N. Ireland BT52 1SA.

*Lindsay, Mrs H., MA, PhD (address unknown).

Lindsay, Colonel Oliver J. M., MBIM, Brookwood House, Brookwood, nr Woking, Surrey.

Linehan, P. A., MA, PhD, St John's College, Cambridge CB2 1TP.

Lipman, V. D., CVO, MA, DPhil, FSA, 9 Rotherwick Road, London NW11 9DG.

Livermore, Professor H. V., MA, Sandycombe Lodge, Sandycombe Road, St Margarets, Twickenham, Middx.

Lloyd, Professor H. A., BA, DPhil, Dept of History, The University, Cottingham Road, Hull HU6 7RX.

Lloyd, Professor T. O., MA, DPhil, Dept of History, The University, Toronto, Canada, M5S 1AI.

Loach, Mrs J., MA, Somerville College, Oxford OX2 6HD.

Loades, Professor D. M., MA, PhD, Dept of History, University College of North Wales, Bangor, Gwynedd LL57 2DG.

Lobel, Mrs M. D., BA, FSA, 16 Merton Street, Oxford.

Lockie, D. McN., MA, 25 Chemin de la Panouche, Saint-Anne, 06130 Grasse, France.

Lockyer, R. W., MA, Dept of History, Royal Holloway and Bedford New College, Egham Hill, Egham, Surrey TW20 0EX.

Logan, F. D., MA, MSD, Emmanuel College, 400 The Fenway, Boston, Mass. 02115, U.S.A.

Logan, O. M. T., MA, PhD, 18 Clarendon Road, Norwich NR2 2PW.

London, Miss Vera C. M., MA, 55 Churchill Road, Church Stretton, Shropshire SY6 6EP.

Longley, D. A., MA, PhD, Dept of History, Taylor Building, King's College, The University, Old Aberdeen AB9 2UB.

Longmate, N. R., MA, 30 Clydesdale Gardens, Richmond, Surrey.

Loomie, Rev. A. J., SJ, MA, PhD, Fordham University, New York, N.Y. 10458, U.S.A.

Lottes, Professor G., MA, DPhil-Habil, Bucher Str. 74, 8500 Nurnberg 10, West Germany.

Loud, G. A., MA, DPhil, School of History, The University, Leeds LS2 9JT.

Louis, Professor William R., BA, MA, DPhil, Dept of History, University of Texas, Austin, Texas 78712, U.S.A.

Lourie, Elena, MA, DPhil, Dept of History, Ben Gurion University of The Negev, P.O. Box 653, Beer Sheva 84105, Israel.

Lovatt, R. W., MA, DPhil, Peterhouse, Cambridge CB2 1RD.

Lovegrove, D. W., MA, BD, PhD, Dept of Ecclesiastical History, St Mary's College, The University, St Andrews, Fife KY16 9JU.

Lovell, J. C., BA, PhD, Eliot College, University of Kent, Canterbury CT2 7NS.

Lovett, A. W., MA, PhD, 26 Coney Hill Road, West Wickham, Kent BR4 9BX.

Lowe, P. C., BA, PhD, The University, Manchester M13 9PL.

Lowe, R, BA, PhD, Dept of Economic and Social History, The University, 13-15 Woodland Road, Bristol BS8 2TJ.

Lowerson, J. R., BA, MA, Centre for Continuing Education, University of Sussex, Brighton.

Loyn, Professor H. R., MA, FBA, FSA, Dept of History, Westfield College, Kidderpore Avenue, London NW3 7ST.

Lucas, C. R., MA, DPhil, Balliol College, Oxford OX1 3BJ.

Lucas, P. J., MA, PhD, Dept of English, University College, Belfield, Dublin 4, Ireland.

*Lumb, Miss S. V., MA, Torr-Colin House, 106 Ridgway, Wimbledon, London SW19.

Lunn, D. C. J., STL, MA, PhD, 25 Cornwallis Avenue, Clifton, Bristol BS8 4PP.

Lunt, Major-General J. D., MA, Hilltop House, Little Milton, Oxfordshire OX9 7PU.

Luscombe, Professor D. E., MA, PhD, FSA, 4 Caxton Road, Broomhill, Sheffield S10 3DE.

Luttrell, A. T., MA, DPhil, 14 Perfect View, Bath BA1 5JY.

Lyman, Professor Richard W., PhD, 350 East 57th Street, Apt 14-B, New York, N.Y. 10022, U.S.A.

Lynch, Professor J., MA, PhD, Inst. of Latin American Studies, University of London, 31 Tavistock Square, London WC1H 9HA.

Lynch, M., MA, PhD, Dept of Scottish History, The University, William Robertson Building, 50 George Square, Edinburgh EH8 9YW.

Lyttelton, The Hon. N. A. O., BA, 30 Paulton's Square, London SW3.

Mabbs, A. W., 32 The Street, Wallington, Herts. SG7 6SW.

Macaulay, J. H., MA, PhD, 11 Kirklee Circus, Glasgow G12 0TW.

McBriar, Professor A. M., BA, DPhil, FASSA, Dept of History, Monash University, Clayton, Victoria 3168, Australia.

McCaffrey, J. F., MA, PhD, Dept of Scottish History, The University, Glasgow G12 8QH.

MacCaffrey, Professor W. T., PhD, 745 Hollyoke Center, Harvard University, Cambridge, Mass. 02138, U.S.A.

McCann, W. P., BA, PhD, 41 Stanhope Gardens, Highgate, London N6.

McCaughan, Professor R. E. M., MA, BArch, Hon. DSc, FSA, FRAnthI, FRIBA, FRSA, 'Rowan Bank', Kingsley Green, Fernhurst, West Sussex GU27 3LL.

McConica, Professor J. K., CSB, MA, DPhil, University of St Michael's College, 81 St Mary's Street, Toronto, Ontario, Canada M5S 1J4.

McCord, Professor N., BA, PhD, 7 Hatherton Avenue, Cullercoats, North Shields, Tyne and Wear NE30 3LG.

McCracken, Professor J. L., MA, PhD, 196 Tenth Street, Morningside, Durban 4001, South Africa.

MacCulloch, D. N. J., MA, PhD, FSA, Wesley College, Henbury Road, Westbury-on-Trym, Bristol BS10 7QD.

MacCurtain, Margaret B., MA, PhD, Dept of History, University College, Belfield, Dublin 4, Ireland.

McCusker, J. J., MA, PhD, Dept of History, University of Maryland, College Park, Maryland 20742, U.S.A.

MacDonagh, Professor O., MA, PhD, Research School of Social Sciences, Institute of Advanced Studies, Australian National University, P.O. Box 4, Canberra, A.C.T. 2601, Australia.

Macdonald, Professor D. F., MA, DPhil, 11 Arnhall Drive, Dundee.

McDowell, Professor R. B., PhD, LittD, Trinity College, Dublin, Ireland.

Macfarlane, A. D. J., MA, DPhil, PhD, King's College, Cambridge CB2 1ST.

Macfarlane, L. J., PhD, FSA, King's College, University of Aberdeen, Aberdeen AB9 1FX.

McGrath, Professor P. V., MA, Dept of History, University of Bristol, Bristol BS8 1RJ.

MacGregor, D. R., MA, ARIBA, FSA, 99 Lonsdale Road, London SW13 9DA.

McGregor, J. F., BA, BLitt, Dept of History, University of Adelaide, SA 5001, Australia.

McGurk, J. J. N., BA, MPhil, PhD, Flat 2, 43 Lulworth Road, Birkdale, Southport, Merseyside, Lancs PR8 2JN.

McGurk, P. M., PhD, 11 Ashdon Close, Woodford Green, Essex IG8 0EF.

McHardy, Alison K., MA, DPhil, Dept of History, Taylor Building, King's College, Aberdeen AB9 1FX.

Machin, G. I. T., MA, DPhil, Dept of Modern History, University of Dundee, Dundee DD1 4HN.

MacIntyre, A. D., MA, DPhil, Magdalen College, Oxford OX1 4AU.

MacKay, A. I. K., MA, PhD, Dept of History, The University, Edinburgh EH8 9YL.

McKendrick, N., MA, Gonville and Caius College, Cambridge CB2 1TA.

McKenna, Professor J. W., MA, PhD, Orchard Hill Farm, Sandown Road, P.O. Box 343, N. Danville, N.H. 03819, U.S.A.

MacKenney, R. S., MA, PhD, Dept of History, University of Edinburgh, William Robertson Building, George Square, Edinburgh EH8 9JY.

MacKenzie, J. MacD., MA, PhD, Dept of History, The University, Bailrigg, Lancaster LA1 4YG.

Mackesy, P. G., MA, DPhil, DLitt, Pembroke College, Oxford OX1 1DW.

McKibbin, R. I., MA, DPhil, St John's College, Oxford OX1 3JP.

McKinley, R. A., MA, 42 Boyers Walk, Leicester Forest East, Leicester LE3 3LN.

McKitterick, Rosamond D., MA, PhD, Newnham College, Cambridge CB3 9DF.

Maclagan, M., MA, FSA, Trinity College, Oxford OX1 3BH.

MacLeod, Professor R. M., AB, PhD, Dept of History, The University of Sydney, Sydney, N.S.W., Australia 2006.

McLynn, F. J., MA, MA, PhD, 46 Grange Avenue, Twickenham, Middlesex TW2 5TW.

*McManners, Professor J., MA, DLitt, FBA, Christ Church, Oxford OX1 1DP.

McMillan, J. F., MA, DPhil, Dept of History, The University, Heslington, York YO1 5DD.

MacNiocaill, Professor G., PhD, DLitt, Dept of History, University College, Galway, Ireland.

McNulty, Miss P. A., BA, 84b Eastern Avenue, Reading RG1 5SF.

Macpherson, Professor C. B., BA, MSc(Econ), DSc(Econ), DLitt, LLD, FRSC, 32 Boswell Avenue, Toronto, Canada M5R 1M4.

Madariaga, Professor Isabel de, PhD, 25 Southwood Lawn Road, London N6.

Madden, A. F., McC, DPhil, Nuffield College, Oxford OX1 1NF.

Maddicott, J. R., MA, DPhil, Exeter College, Oxford OX1 3DP.

Maehl, Professor W. H., PhD, The Fielding Institute, 2112 Santa Barbara Street, Santa Barbara, CA 93105, U.S.A.

Maffei, Professor Domenico, MLL, DrJur, Via delle Cerchia 19, 53100 Siena, Italy.

Magnus-Allcroft, Sir Phillip, Bt., CBE, FRSL, Stokesay Court, Craven Arms, Shropshire SY7 9BD.

Maguire, W. A., MA, PhD, 18 Harberton Park, Belfast, N. Ireland BT9 6TS.

Mahoney, Professor T. H. D., AM, PhD, MPA, 130 Mt. Auburn Street, #410, Cambridge, Mass. 02138, U.S.A.

*MAJOR, Miss K., MA, BLitt, LittD, FBA, FSA, 21 Queensway, Lincoln LN2 4AJ.

Malcolm, Joyce L., 1264 Beacon Street, Brookline, Mass. 02146, U.S.A.

Mallett, Professor M. E., MA, DPhil, Dept of History, University of Warwick, Coventry CV4 7AL.

Mallia-Milanes, V., BA, MA, PhD, 135 Zabbar Road, Paola, Malta.

Mangan, James A., BA, PhD, PGCE, ACSE, DLC, 39 Abercorn Drive, Hamilton, Scotland.

Manning, Professor A. F., Bosweg 27, Berg en Dal, The Netherlands.

Manning, Professor B. S., MA, DPhil, Dept of History, New University of Ulster, Coleraine, Co. Londonderry, Northern Ireland BT52 1SA.

Manning, Professor R. B., PhD, 2848 Coleridge Road, Cleveland Heights, Ohio 44118, U.S.A.

Mansergh, Professor P. N. S., OBE, MA, DPhil, DLitt, LittD, FBA, St John's College, Cambridge CB2 1TP.

Maprayil, C., BD, LD, DD, MA, PhD, c/o Institute of Historical Research, Senate House, London WC1E 7HU.

Marchant, The Rev. Canon R. A., PhD, BD, Laxfield Vicarage, Woodbridge, Suffolk IP13 8DT.

Marett, W. P., BA, MA, PhD, BSc(Econ), BCom, 20 Barrington Road, Stoneygate, Leicester LE2 2RA.

Margetts, J., MA, DipEd, DrPhil, 5 Glenluce Road, Liverpool L19 3BX.

Markus, Professor Emeritus R. A., MA, PhD, 100 Park Road, Chilwell, Beeston, Nottingham NG9 4DE.

Marquand, Professor D., MA, Dept of Politics and Contemporary History, The University, Salford M5 4WT.

Marriner, Sheila, MA, PhD, Dept of Economic History, University of Liverpool, Eleanor Rathbone Building, Myrtle Street, P.O. Box 147, Liverpool L69 3BX.

Marsh, Professor Peter T., PhD, Dept of History, Syracuse University, Syracuse, New York 13210, U.S.A.

Marshall, J. D., PhD, Brynthwaite, Charney Road, Grange-over-Sands, Cumbria LA11 6BP.

Marshall, Professor P. J., MA, DPhil, King's College London, Strand, London WC2R 2LS.

Martin, E. W., Crossways, Editha Cottage, Black Torrington, Beaworthy, Devon EX21 5QF.

Martin, G. H., CBE, MA, DPhil, Public Record Office, Chancery Lane, London WC2A 1LR.

Martin, Professor Miguel, P.O. Box 1696, Zone 1, Panama 1, Republic of Panama.

Martindale, Jane P., MA, DPhil, School of English and American Studies, University of East Anglia, University Plain, Norwich NR4 7TJ.

Marwick, Professor A. J. B., MA, BLitt, Dept of History, The Open University, Walton Hall, Milton Keynes, Bucks MK7 6AA.

Mason, A., BA, PhD, 1 Siddeley Avenue, Kenilworth, Warwickshire CV8 1EW.

Mason, E. Emma, BA, PhD, Dept of History, Birkbeck College, Malet Street, London WC1E 7HX.

Mason, F. K., Beechwood, Watton, Norfolk IP25 6AB.

Mason, J. F. A., MA, DPhil, FSA, Christ Church, Oxford OX1 1DP.

Mate, Professor Mavis E, MA, PhD, Dept of History, University of Oregon, Eugene, OR 97405, U.S.A.

Mather, Professor F. C., MA, 69 Ethelburt Avenue, Swaythling, Southampton.

Mathew, W. M., MA, PhD, School of English and American Studies, University of East Anglia, University Plain, Norwich NR4 7TJ.

Mathias, Professor P., CBE, MA, DLitt, FBA, Downing College, Cambridge, CB2 1DQ.

*Mathur-Sherry, Tikait Narain, BA, LLB, 3/193-4 Prem-Nagar, Dayalbagh, Agra-282005 (U.P.), India.

Matthew, Professor D. J. A., MA, DPhil, Dept of History, The University, Reading RG6 2AA.

MATTHEW, H. C. G., MA, DPhil, (*Literary Director*), St Hugh's College, Oxford OX2 6LE.

Matthews, J. F., MA, DPhil, Queen's College, Oxford OX1 4AW.

Mattingly, Professor H. B., MA, Dept of Ancient History, The University, Leeds LS2 9JT.

Le May, G. H. L., MA, Worcester College, Oxford OX1 2HB.

Mayhew, G. J., BA, DPhil, 29 West Street, Lewes, East Sussex BN7 2NZ.

Mayhew, N. J. MA, 101 Marlborough Road, Oxford OX1 4LX.

Mayr-Harting, H. M. R. E., MA, DPhil, St Peter's College, Oxford OX1 2DL.

Mbaeyi, P. M., BA, DPhil, Alvan Ikoku College of Education, Dept of History, PMB 1033, Owerri, Imo State, Nigeria.

Meek, Christine E., MA, DPhil, 3145 Arts Building, Trinity College, Dublin 2, Ireland.

Meek, D. E., MA, BA, Dept of Celtic, University of Edinburgh, David Hume Tower, George Square, Edinburgh EH8 9JX.

Meller, Miss Helen E., BA, PhD, 2 Copenhagen Court, Denmark Grove, Alexandra Park, Nottingham NG3 4LF.

Merson, A. L., MA, Flat 12, Northerwood House, Swan Green, Lyndhurst, Southampton SO4 17DT.

Metcalf, Professor M, History Dept, 614 Social Sciences, 267 19th Avenue South, Minneapolis, Minn 55455, U.S.A.

Mettam, R. C., BA, MA, PhD, Dept of History, Queen Mary College, Mile End Road, London E1 4NS.

Mews, Stuart, PhD, Dept of Religious Studies, Cartmel College, Bailrigg, Lancaster.

Micklewright, F. H. A., PhD, 4 Lansdowne Court, 1 Lansdowne Road, Ridgway, Wimbledon, London SW20.

Middlebrook, Norman M., 48 Linden Way, Boston, Lincs. PE21 9DS.

Midgley, Miss L. M., MA, 84 Wolverhampton Road, Stafford ST17 4AW.

Miller, Professor A., BA, MA, PhD, Dept of History, University of Houston, Houston, Texas, U.S.A.

Miller, E., MA, LittD, 36 Almoners Avenue, Cambridge CB1 4PA.

Miller, Miss H., MA, University College of North Wales, Bangor, Gwynedd LL57 2DG.

Miller, J., MA, PhD, Dept of History, Queen Mary College, Mile End Road, London E1 4NS.

Milne, A. T., MA, 9 Frank Dixon Close, London SE21 7BD.

Milne, Miss D. J., MA, PhD, King's College, Aberdeen, AB9 1FX.

Milsom, Professor S. F. C., MA, FBA, 113 Grantchester Meadows, Cambridge CB3 9JN.

Minchinton, Professor W. E., BSc(Econ), 53 Homefield Road, Exeter, Devon, EX1 2QX.

Mingay, Professor G. E., PhD, Mill Field House, Selling Court, Selling, nr Faversham, Kent.

Mitchell, C., MA, BLitt, LittD, Woodhouse Farmhouse, Fyfield, Abingdon, Berks.

Mitchell, L. G., MA, DPhil, University College, Oxford OX1 4BH.

Mitchison, Professor Rosalind, MA, Great Yew, Ormiston, East Lothian EH35 5NJ.

Miyoshi, Professor Yoko, 1-29-2 Okayama, Meguro, Tokyo 152, Japan.

Moloney, Thomas M., PhD, 9 Treetops, Sydney Road, Woodford Green, Essex IG8 0SY.

Mommsen, Professor Dr W. J., Leuchtenberger Kirchweg 43, 4000 Dusseldorf-Kaiserswerth, West Germany.

Mondey, D. C., 175 Raeburn Avenue, Surbiton, Surrey KT5 9DE.

Money, Professor J., PhD, 912 St Patrick Street, Victoria, B.C., Canada V8S 4X5.

Moody, Professor Michael E., PhD, 2713 Third Street, La Verne, Calif. 91750, U.S.A.

Moore, B. J. S., BA, University of Bristol, 67 Woodland Road, Bristol BS8 1UL.

Moore, Professor D. Cresap, 935 Memorial Drive, Cambridge, Mass. 02138, U.S.A.

Moore, R. I., MA, Dept of History, The University, Sheffield S10 2TN.

Moore, Professor R. J., DLit, PhD, BA, MA, School of Social Sciences, Flinders University of South Australia, Bedford Park, South Australia 5042, Australia.

*Moorman, Mrs M., MA, 22 Springwell Road, Durham DH1 4LR.

Morey, Rev. Dom R. Adrian, OSB, MA, DPhil, LittD, Benet House, Mount Pleasant, Cambridge CB3 0BL.

Morgan, B. G., BArch, PhD, Tan-y-Fron, 43 Church Walks, Llandudno, Gwynedd.

Morgan, D. A. L., Dept of History, University College London, Gower Street, London WC1E 6BT.

Morgan, David R., MA, PhD, Dept of Politics, Roxby Building, The University, P.O. Box 147, Liverpool L69 3BX.

Morgan, K. O., MA, DPhil, FBA, The Queen's College, Oxford OX1 4AW.

Morgan, Miss P. E., 1a The Cloisters, Hereford HR1 2NG.

Morgan, P. T. J., MA, DPhil, Dept of History, University College of Swansea, Singleton Park, Swansea SA2 7BR.

Morgan, Victor F. G., BA, School of English and American Studies, University of East Anglia, Norwick NR4 7TJ.

Morioka, Professor K., BA, 3-12 Sanno 4 Chome, Ota-Ku, Tokyo 143, Japan.

Morrell, J. B., BSc., MA, Dept of Social Sciences, The University, Richmond Road, Bradford BD7 1DP.

Morrill, J. S., MA, DPhil, Selwyn College, Cambridge CB3 9DQ.

Morris, The Rev. Professor C., MA, 53 Cobbett Road, Bitterne Park, Southampton SO2 4HJ.

Morris, G. C., MA, King's College, Cambridge CB2 1ST.

Morris, L. P., BA, PhD, Dept of History and Archaeology, The University, Queen's Drive, Exeter EX4 4QH.

Mortimer, R., PhD, 10 Orchard Avenue, Cambridge CB2 4AH.

Mosse, Professor W. E. E., MA, PhD, Dawn Cottage, Ashwellthorpe, Norwich, Norfolk.

Mullins, E. L. C., OBE, MA, Institute of Historical Research, University of London, Senate House, London WC1E 7HU.

Munro, D. J., MA, 65 Meadowcroft, St Albans, Herts. AL1 1UF.

Murdoch, D. H., MA, School of History, The University, Leeds LS2 9JT.

Murray, A., MA, BA, BPhil, University College, Oxford OX1 4BH.

Murray, Athol L., MA, LLB, PhD, 33 Inverleith Gardens, Edinburgh EH3 5PR.

Murray, Professor B. K., PhD, BA, History Department, University of Witwatersrand, Johannesburg, South Africa.

Myatt-Price, Miss E. M., BA, MA, 20 Highfield Drive, Epsom, Surrey KT19 0AS.

Myerscough, J., MA, 39 Campden Street, London W8 7ET.

Myres, J. N. L., CBE, LLD, DLitt, DLit, FBA, FSA, The Manor House, Kennington, Oxford OX1 5PH.

Nef, Professor J. U., PhD, 2726 N Street NW, Washington, D.C. 20007, U.S.A.

Nelson, Janet L., BA, PhD, Dept of History, King's College London, Strand, London WC2R 2LS.

Neveu, Dr Bruno, 30 rue Jacob, Paris VIe, France.

New, Professor J. F. H., Dept of History, Waterloo University, Waterloo, Ontario, Canada.

Newbury, C. W., MA, PhD, Linacre College, Oxford OX1 3JA.

Newitt, M. D. D., BA, PhD, Queen's Building, University of Exeter, Exeter, Devon EX4 4QH.

Newman, Professor A. N., MA, DPhil, 33 Stanley Road, Leicester.

Newman, P. R., BA, DPhil, 1 Ainsty Farm Cottage, Bilton in Ainsty, York YO5 8NN.

Newsome, D. H., MA, LittD, Master's Lodge, Wellington College, Crowthorne, Berks. RG11 7PU.

Nicholas, Professor David, PhD, Dept of History, University of Nebraska, Lincoln, Nebraska 68588, U.S.A.

Nicholas, Professor H. G., MA, FBA, New College, Oxford OX1 3BN.

Nicholls, A. J., MA, BPhil, St Antony's College, Oxford OX2 6JF.

Nicol, Mrs A., MA, BLitt, Public Record Office, Chancery Lane, London WC2A 1LR.

Nicol, Professor D. M., MA, PhD, King's College London, London WC2R 2LS.

Nightingale, Pamela, MA, PhD, 20 Beaumont Buildings, Oxford OX1 2LL.

Noakes, J. D., BA, MA, DPhil, Dept of History, Queen's Bldg., The University, Exeter EX4 4QH.
Norman, E. R., MA, PhD, Christ Church College, Canterbuty, Kent CT1 1QU.

Obolensky, Professor Sir Dimitri, MA, PhD, DLitt, FBA, FSA, Christ Church, Oxford OX1 1DP.
O'Brien, M. G. R., BA, MA, PhD, Magee College, University of Ulster, Northlands Road, Londonderry, Northern Ireland.
O'Brien, P. K., MA, DPhil, BSc(Econ), St Antony's College, Oxford OX2 6JF.
O'Day, A., BA, MA, PhD, Polytechnic of North London, Prince of Wales Road, London NW5.
O'Day (Englander), Mrs M. R., BA, PhD, 14 Marshworth, Tinkers Bridge, Milton Keynes MK6 3DA.
*Offler, Professor H. S., MA, 28 Old Elvet, Durham DH1 3HN.
O'Gorman, F., BA, PhD, The University, Manchester M13 9PL.
O'Higgins, The Rev. J., SJ, MA, DPhil, Campion Hall, Oxford.
Okey, R. F. C., MA, DPhil, 10 Bertie Road, Kenilworth, Warwickshire CU8 1JP.
Olney, R. J., MA, DPhil, Historical Manuscripts Commission, Quality House, Quality Court, Chancery Lane, London WC2A 1HP.
Orde, Miss A. W., MA, PhD, Dept of History, University of Durham, 43 North Bailey, Durham DH1 3EX.
Orme, Professor N. I., MA, DPhil, DLitt, FSA, Dept. of History and Archaeology, University of Exeter, Exeter EX4 4QH.
*Orr, J. E., MA, ThD, DPhil, 11451 Berwick Street, Los Angeles, Calif. 90049, U.S.A.
Ó Tuathaigh, M. A. G., MA, Dept of History, University College, Galway, Ireland.
Otway-Ruthven, Professor A. J., MA, PhD, 7 Trinity College, Dublin, Ireland.
Outhwaite, R. B., MA, PhD, Gonville and Caius College, Cambridge CB2 1TA.
Ovendale, R., MA, DPhil, Dept of International Politics, University College of Wales, Aberystwyth SY23 3DY.
Owen, A. E. B., MA, 35 Whitwell Way, Coton, Cambridge CB3 7PW.
Owen, Mrs D. M., MA, LittD, FSA, 35 Whitwell Way, Coton, Cambridge CB3 7PW.
Owen, G. D., MA, PhD, 21 Clifton Terrace, Brighton, Sussex BN1 3HA.
Owen, J. B., BSc, MA, DPhil, 24 Hurdeswell, Long Hanborough, Oxford OX7 2DH.

Pagden, A. R. D., BA, 172 Sturton Street, Cambridge CB1 2QF.
Palgrave, D. A., MA, CChem, FRSC, FSG, 210 Bawtry Road, Doncaster, S. Yorkshire DN4 7BZ.
Palliser, Professor D. M., MA, DPhil, FSA, Dept of History, The University, Hull HU6 7RX.
Palmer, J. G. MA, MSc(Econ), MPhil, 78 Norroy Road, London SW15 1PG.
Palmer, J. J. N., BA, BLitt, PhD, 59 Marlborough Avenue, Hull.
Palmer, Sarah, PhD, MA, MA, Dept of History, Queen Mary College, Mile End Road, London E1 4NS.

Paret, Professor P., Inst. for Advanced Study, School of Historical Studies, Princeton, N.J. 08540, U.S.A.

Parish, Professor P. J., BA, Institute of U.S. Studies, 31 Tavistock Square, London WC1H 9EZ.

Parker, Professor N. G., MA, PhD, LittD, FBA, Dept of History, University of Illinois, 309 Gregory Hall, 810 South Wright Street, Urbana, Ill. 61801, U.S.A.

Parker, R. A. C., MA, DPhil, The Queen's College, Oxford OX1 4AW.

Parkes, M. B., BLitt, MA, FSA, Keble College, Oxford OX1 3PG.

*Parkinson, Professor C. N., MA, PhD, 45 Howe Road, Onchan, Douglas, Isle of Man.

Parris, H. W., MA, PhD, Warwick House, 47 Guildhall Street, Bury St Edmunds, Suffolk IP33 1QF.

Parry, G. J. R., MA, PhD, History Dept, University College of North Wales, Bangor, Gwynedd, LL57 2DG.

Patrick, Rev. J. G., MA, PhD, DLitt, 8 North Street, Braunton, N. Devon EX33 1AJ.

Pavlowitch, Stevan K., MA, LesL, Dept of History, The University, South-ampton SO9 5NH.

Payne, Mrs. Ann, BA, 138 Culford Road, London N1 4HU.

Payne, Professor Peter L., BA, PhD, 68 Hamilton Place, Aberdeen AB2 4BA.

Paz, Denis G., PhD, Dept of History, Clemson University, Clemson, South Carolina 29634-1507, U.S.A.

Peake, Rev. F. A., DD, DSLitt, 310 Dalehurst Drive, Nepean, Ontario, Canada K2G 4E4.

Pearl, Mrs Valerie L., MA, DPhil, FSA, New Hall, Cambridge CB3 0DF.

Peck, Professor Linda L., PhD, Dept of History, Purdue University, University Hall, West Lafayette, Indiana 47907, U.S.A.

Peden, G. C., MA, DPhil, School of History, University of Bristol, 13-15 Woodland Road, Bristol BS8 1TB.

Peek, Miss H. E., MA, FSA, FSAScot, Taintona, Moretonhampstead, Newton Abbot, Devon TQ13 8LG.

Peel, Lynnette J., BAgrSc, MAgrSc, PhD, 49 Oaklands, Hamilton Road, Reading RG1 5RN.

Peele, Miss Gillian R., BA, BPhil, Lady Margaret Hall, Oxford OX2 6QA.

Pelling, Margaret, BA, MLitt, Wellcome Unit for the History of Medicine, University of Oxford, 45-47 Banbury Road, Oxford OX2 6PE.

Pennington, D. H., MA, Balliol College, Oxford OX1 3BJ.

Perkin, Professor H. J., MA, Dept of History, Northwestern University, Evanston, Illinois 60201, U.S.A.

Perry, Norma, BA, PhD, 2 Crossmead Villas, Dunsford Road, Exeter, Devon, EX2 9PU.

Peters, Professor E. M., PhD, Dept of History, University of Pennsylvania, Philadelphia 19174, U.S.A.

Pettegree, A. D. M., MA, DPhil, Dept. of Modern History, St Andrews University, St Andrews, Fife KY16 9AL.

Pfaff, Professor Richard W., MA, DPhil, Dept of History, Hamilton Hall 070A, University of North Carolina, Chapel Hill, N.C. 27514, U.S.A.

Phillips, Sir Henry (E. I.), CMG, MBE, MA, 34 Ross Court, Putney Hill, London SW15.

Phillips, Assoc. Professor John A., PhD, Dept of History, University of California, Riverside, Calif. 92521, U.S.A.

Phillips, J. R. S., BA, PhD, FSA, Dept of Medieval History, University College, Dublin 4, Ireland.

Phillipson. N.T., MA, PhD, Dept of History, The University George Square, Edinburgh EH8 9JY.

Phythian-Adams, C. V., MA, Dept of English Local History, The University, University Road, Leicester LE1 7RH.

Pierce, Professor G. O., MA, Dept of History of Wales, University College, P.O. Box 95, Cardiff CF1 1XA.

Piggin, F. S., BA, BD, DipEd, PhD, AKC, Dept of History, University of Wollongong, Wollongong, N.S.W., Australia 2500.

Pitt, H. G., MA, Worcester College, Oxford OX1 2HB.

Platt, Professor C. P. S., MA, PhD, FSA, Dept of History, The University, Southampton SO9 5NH.

Platt, Professor D. C. St M., MA, DPhil, St Antony's College, Oxford OX2 6JF.

Plumb, Sir John, PhD, LittD, FBA, FSA, Christ's College, Cambridge CB2 3BU.

Pocock, Professor J. G. A., PhD, Johns Hopkins University, Baltimore, Md. 21218, U.S.A.

Pogge von Strandmann, H. J. O., MA, DPhil, University College, Oxford OX1 4BH.

Pole, Professor J. R., MA, PhD, St Catherine's College, Oxford OX1 3UJ.

Pollard, A. J., BA, PhD, 22 The Green, Hurworth-on-Tees, Darlington, Co. Durham DL2 2AA.

Pollard, Professor D. S., BSc(Econ), PhD, Abteilung Geschichte, Fakultät für Geschichtswissenschaft und Philosophie, Univer. Bielefeld, Postfach 8640, 4800 Bielefeld 1.

Polonsky, A. B., BA, DPhil, Dept of International History, London School of Economics, Houghton Street, London WC2A 2AE.

Port, Professor M. H., MA, BLitt, FSA, Dept of History, Queen Mary College, Mile End Road, London E1 4NS.

PORTER, A. N., MA, PhD (*Hon. Secretary*), Dept of History, King's College London, Strand, London WC2R 2LS.

Porter, B. E., BSc(Econ), PhD, Merville, Allan Road, Seasalter, Whitstable, Kent CT5 4AH.

Porter, H. C., MA, PhD, Faculty of History, West Road, Cambridge CB3 9EF.

Porter, J. H., BA, PhD, Dept of Economic History, The University, Amory Buildings, Rennes Drive, Exeter EX4 4RJ.

Porter, S., BA, MLitt, PhD, Royal Commission on Historical Monuments, Newlands House, 37-40 Berners Street, London W1P 4BP.

Post, J., MA, PhD, Public Record Office, Chancery Lane, London WC2A 1LR.

Potter, J., BA, MA(Econ), London School of Economics, Houghton Street, London WC2A 2AE.

Powell, W. R., BLitt, MA, FSA, 2 Glanmead, Shenfield Road, Brentwood, Essex CM15 8ER.

Power, M. J., BA, PhD, School of History, The University, P.O. Box 147, Liverpool L69 3BX.

Powicke, Professor M. R., MA. 67 Lee Avenue, Toronto, Ontario, Canada, M43 2P1.

Powis, J. K. MA, DPhil, Balliol College, Oxford OX1 3BJ.

Prall, Professor Stuart E., MA, PhD, Dept of History, Queens College, C.U.N.Y., Flushing, N.Y. 11367, U.S.A.

. Prentis, Malcolm D., BA, MA, PhD, 3 Marina Place, Belrose, New South Wales 2085, Australia.

Prest, W. R., MA, DPhil, Dept of History, University of Adelaide, North Terrace, Adelaide 5001, S. Australia.

Preston, Professor P., MA, DPhil, MA, Dept of History, Queen Mary College, Mile End Road, London E1 4NS.

*Preston, Professor R. A., MA, PhD, Duke University, Durham, N.C., U.S.A.

Prestwich, J. O., MA, 18 Dunstan Road, Old Headington, Oxford OX3 9BY.

Prestwich, Mrs M., MA, St Hilda's College, Oxford OX4 1DY.

Prestwich, Professor M. C., MA, DPhil, Dept of History, The University, 43/46 North Bailey, Durham DH1 3EX.

Price, A. W., PhD, 19 Bayley Close, Uppingham, Leicestershire LE15 9TG.

Price, Rev. D. T. W., MA, St David's University College, Lampeter, Dyfed SA48 7ED.

Price, F. D., MA, BLitt, FSA, Keble College, Oxford OX1 3PG.

Price, Professor Jacob M., AM, PhD, University of Michigan, Ann Arbor, Michigan 48104, U.S.A.

Price, R. D., BA, DLitt, School of Modern Languages & European History, University of East Anglia, Norwich NR4 7TJ.

Prichard, Canon T. J., MA, PhD, Tros-yr-Afon, Llangwnnadl, Pwllheli, Gwynedd LL53 8NS.

Prins, G. I. T., MA, PhD, Emmanuel College, Cambridge CB2 3AP.

Pritchard, Professor D. G., PhD, 11 Coed Mor, Sketty, Swansea, W. Glam. SA2 8BQ.

Pritchard, R. J., PhD, 28 Star Hill, Rochester, Kent ME1 1XB.

Prochaska, Alice M. S., MA, DPhil, 9 Addison Bridge Place, London W14 8XP.

Pronay, N., BA, School of History, The University, Leeds LS2 9JT.

Prothero, I. J., BA, PhD, The University, Manchester M13 9PL.

Pugh, T. B., MA, BLitt, 28 Bassett Wood Drive, Southampton SO2 3PS.

Pullan, Professor B. S., MA, PhD, FBA, Dept of History, The University, Manchester M13 9PL.

Pulman, M. B., MA, PhD, AB, History Dept, University of Denver, Colorado 80210, U.S.A.

Pulzer, Professor P. G. J., MA, PhD, All Souls College, Oxford OX1 4AL.

Quested, Rosemary K. I., MA, PhD, 30 Woodford Court, Birchington, Kent CT7 9DR.

Quinault, R. E., MA, DPhil, 21 Tytherton Road, London N19.

QUINN, Professor D. B., MA, PhD, DLit, DLitt, DLitt, DLitt, LLD, MRIA, DHL, Hon. FBA, 9 Knowsley Road, Liverpool L19 0PF.

Quintrell, B. W., MA, PhD, School of History, The University, P.O. Box 147, Liverpool L69 3BX.

Raban, Mrs S. G., MA, PhD, Trinity Hall, Cambridge CB2 1TJ.

Rabb, Professor T. K., MA, PhD, Princeton University, Princeton, N.J. 08540, U.S.A.

Radford, C. A. Ralegh, MA, DLitt, FBA, FSA, Culmcott, Uffculme, Cullompton, Devon EX15 3AT.

*Ramm, Miss A., MA, DLitt, Metton Road, Roughton, Norfolk NR11 8QT.

*Ramsay, G. D., MA, DPhil, 15 Charlbury Road, Oxford OX2 6UT.

Ramsden, J. A., MA, DPhil, Dept of History, Queen Mary College, Mile End Road, London E1 4NS.

Ramsey, Professor P. H., MA, DPhil, Taylor Building, King's College, Old Aberdeen AB9 1FX.

Ranft, Professor B. McL., MA, DPhil. 32 Parkgate, Blackheath, London SE3 9XF.

Ransome, D. R., MA, PhD, 10 New Street, Woodbridge, Suffolk.

Ratcliffe, D. J., MA, BPhil, PhD, Dept of History, The University, 43 North Bailey, Durham DH1 3EX.

Rawcliffe, Carole, BA, PhD, 24 Villiers Road, London NW2.

Rawley, Professor J. A., PhD, University of Nebraska, Lincoln, Nebraska 68508, U.S.A.

Ray, Professor R. D., BA, BD, PhD, Dept of History, University of Toledo, 2801 W. Bancroft Street, Toledo, Ohio 43606, U.S.A.

Read, Professor D., BLitt, MA, PhD, Darwin College, University of Kent at Canterbury, Kent CT2 7NY.

Reader, W. J., BA, PhD, 46 Gough Way, Cambridge CB3 9LN.

Reay, B. G., BA, DPhil, Dept of History, University of Auckland, Auckland, New Zealand.

Reed, Michael A., MA, LLB, PhD, 1 Paddock Close, Quorn, Leicester LE12 8BJ.

Reeves, Professor A. C., MA, PhD, Dept of History, Ohio University, Athens, Ohio 45701, U.S.A.

Reeves, Miss M. E., MA, PhD, 38 Norham Road, Oxford OX2 6SQ.

Reid, B. H., MA, PhD, Dept of War Studies, Kings College London, Strand, London WC2R 2LS.

Reid, F., MA, DPhil, 24 Station Road, Kenilworth, Warwickshire.

Reid, Professor L. D., MA, PhD, 200 E. Brandon Road, Columbia, Mo. 65201, U.S.A.

Reid, Professor W. S., MA, PhD, University of Guelph, Guelph, Ontario, Canada.

Rempel, Professor R. A., DPhil, Dept of History, McMaster University, 1280 Main Street West, Hamilton, Ontario, Canada L8S 4L9.

Renold, Miss P., MA, 51 Woodstock Close, Oxford OX2 8DD.

Renshaw, P. R. G., MA, Dept of History, The University, Sheffield S10 2TN.

Reuter, T. A., MA, DPhil, Monumenta Germaniae Historica, Ludwig-strasse 16, 8 München 34, West Germany.

Reynolds, D. J., MA, PhD, Christ's College, Cambridge CB2 3BU.

Reynolds, Miss S. M. G., MA, 26 Lennox Gardens, London SW1.

Richards, J. M., MA, Dept of History, The University, Bailrigg, Lancaster LA1 4YG.

Richards, Rev. J. M., MA, BLitt, STL, St Mary's, Cadogan Street, London SW3 2QR.

Richardson, P. G. L., BA, PhD, 16 Tanner Grove, Northcote, Victoria 3070, Australia.

Richardson, R. C., BA, PhD, King Alfred's College, Winchester.

Richter, Professor M., DrPhil. habil, Universität Konstanz, Postfach 5560, D-7750 Konstanz 1, Germany.

Riden, Philip J., MA, MLitt, Dept of Extramural Studies, University College, P.O. Box 78, Cardiff CF1 1XL.

Ridgard, J. M., PhD, Dennington Place, Dennington, Woodbridge, Suffolk IP13 8AN.

Riley, P. W. J., BA, PhD, The University, Manchester M13 9PL.

Riley-Smith, Professor J. S. C., MA, PhD, Royal Holloway and Bedford New College, Egham Hill, Egham, Surrey TW20 0EX.

Rimmer, Professor W. G., MA, PhD, University of N.S.W., P.O. Box 1, Kensington, N.S.W. 2033, Australia.

Ritcheson, Professor C. R., DPhil, Dept of History, University of Southern California, University Park, Los Angeles 90007, U.S.A.

Ritchie, J. D., BA, DipEd, PhD, 74 Banambila Street, Aranda, ACT 2614, Australia.

Rizvi, S. A. G., MA, DPhil, 7 Portland Road, Summertown, Oxford.

Roach, Professor J. P. C., MA, PhD, 1 Park Crescent, Sheffield S10 2DY.

Robbins, Professor Caroline, PhD, 815 The Chetwynd, Rosemount, Pa. 19010, U.S.A.

Robbins, Professor K. G., MA, DPhil, DLitt, Dept of History, The University, Glasgow G12 8QQ.

Roberts, J. M., MA, DPhil, Merton College, Oxford OX1 4JD.

Roberts, Professor M., MA, DPhil, DLit, FilDr, FBA, 1 Allen Street, Grahamstown 6140, C.P., South Africa.

Roberts, P. R., MA, PhD, FSA, Keynes College, The University, Canterbury, Kent CT2 7NP.

Roberts, Professor R. C., PhD, 284 Blenheim Road, Columbus, Ohio 43214, U.S.A.

Roberts, Professor R. S., PhD, History Dept, University of Zimbabwe, P.O. Box MP 167, Harare, Zimbabwe.

Roberts, Stephen K., BA, PhD, East View, Iron Cross, Salford Priors, Evesham, Worcs. WR11 5SH.

Robertson, J. C., MA, DPhil, St Hugh's College, Oxford OX2 6LE.

Robinson, F. C. R., MA, PhD, Alderside, Egham Hill, Egham, Surrey TW20 0BD.

Robinson, K. E., CBE, MA, DLitt, LLD, The Old Rectory, Church Westcote, Kingham, Oxford OX7 6SF.

Robinson, R. A. H., BA, PhD, School of History, The University, Birmingham B15 2TT.

Robinton, Professor Madeline R., MA, PhD, 210 Columbia Heights, Brooklyn 1, New York, U.S.A.

Robson, Professor Ann P. W., PhD, 28 McMaster Avenue, Toronto, Ontario, Canada M4V 1A9.

Rodger, N. A. M., MA, DPhil, 40 Grafton Road, Acton, London W3.

*Rodkey, F. S., AM, PhD, 152 Bradley Drive, Santa Cruz, Calif., U.S.A.

Rodney, Professor W., MA, PhD, Royal Roads Military College, FMO, Victoria, B.C., Canada V0S 1B0.

Roebuck, Peter, BA, PhD, Dept of History, New University of Ulster, Coleraine, N. Ireland BT48 7JL.

Rogers, Professor A., MA, PhD, FSA, Ulph Cottage, Church Plain, Burnham Market, Kings Lynn, Norfolk PE31 8EL.

Rogister, J. M. J., MA, DPhil, 4 The Peth, Durham DH1 4PZ.

Rolo, Professor P. J. V., MA, The University, Keele, Staffordshire ST5 5BG.

Rompkey, R. G., MA, BEd, PhD, Dept of English, Memorial University, St John's, Newfoundland, Canada A1C 5S7.

Roots, Professor I. A., MA, FSA, Dept of History, University of Exeter, Queen's Building, The Queen's Drive, Exeter EX4 4QH.

Roper, M., MA, Public Record Office, Ruskin Avenue, Kew, Richmond, Surrey TW9 4DU.

Rose, Margaret A., BA, PhD, c/o H.P.S. Faculty of Arts University of Melbourne, Parkville, Victoria 3052, Australia.

Rose, Professor P. L., MA, DenHist (Sorbonne), Dept of General History, University of Haifa, Haifa, Israel.

Rosenthal, Professor Joel T., PhD, Dept of History, State University, Stony Brook, New York 11794, U.S.A.

Roseveare, Professor H. G., PhD, King's College London, Strand, London WC2R 2LS.

Roskell, Professor J. S., MA, DPhil, FBA, The University, Manchester M13 9PL.

Rothblatt, Professor Sheldon, PhD, Dept of History, University of California, Berkeley, Calif. 94720, U.S.A.

Rothermund, Professor D., MA, PhD, DPhil Habil, Oberer Burggarten 2, 6915 Dossenheim, West Germany.

Rothney, Professor G. O., MA, PhD, LLD, St John's College, University of Manitoba, Winnipeg, Canada R3T 2M5.

Rothrock, Professor G. A., MA, PhD, Dept of History, University of Alberta, Edmonton, Alberta, Canada T6G 2H4.

Rousseau, P. H., MA, DPhil, Dept of History, University of Auckland, Private Bag, Auckland, New Zealand.

*Rowe, Miss B. J. H., MA, BLitt, St Anne's Cottage, Winkton, Christchurch, Hants.

Rowe, W. J., DPhil, Rock Mill, Par, Cornwall PL25 2SS.

Rowse, A. L., MA, DLitt, DCL, FBA, Trenarren House, St Austell, Cornwall.

Roy, I., MA, DPhil, Dept of History, King's College London, Strand, London WC2R 2LS.

Roy, Professor R. H., MA, PhD, 2841 Tudor Avenue, Victoria, B.C., Canada V8N 1L6.

Royle, E., MA, PhD, Dept of History, The University, Heslington, York YO1 5DD.

Rubens, A., FRICS, FSA, 16 Grosvenor Place, London SW1.

Rubini, D. A., DPhil, Temple University, Philadelphia 19122, Penn., U.S.A.

Rubinstein, Professor N., PhD, Westfield College, Kidderpore Avenue, London NW3 7ST.

Rubinstein, Assoc. Professor W. D., BA, PhD, School of Social Sciences, Deakin University, Victoria 3217, Australia.

Ruddock, Miss A. A., PhD, FSA, Wren Cottage, Heatherwood, Midhurst, W. Sussex GU29 9LH.

Rudé, Professor G. F. E., MA, PhD, The Oast House, Hope Farm, Beckley, nr Rye, E. Sussex.

Rule, Professor John C., MA, PhD, Dept of History, Ohio State University, 230 West 17th Avenue, Colombus, Ohio 43210, U.S.A.

Rule, J. G., MA, PhD, Dept of History, The University, Southampton SO9 5NH.

Rumble, A. R., BA, PhD, Dip Arch Admin., Dept of Palaeography, University of Manchester, Oxford Road, Manchester M13 8PL.

*RUNCIMAN, The Hon. Sir Steven, CH, MA, DPhil, LLD, LittD, DLitt, LitD, DD, DHL, FBA, FSA, Elshieshields, Lockerbie, Dumfriesshire.

Runyan, Professor Timothy J., Dept of History, Cleveland State University, Cleveland, Ohio 44115, U.S.A.

Rupke, N. A., MA, PhD, Wolfson College, Oxford OX2 6UD.

Russell, Professor C. S. R., MA, Dept of History, University College London, Gower Street, London WC1E 6BT.
Russell, Mrs J. G., MA, DPhil, St Hugh's College, Oxford OX2 6LE.
Russell, Professor P. E. L. R., MA, FBA, 23 Belsyre Court, Woodstock Road, Oxford OX2 6HU.
Ryan, A. N., MA, School of History, University of Liverpool, P.O. Box 147, Liverpool L69 3BX.
Ryan, Professor S., PhD, Dept of History, Memorial University, St John's Newfoundland, Canada A1C 5S7.
Rycraft, P., BA, Dept of History, The University, Heslington, York YO1 5DD.
Ryder, A. F. C., MA, DPhil, Dept of History, University of Bristol, Wills Memorial Building, Queen's Road, Bristol BS8 1RJ.

Sachse, Professor W. L., PhD, 4066 Whitney Avenue, Mt Carmel, Conn. 06518, U.S.A.
Sainty, Sir John, KCB, MA, 22 Kelso Place, London W8.
*Salmon, Professor E. T., MA, PhD, 36 Auchmar Road, Hamilton, Ontario, Canada LPC 1C5.
Salmon, Professor J. H. M., MA, MLitt, DLit, Bryn Mawr College, Bryn Mawr, Pa. 19101, U.S.A.
*Saltman, Professor A., MA., PhD, Bar Ilan University, Ramat Gan, Israel.
Salvadori, Max W., Dr Sc, LittD, 36 Ward Avenue, Northampton, Mass. 01060, U.S.A.
Samuel, E. R., BA, MPhil, Flat 4, Garden Court, 63 Holden Road, Woodside Park, London N12 7DG.
Sanderson, Professor G. N., MA, PhD, 2 Alder Close, Englefield Green, Surrey TW20 0LU.
Sar Desai, Professor Damodar R., MA, PhD, Dept of History, University of California, Los Angeles, Calif. 90024, U.S.A.
Saul, N. E., MA, DPhil, Dept of History, Royal Holloway and Bedford New College, Egham Hill, Egham, Surrey TW20 0EX.
Saunders, A. D., MA, FSA, 12 Ashburnham Grove, Greenwich, London SE10 8UH.
Saville, Professor J., BSc(Econ), Dept of Economic and Social History, The University, Hull HU6 7RX.
Sawyer, Professor P. H., MA, Viktoriagatan 18, 441 33 Alingsas, Sweden.
Sayers, Miss J. E., MA, BLitt, PhD, FSA, University College London, Gower Street, London WC1E 6BT.
Scammell, G. V., MA, Pembroke College, Cambridge CB2 1RF.
Scammell, Mrs Jean, MA, Clare Hall, Cambridge.
Scarisbrick, Professor J. J., MA, PhD, 35 Kenilworth Road, Leamington Spa, Warwickshire.
Schofield, A. N. E. D., PhD, 57 West Way, Rickmansworth, Herts. WD3 2EH.
Schofield, R. S., MA, PhD, 27 Trumpington Street, Cambridge CB2 1QA.
Schreiber, Professor Roy E., PhD, Dept of History, Indiana University, P.O.B. 7111, South Bend, Indiana 46634, U.S.A.
Schreuder, Professor D. M., BA, DPhil, Dept of History, The University of Sydney, N.S.W. 2006, Australia.
Schroder, Professor H.-C., DPhil, Technische Hochschule Darmstadt, Institut fur Geschichte, Schloss, 6100 Darmstadt, West Germany.
Schurman, Professor D. McK., MA, MA, PhD, 191 King Street East, Kingston, Ontario, Canada K7L 3A3.

Schweizer, Karl W., MA, PhD, 4 Harrold Drive, Bishop's University, Lennoxville, Quebec, Canada.

Schwoerer, Professor Lois G., PhD, 7213 Rollingwood Drive, Chevy Chase, Maryland 20015, U.S.A.

Scott, Dom Geoffrey, MA, PhD, Dip Theol, Douai Abbey, Upper Woolhampton, Reading RG7 5TH.

Scott, H. M., MA, PhD, Dept of Modern History, The University, St Salvator's College, St Andrews, Fife.

Scott, Tom, MA, PhD, School of History, The University, P.O. Box 147, Liverpool L69 3BX.

Scouloudi, Miss I., MSc(Econ), FSA, 82, 3 Whitehall Court, London SW1A 2EL.

Scribner, R. W., MA, PhD, Clare College, Cambridge CB2 1TL.

Seaborne, M. V. J., MA, Penylan, Cilcain Road, Pantymwyn, Mold, Clwyd CH7 5NJ.

Searle, A., BA, MPhil, Dept of Manuscripts, British Library, London WC1B 3DG.

Searle, Professor Eleanor, AB, PhD, 431 S. Parkwood Avenue, Pasadena, Calif. 91107, U.S.A.

Searle, G. R., MA, PhD, School of English and American Studies, University of East Anglia, University Plain, Norwich NR4 7TJ.

Seaver, Professor Paul S., MA, PhD, Dept of History, Stanford University, Stanford, Calif. 94305, U.S.A.

Seddon, P. R., BA, PhD, Dept of History, The University, Nottingham NG7 2RD.

Sell, Rev. Professor A. P. F., BA, BD, MA, PhD, Dept of Religious Studies, Faculty of Humanities, 2500 University Drive NW, Calgary, Alberta, Canada T2N 1N4.

Sellar, W. D. H., BA, LLB, 6 Eildon Street, Edinburgh EH3 5JU.

Semmell, Professor Bernard, PhD, Dept of History, State University of New York at Stony Brook, N.Y. 11790, U.S.A.

Serjeant, W. R., BA, 51 Derwent Road, Ipswich, Suffolk IP3 0QR.

Seton-Watson, C. I. W., MC, MA, Oriel College, Oxford OX1 4EW.

Shannon, Professor R. T., MA, PhD, Dept of History, University College of Swansea, Swansea SA2 8PP.

Sharpe, J. A., MA, DPhil, Dept of History, The University, Heslington, York YO1 5DD.

Sharpe, K. M., MA, DPhil, Dept of History, University of Southampton, Highfield, Southampton SO9 5NH.

Sharpe, R., MA, PhD, 35 Norreys Avenue, Oxford OX1 4ST.

Shaw, I. P., MA, 3 Oaks Lane, Shirley, Croydon, Surrey CR0 5HP.

Shead, N. F., MA, BLitt, 8 Whittliemuir Avenue, Muirend, Glasgow G44 3HU.

Sheils, W. J., PhD, Goodricke Lodge, Heslington Lane, York YO1 5DD.

Shennan, Professor J. H., PhD, Dept of History, University of Lancaster, Furness College, Bailrigg, Lancaster LA1 4YG.

Sheppard, F. H. W., MA, PhD, FSA, 10 Albion Place, West Street, Henley-on-Thames, Oxon RG9 2DT.

Sherborne, J. W., MA, 26 Hanbury Road, Bristol BS8 2EP.

Sheridan, Professor R. B., BS, MS, PhD, Dept of Economics, University of Kansas, Lawrence, Kansas 66045, U.S.A.

Sherwood, R. E., 22 Schole Road, Willingham, Cambridge CB4 5JD.

Short, K. R. MacD., BA, MA, BD, EdD, DPhil, 89 Bicester Road, Kidlington, Oxford OX5 2LD.

Shukman, H., BA, DPhil, MA, St Antony's College, Oxford OX2 6JF.

Simpson, D. H., MA, Royal Commonwealth Society, 18 Northumberland Avenue, London WC2.

Simpson, G. G., MA, PhD, FSA, Taylor Building, King's College, Old Aberdeen AB9 2UB.

Sinar, Miss J. C., MA, 60 Wellington Street, Matlock, Derbyshire DE4 3GS.

Siney, Professor Marion C., MA, PhD, 1890 East 107th Street, Apt 534, Cleveland, Ohio 44106, U.S.A.

Sked, A., MA, DPhil, Flat 3, Aberdeen Court, 68 Aberdeen Park, London N5 2BH.

Skidelsky, Professor R. J. A., BA, PhD, Tilton House, Selmeston, Firle, Sussex.

Skinner, Professor Q. R. D., MA, FBA, Christ's College, Cambridge CB2 3BU.

Slack, P. A., MA, DPhil, Exeter College, Oxford OX1 3DP.

Slade, C. F., PhD, FSA, 28 Holmes Road, Reading, Berks.

Slater, A. W., MSc(Econ), 146 Castelnau, London SW13 9ET.

Slatter, Miss M. D., MA, 2 Tuscan Close, Tilehurst, Reading, Berks. RG3 6DF.

Slaven, Professor A, MA, BLitt, Dept of Economic History, University of Glasgow, Adam Smith Building, Glasgow G13 8RT.

Slavin, Professor A. J., PhD, College of Arts & Letters, University of Louisville, Louisville, Kentucky 40268, U.S.A.

Slee, P. R. H., PhD, BA, 10 Burghley Lane, Stamford, Lincolnshire.

Smith, A. G. R., MA, PhD, 5 Cargil Avenue, Kilmacolm, Renfrewshire.

Smith, A. Hassell, BA, PhD, School of English and American Studies, University of East Anglia, Norwich NR4 7TJ.

Smith, B. S., MA, FSA, Historical Manuscripts Commission, Quality House, Quality Court, Chancery Lane, London WC2A 1HP.

Smith, D. M., MA, PhD, FSA, Borthwick Institute of Historical Research, St Anthony's Hall, York YO1 2PW.

Smith, E. A., MA, Dept of History, Faculty of Letters, The University, Whiteknights, Reading RG6 2AH.

Smith, F. B., MA, PhD, Research School of Social Sciences, Institute of Advanced Studies, Australian National University, G.P.O. Box 4, Canberra, A.C.T. 2601, Australia.

Smith, Professor Goldwin A., MA, PhD, DLitt, Wayne State University, Detroit, Michigan 48202, U.S.A.

Smith, J. Beverley, MA, University College, Aberystwyth SY23 2AX.

Smith, Joseph, BA, PhD, Dept of History, The University, Exeter EX4 4QH.

Smith, Julia M. H., MA, DPhil, Dept of History, Trinity College, Hartford, Conn. 06106, U.S.A.

Smith, Professor L. Baldwin, PhD, Northwestern University, Evanston, Ill. 60201, U.S.A.

Smith, Professor P., MA, DPhil, Dept of History, The University, Southampton SO9 5NH.

Smith, Professor R. E. F., MA, Dept of Russian, The University, P.O. Box 363, Birmingham B15 2TT.

Smith, Richard M., BA, PhD, All Souls College, Oxford OX1 4AL.

Smith, R. S., MA, BA, 7 Capel Lodge, 244 Kew Road, Kew, TW9 3JU.

Smith, S., BA, PhD, Les Haies, 40 Oatlands Road, Shinfield, Reading, Berks.

Smith, Professor T. A., BSc(Econ), Queen Mary College, Mile End Road, London E1 4NS.

Smith, W. H. C., BA, PhD, Erin Lodge, Symons Hill, Falmouth TR11 2SX.

Smith, W. J., MA, 5 Gravel Hill, Emmer Green, Reading, Berks. RG4 8QN.

Smyth, A. P., BA, MA, DPhil;, FSA, Keynes College, The University, Canterbury CT2 7NP.

Snell, L. S., MA, FSA, FRSA, 27 Weoley Hill, Selly Oak, Birmingham B29 4AA.

Snow, Professor V. F., MA, PhD, Dept of History, Syracuse University, 311 Maxwell Hall, Syracuse, New York 13244, U.S.A.

Snyder, Professor H. L., MA, PhD, 5577 Majestic Court, Riverside, Calif. 92506, U.S.A.

Soden, G. I., MA, DD, Buck Brigg, Hanworth, Norwich, Norfolk.

Soffer, Professor Reba N., PhD, 665 Bienveneda Avenue, Pacific Palisades, California 90272, U.S.A.

Somers, Rev. H. J., JCB, MA, PhD, St Francis Xavier University, Antigonish, Nova Scotia, Canada.

Somerville, Sir Robert, KCVO, MA, FSA, 2 Hunt's Close, Morden Road, London SE3 0AH.

Sommerville, Johann P., MA, PhD, Dept. of History, University of Wisconsin-Madison. 3211 Humanities Building, 455 North Street, Madison, Wisconsin 53706, U.S.A.

Sorrenson, Professor M. P. K., MA, DPhil, History Dept, University of Auckland, Private Bay, Auckland, New Zealand.

SOUTHERN, Sir Richard (W.), MA, DLitt, LittD, DLitt, FBA, 40 St John Street, Oxford OX1 2LH.

Southgate, D. G., BA, DPhil, The Old Harriers, Bridford, nr Exeter, Devon EX6 7HS.

Spalding, Miss R., MA, 34 Reynards Road, Welwyn, Herts.

Speck, Professor W. A., MA, DPhil, School of History, The University, Leeds LS2 9JT.

Spencer, B. W., BA, FSA, 6 Carpenters Wood Drive, Chorleywood, Herts.

Spiers, E. M., MA, PhD, 170 Alwoodley Lane, Leeds, West Yorkshire LS17 7PF.

Spinks, Revd B. D., BA, MTh, BD, Churchill College, Cambridge CB3 0DS.

Spinner, Professor T. J. Jr., PhD, Dept of History, University of Vermont, 314 Wheeler House, Burlington, Vermont 05405, U.S.A.

Spooner, Professor F. C., MA, PhD, LittD, FSA, 31 Chatsworth Avenue, Bromley, Kent BR1 5DP.

Spring, Professor D., PhD, Dept of History, Johns Hopkins University, Baltimore, Md. 21218, U.S.A.

Spufford, Mrs H. M., MA, PhD, LittD, Newnham College, Cambridge CB3 9DF.

Spufford, P., MA, PhD, Queens' College, Cambridge CB3 9ET.

Squibb, G. D., QC, FSA, The Old House, Cerne Abbas, Dorset DT2 7JQ.

Stacey, Assistant Professor R. C., BA, MA, PhD, Dept of History, Yale University, New Haven, Connecticut 06520, U.S.A.

Stachura, P. D., MA, PhD, Dept of History, The University, Stirling FK9 4LA.

Stacpoole, Dom Alberic J., OSB, MC, MA, DPhil, Saint Benet's Hall, Oxford OX1 3LN.

Stafford, Pauline A., BA, DPhil, Athill Lodge, St Helen's Lane, Adel, Leeds LS16 8BS.

Stanley, The Hon. G. F. G., MA, BLitt, DPhil, PO Box 790, Sackville, N.B., Canada EoA 3Co.

Stansky, Professor Peter, PhD, Dept of History, Stanford University, Stanford, Calif. 94305, U.S.A.

Starkey, D. R., MA, PhD, 49 Hamilton Park West, London N5 1AE.

Steele, E. D., MA, PhD, School of History, The University, Leeds LS2 9JT.

Steinberg, J., MA, PhD, Trinity Hall, Cambridge CB2 1TJ.

Steiner, Mrs Zara S., MA, PhD, New Hall, Cambridge CB3 0DF.

Stephens, J. N., MA, DPhil, Dept of History, University of Edinburgh, William Robertson Building, George Square, Edinburgh EH8 9JY.

Stephens, W. B., MA, PhD, FSA, 37 Batcliffe Drive, Leeds 6.

Stephenson, Mrs Jill, MA, PhD, Dept of History, University of Edinburgh, William Robertson Building, George Square, Edinburgh EH8 9JY.

Steven, Miss M. J. E., PhD, 3 Bonwick Place, Garran, A.C.T. 2605, Australia.

Stevenson, David, MA, PhD, Dept of International History, London School of Economics, Houghton Street, Aldwych, London WC2A 2AE.

Stevenson, D., BA, PhD, Dept of History, Taylor Buildings, King's College, Old Aberdeen AB1 0EE.

Stevenson, Miss J. H., BA, c/o Institute of Historical Research, Senate House, Malet Street, London, WC1E 7HU.

Stevenson, J., MA, DPhil, Dept of History, The University, Sheffield S10 2TN.

Stewart, A. T. Q., MA PhD, Dept of Modern History, The Queen's University, Belfast BT7 1NN.

Stitt, F. B., BA, BLitt, DLitt, 2 Ashtree Close, Little Haywood, Stafford ST18 0NL.

Stockwell, A. J., MA, PhD, Dept of History, Royal Holloway and Bedford New College, Egham Hill, Egham, Surrey TW20 0EX.

Stone, E., MA, DPhil, FSA, Keble College, Oxford OX1 3PG.

Stone, Professor L., MA, Princeton University, Princeton, N.J. 08540, U.S.A.

Storey, Professor R. L., MA, PhD, 19 Elm Avenue, Beeston, Nottingham NG9 1BU.

Storry, J. G., The Eyot House, Sonning Eye, Reading RG4 0TN.

Story, Professor G. M., BA, DPhil, 335 Southside Road, St John's Newfoundland, Canada.

Stourzh, Professor G., DPhil, Brechergasse 14, A-1190 Vienna, Austria.

*Stoye, J. W., MA, DPhil, Magdalen College, Oxford OX1 4AU.

Street, J., MA, PhD, Badgers' Wood, Cleveley, Forton, Garstang, Preston PR3 1BY.

Stringer, K. J., BA, MA, PhD, Dept of History, Furness College, The University, Lancaster LA1 4YG.

Strong, Mrs F., MA, Traigh Gate, Arisaig, Inverness-shire PH39 4N1.

Strong, Sir Roy, BA, PhD, FSA, 3cc Morpeth Terrace, London SW1P 1EW.

Stuart, C. H., MA, Christ Church, Oxford OX1 1DP.

Studd, J. R., PhD, Dept of History, The University, Keele, Staffs. ST5 5BG.

Sturdy, D. J., BA, PhD, Dept of History, New University of Ulster, Coleraine, N. Ireland BT52 1SA.

Supple, Professor B. E., BSc(Econ), PhD, MA, St Catharine's College, Cambridge CB2 1RL.

Sutcliffe, Professor A. R., MA, DU, Dept of Economic and Social History, The University, 21 Slayleigh Avenue, Sheffield S10 3RA.

Sutherland, Gillian, MA, DPhil, MA, PhD, Newnham College, Cambridge CB3 9DF.

Swanson, R. N., MA, PhD, School of History, The University, P.O. Box 363, Birmingham B15 2TT.

Swanton, Professor M. J., BA, PhD, FSA, Queen's Building, The University, The Queen's Drive, Exeter EX4 4QH.

Swart, Professor K. W., PhD, LittD, University College London, Gower Street, London WC1 6BT.

Sweet, D. W., MA, PhD, Dept of History, The University, 43 North Bailey, Durham.

Sweetman, J., MA, PhD, 98 Kings Ride, Camberley, Surrey GU15 4LN.

Swenarton, M. C., BA, PhD, 10d Barnsbury Terrace, London N1 1JH.

Swift, R. E., PhD, MA, 14 Holly Drive, Penyfford, nr Chester, Clwyd.

Swinfen, D. B., MA, DPhil, 14 Cedar Road, Broughty Ferry, Dundee.

Sydenham, Professor Emeritus M. J., PhD, Dept of History, Carleton University, Ottawa, Canada K1S 5B6.

Syrett, Professor D., PhD, 329 Sylvan Avenue, Leonia, NJ 07605, U.S.A.

Szechi, D., BA, DPhil, 19 Henry Road, Oxford OX2 0DG.

Taft, Barbara, PhD, 3101 35th Street, Washington, D.C. 20016, U.S.A.

Talbot, C. H., PhD, BD, FSA, 47 Hazlewell Road, London SW15.

Tamse, Coenraad Arnold, DLitt, De Krom, 12 Potgieterlaan, 9752 Ex Haren (Groningen), The Netherlands.

Tanner, J. I., CBE, MA, PhD, DLitt, Flat One, 57 Drayton Gardens, London SW10 9RU.

Tarling, Professor P. N., MA, PhD, LittD, University of Auckland, Private Bag, Auckland, New Zealand.

Tarn, Professor J. N., B.Arch, PhD, FRIBA, Dept of Architecture, The University, Leverhulme Building, Abercromby Square, P.O. Box 147, Liverpool L69 3BX.

Taylor, Arnold J., CBE, MA, DLitt, FBA, FSA, Rose Cottage, Lincoln's Hill, Chiddingfold, Surrey GU8 4UN.

Taylor, Professor Arthur J., MA, School of History, The University, Leeds LS2 9JT.

Taylor, Rev. Brian, MA, FSA, The Rectory, The Flower Walk, Guildford GU2 5EP.

Taylor, J., MA, School of History, The University, Leeds LS2 9JT.

Taylor, J. W. R., 36 Alexandra Drive, Surbiton, Surrey KT5 9AF.

Taylor, P. M., BA, PhD, School of History, The University, Leeds LS2 9JT.

Taylor, R. T., MA, PhD, Dept of Political Theory and Government, University College of Swansea, Swansea SA2 8PP.

Taylor, W., MA, PhD, FSAScot, 25 Bingham Terrace, Dundee.

Teichova, Professor Alice, BA, PhD, University of East Anglia, University Plain, Norwich NR4 7TJ.

Temperley, H., BA, MA, PhD, School of English and American Studies, University of East Anglia, University Plain, Norwich NR4 7TJ.

Temple, Nora C., BA, PhD, Dept of History, University College, P.O. Box 78, Cardiff CF1 1XL.

Terraine, J. A., 74 Kensington Park Road, London W11 2PL.

Thacker, A. T., MA, DPhil, Flat 1, 6 Liverpool Road, Chester, Cheshire.

Thackray, Professor Arnold W., PhD, E. F. Smith Hall D-6, University of Pennsylvania, Philadelphia 19104, PA, U.S.A.

Thane, Patricia M., BA, PhD, 5 Twisden Road, London NW5 1DL.

Thirsk, Mrs I. Joan, PhD, FBA, 1 Hadlow Castle, Hadlow, Tonbridge, Kent TN11 0EG.

Thistlethwaite, Professor F., CBE, DCL, LHD, 15 Park Parade, Cambridge CB5 8AL.

Thomas, Professor A. C., MA, DipArch, FSA, Hon. MRIA, Lambessow, St Clement, Truro, Cornwall.

Thomas, D. O., MA, PhD, Orlandon, 31 North Parade, Aberystwyth, Dyfed SY23 2JN.

Thomas, E. E., BA, The Shippen, Pilgrim's Way, Westhumble, Dorking, Surrey RH5 6AW.

Thomas of Swynnerton, Lord, MA, 29 Ladbroke Grove, London W11 3BB.

Thomas, J. H., BA, PhD, School of Social and Historical Studies, Portsmouth Polytechnic, Bellevue Terrace, Southsea, Portsmouth PO5 3AT.

Thomas, K. V., MA, DLitt, FBA, Corpus Christi College, Oxford OX1 4JF.

Thomas, Professor P. D. G., MA, PhD, Dept of History, Hugh Owen Building, University College of Wales, Aberystwyth SY23 2AU.

Thomas, W. E. S., MA, Christ Church, Oxford OX1 1DP.

Thomis, Professor M. I., MA, PhD, University of Queensland, St Lucia, Brisbane 4067, Australia.

Thompson, A. F., MA, Wadham College, Oxford OX1 3PN.

Thompson, C. L. F., BA, Colne View, 69 Chaney Road, Wivenhoe, Essex.

Thompson, Mrs D. K. G., MA, Wick Episcopi, Upper Wick, Worcester WR2 5SY.

Thompson, D. M., MA, PhD, Fitzwilliam College, Cambridge CB3 0DG.

Thompson, E. P., MA, Wick Episcopi, Upper Wick, Worcester WR2 5SY.

Thompson, Professor F. M. L., MA, DPhil, FBA, Institute of Historical Research, Senate House, London WC1E 7HU.

Thompson, I. A. A., MA, PhD, PhD, Dept of History, The University, Keele, Staffs. ST5 5BG.

Thompson, J. A., MA, PhD, St Catharine's College, Cambridge CB2 1RL.

Thompson, R. F., MA, School of English and American Studies, University of East Anglia, Norwich NR4 7TJ.

Thomson, J. A. F., MA, DPhil, The University, Glasgow G12 8QQ.

Thomson, R. M., MA, PhD, Dept of History, University of Tasmania, Box 252C, GPO, Hobart, Tasmania 7001, Australia.

Thorne, C. G., MA, DLitt, FBA, School of European Studies, University of Sussex, Falmer, Brighton BN1 9QN.

Thornton, Professor A. P., MA, DPhil, University College, University of Toronto, Toronto, Canada, M5S 1A1.

*Thrupp, Professor S. L., MA, PhD, 57 Balsam Lane, Princeton, New Jersey 08540, U.S.A.

Thurlow, The Very Rev. A. G. G., MA, FSA, 2 East Pallant, Chichester, West Sussex PO19 1TR.

Tite, C. G. C., BA, MA, PhD, 12 Montagu Square, London W1H 1RB.

Tomizawa, Professor Reigan, MA, DLitt, Dept of History, Kansai University, 3-10-12 Hiyoshidai, Taksukishi, Osaka 569, Japan.

Tomkeieff, Mrs O. G., MA, LLB, 88 Moorside North, Newcastle upon Tyne NE4 9DU.

Tomlinson, H. C., BA, DPhil, The Cathedral School, Old College, 29 Castle Street, Hereford HR1 2NN.

Tonkin, J. M., BA, BD, PhD, Dept of History, University of Western Australia, Nedlands, Western Australia 6009.

Townshend, C. J. N., MA, DPhil, 62 The Covert, Keele, Staffs.

Trainor, L., BA, PhD, History Dept, University of Canterbury, Private Bag, Christchurch, New Zealand.

Trebilcock, R. C., MA, Pembroke College, Cambridge CB2 1RF.

Tsitsonis, S. E., PhD, 31 Samara Street, Paleo Psyhico, (15452), Athens, Greece.

Tuck, J. A., MA, PhD, Dept of History, The University, 13–15 Woodland Road, Bristol BS8 1TB.

Turnbull, Professor Constance M., BA, PhD, 36 Stoneleigh Avenue, Coventry, CV5 6BZ.

Turner, Mrs Barbara D. M. C., BA, 27 St Swithuns Street, Winchester, Hampshire.

Turner, G. L'E., FSA, DSc, The Old Barn, Mill Street, Islip, Oxford OX5 2SY.

Turner, J. A., MA, DPhil, 31 Devereux Road, London SW11 6JR.

Turner, Professor Ralph V., MA, PhD, History Department, Florida State University, Tallahassee, Florida 32306 U.S.A.

Tyacke, N. R. N., MA, DPhil, 1a Spencer Rise, London NW5.

Tyerman, C. J., MA, DPhil, Exeter College, Oxford OX1 3DP.

Tyler, P., BLitt, MA, DPhil, University of Western Australia, Nedlands, Western Australia 6009.

Ugawa, Professor K., BA, MA, PhD, Minami-Ogikubo, 1-chome 25-15, Suginami-Ku, Tokyo 167, Japan.

Underdown, Professor David, MA, BLitt, DLitt, Dept of History, Yale University, P.O. Box 1504A, Yale Station, New Haven, Conn. 06520, U.S.A.

Upton, A. F., MA, 5 West Acres, St Andrews, Fife.

Vaisey, D. G., MA, FSA, 12 Hernes Road, Oxford.

Vale, M. G. A., MA, DPhil, St John's College, Oxford OX1 3JP.

Van Caenegem, Professor R. C., LLD, PhD, Veurestraat 47, B9821 Gent-Afsnee, Belgium.

Van Houts, Elisabeth, DLitt, Girton College, Cambridge CB3 0JG.

Van Roon, Professor Ger, Dept of Contemporary History, Vrije Universiteit, Amsterdam, Koningslaan 31–33, The Netherlands.

Vann, Professor Richard T., PhD, Dept of History, Wesleyan University, Middletown, Conn. 06457, U.S.A.

*Varley, Mrs J., MA, FSA, 164 Nettleham Road, Lincoln.

Vaughan, Sir (G) Edgar, KBE, MA, 9 The Glade, Sandy Lane, Cheam, Sutton, Surrey SM2 7NZ.

Veale, Elspeth M., BA, PhD, 31 St Mary's Road, Wimbledon, London SW19 7BP.

Véliz, Professor C., BSc, PhD, Dept. of Sociology, La Trobe University, Melbourne, Victoria 3083, Australia.

Vessey, D. W. T. C., MA, PhD, Dept of Classics, King's College London, Strand, London WC2R 2LS.

Vincent, D. M., BA, PhD, Dept of History, The University, Keele, Staffs ST5 5BG.

Vincent, Professor J. R., MA, PhD, Dept of History, The University, 13 Woodland Road, Bristol BS8 1TB.

Virgoe, R., BA, PhD, School of English and American Studies, University of East Anglia, Norwich NR4 7TJ.

Waddell, Professor D. A. G., MA, DPhil, Dept of History, University of Stirling, Stirling FK9 4LA.

*Wagner, Sir Anthony (R.), KCVO, MA, DLitt, FSA, College of Arms, Queen Victoria Street, London EC4.

Waites, B. F., MA, FRGS, 6 Chater Road, Oakham, Leics. LE15 6RY.

Wakelin, M. F., Royal Holloway and Bedford New College, Egham Hill, Egham, Surrey TW20 0EX.

Walford, A. J., MA, PhD, FLA, 45 Parkside Drive, Watford, Herts WD1 3AU.

Walker, Rev. Canon D. G., DPhil, FSA, University College of Swansea, Swansea SA2 8PP.

Walker, Professor Sue S., MA, PhD, History Department, Northeastern Illinois University, Chicago, Illinois 60625, U.S.A.

Wallace, Professor W. V., MA, Institute of Soviet and East European Studies, University of Glasgow, 9-11 Southpark Terrace, Glasgow G12 8LQ.

Waller, P. J., BA, MA, Merton College, Oxford OX1 4JD.

Wallis, Miss H. M., OBE, MA, DPhil, FSA, 96 Lord's View, St John's Wood Road, London NW8 7HG.

Wallis, P. J., MA, 43 Briarfield Road, Newcastle upon Tyne NE3 3UH.

Walne, P., MA, FSA, County Record Office, County Hall, Hertford.

Walsh, T. J., MA, PhD, MB, BCh, LittD, (Hon.) FFA, RCSI, 5 Lower George Street, Wexford, Ireland.

Walton, J. K., BA, PhD, Dept of History, Furness College, The University, Lancaster LA1 4YG.

Walvin, J., BA, MA, DPhil, Dept of History, The University, Heslington, York YO1 5DD.

Wangermann, Professor E., MA, DPhil, Institut of Geschichte, Universität Salzburg, A-5020 Salzburg.

Wanklyn, M. D., BA, MA, PhD, Dept of Arts, The Polytechnic, Wulfruna Street, Wolverhampton, West Midlands.

Ward, Jennifer, C., MA, PhD, 51 Hartswood Road, Brentwood, Essex CM14 5AG.

Ward, Professor W. R., DPhil, 21 Grenehurst Way, The Village, Petersfield, Hampshire GU31 4AZ.

Warner, Professor G., MA, Arts Faculty, The Open University, Walton Hall, Milton Keynes MK7 6AA.

Warren, A. J., MA, DPhil, Vanbrugh Provost's House, 1 Bleachfield, Heslington, York YO1 5DD.

Warren, Professor W. L., MA, DPhil, FRSL, Dept of Modern History, The Queen's University, Belfast, N. Ireland BT7 1NN.

Wasserstein, Professor B. M. J., MA, DPhil, Dept of History, Brandeis University, Waltham, Mass. 02254, U.S.A.

Wasserstein, D. J., MA, DPhil, Dept of Semitic Languages, University College, Belfield, Dublin 4, Ireland.

*Waters, Lt-Commander D. W., RN, FSA, Jolyons, Bury, nr Pulborough, W. Sussex.

Wathey, A. B., MA, DPhil, Downing College, Cambridge CB2 1DG.

Watkin, The Rt Rev. Abbot Aelred, OSB, MA, FSA, St Benet's, Beccles, Suffolk NR34 9NR.

WATSON, Professor A. G., MA, DLit, BLitt, FSA (*Hon Librarian*), University College London, Gower Street, London WC1 6BT.

Watson, D. R., MA, BPhil, Dept of Modern History, The University, Dundee DD1 4HN.

Watt, Professor D. C., MA, London School of Economic, Houghton Street, London WC2A 2AE.

Watt, Professor D. E. R., MA, DPhil, Dept of Mediaeval History, St Salvator's College, St Andrews, Fife KY16 9AJ.

Watt, Professor J. A., BA, PhD, Dept of History, The University, Newcastle upon Tyne NE1 7RU.

Watts, D. G., MA, BLitt, 34 Greenbank Crescent, Bassett, Southampton SO1 7FQ.

Watts, M. R., BA, DPhil, Dept of History, The University, University Park, Nottingham NG7 2RD.

Webb, Professor Colin de B., BA, MA, University of Natal, King George V Avenue, Durban 4001, S Africa.

Webb, J. G., MA, 11 Blount Road, Pembroke Park, Old Portsmouth, Hampshire PO1 2TD.

Webb, Professor R. K., PhD, 3309 Highland Place NW., Washington, D.C. 20008, U.S.A.

Webster (A.) Bruce, MA, FSA, 5 The Terrace, St Stephens, Canterbury.

Webster, C., MA, DSc, FBA, Corpus Christi College, Oxford OX1 4JF.

Wedgwood, Dame (C.) Veronica, OM, DBE, MA, LittD, DLitt, LLD, Whitegate, Alciston, nr Polegate, Sussex.

Weinbaum, Professor M., PhD, 133-33 Sanford Avenue, Flushing, N.Y. 11355, U.S.A.

Weinstock, Miss M. B., MA, 26 Wey View Crescent, Broadway, Weymouth, Dorset.

Wellenreuther, H., PhD, 33 Merkel Str., 34 Gottingen, Germany.

Wells, R. A. E., BA, DPhil, Dept of Humanities, Brighton Polytechnic, Falmer, Brighton, Sussex.

Wende, Professor P. P., DPhil, Historisches Seminar der Johann Wolfgang Goethe-Universtat, 8 Frankfurt am Main, Benchenbergantage 31, West Germany.

Wendt, Professor Bernd-Jurgen, DrPhil, Beim Andreasbrunnen 8, 2 Hamburg 20, West Germany.

Wernham, Professor R. B., MA, Marine Cottage, 63 Hill Head Road, Hill Head, Fareham, Hants.

*Weske, Mrs Dorothy B., AM, PhD, Oakwood, Sandy Spring, Maryland 20860, U.S.A.

West, Professor F. J., PhD, Pro Vice Chancellor's Office, Deakin University, Victoria 3217, Australia.

Weston, Professor Corinne C., PhD, 200 Central Park South, New York, N.Y. 10019, U.S.A.

Whaley, Joachim, MA, PhD, Gonville and Caius College, Cambridge CB2 1TA.

Whatley, C. A., BA, PhD, Dept of Modern History, The University, Dundee DD1 4HN.

White, Rev. B. R., MA DPhil, 55 St Giles', Regent's Park College, Oxford.

White, G. J., MA, PhD, Chester College, Cheyney Road, Chester CH1 4BJ.

Whiteman, Miss E. A. O., MA, DPhil, FSA, Lady Margaret Hall, Oxford OX2 6QA.

Whiting, J. R. S., MA, DLitt, 15 Lansdown Parade, Cheltenham, Glos.

Whiting, R. C., MA, DPhil, School of History, The University, Leeds LS2 9JT.

Whittam, J. R., MA, BPhil, PhD, Dept of History, University of Bristol, Senate House, Bristol BS8 1TH.

Wickham, C. J., MA, DPhil, School of History, The University, P.O. Box 363, Birmingham B15 2TT.

Wiener, Professor J. H., BA, PhD, Dept of History, City College of New York, Convent Avenue at 138th Street, N.Y. 10031, U.S.A.

Wiener, Professor M. J., PhD, Dept of History, Rice University, Houston, Texas 77251, U.S.A.

Wilkie, Rev. W., MA, PhD, Dept of History, Loras College, Dubuque, Iowa 52001, U.S.A.

Wilks, Professor M. J., MA, PhD, Dept of History, Birkbeck College, Malet Street, London WC1 7HX.

*Willan, Professor T. S., MA, DPhil, 3 Raynham Avenue, Didsbury, Manchester M20 oBW.

Williams, D., MA, PhD, DPhil, University of Calgary, Calgary, Alberta, Canada T2N 1N4.

Williams, Daniel T., BA, PhD, Dept of History, The University, Leicester LE1 7RH.

Williams, Sir Edgar (T.), CB, CBE, DSO, MA, 94 Lonsdale Road, Oxford OX2 7ER.

Williams, (Elisabeth) Ann, BA, PhD, 77 Gordon Road, Wanstead, London E11 2RA.

Williams, Gareth W., MA, MSc(Econ), Dept of History, Hugh Owen Building, University College of Wales, Aberystwyth SY23 3DY.

Williams, Professor Glanmor, MA, DLitt, 11 Grosvenor Road, Swansea SA2 oSP.

Williams, Professor Glyndwr, BA, PhD, Dept of History, Queen Mary College, Mile End Road, London E1 4NS.

Williams, Professor G. A., MA, PhD, 66 De Burgh Street, Cardiff CF1 8LD.

Williams, J. A., MA, BSc(Econ), 44 Pearson Park, Hull, HU5 2TG.

Williams, J. D., BA, MA, PhD, 56 Spurgate, Hutton Mount, Brentwood, Essex CM13 2JT.

Williams, Patrick L, BA, PhD, 30 Andover Road, Southsea, Hants. PO4 9QG.

Williams, P. H., MA, DPhil, New College, Oxford OX1 3BN.

Williams, T. I., MA, DPhil, 20 Blenheim Drive, Oxford OX2 8DG.

Williamson, P. A., PhD, Dept of History, The University, 43/46 North Bailey, Durham DH1 3EX.

Willmott, H. P. MA, 13 Barnway, Englefield Green, Egham, Surrey TW20 oQU.

WILSON, Professor C. H., CBE, MA, LittD, DLitt, DLitt, DLitt, FBA, Jesus College, Cambridge CB5 8BL.

Wilson, Sir David M., MA, LittD, FilDr, DrPhil, FBA, FSA, The Director's Residence, The British Museum, London WC1B 3DG.

Wilson, H. S., BA, BLitt, Dept of History, The University, Heslington, York YO1 5DD.

Wilson, R. G., BA, PhD, University of East Anglia, School of Social Studies, University Plain, Norwich NR4 7TJ.

Wilson, Professor T. G., MA, DPhil, Dept of History, University of Adelaide, Adelaide, South Australia.

Winch, Professor D. N., PhD, BSc(Econ), FBA, University of Sussex, Brighton BN1 9QN.

Winks, Professor R. W. E., MA, PhD, 648 Berkeley College, Yale University, New Haven, Conn. 06520, U.S.A.

Winstanley, M. J., BA, MA, Dept of History, Furness College, The University, Bailrigg, Lancaster LA1 4YG.

Winter, J. M., BA, PhD, Pembroke College, Cambridge CB2 1RF.

Wiswall, Frank L., Jr., BA, JuD, PhD, Meadow Farm, Castine, Maine 04421 U.S.A.

Withrington, D. J., MA, MEd, Dept of History, University of Aberdeen, Taylor Building, King's College, Old Aberdeen AB9 2UB.

Wong, John Yue-Wo, BA, DPhil, Dept of History, University of Sydney, N.S.W., Australia 2006.

*Wood, Rev. A. Skevington, PhD, 17 Dalewood Road, Sheffield S8 0EB.

Wood, Diana, BA, PhD, 8 Bartlemas Close, Oxford OX4 2AE.

Wood, I. N., MA, DPhil, School of History, The University, Leeds LS2 9JT.

Wood, Mrs S. M., MA, BLitt, Greengables, Earisley, Herefordshire HR3 6PQ.

Woolf, Professor, S. J., MA, DPhil, Dept of History, University of Essex, Wivenhoe Park, Colchester CO4 3SQ.

Woolrych, Professor A. H., BLitt, MA, Patchetts, Caton, nr Lancaster.

Wootton, Assoc. Professor D. R. J., Dept of Political Science, Faculty of Social Science, Social Science Centre, The University of Western Ontario, London, Canada N6A 5C2.

WORDEN, A. B., MA, DPhil (*Literary Director*), St Edmund Hall, Oxford OX1 4AR.

Wordie, James R., MA, PhD, St. Andrew's Hall, Redlands Road, Reading, Berks. RG1 5EY.

Wormald, B. H. G., MA, Peterhouse, Cambridge CB2 1RD.

Wormald, C. Patrick, MA, 60 Hill Top Road, Oxford OX4 1PE.

Wormald, Jennifer, MA, PhD, St Hilda's College, Oxford OX4 1DY.

Wortley, The Rev. Professor J. T., MA, PhD, DD, History Dept, University of Manitoba, Winnipeg, Manitoba, Canada R3T 2N2.

Wright, A. D., MA, DPhil, School of History, The University, Leeds LS2 9JT.

Wright, C. J., MA, PhD, 8 Grove Road, East Molesey, Surrey KT8 9JS.

Wright, D. G., BA, PhD, Dip Ed. 9 Victoria Park, Shipley, West Yorkshire BD18 4RL.

Wright, Professor E., MA, Institute of United States Studies, 31 Tavistock Square, London WC1H 9EZ.

Wright, Rev. Professor J. Robert, DPhil, General Theological Seminary, 175 Ninth Avenue, New York, N.Y. 10011, U.S.A.

Wright, Professor Maurice W., BA, DPhil, Dept of Government, Dover Street, Manchester M13 9PL.

Wrightson, K,. MA, PhD, Jesus College, Cambridge CB5 8BL.

Wroughton, J. P., MA, 6 Ormonde House, Sion Hill, Bath BA1 2UN.

Yale, D.E.C., MA, LLB, FBA, Christ's College, Cambridge CB2 3BU.

Yates, W. N., MA, Kent Archives Office, County Hall, Maidstone, Kent ME14 1XH.

Yorke, Barbara A. E., BA, PhD, King Alfred's College of Higher Education, Sparkford Road, Winchester SO22 4NR.

Youings, Professor Joyce A., BA, PhD, 5 Silver Street, Thorberton, Exeter EX5 5LT.

Young, J. W., BA, PhD, Dept of International History, London School of Economics, Houghton Street, London WC2A 2 AE.

Young, K. G., BSc(Econ), MSc, PhD, (address unknown).

Young, Mrs Susan H. H., BA, 78 Holland Road, Ampthill, Beds. MK45 2RS.

Youngs, Professor F. A., Jr., Dept of History, Louisiana State University, Baton Rouge, Louisiana 70803, U.S.A.

Zagorin, Professor P., PhD, Dept of History, College of Arts and Science, University of Rochester, River Campus Station, Rochester, N.Y. 14627, U.S.A.

Zeldin, T., MA, DPhil, St Antony's College, Oxford OX2 6JF.

Zeman, Zbynek A. B., MA, DPhil, St Edmund Hall, Oxford OX1 4AR.

Ziegler, P. S., FRSL, 22 Cottesmore Gardens, London W8.

ASSOCIATES OF THE
ROYAL HISTORICAL SOCIETY

Abela, Major A. E., MBE, 21 Borg Olivier Street, Sliema, Malta.

Addy, J., MA, PhD, 66 Long Lane, Clayton West, Huddersfield, HD8 9PR.

Aitken, Rev. Leslie R., MBE, 36 Ethelbert Road, Birchington, Kent CT7 9PY.

Ayrton, Lt-Col. M. McI., HQ Mess, The School of Signals, Blandford Camp, Dorset DT11 8RH.

Ayton, A. C., BA, Dept of History, The University, Cottingham Road, Hull HU6 7RX.

Begley, M. R., 13 Adelaide Avenue, King's Lynn, Norfolk PE30 3AH.

Birchenough, Mrs F. J., 6 Cheyne Walk, Bramblefield Estate, Longfield, Kent.

Bird, E. A., 29 King Edward Avenue, Rainham, Essex RN13 9RH.

Blackwood, B., FRIBA, FRTPI, FSAScot, DipTP, Dip Con Studies, Ebony House, Whitney Drive, Stevenage SG1 4BL.

Bottomley, A. F., BA, MA, Eversley School, Southwold, Suffolk IP18 6AH.

Boyes, J. H., 129 Endlebury Road, Chingford, London E4 6PX.

Bratt, C., 65 Moreton Road, Upton, Merseyside L49 4NR.

Bryant, W. N., MA, PhD, College of S. Mark and S. John, Derriford Road, Plymouth, Devon.

Butler, Mrs M. C., MA, 4 Castle Street, Warkworth, Morpeth, Northumberland NE65 0UW.

Cairns, Mrs W. N., MA, Alderton House, New Ross, Co. Wexford, Ireland.

Carter, F. E. L., CBE, MA, FSA, 8 The Leys, London N2 0HE.

Cary, Sir Roger, Bt, BA, 23 Bath Road, London W4.

Chandra, Shri Suresh, MA, MPhil, B$\frac{1}{2}$ Havelock Road Colony, Lucknow 226001, India.

Chappell, Rev. M. P., MA, St Luke's Vicarage, 37 Woodland Ravine, Scarborough YO12 6TA.

Clifton, Mrs Gloria C., BA, 13 Fontaine Road, London SW16 3PB.

Cobban, A. D., 11 Pennyfields, Warley, Brentwood, Essex CM14 5JP.

Coleby, A. M., BA, Dept of History, The University, Sheffield S10 2TN.

Condon, Miss M. M., BA, 56 Bernard Shaw House, Knatchbull Road, London NW10.

Cooksley, P. G., 4 Ellerslie Court, Beddington Gardens, Wallington, Surrey SM6 0JD.

Cowburn-Wood, J. O. BA, MEd, The Dolphins, 131 King Edward Road, Onchan, Isle of Man.

Cox, A. H., Winsley, 11a Bagley Close, West Drayton, Middlesex.

Creighton-Williamson, Lt-Col. D., 1 The Pines, Westend Lane, Hucclecote, Gloucester GL3 3SH.

d'Alton, Ian, MA, PhD, 30 Kew Park Avenue, Lucan, Co. Dublin, Ireland.

Daniels, C. W., MEd, Culford School, Bury St Edmunds, Suffolk IP28 6TX.

Davies, G. J., BA, PhD, FSA, 16 Melcombe Avenue, Weymouth, Dorset DT4 7TH.

Davies, P. H., BA, Erskine House, Homesfield, Erskine Hill, London NW11 6HN.

Davis, J. M., BA, MA, MSc, 6 Ellerslie Court, Gladstone Road, Crowborough, East Sussex TN6 1PL.

Davis, Virginia G., BA, PhD, Dept of History, The University, Cottingham Road, Hull HU6 7RX.

Denton, Barry, 10 Melrose Avenue, Off Bants Lane, Northampton NN5 5PB.

Downie, W. F., BSc, CEng, FICE, FINucE, MIES, 10 Ryeland Street, Strathaven, Lanarkshire ML10 6DL.

Dowse, Rev. I. R., 23 Beechfield Road, Hemel Hempstead HP1 1PP.

Edgell, The Revd H. A. R., SB, StJ, Horning Vicarage, Norwich NR12 8PZ.

Elliott, Rev. W., BA, 8 Lea View, Cleobury Mortimer, Kidderminster, Worcs. DY14 8EE.

Enoch, D. G., BEd, MEd, Treetops, 14 St David's Road, Miskin, Pontyclun CF7 8PW.

Firth, P. J. C., 59 Springfield Road, London NW8 0QJ.

Fitzgerald, R., PhD, BA, 32 Kynaston Road, Enfield, Middlesex EN2 0DB.

Foster, J. M., MA, 3 Marchmont Gardens, Richmond, Surrey TW10 6ET.

Franco de Baux, Don Victor, KCHS, KCN, Flat 2, 28 St Stephens Avenue, London W12 8JH.

Frazier, R. Ll., BA, Dept of History, The University, Nottingham NG7 2RD.

Freeman, Miss J., 5 Spencer Close, Stansted Mountfitchet, Essex.

Granger, E. R., Bluefield, Blofield, Norfolk.

Green, P. L., MA, 9 Faulkner Street, Gate Pa, Taurange, New Zealand.

Grosvenor, Ian D., BA, 78 Willows Crescent, Cannon Hill, Birmingham B12 9ND.

Gurney, Mrs S. J., 'Albemarle', 13 Osborne Street, Wolverton, Milton Keynes MK12 5HH.

Guy, Rev. J. R., BA, Selden End, Ash, nr Martock, Somerset TA12 6NS.

Hall, P. T., Accrington and Rosendale College, Sandy Lane, Accrington, Lancs. BB5 2AW.

Hamilton-Williams, D. C., BSc, SRN, MRSH, 6 Faraday Avenue, East Grinstead, West Sussex RH19 4AX.

Hanawalt, Professor Barbara A., MA, PhD, Dept of History, University of Minnesota, Minneapolis, M.N. 55455, U.S.A.

Hawkes, G. I., BA, MA, PhD, Linden House, St Helens Road, Ormskirk, Lancs.

Hawtin, Miss V. G., BA, PhD, FSAScot, FRSAI, Honey Cottage, 5 Clifton Road, London SW19 4QX.

Henderson-Howat, Mrs A. M. D., 9 Capel Court, The Burgage, Prestbury, Cheltenham, Glos GL52 3EL.

Hendrie, A. W. A., BA, ACP, Sandy Ridge, Amberley Road, Storrington, West Sussex RH20 4JE.

Hillman, L. B., BA, 18 Creswick Walk, Hampstead Garden Suburb, London NW11 6AN.

Hoare, E. T., 70 Addison Road, Enfield, Middlesex.

Hodge, Mrs G., 85 Hadlow Road, Tonbridge, Kent.

Hope, R. B., MA, MEd, PhD, 5 Partis Way, Newbridge Hill, Bath, Avon BA1 3QG.

Jackson, A., BA, 14 Latimer Lane, Guisborough, Cleveland.

James, T. M., BA, MA, PhD, 36 Heritage Court, Boley Park, Lichfield, Staffs. WS14 9ST.

Jarvis, L. D., Middlesex Cottage, 86 Mill Road, Stock, Ingatestone, Essex.

Jennings, T. S., GTCL, The Willows, 54 Bramcote Road, Loughborough LE11 2AS.

Jermy, K. E., MA, Cert. Archaeol., CEng, MIM, FISTC, AIFA, FRSA, 5 Far Sandfield, Churchdown, Gloucester GL3 2JS.

Jerram-Burrows, Mrs L. E., Parkanaur House, 88 Sutton Road, Rochford, Essex.

Johnston, F. R., MA, 20 Russell Street, Eccles, Manchester.

Johnstone, H. F. V., 119 Kingsbridge Road, Parkstone, Poole, Dorset BH14 8TL.

Jones, Rev. D. R., BA, MA, Chaplain's Office, St. George's Church, HQ Dhekelia, British Forces Post Office 58.

Jones, Dr N. L., Dept of History & Geography, Utah State University, UMC 07, Logan, Utah 84322, U.S.A.

Keir, Mrs G. I., BA, BLitt, 17 Battlefield Road, St Albans Herts. AL1 4DA.

Kennedy, M. J., BA, Dept of Medieval History, The University, Glasgow G12 8QQ.

Kilburn, T., BSocSc, MA, Pineacres, Grove Lane, Hackney, Matlock, Derbyshire DE4 2QF.

Knight, G. A., BA, PhD, DAA, MIInfSc, 17 Lady Frances Drive, Market Rasen, Lincs. LN8 3JJ.

Land, N., 44 Lineholt Close, Oakenshaw South, Redditch, Worcs.

Lazarus, D., JP, CA, P.O. Box 449, East London 5200, S. Africa.

Leckey, J. J., MSc(Econ), LCP, FRSAI, Vestry Hall, Ballygowan, Co. Down, N. Ireland BT23 6HQ.

Lee, Professor M. du P., PhD, Douglass College, Rutgers University, NB, NJ 08903, U.S.A.

Lewin, Mrs J., MA, 3 Sunnydale Gardens, Mill Hill, London NW7.

Lewis, J. B., MA, CertEd, FRSA, 93 Five Ashes Road, Westminster Park, Chester CH4 7QA.

McDowell, W. H., MA, MSc, BA, 13 Saughtonhall Avenue, Edinburgh EH12 5RJ.

McIntyre, Miss S. C., BA, DPhil, West Midlands College of Higher Education, Walsall, West Midlands.

McKenna, Rev. T. J., P.O. Box 979, Quean Beyan, NSW 2620, Australia.

McLeod, D. H., BA, PhD, Dept of Theology, The University, P.O. Box 363, Birmingham B15 2TT.

Meatyard, E., BA, DipEd, Guston, Burial Lane, Church Lane, Llantwit Major, S. Glam.

Metcalf, D. M., MA, DPhil, 40 St Margaret's Road, Oxford OX2 6LD.

Morris, A. R., BSc(Econ), MA, Woolpit End, Duke of Kent School, Ewhurst, Surrey GU6 7NS.

Munson, K. G., 'Briar Wood', 4 Kings Ride, Seaford, Sussex BN25 2LN.

Nagel, L. C. J., BA, (address unknown).

Newman, L. T., MSc, DIC, CEng, 27 Mallow Park, Pinkneys Green, Maidenhead, Berks.

Noonan, J. A., BA, MEd, HDE, St Patrick's Comprehensive School, Curriculum Development Centre, Shannon, Co. Clare, Ireland.

Oggins, R. S., PhD, Dept of History, State University of New York, Binghamton 13901, U.S.A.

Osborne, Irving, BEd, Adv.DipEd, FRSA, FRGS, FCollP, 169 Goodman Park, Slough SL2 5NR.

Pam, D. O., 44 Chase Green Avenue, Enfield, Middlesex EN2 8EB.

Paton, L. R., 49 Lillian Road, Barnes, London SW13.

Paulson, E., BSc(Econ), 11 Darley Avenue, Darley Dale, Matlock, Derbys. DE4 2GB.

Perry, E., FSAScot, 11 Lynmouth Avenue, Hathershaw, Oldham OL8 3 ES.

Perry, K., MA, 14 Highland View Close, Colehill, Wimborne, Dorset.

Powell, Mrs A. M., 129 Blinco Grove, Cambridge CB1 4TX.

Priestley, Captain E. J., MA, MPhil, 7 Inverleith Place, Edinburgh EH3 5QE.

Raspin, Miss A., London School of Economics, Houghton Street, London WC2A 2AE.

Rees, Rev. D. B., BA, BD, MSc(Econ), PhD, 32 Garth Drive, Liverpool L18 6HW.

Reid, N. H., MA, Wingate, Church Brae, Limekilns, Fife.

Rendall, Miss J., BA, PhD, Dept of History, University of York, Heslington, York YO1 5DD.

Richards, N. F., PhD, 376 Maple Avenue, St Lambert, Prov. of Quebec, Canada J4P 2S2.

Roberts, S. G., MA, DPhil, 23 Beech Avenue, Radlett, Herts. WD7 7DD.

Rosenfield, M. C., AB, AM, PhD, Box 395, Mattapoisett, Mass. 02739, U.S.A.

Russell, Mrs E., BA, c/o Dept of History, University College London, Gower Street, London WC1E 6BT.

Sabben-Clare, E. E., MA, 4 Denham Close, Abbey Hill Road, Winchester SO23 7BL.

Sainsbury, F., 16 Crownfield Avenue, Newbury Park, Ilford, Essex.

Scannura, C. G., MA, 1/11 St Dominic Street, Valletta, Malta.

Scott, The Rev. A. R., MA, BD, PhD, Sunbeam Cottage, 110 Mullalelish Road, Richhill, Co Armagh, N. Ireland BT61 9LT.

Sellers, J. M., MA, 9 Vere Road, Pietermaritzburg 3201, Natal, S. Africa.

Shores, C. F., ARICS, 40 St Mary's Crescent, Hendon, London NW4 4LH.

Sorensen, Mrs M. O., MA, 8 Layer Gardens, London W3 9PR.

Sparkes, I. G., FLA, 124 Green Hill, High Wycombe, Bucks.

Starr, C. R., 63 Abbey Gardens, London W6 8QR.

Teague, D. C., ARAeS, MIMM, 1 Fisher Road, Stoke, Plymouth PL2 3BA.

Thomas, D. L., BA, Public Record Office, Chancery Lane, London WC2A 1LR.

Thomas, Miss E. J. M., BA, 8 Ravenscroft Road, Northfield End, Henley-on-Thames, Oxon. RG9 2DH.

Thompson, L. F., Colne View, 69 Chaney Road, Wivenhoe, Essex.

Tracy, J. N., BA, MPhil, PhD, Dept of History, National University of Singapore, Kent Ridge, Singapore 0511.

Tudor, Victoria M., BA, PhD, 33 Convent Close, Hitchin, Herts. SG5 1QN.

Waldman, T. G., MA, 620 Franklin Bldg./I6, University of Pennsylvania, Philadelphia, Pa. 19104, U.S.A.

Walker, J. A., 1 Sylvanus, Roman Wood, Bracknell, Berkshire RG12 4XX.

Wall, Rev. J., BD, MA, PhD, 10 Branksome Road, Norwich NR4 6SN.

Ward, R. C., BA, MPhil, 192 Stortford Hall Park, Bishop's Stortford, Herts. CM23 5AS.

Warren, Ann K., PhD, Dept of History, Case Western Reserve University, Cleveland, Ohio 44106, U.S.A.

Warrillow, E. J. D., MBE, FSA, Hill-Cote, Lancaster Road, Newcastle, Staffs.

Weise, Selene H. C., PhD, 22 Hurd Street, Mine Hill, New Jersey 07801, U.S.A.

Welbourne, D. J., 57 West Busk Lane, Otley, West Yorkshire LS21 3LY.

Westlake, R. A., 140 Wyld Way, Wembley, Middlesex HA9 6PU.

Wickham, David E., MA, 116 Parsonage Manorway, Belvedere, Kent.

Wilkinson, F. J., 40 Great James Street, Holborn, London WC1N 3HB.

Williams, A. R., BA, MA, 5 Swanswell Drive, Granley Fields, Cheltenham, Glos. GL51 6LL.

Williams, C. L. Sinclair, ISO, The Old Vicarage, The Green, Puddletown, nr Dorchester, Dorset.

Williams, G., FLA, 32 St John's Road, Manselton, Swansea SA5 8PP.

Williams, P. T., FSAScot, FRSA, FFAS, Bryn Bueno, Whitford Street, Holywell, Clwyd, North Wales.

Wilson, A. R., BA, MA, 80 Apedale Road, Wood Lane, Bignall End, Stoke-on-Trent ST7 8PH.

Windrow, M. C., West House, Broyle Lane, Ringmer, nr Lewes, Sussex.

Winterbottom, D. O., MA, BPhil, Clifton College, Bristol BS8 3JH.

Wood, A. W., A.Dip.R, 11 Blessington Close, London SE13.

Woodall, R. D., BA, Bethel, 7 Wynthorpe Road, Horbury, nr Wakefield, Yorks. WF4 5BB.

Worsley, Miss A. V., BA, 3d St George's Cottages, Glasshill Street, London SE1.

Young, Assoc., Professor M. B., BA, MA, PhD, Dept of History, Illinois Wesleyan University, Bloomington, Illinois 61701, U.S.A.

Zerafa, Rev. M. J., St Dominic's Priory, Valletta, Malta.

CORRESPONDING FELLOWS

Ajayi, Professor J. F. Ade, University of Ibadan, Ibadan, Nigeria, West Africa.

Berend, Professor T. Ivan, Hungarian Academy of Sciences, 1361 Budapest V, Roosevelt-tèr 9, Hungary.

Bischoff, Professor B., DLitt, 8033 Planegg C., Ruffini-Alee 27, München, West Germany.

Boorstin, Daniel J., MA, LLD, 3541 Ordway Street, N.W., Washington, DC 20016, U.S.A.

Boyle, Monsignor Leonard E., OP, Biblioteca Apostolica Vaticana, Vatican City, Rome, Italy.

Cipolla, Professor Carlo M., University of California, Berkeley Campus, Berkeley, Calif. 94720, U.S.A.

Constable, Giles, PhD, School of Historical Studies, The Institute for Advanced Study, Princeton, N.J. 08540, U.S.A.

Crouzet, Professor F. M. J., 6 rue Benjamin Godard, 75016 Paris, France.

Duby, Professor G., Collège de France, 11 Place Marcelin-Berthelot, 75005 Paris, France.

Garin, Professor Eugenio, via Francesco Crispi 6, 50129 Firenze F, Italy.

Gieysztor, Professor Aleksander, Polska Akademia Nauk, Wydzial I Nauk, Rynek Starego Miasta 29/31, 00-272 Warszawa, Poland.

Giusti, Rt Rev. Mgr M., JCD, Archivio Segreto Vaticano, Vatican City, Italy.

Glamann, Professor K., DPhil, DLitt, The Carlsberg Foundation, H.C. Andersens Boulevard 35, 1553 København, V, Denmark.

Gopal, Professor S., MA, DPhil, Centre for Historical Studies, Jawaharlal Nehru University, New Mehrauli Road, New Delhi-110067, India.

Guenée, Professor Bernaerd, 8 rue Huysmans, 75006 Paris, France.

Hancock, Professor Sir Keith, KBE, MA, DLitt, FBA, Australian National University, Box 4, P.O., Canberra, ACT, Australia.

Hanke, Professor L. U., PhD, University of Massachusetts, Amherst, Mass. 01002, U.S.A.

Heimpel, Professor Dr H., DrJur, Dr Phil, former Direktor des Max Planck-Instituts für Geschichte, Gottingen, Dahlmannstr. 14, West Germany.

Inalcik, Professor Halil, PhD, The University of Ankara, Turkey.

Inglis, Professor K. S., DPhil (History Dept.) The Australian National University, GPO Box 4, Canberra, ACT 2601, Australia, The Research School of Social Sciences.

Klingenstein, Professor Grete, Paniglgasse 19 A/31, A-1040 Wien IV, Austria.

Kossmann, Professor E. H., DLitt, Rijksuniversiteit te Groningen, Groningen, The Netherlands.
Kuttner, Professor S., MA, JUD, SJD, LLD, Institute of Medieval Canon Law, University of California, Berkeley, Calif. 94720, U.S.A.

Ladurie, Professor E. B. LeRoy, Collège de France, 11 Place Marcelin-Berthelot, 75005 Paris, France.
Leclercq, The Rev. Dom Jean L., OSB, Abbaye St-Maurice, L-9737 Clervaux, Luxembourg.

McNeill, Professor William H., 1126 East 59th Street, Chicago, Illinois 60637, U.S.A.
Maruyama, Professor Masao, 2-44-5 Higashimachi, Kichijoji, Musashi-noshi, Tokyo 180, Japan.
Michel, Henri, 12 Rue de Moscou, 75008 Paris, France.
Morgan, Professor Edmund S., Department of History, P.O. Box 1504A Yale Station, New Haven, Conn. 06520-7425, U.S.A.

Peña y Cámara, J. M. de la, Avenida Reina, Mercedes 65, piso 7-B, Seville 12, Spain.
Prawer, Professor J., Department of Medieval History, Hebrew University, Il-Jerusalem, Israel.

Slicher van Bath, Professor B. H., Gen. Fouldesweg 113, Wageningen, The Netherlands.

Thapar, Professor Romila, Dept of Historical Studies, Jawaharlal Nehru University, New Mehrauli Road, New Delhi-110067, India.
Thorne, Professor S. E., MA, LLB, LittD, LLD, FSA, Law School of Harvard University, Cambridge, Mass. 02138, U.S.A.

Van Houtte, Professor J. A., PhD, FBA, Termunkveld, Groeneweg, 51, Egenhoven, Heverlee, Belgium.
Verlinden, Professor C., PhD, 3 Avenue du Derby, 1050 Brussels, Belgium.

Wang, Professor Juefei, Nanjing University, China.
Wolff, Professor Philippe, Edifici Roureda Tapada, 2ª,7, Santa Coloma (Principality of Andorra), France.
Woodward, Professor C. Vann, PhD, Yale University, 104 Hall of Graduate Studies, New Haven, Conn. 06520, U.S.A.

Zavala, S., LLD, Montes Urales 310, Mexico 10, D.F., Mexico.

TRANSACTIONS AND PUBLICATIONS

OF THE

ROYAL HISTORICAL SOCIETY

The publications of the Society consist of the *Transactions*, supplemented in 1897 by the *Camden Series* (formerly the Camden Society, 1838–97); since 1937 by a series of *Guides and Handbooks* and, from time to time, by miscellaneous publications. The Society also began in 1937 an annual bibliography of *Writings on British History*, for the continuation of which the Institute of Historical Research accepted responsibility in 1965; it publishes, in conjunction with the American Historical Association, a series of *Bibliographies of British History*.

List of series published

The following are issued in collaboration with the distributor/publisher indicated:

Annual Bibliography of British and Irish History	
All titles	Harvester Press
Bibliographies of British History	
All except 1485–1603, 1714–1789	Oxford University Press
1485–1603, 1714–1789	Harvester Press
Camden Series	
Old Series and New Series	Johnson Reprint
Third and Fourth Series*	Boydell and Brewer
Guides and Handbooks	
Main Series*	Boydell and Brewer
Supplementary Series*	Boydell and Brewer
Miscellaneous titles	Boydell and Brewer
Studies in History	
All titles	Boydell and Brewer
Transactions of the Royal Historical Society	
Up to *Fifth Series*, Vol. 19	Kraus Reprint
Fifth Series, Vol. 20 onwards*†	Boydell and Brewer
Writings on British History	
Up to 1946	Dawson Book Service
1946–1974	Instititute of Historical Research

Members' entitlements

Fellows and Subscribing Libraries receive free copies of new volumes of series marked*.

Corresponding Fellows, Retired Fellows and Associates receive free copies of new volumes of this series marked†.

Terms for members' purchase of individual titles are listed below.

Methods of Ordering Volumes

Institute of Historical Research—an invoice will be sent with volume.
In all other cases pre-payment is required. If correct price is not known, a cheque made payable to the appropriate supplier, in the form 'Not exceeding £   ' may be sent with the order. Otherwise a pro-forma invoice will be sent.

LIST OF TITLES
ARRANGED BY DISTRIBUTOR

BOYDELL & BREWER

Address for orders: P.O. Box 9, Woodbridge, Suffolk IP12 3DF.

Camden Third Series: All titles now available; a list can be sent on request. Prices range from £10 for original volumes to £30 for the largest reprinted volumes. (£7.50–£22.50 to Members).

Camden Fourth Series: The following titles are available price £10. (£7.50 to Members) unless otherwise indicated:

1. Camden Miscellany, Vol. XXII: 1. Charters of the Earldom of Hereford, 1095–1201. Edited by David Walker. 2. Indentures of Retinue with John of Gaunt, Duke of Lancaster, enrolled in Chancery, 1367–99. Edited by N. B. Lewis. 3. Autobiographical memoir of Joseph Jewell, 1763–1846. Edited by A. W. Slater. 1964. £25.00.
2. Documents illustrating the rule of Walter de Wenlock, Abbot of Westminster, 1283–1307. Edited by Barbara Harvey. 1965.
3. The early correspondence of Richard Wood, 1831–41. Edited by A. B. Cunningham. 1966. £25.00.
4. Letters from the English abbots to the chapter at Cîteaux, 1442–1521. Edited by C. H. Talbot. 1967.
5. Select writings of George Wyatt. Edited by D. M. Loades. 1968.
6. Records of the trial of Walter Langeton, Bishop of Lichfield and Coventry (1307–1312). Edited by Miss A. Bearwood. 1969.
7. Camden Miscellany, Vol. XXIII: 1. The Account Book of John Balsall of Bristol for a trading voyage to Spain, 1480. Edited by T. F. Reddaway and A. A. Ruddock. 2. A Parliamentary diary of Queen Anne's reign. Edited by W. A. Speck. 3. Leicester House politics, 1750–60, from the papers of John second Earl of Egmont. Edited by A. N. Newman. 4. The Parliamentary diary of Nathaniel Ryder, 1764–67. Edited by P. D. G. Thomas. 1969.
8. Documents illustrating the British Conquest of Manila, 1762–63. Edited by Nicholas P. Cushner. 1971.
9. Camden Miscellany, Vol XXIV: 1. Documents relating to the Breton succession dispute of 1341. Edited by M. Jones. 2. Documents relating to the Anglo-French negotiations, 1439. Edited by C. T. Allmand. 3. John Benet's Chronicle for the years 1400 to 1462. Edited by G. L. Harriss. 1972.
10. Herefordshire Militia Assessments of 1663. Edited by M. A. Faraday. 1972.
11. The early correspondence of Jabez Bunting, 1820–29. Edited by W. R. Ward. 1972.
12. Wentworth Papers, 1597–1628. Edited by J. P. Cooper, 1973.
13. Camden Miscellany, Vol. XXV: 1. The Letters of William, Lord Paget. Edited by Barrett L. Beer and Sybil Jack. 2. The Parliamentary Diary of John Clementson, 1770–1802. Edited by P. D. G. Thomas. 3. J. B. Pentland's Report on Bolivia, 1827. Edited by J. V. Fifer, 1974.
14. Camden Miscellany, Vol. XXVI: 1. Duchy of Lancaster Ordinances, 1483. Edited by Sir Robert Somerville. 2. A Breviat of the Effectes

devised for Wales. Edited by P. R. Roberts. 3. Gervase Markham, The Muster-Master. Edited by Charles L. Hamilton. 4. Lawrence Squibb, A Book of all the Several Offices of the Court of the Exchequer (1642). Edited by W. H. Bryson. 5. Letters of Henry St John to Charles, Earl of Orrery, 1709-11. Edited by H. T. Dickinson. 1975.

15. Sidney Ironworks Accounts, 1541-73. Edited by D. W. Crossley. 1975.
16. The Account-Book of Beaulieu Abbey. Edited by S. F. Hockey. 1975.
17. A calendar of Western Circuit Assize Orders, 1629-48. Edited by J. S. Cockburn. 1976.
18. Four English Political Tracts of the later Middle Ages. Edited by J.-Ph. Genet. 1977.
19. Proceedings of the Short Parliament of 1640. Edited by Esther S. Cope in collaboration with Willson H. Coates. 1977.
20. Heresy Trials in the Diocese of Norwich, 1428-31. Edited by N. P. Tanner. 1977.
21. Edmund Ludlow: A Voyce from the Watch Tower (Part Five: 1660-1662). Edited by A. B. Worden. 1978.
22. Camden Miscellany, Vol. XXVII: 1. The Disputed Regency of the Kingdom of Jerusalem, 1264/6 and 1268. Edited by P. W. Edbury. 2. George Rainsford's *Ritratto d'Ingliterra* (1556). Edited by P. S. Donaldson. 3. The Letter-Book of Thomas Bentham, Bishop of Coventry and Lichfield, 1560-1561. Edited by Rosemary O'Day and Joel Berlatsky. 1979.
23. The Letters of the Third Viscount Palmerston to Laurence and Elizabeth Sulivan, 1804-63. Edited by Kenneth Bourne. 1979.
24. Documents illustrating the crisis of 1297-98 in England. Edited by M. Prestwich. 1980.
25. The Diary of Edward Goschen, 1900-1914. Edited by C. H. D. Howard. 1980.
26. English Suits before the Parlement of Paris, 1420-36. Edited by C. T. Allmand and C. A. J. Armstrong. 1982.
27. The Devonshire Diary, 1759-62. Edited by P. D. Brown and K. W. Schweizer. 1982.
28. Barrington Family Letters, 1628-1632. Edited by A. Searle. 1983.
29. Camden Miscellany XXVIII: 1. The Account of the Great Household of Humphrey, first Duke of Buckingham, for the year 1452-3. Edited by Mrs M. Harris. 2. Documents concerning the Anglo-French Treaty of 1550. Edited by D. L. Potter. 3. *Vita Mariae Reginae Anglie.* Edited by D. MacCulloch. 4. Despatch of the Count of Feria to Philip II, 1558. Edited by S. L. Adams and M. J. Rodriguez-Salgado. 1983.
30. Gentlemen of Science: Early correspondence of the British Association for the Advancement of Science. Edited by A. W. Thackray and J. B. Morrell. 1984.
31. Reading Abbey Cartularies, Vol. I. Edited by B. R. Kemp. 1986.
32. The Letters of the First Viscount Hardinge of Lahore to Lady Hardinge and Sir Walter and Lady James 1844-1847. Edited by Bawa Satinder Singh. 1986.
33. Reading Abbey Cartularies, Vol. II. Edited by B R. Kemp. 1987.
34. Camden Miscellany, Vol. XXIX: 1. Computus Rolls of the English Lands of the Abbey of Bec (1272-1289). Edited by Marjorie Chibnall. 2. Financial Memoranda of the Reign of Edward V. Edited by Rosemary Horrox. 3. A collection of several speeches and treatises of the late Treasurer Cecil. Edited by Pauline Croft. 4. John Howson's Answers to Archbishop Abbot's Accusations, 1615. Edited by Nicholas Cranfield

and Kenneth Fincham. 5. Debates in the House of Commons 1697–1699. Edited by D. W. Hayton. 1987.

35. The Short Parliament (1640) Diary of Sir Thomas Aston. Edited by Judith D. Maltby. 1988.